Beethoven

The Piano Concertos

Their Creation, Origins and Reception History

BEETHOVEN

As depicted by the life mask taken by Franz Klein in 1812

(derived from a copy in the author's possession)

BEETHOVEN

THE PIANO CONCERTOS

THEIR
CREATION, ORIGINS
AND
RECEPTION HISTORY

Incorporating Contextual Accounts of
Beethoven and his Contemporaries

Terence M. Russell

Jelly Bean Books

CONTENTS

AUTHOR'S
NOTE

I have cherished the idea of making a study of the life and work of Beethoven for many years. This statement requires a few words of personal reflection. I first encountered Beethoven in my early piano lessons — Minuet in G major, WoO 10, No. 2. At the same time I became acquainted with his piano pupil Carl Czerny — *Book One, Piano Studies.* My heart sank when I discovered the rear cover advertised a further *99* books in the same series — scales, arpeggios studies for the left hand, studies for the right hand — all the way to his Op. 824! By coincidence, my *Czerny Book One* was edited by Alec Rowley — who had the same surname as my music teacher. In my childish innocence, I often wondered why *he himself* never appeared to give me a lesson!

In my teenage years I found myself drawn ever closer to Beethoven's music in the manner that ferromagnetic materials are ineluctably held captive in the sway of a magnetic field. The impulse to which I yielded is well described in words the conductor Bruno Walter gave in one of his rare public addresses: 'It is my belief that young people at that age are more easily impressed by what is heroic and grandiose; that they more easily understand works of art in which passionate feelings are violently uttered in raised accents, and that the lighter sounds of cheerfulness are less impressive to them.' I do indeed recall the stirring effect made on me on first hearing the Overture *Egmont*, the unfolding drama of the Fifth Symphony and the declamatory opening chords of the *Emperor* Piano Concerto.

I resolved to read everything I could about Beethoven, starting with Marion Scott's pioneering English-language study of the composer in *The Master Musicians series*. My father took out a subscription for me for *The Gramophone* magazine, enabling me to read reviews of the new 'LP' recordings — none of which though I could afford! The LP was then — 1950s — beginning to supplant the 78 rpm shellac records, stacks of which could be purchased for as little as six pence each in 'old' money. I listed to the radio to hear Anthony Hopkins 'Talking about music' and to other musicological luminaries including Howard Fergusson, Hans Keller, Paul Hamburger, Denis Matthews, and Peter Stadlen.

At this same time I had the privilege of hearing Beethoven's music performed by the *Hallé Orchestra* under the baton of Sir John Barbirolli, and experienced the *Carl Rosa Opera Company* perform the composer's only opera *Fidelio*; I borrowed the piano-reduction score from the City Library to become better acquainted with this moving work — only to find the score's fists full of notes were well beyond my capabilities. Nonetheless, since then *Fidelio's* every note has been woven into my DNA. I also recall the period when the *London Promenade Concerts* were designated 'Friday night is Beethoven night'.

II

Through these influences I resolved to visit Vienna to see where Beethoven had lived and worked. But how? The support for such travel was beyond the means of my family. Fortunately in my final year at school (1959) an opportunity presented itself. I saw a poster that stated *WUS — World University Service* — required volunteers to work in the Austrian town of Linz to help relocate refugees who were living there in improvised wooden shacks — displaced and dispossessed victims of the Second World War. To those participating all expenses would be paid together with free accommodation — in one of the crumbling wooden shacks! From Linz, I planned to make my way to Vienna.

I applied to *WUS* and, despite being a mere school-leaver, I was accepted. The *WUS* authorities doubtless reasoned the building-trade skills I had acquired during my secondary education in the building department of a technical school would be useful. This proved to be the case. At the refugee camp I dug trenches and was allowed to assist as a bricklayer. All about me were wide-eyed children eager to help but mostly getting in the way. I recall one afternoon when a reporter from *The Observer* newspaper paid a visit to our construction site to gather material for an article he was writing on European post-war recovery — he generously admired my trenches and brickwork!

Of lasting significance was another visit, this time from a Belgian priest. He took a group of us to the nearby *Mauthausen* Concentration Camp, recently opened as a silent and solemn memorial to those who had perished there. It was a deeply moving experience. Years later I learned of the views of the ardent Beethovenian Sir Michael Tippet. After the horrors of the *Holocaust,* he posed the question for mankind: 'What price Beethoven now?' He posited: 'Could we any longer find solace in Beethoven's setting of Schiller's *Ode to Joy* and its utopian vision — "Be embraced you Millions"?'

My refugee contribution duly came to end and Vienna beckoned. On arrival there I found scenes reminiscent of *The Third Man* and *Harry Lime*. I recall, for example, encountering cobblestones piled high in the streets waiting to be replaced after having been disturbed by the heavy armoured vehicles that had so recently passed over them. But Vienna was welcoming. I visited the houses where Beethoven had lived and worked and paused outside others associated with him that were identified by a commemorative plaque and the Austrian flag. A particularly memorable occasion was attending a recital in the great salon within the palace of Beethoven's noble patron Prince Lobkowitz — the very one where the *Eroica* Symphony had been premiered. Ultimately, my steps led me to the composer's first resting place in the *Währinger Ortsfriedhof.* I paid silent homage to the great man and, as I did so, discovered nearby the resting place of Franz Schubert to whom Beethoven was an endless source of admiration and inspiration.

I felt a youthful impulse to discover yet more about Beethoven and his music. But absorption in musicology would have to take second place. My chosen career beckoned in the guise of architecture — 'the mother of the arts' and 'the handmaid of society'. There was room though for Beethoven's music and from that time on it has been my constant companion through attendance at recitals, in concerts and music-making in the home. And at home a reproduction of Franz Kline's 1812 study of the composer has greeted me each day for more than half a century.

On my retirement from a career in architectural practice, research and university teaching, the opportunity finally presented itself for me to devote time to researching Beethoven musicology. Having attained my eightieth year also emboldened me to make progress with my good intentions!

With these autobiographical remarks outlined I will say a few remarks about my working method— see also the comments made in *Editorial Principles*.

As a member of staff of The University of Edinburgh, I had the good fortune to have access to the *Reid Music Library*, formed from a nucleus of books bequeathed by General John Reid and augmented over the years by such custodians as Sir Donald Francis Tovey, sometime *Reid Professor of Music* and renowned Beethoven scholar. Over a period of three years, I made a survey of the many works in the Reid collection. I consulted each item in turn making records on paper slips — many hundreds — that I deemed to be relevant for my researches. I confined my searches to book-publications, as reflected in my accompanying bibliography. All of this was quite some years ago, the cut-off date for my researches being 2007. Beyond this date I have not surveyed any further works. I am mindful though that Beethoven musicology and related publication continue to be a major field of endeavour in the manner of the proverbial 'ever rolling stream'.

In the intervening years since completing my archival researches, personal tribulations associated with family illness and bereavement slowed my progress in giving expression to my projected intentions. Latterly, however, with renewed energy, and more time at my disposal, I have been able to make progress. My studies take the form of a set of monographs. The first set of these, trace the creation origins and reception history of each of Beethoven's piano sonatas and string quartets. The resulting texts also incorporate contextual accounts of Beethoven and his contemporaries. Also included in my musicological surveys are two related Beethoven anthologies. The set of monographs in question, identified by short title, are:

Beethoven: An anthology of selected writings.
Beethoven: The piano sonatas: An anthology of selected
   writings.

The Piano Sonatas:
Op. 2—Op. 28
Op. 31—Op. 81a
Op. 90—Op. 111

The String Quartets:
Op. 18, Nos. 1—6
Op. 59, Nos. 1—3 (Razumovsky); Op. 74 (The Harp);
   Op. 95 (Quartetto serioso)
Op. 127, Op. 132 and Op. 130 (Galitzin)
Op. 131, Op. 135; Grosse Fuge, Op. 133 and Op. 134
   (Fugue transcription)

I provide further information about these studies in the introduction to each individual monograph. Suffice it for me to state here the basic premise upon which my work is founded. I believe it is rewarding, concerning the life of a great artist, to find connections between who he *was* and what he *did*; in Martin Cooper's words 'between his personality, as expressed on the one hand in human relationships, and on the other in artistic creation'. (*Beethoven, The Last Decade*) That is not to say I consider it essential to the enjoyment of Beethoven's music to know this or that fact about it. His music can be enjoyed, as millions do, with — in Robert Simpson's apt phrase —'an innocent ear', for what it is and how it reaches out to us in purely musical terms without any prejudging of its merits based upon extra-musicological facts. Maynard Solomon expresses similar thoughts: 'It is doubtless true that we need have no knowledge whatever of a composer's biography, or knowledge of any other motivating factor of any kind, to appreciate the artwork on some fundamental level.' (*Beethoven Essays*, 1988, p. 116)

I must make a further point. I am mindful that a scholar who ventures into a field of study that is not rightly his may be regarded with some suspicion. In this regard I can but ask the reader to place his or her trust in me in the following way. I have attempted to bring to my work the care which publishers and their desk editors have required of me in my book writings relating to architecture – listed elsewhere.

As inferred, it is now more than sixty years since I paid homage to Beethoven in Vienna's *Währinger Ortsfriedhof* and my warmth of feeling towards the composer and his music have grown with the passing of the years. My studies are not intended to be propaedeutic – that would be pretentious. However, if in sharing with others what I have to say contributes to their knowledge and understanding of the composer, and thereby increases their own feelings towards him and his works, my own pleasure in bringing my work to completion will be all the more enhanced.

When Beethoven arrived in Vienna, he was unknown. He was armed though with a note of encouragement from his youthful friend and benefactor Count Ferdinand Waldstein. It contained the often-quoted words: 'Receive Mozart's spirit from Haydn's hands.' Some forty years later Beethoven passed away in the House of the black-robed Spaniards at 200 *Alservorstädter*, the *Glacis* where he had lived since the autumn of 1825. Soldiers had to be called to secure the doors to the inner courtyard of the house from the pressure of onlookers. His body was blessed in the *Alservorsttädt Parish Church*, schools were closed and perhaps as many as 10,000 people formed a funeral procession – an honour ordinarily reserved for monarchs. The *Marcia Funebre* from the composer's Op. 26 Piano

Sonata was performed at the funeral ceremony. Franz Grillparzer read the funeral oration. Franz Schubert, who, as remarked in life so admired Beethoven, was one of the pallbearers. The composer's mortal remains were lowered into a simple vault. Beethoven now belonged to history.

Dr Terence M. Russell
Edinburgh 2020

To the foregoing I am pleased to add the following works:

The Piano Concertos
The Symphonies: An Anthology of Selected Writings
Symphony No. 1 In C Major, Op. 21
Symphony No. 2 in D Major, Op. 36
Symphony No. 3 in E-flat Major, Op. 55
Symphony No. 4 in B-flat Major, Op. 60

TMR
2024

INTRODUCTION

B eethoven first played the piano in public when he was seven, and by the age of eleven he was already something of a local celebrity in his hometown of Bonn. Under the tutelage of his teacher Christian Gottlob Neefe, he mastered *The Well-Tempered Clavier* of J.S. Bach and it was Neefe who allowed his youthful protégé to deputise for him as Court Organist and *cembalist*. These duties entailed directing the orchestra from the keyboard and playing at sight from the score. It was Neefe who also arranged for the publication of Beethoven's earliest compositions. These included: the variations for piano on a march by Dressler (WoO 63, 1782); the three *Kurfürsten* Sonatas, WoO 47 (1783) — published with a dedication to Maximilian Friedrich; the three Piano Quartets, WoO, 36 (1785); the Rondos in C major, WoO 48 and in A major, WoO 49 (1782–85); and the Piano Concerto in E-flat major, WoO 4 (1784). Regarding the latter, for a thirteen-year old it displays remarkable self-assurance and technical display, and is the work with which we commence our discussion of Beethoven's writing for the genre of the piano concerto.

Beethoven moved to Vienna in November 1792, just before his twenty-second birthday, and was soon acknowledged in the salons of the nobility for being a virtuoso pianist. In particular, it was his unrivalled powers of improvisation for which he was most admired. He reached wider audiences, beyond the salons, through the public performance of his piano concertos — until deafness compelled him to withdraw from the concert platform. In 1795, Beethoven performed a piano concerto by Mozart at a concert in Vienna given, for the benefit of Mozart's widow Constanze. The work in question was probably the Concerto in D minor, K. 466 that Beethoven is known to have held in high regard, and for which he supplied cadenzas — that are still admired and performed today.

For Beethoven, as for Mozart before him, the concerto for piano was a dramatic genre of music-making that provided him, in the role of soloist, with the opportunity to display his skills as a virtuoso pianist. As Dennis Matthews remarks: '[The] concerto is one of the most dramatic art-forms ever devised ... The player must know, follow and experience the content and logic of the [orchestra's] unfolding, not only as so-much material for discussion and development, but as a challenge to his wits ... Therein lie the seeds of the drama.' (Dennis Matthews, *In Pursuit of Music*)

In the first of his three piano concertos, to which he gave opus numbers, Beethoven had to confront, and reconcile, the challenge of achieving a balance between the soloist and orchestra. The pianoforte of the period, with its lightweight structure and diminutive five-octave keyboard, meant the soloist could not compete with the orchestra on equal terms.

As instruments of greater sonority, and more extended compass, came available Beethoven was able to exploit these features, notably, in his Fourth and Fifth Concertos. Beethoven played and directed the first performances of his first four piano concertos for which he would have improvised cadenzas. Only with the Piano Concerto in E-flat major, the *Emperor*, did he relinquish the role of soloist — in favour of his pupil Carl Czerny — and for which he supplied fully written-out cadenza passages. Moreover, it was with the *Emperor* Concerto that Beethoven felt he could write for the piano in a manner that enabled the piano to hold its own against the orchestra.

The orchestra itself was changing. In 1808, when the Fourth Piano Concerto was being performed. The typical orchestra, of the kind that would be heard in the Theater an der Wien, consisted of, 12 violins, 4 violas, 3 cellos, 3 basses, 2 each of flutes, oboes, clarinets, bassoons, horns, trumpets, and timpani. By 1825, the orchestra of Vienna's Redoutensaal had strings comprising 36 violins, 14 violas, 12 cellos, and 17 double basses. (Barry Cooper, *The Beethoven compendium*)

The Piano Concerto in B-flat Major, Op. 19 was the first of Beethoven's five piano concertos, bearing opus numbers, to be composed but due to delays in its publication it was designated as being 'No. 2'. Beethoven held it back from publication, in part, to avoid pirate editions from appearing so that he could retain personal control over the work as long as possible. He was given to saying: 'Musical policy demands that one should keep one's ... concertos to oneself for a time.' Beethoven also made changes to the score from that conceived at its initial period of gestation in the 1780s; in its final form, in 1809, he supplied the music with cadenza-writing.

Not surprisingly, Beethoven, the young composer, was

reliant upon Mozart for his model; Op. 19 shares the same key and restrained orchestration — no clarinets, trumpets or timpani — with Mozart's last Piano Concerto No 27, K. 595. By Beethoven's later standards, the Concerto is considered to be somewhat modest and conventional, although revealing a distinct advance on his WoO 4. Beethoven himself, writing in 1801 to his Leipzig publisher Breitkopf and Härtel, admitted it was 'not one of his best compositions' and offered it to him at a reduced price. Nevertheless, the B-flat Major Concerto has its admirers who consider its Mozartian traits are 'more robust, wilful and explosive' (Denis Matthews); is possessed of 'charm and good humour' (Michael Steinberg); and its *Adagio* 'harbours surprising intensity and a compelling rhetorical expression'. (William Kinderman)

In the C major Piano Concerto, Op. 15, Beethoven once more followed Mozart's precedent in both formal and musicological terms. The piano, more correctly the fortepiano, is not yet given the role of a dominant force to rule over the orchestra, but is more of an equal among equals, although it is assigned its special tasks. Like Mozart, Beethoven sets out the work in three movements. Despite this attachment to tradition, as Czerny remarks of Beethoven's piano music: 'The general character of Beethoven's works is fervent, grand, energetic, noble, and replete with feeling; often also humorous and sportive, occasionally even eccentric, but always intellectual ... never effeminately elegant, or whiningly sentimental' (Carl Czerny, *On the Proper Performance of Beethoven's Compositions for Piano*). With his Op. 15, Beethoven expanded the concerto form to new proportions. It was the longest piano concerto so-far composed with an expanded orchestra augmented with parts for clarinets, trumpets, and timpani. Perhaps a military character can be discerned?

Despite the innovations in his Op. 15, Beethoven once more did not consider the C major Concerto to be one of his more worthy creations. He remarked to this effect to the publisher Franz Hoffmeister when he requested just ten ducats for it — only half his usual price for such an orchestral composition. The fact that the work has long-been established in the concert-pianists' repertoire is indicative that the composer's self-disparagement was not wholly justified. Critics have variously praised Beethoven's creation for its 'outstanding freshness of inspiration' (R. Kinloch Anderson), its 'thoughtful slow movement' and 'high spirited rondo finale' (William Kinderman), and for exhibiting 'the confidence of a young master in his own strength ... holding the seeds of a new power ... that became fully exerted only later' (Robert Simpson).

In the words of Anthony Hopkins, with his Third Piano Concerto in C minor, Op. 37 'Beethoven came of age' as a composer of works for soloist and orchestra. Moreover, on a personal level, the C minor Concerto was conceived at one of the happiest and most successful periods in the composer's life. It was 1800, the start of a new century, Beethoven was in his thirtieth year and, in the role of virtuoso pianist, had made a successful concert tour of Prague. He wrote to his brother Johann enthusiastically: 'My art is winning me friends and renown, and what more do I want? I shall make a good deal of money.'

The key of C minor held special significance for Beethoven. He had already given expression to it in the Piano Trio, Op.1, No. 3 (1795); the Piano Sonata, Op. 10, No. 1 (1798); the Piano Sonata, Op. 13, *Pathétique* (1798); the String Trio, Op. 9 (1798); and the String Quartet, Op. 18, No. 4 (1799). In addition to the Piano Concerto Op. 37, he soon gave further expression to C minor in such works as: the Violin Sonata, Op. 30, No. 2 (1803); the *Eroica*

Symphony — funeral march (1803–04); and Overture *Coriolan*, Op. 62 (1807). C minor would also become Beethoven's *heroic* key in such works for piano as the Thirty-Two Variations, WoO 80, (1806) and would reach a point of consummation in the Fifth Symphony, Op. 67, (1808). Towards the end his life he returned to C minor for his final great Piano Sonata, Op. 111 (1822).

Beethoven composed the C minor Piano Concerto at the same time as he worked on the Second Symphony, Op. 36. For both of these works he resorted to the standard classical orchestra comprising, pairs of flutes, oboes, clarinets, bassoons, horns, trumpets, and kettledrums.

The C minor Concerto was first performed in Vienna on 5 April 1803. Following a performance in 1805, the music critic of the *Allgemeine musikalische Zeitung* enthused: 'The present grand concerto belongs to the most significant works that have appeared from this ingenious master for several years, and in several respects it might distinguish itself from all the rest to its advantage. In addition to such a total sum of beautiful and noble ideas, the reviewer finds, at the very least, in none of his newest works such a thorough working out, yet without becoming turgid or overly learned, a character so solidly maintained without excess, and such unity in workmanship. It will, and must, have the greatest and most beautiful effect everywhere that it can be well performed.'

Czerny, who performed the C minor Concerto, similarly enthused: 'The style and character of this Concerto are much more grand and fervent than in the former two.' In the 'Special Issue' of *The Musical Times*, published to coincide with Beethoven's Death Centenary (1927), the pianist Fanny Davies (a pupil of Clara Schuman) wrote: 'The C minor, a great concerto, is a glorious link between the early Beethoven and the later. The very first theme of the *tutti* is cast in Beethoven's heroic mould. The writing is still mostly that of the earlier concertos, the solo standing against the orchestra, rather than working-in with it, but there are moments when it breaks away from this.'

In her pioneering study *Beethoven* (*The Master Musicians*), Marion Scott reflected: 'With the Concerto No. 3, in C minor, Op. 37 (composed in 1800) we reach Beethoven the tone-poet. Conventional elements are still retained in the disposition of the orchestral *tutti*, and the cadenza for the piano, etc., and even in the idiom of the subject, the impassioned quietude of the *Largo*, the biting brilliance of the *Rondo* and the subtle key-scheme underlying the whole work are pure Beethoven. Indeed, I sometimes think this whole Concerto is as much a self-portrait of Beethoven at thirty as the *Eroica* is of Beethoven at thirty-three.'

Beethoven authority Maynard Solomon describes the C minor Concerto as representing 'a marked advance over its predecessors' and, more significantly, considers it became 'an established model of Classic-Romantic concerto-form for the nineteenth century' (Maynard Solomon, *Beethoven*). In the same spirit, Anthony Hopkins contends: 'The work is essentially forward-looking, and it might be said to have laid the foundation on which the great Romantic concertos of the nineteenth century were ultimately built.' (Anthony Hopkins, *The Seven Concertos of Beethoven*)

When Beethoven composed his Piano Concerto No. 4, in G major, Op. 58 he was in his mid thirties. He was celebrated in Vienna as a virtuoso pianist and, despite the onset of deafness, was still able to perform in public. His fame as a composer — of daring and innovative works — was recognised at home and abroad and publishers were prepared to pay the high prices he demanded for his compositions. Notwithstanding his unconventional demeanour, his capacity for making acerbic remarks, and his pronounced

Bonn accent, he had secured the attention, friendship and financial support of a number of Vienna's musically-minded aristocracy. At the close of the period under consideration, he would soon count no less than the Archduke Rudolph — the Emperor's son — as his composition pupil and who would in due course be the recipient of the dedication to many of his greatest works.

To cite Maynard Solomon once more, he characterises Beethoven's creativity at the period of composition of the G major Concerto as 'an explosive inauguration of [his] post-Heiligenstadt style'. Solomon is making reference here to the intensely personal document Beethoven wrote with the realization of his increasing deafness, his contemplation of taking his life, and his resolve to overcome his physical and emotional impediments in fulfilment of his artistic destiny. The Austrian, medically-qualified musicologist Anton Neumayr has considered the many illnesses that afflicted Beethoven throughout his adult life. Reflecting on his poor state of health, he describes the composer's musical output as 'astonishing'. (Anton Neumayr, *Music and Medicine*)

The following compositions had their genesis around the period of composition of the G major Concerto and are illustrative of Beethoven's capacity, and predilection, for working on several works at the same time: two Sonatas for Piano, Op. 49; Piano Sonata, Op. 53, dedicated to Count Ferdinand von Waldstein; the Triple Concerto, Op. 56; Piano Sonata in F minor, Op. 57 — *Appassionata*; three *Razumovsky* String Quartets, Op. 59; work on the Fourth Symphony, Op. 60; Violin Concerto in D major, Op.61; and *Ah! perfido*, for Soprano and Orchestra, Op. 65. In 1807 and 1808 he completed the Fifth Symphony in C minor, Op. 67 and the Sixth Symphony in F major, Op. 68 — the *Pastoral*. Mention may also be made of the first and second *Leonora* Overtures; the Andante in F major, for Piano, WoO57; and the Thirty-two Variations for Piano, WoO 80. In the words of the Viennese-born musicologist Joseph Braunstein – who attained the great age of 104: 'Every work in this list ... is a seminal masterpiece, and everyone breaks new ground.' (Joseph Braunstein, *Musica Aeterna*)

The facial representation of Beethoven, taken by the sculptor Franz Klein, has contributed to the popular image of the composer as being a furrow-browed, scowling, at odds-with-the-world, fist-shaking misanthrope. Nothing could be further from the truth. The taking of Klein's image involved considerable discomfort, inducing Beethoven to distort his features. Beethoven's contemporary portraits reveal a more serene countenance. (See: H. C. Robbins Landon, 'Beethoven Gallery' in, *Beethoven*) Nor is Beethoven forever hurling C minor thunderbolts in his music. Tranquillity is also to be found, as in the Fourth Piano Concerto, the Violin Concerto, and the *Pastoral* Symphony – notwithstanding that the latter does happen to include a thunderstorm! Collectively, this is music imbued with 'a sense of spaciousness with moments of profound reflective stillness'. (Richard Wigmore, BBC, Radio Three, 2005, *The Beethoven Experience*) The Piano Concerto in G major, in particular, 'breathes warmth of heart and serenity'. (Denis Matthews, *Beethoven, The Master Musicians*) The lyricism inherent within the G major Concerto is all the more remarkable since it was composed when Beethoven was emerging from his 'dark night of the soul', as expressed in the poignancy of the *Heiligenstadt Testament*. From the mid-nineteenth century, writers have likened the manner in which the piano triumphs over the orchestra to 'Orpheus taming the Furies'.

Beethoven was the soloist in the Concerto's premiere

on the occasion of his marathon concert held on 22 December 1808 at Vienna's Theater an der Wien. This proved to be his last appearance as a piano-concerto soloist. Thereafter, the work appears to have languished until Felix Mendelssohn performed it in Leipzig in 1836. Robert Schumann was in the audience and later wrote of the experience: 'This day Mendelssohn played the G major Concerto of Beethoven with a power and finish that transported us all. I received a pleasure from it as I have never enjoyed; I sat in my place without moving a muscle or even breathing – afraid of making a noise!' Many other admirers of the music have since felt similarly inclined.'

Beethoven's Fifth Piano Concerto in E-flat major, Op. 73 is popularly known to English-speaking audiences as *The Emperor*. The origins of the work's nickname are uncertain but some authorities attribute it to the German-born, London-based pianist and publisher Johann Baptist Cramer. Beethoven and Cramer were on friendly terms – most of the time. Beethoven is reported to have remarked that Cramer had given him greater pleasure than any other pianist and, for his part, Cramer considered Beethoven to be 'the supreme improviser'.

The sobriquet *Emperor* is in many ways appropriate – albeit indirectly – insofar as it captures something of the turbulent atmosphere prevailing at the period of the music's composition. 1809, the period of gestation of Beethoven's Op. 73, was an inauspicious one for Austria's musical capital; Austria was at war with France. On 10 May, the French surrounded the city that the Archduke Maximilian had ordered to be defended. On learning of his refusal to capitulate, the following day the French artillery opened their bombardment of the city's defensive walls. The windows of Haydn's apartment were shattered and a shell exploded in the grounds of the school then attended by the eleven-year old Franz Schubert. At this time, Beethoven resided near the defensive city-wall (*Wasserkunst Bastei*) that became a specific target and blasts were discharged close to the windows of his apartment. Beethoven's biographer Alexander Wheelock Thayer comments: 'Every shot directed ... was liable to plunge into Beethoven's windows.' Beethoven eventually sought refuge in the basement of the house of his younger brother Caspar Carl (Kaspar Karl), protecting his remaining hearing with cushions that he placed over his ears.

Perhaps the exalted nature of the *Emperor* Concerto may be regarded as Beethoven's psychological response to the turbulent events of the time? In his *Music and Medicine*, Anton Neumayr suggests this may be the case. Beethoven, though, cautioned against seeking 'inner significance' in his music. He gave few interpretive titles to his works and it is unlikely he would have approved of the nickname *Emperor* for his Op. 73 Concerto. The title is, however, appropriate to the grandeur of the music, conceived as it is on the scale of the *Eroica* Symphony — originally dedicated to Napoleon.

In the E-flat major Concerto, the piano is presented on equal terms with the orchestra. From the outset it is prominent, in the foreground, but not muted, as with the G major Concerto, but resplendent with opening cadenza-like flourishes. Beethoven now had access to a piano having a six-octave keyboard and one capable of greater sonority than its diminutive, five-octave predecessors. Moreover, notwithstanding his deafness, he was now the supreme master of his pianistic craft. In the piano writing he exploits this by giving the soloist virtuoso scale-passages, declamatory arpeggios, and elaborate decorations. But he was also determined to retain control over such elaborations. Hitherto, in the previous four concertos, he had provided opportunities for the soloist to give expression to his, or her, virtuosity in the form of free improvisation. But here, in the *Emperor*

Concerto, he wrote his own cadenzas into the score, dissuading others with the injunction *Non 'si fa cadenza, ma s'attacca subito il seguenti* — 'Do not play a cadenza, but attack the following at once'.

1809 may be considered as Beethoven's E-flat major year. In addition to the *Emperor* Concerto, he also composed the so-called *Harp* String Quartet, Op. 74 and the Piano Sonata, Op. 81a, to which Beethoven himself gave the title *Les Adieux* — 'The Farewell'. This may be seen as an expression of concern, set in programmatic music, for his pupil the Archduke Rudolph — the dedicatee of Op. 73 — as he prepared to leave Vienna to escape the threat of the invasion.

Because of his deafness, Beethoven did not premiere the *Emperor* Concerto. This honour went to Friedrich Schneider who performed the work on 28 November 1811 at a Gewandhaus concert in Leipzig. Vienna had to wait until 11 February, the following year, when Carl Czerny played the work, under Beethoven's guidance, at Vienna's Opera House. The audience's response to the Concerto was muted, according to the report in the Journal *Thalia* — dedicated to all that was 'flourishing' and possessed of 'beauty and charm'. The music correspondent stated: 'If this composition ... failed to receive the applause which it deserved, the reason is to be sought partly in the subjective character of the work, partly in the objective nature of the listeners.' He justified his reasoning: 'Beethoven, full of proud confidence in himself, never writes for the multitude; he demands understanding and feeling, and because of the intentional difficulties, he can receive these only on the hands of the knowing minority, of whom is not to be found on such occasions.'

Such reservations have long been set aside, and support for the *Emperor* Concerto has sometimes come from unlikely sources. When he was preparing for his London concert tour in 1897, Percy Grainger wrote to his friend Dr. Henry O'Hara – in his hometown of Melbourne: 'Concertos are lovely things to practice and Beethoven was such a master of them, for instance his glorious E-flat major is a real masterpiece.' The pianist-composer James Butt recalls an occasion when he was receiving composition lessons from Benjamin Britten, who is considered to have had some antipathy towards Beethoven – though not entirely justified. When Butt mentioned the *Emperor* Concerto, it prompted Britten to enthuse 'Ah yes', and, as Butt relates, he turned to the piano remarking: 'I think this has always been rather a lovely sound' and played the closing bars of the last movement 'most gracefully and without effort'. (Donald Mitchell, editor, *Letters from a Life: The Selected Letters and Diaries of Benjamin Britten 1913–1976*, 1991. Vol. 2) More predictably, the ardent Beethovenian Donald Francis Tovey enthused: 'Nobody with a sense of style has the slightest doubt that Beethoven's three greatest concertos, the G major, Op. 58, the E-flat major, Op. 73, and the Violin Concerto, Op. 61, are among his grandest works.' (Donald Francis Tovey, *Beethoven*)

It may be argued Beethoven's *Emperor* Concerto served as a blueprint, or palimpsest, for the composers of Romantic concertos that followed in the nineteenth century.

The Italian-born English composer, pedagogue, and music publisher Muzio Clementi met Beethoven when on a business trip to Vienna in April 1807. After some initial aloofness, the two soon became friends and established a working-relationship. Clementi wrote home to William Frederick Collard, his business partner in London: 'By a little management ... I have at last made a complete conquest of that *haughty beauty* [Clementi's italics] Beethoven'. Clementi explains how he had persuaded the composer to have several of his works published in England (London) and how well his publishing house would take care of him. The works in question included the Fourth Piano Concerto, Op. 58 and the Violin Concerto, Op. 60. Concerning the latter, he asked Beethoven to adapt the music for pianoforte that would, thereby, become Piano Concerto, Op. 61a. Notwithstanding his reluctance for making such arrangements and transcriptions of his music, Beethoven consented to Clementi's request. Critics of the outcome exonerate him on the grounds that he was, doubtless, motivated be a desire to further the popularity of his Violin Concerto and, ever relevant to his personal circumstances, the pressing need to earn additional money from his labours.

In the piano transcription, Beethoven retained the original orchestral accompaniment whilst adapting the solo part to the idiomatic requirements of the keyboard — notably in the lower register of the instrument. The closing pages are of interest. The piano engages in duet-like exchanges with the timpani that call to mind the emergence of the timpani at the close of the *Emperor* Concerto. Beyond such moments, Op. 61a is considered to be little more than a musical curiosity, reminding us of the adage, 'Even Homer sometimes nods' — which may be taken to mean, 'Even the most scrupulous and exact person may fall victim to mistakes and errors'. Writing of Beethoven's adaptation, the American musicologist Leon Plantinga remarks: 'What counts in transcribing music, from the one instrument to the other, is the invention of textures that sound convincing on the piano, an art in which Beethoven's solo piano works of course excel. This virtue is conspicuously missing in the transcription of the Violin Concerto. (Leon Plantinga, *Beethoven's Concertos*)

Beethoven did not intend the *Emperor* to be his last piano concerto. In late 1814 and early 1815 he turned his mind once more to the genre. Some 70 pages of sketches survive, together with the start of a full score, for a Concerto in D major. These are preserved as 'MS Artaria 184' in the Catalogue of the Staatsbibliothek, Berlin. Beethoven appears to have become dissatisfied with the work and left it incomplete. In 1987, Nicholas Cook and Kelina Kwan reconstructed a performing edition of the first movement. The music may also be heard in the form of Hess 15.

In the eloquent words of Robert Simpson: 'Here he stopped, and to try to imagine what kind of concertos Beethoven would have written, in the period of the late quartets, can be no more than frustrating. Perhaps he was no longer interested in works with elements of display — yet who knows? If someone had commissioned a concerto, how might he have responded? There can be no doubt that he would have explored new and profound aspects of the relationship between the individual and the mass, and that no one since has moved into the regions he alone knew.' (Robert Simpson, *Beethoven and the Concertos*, in: *A Guide to the Concerto*

TMR

EDITORIAL
PRINCIPLES

B y its very nature a study of this kind draws extensively on the work of others. Every effort has been made to acknowledge this in the text by indicating words directly quoted or adapted with single quotation marks. Wherever possible, for the sake of consistency, I have retained the orthography of quoted texts making only occasional silent changes of spelling and capitalization. Deleted words are identified by means of three ellipsis points ... and interpolations are encompassed within square brackets [ ]. Quoted words, phrases and longer cited passages of text remain the intellectual property of their copyright holders.

The texts to each piano concerto are presented 'free-standing' so they can be read independently of each other – rather in the manner of a recital programme-note. However, the circumstances bearing on Beethoven's life, and the origins of his compositions, unite his works in various ways. With this in mind, the reader, so inclined, may read this book in the conventional way — from cover to cover. Thereby, insights may be gained into the nature of the interrelationships between the various piano concertos and the circumstances bearing on their creation origins. A number of individuals recur in our narratives. To introduce these afresh, in the text to each concerto, would become repetitive. I have therefore adopted the principle of describing a particular individual at their *first* appearance with subsequent citations being made in summary form. I occasionally make cross-references between texts, but these have been kept to a minimum. The Index is presented in the form of a timeline and serves as a guide to who and what appears in the texts in their chronological sequence.

I address the reader in the second person notwithstanding that the work is my own — produced without the benefit of a desk editor. It follows that I must bear the responsibility for any errors of misunderstanding or misinterpretation for which I ask the reader's forbearance. A collaboration I must acknowledge is the help I received from the librarians of the **Reid Music Library** at the University of Edinburgh. Over the three-year period it took me to compile my reference sources, they served me with unfailing courtesy, often supplying me with twenty or more books at a time. In converting my manuscript into book-format, I wish to thank my editorial coordinator, William Rees, for his support and painstaking care. I would also like to thank Shaun Russell (no relation) for his work designing the covers for each of the volumes.

My admiration for Beethoven provided the initial impulse to commence this undertaking and has sustained me over the several years it has taken to bring my enterprise to completion. That said I am no Beethoven idolater. I am mindful of the danger that awaits one who ventures to chronicle the work of a great artist. I believe it was Sigmund

Freud who suggested that biographers may become so disposed to their subject, and their emotional involvement with their hero, that their work becomes an exercise in idealisation. In response to such a putative charge let me say. First, I am no biographer. I do however make reference to Beethoven's personal life and his relationships with his contemporaries, consistent with my sub-title. Second, I acknowledge Beethoven has his detractors. Accordingly, I have not shrunk from allowing dissentient voices, critical of Beethoven and his work, to be heard. These, however, are few and are silenced amidst the adulation that awaits the reader in support of the endeavours of one of humanity's great creators and one who courageously showed the way in overcoming personal adversity.

TMR

BEETHOVEN'S
FINANCIAL
TRANSACTIONS

Beethoven's negotiations with his music publishers make many references to his compositions. Today they are recognised for what they are — enduring works of art — but referred to in his business correspondence they appear almost as though they were mere everyday commodities — for which he required an appropriate remuneration. Beethoven resented the time he had to devote to the business-side of his affairs. He believed an agency should exist, for fellow artists such as himself, from which a reasonable sum could be paid for the work (composition) submitted, leaving more time for creative enterprises. In the event Beethoven, like Mozart before him, had to deal with publishers largely on his own. Beethoven, though, did benefit in his business dealings from the help he received from his younger brother Kasper Karl (Caspar Carl). From 1800, Carl worked as a clerk in Vienna's Department of

Finance, in which capacity he found time to correspond with publishers to offer his brother's works for sale and — importantly — to secure the best prices he could. In April 1802, Beethoven wrote to the Leipzig publishers Breitkopf & Härtel: '[You] can rely entirely on my brother who, in general, attends to my affairs.' Whilst Carl promoted Beethoven's interests with determination, he appears to have lacked tact and made enemies. For example, Beethoven's piano pupil Ferdinand Ries — who for a while also helped the composer with his business negotiations — is on record as describing Carl as being 'the biggest skinflint in the world'. The currencies most referred to in Beethoven's correspondence are as follows:

> Silver gulden and florin: these were interchangeable and had a value of about two English shillings.
> Ducat: 4 1/2 gulden / florins: valued at about nine shillings.
> Louis d'or: This gold coin was adopted during the Napoleonic wars and the French occupation of Vienna and Austria more widely. It had a value of about two ducats or approximately twenty shillings, or one-pound sterling.

Beethoven was never poor — in the romantic sense of 'an artist starving in a garret'. On arriving in Vienna, in 1792, he was fortunate to receive financial support from his patron Prince Karl Lichnowsky who conferred on him an annuity of 600 florins — that he maintained for several years. Between the months of February and July of 1796, Beethoven undertook a concert tour taking in Prague, Dresden, Leipzig and Berlin. He was well-received and wrote to his other younger brother Nikolaus Johann: 'My art is winning me friends and what more do I want? ... I shall make a good deal of money.' Later on, in 1809, Napoleon Bonaparte's youngest brother Jérôme Bonaparte offered Beethoven an appointment at his Court with the promise of an income of 4,000 florins. Alarmed at the prospect of losing Beethoven — now the most celebrated composer in Europe — three of Vienna's most notable citizens, namely, the Archduke Rudolph (Beethoven's only composition pupil), Prince Kinsky and Prince Lobkowitz settled on the composer the same sum of 4,000 florins. Inflation, however, brought about by the Napoleonic wars, soon eroded its value; personal misfortune to Lobkowitz and Kinsky also took its toll.

Beethoven undoubtedly had to work hard to secure a reasonable standard of living. Notwithstanding, despite his occasional straitened circumstances, he contributed generously to the needs of others. For example, he allowed his works to be performed at charitable concerts without seeking any benefit to himself; in 1815 his philanthropy earned for him the honour of Bürgerrecht — 'freedom of the City'.

Beethoven earned a great deal of money when his music was performed, to considerable acclaim, at several concerts held in association with the Congress of Vienna (1814–15). He did not, though, benefit from it personally; he invested it on behalf of his nephew Karl. It is one of the misfortunes of Beethoven's life that in money-matters he was in some ways culpably improvident. This is poignantly evident in a letter he wrote on 18 March 1827 to the Philharmonic Society of London — just one week before his death; the Society had made him a gift of £100. He sent the Society 'His most heartfelt thanks for their particular sympathy and support'.

TMR

'[The] concerto is one of the most dramatic art-forms ever devised. This drama starts from the first note of the work, which usually happened to be the orchestra's note until Beethoven "emancipated" the soloist in his G major Concerto — but even there, and in the Emperor, the main task of exposition was still the orchestra's role. The player must know, follow and experience e the constant logic of this unfolding, not only as so much material for discussion and development, but as a challenge to his wits. How can he cope with it, embellish it, interrupt, or even show his independence by breaking away from it? Therein lie the seeds of the drama, and though you may argue that it is no longer dramatic for you, because the composer has written it all down and your job is simply to obey orders, it is imperative to re-live it to the full if the playing of notes is to become the performance of music.'

Dennis Matthews, In Pursuit of Music, *1968*

PIANO CONCERTO
E-FLAT MAJOR,
WoO 4

'The Concerto WoO 4 is a competent essay in
the gallant style of J.C. Bach and the South
German School.'

Basil Deane *The Concertos* in: Denis Arnold and Nigel
Fortune editors, *The Beethoven Companion*, 1973, p. 318.

'The Concerto for Piano and Orchestra, WoO
4 of 1784 is formally diffuse and melodically
uninteresting despite moments of folk-like gaiety
in the closing movement; although composed in
emulation of the early C major style of J. C. Bach
and the South Germans, it lacks their craftsmanship and elegance.'

Maynard Solomon, *Beethoven*, 1977, p. 47.

'[Beethoven composed a piano concerto in E-flat major in 1784 in Bonn, and no doubt played it on several occasions. It was in his bag when he went to Vienna in 1792. Beethoven, aware of the superiority of his more mature works and the towering importance of Mozart's concertos, decided to shelve this early work, which came to light after his death. Only the piano part was preserved; the orchestral score for two flutes, oboes, and strings had to be reconstructed on the basis of relevant entries in the piano part in order to make this early piece available for perform-ance.'

Joseph Braunstein, *Musica Aeterna, Program Notes for 1971–1976, Vol. 2*, 1978, p. 19.

'Its musical value is slight, though the orchestra of two flutes, two horns and strings is unusual, and the florid but discursive keyboard writing testifies to the skill of the young virtuoso.'

Denis Matthews, *Beethoven, The Master Musicians*, 1985, p. 172.

'Although the work, lacking in formal integrity and thematic interest, is that of an immature composer, it does contain elements that were to emerge in a better developed form in later works. One element worthy of note is the appearance of brilliant keyboard figuration. Another more specific element of special inter-est is the use of the minor mode in the second episode in the rondo, a gesture that was to

2

remain a striking feature of Beethoven's concerto rondos.'

Michael Broyles, *Beethoven: The Emergence and Evolution of Beethoven's Heroic Style*, 1987, p. 179.

'As usual with the young Beethoven, the piano part bears extensive articulation marks which demonstrate his great attention to detail. It is also strikingly virtuosic, with bravura figuration in all three movements, sometimes exceeding that which Mozart demanded in his concertos ... [It] is an ambitious and far from unsuccessful attempt at coming to grips with one of the most important musical genres.'

Barry Cooper, *Beethoven: The Master Musicians*, 2000, p. 16.

The earliest accounts of the youthful Beethoven derive from the recollections of Gottfried Fischer. His family owned a house in the Rheingasse in Bonn (destroyed in 1944) in which Beethoven lived from about 1775. Fischer recalls Beethoven having lessons on the violin, viola and piano, becoming particularly proficient in the case of the latter. Such was his precocity at the keyboard that, to the annoyance of his father, he was prone to 'playing after his own fashion' — that years later would find its fullest expression in his powers of extemporisation at which his contemporaries acknowledged he was without equal.[1]

By June 1784, Beethoven was an official member of the Electoral musical establishment at Bonn. As such he was eligible — one might say obliged — to wear the court musicians' livery consisting of a sea-green frock-coat, green knee-breaches, stockings, shoes with bows, a gold embroidered waistcoat, hat — and a sword! The artist Joseph Neesen made a silhouette portrait of the youthful composer that is thought to date from about 1786 when he would have been sixteen years old. His lace-trimmed neckerchief and pigtail perruque are clearly discernible. The silhouette, most probably derived from an ink drawing, is said to have been created one evening in the house of the respected von Breuning family who rendered many services to the young Beethoven; he was almost treated as a member of the family. Beethoven considered the Breunings to be 'the guardian angels of his youth'.[2] Franz Wegeler and Ferdinand Ries adopted Neesen's image for the frontispiece to their pioneering study *Biographische, Notizen über Ludwig van Beethoven* that was published in Koblenz in 1838 and Oscar G. Sonneck's, *Beethoven, Impressions by his Contemporaries* (1927 reprint 1967) also included the image.[3] Neesen's silhouette was once considered to be the earliest known surviving likeness of Beethoven until 1952 when an anonymous portrait of the composer came to light. It is thought to portray him as a boy aged thirteen.[4]

Beethoven's musical appointment was significant. The Elector, Maximilian Franz, was resident at Bonn — Beethoven's birthplace — and was also Archbishop of Cologne. The Electoral Court at Bonn embraced the affairs of the church and state in a fusion of musicians' duties in the genres of music for the church, the theatre, and the concert room. Beethoven's name appears in the Court Calendar of 1788 where he is listed as a viola player. As the composer's pioneering biographer Alexander Wheelock Thayer remarks:

'Thus, for a period of full four years, he had the opportunity of studying, practically, compositions in the best of all schools — the orchestra itself.'[5]

4

Leon Plantinga reminds us that Beethoven's position was not that of a liveried-musician, comparable to that of Haydn and Mozart. He was free to pursue his real musical career in his own time — 'this was surely the case in his cultivation as composer and player of the concerto'.[6]

Notwithstanding the reference to Beethoven as violist, it was the piano — more correctly the keyboard — that was central to his musical development both as composer and emerging virtuoso. Under the tutelage of his teacher Christian Gottlob Neefe, at an early age Beethoven mastered *The Well-Tempered Clavier* of J.S. Bach — 'Bach was to be a presence, a beneficent spirit, all his life'.[7] Moreover, such was the youthful Beethoven's prowess that Neefe occasionally allowed his protégé to deputise for him as Court Organist and *cembalist* that involved directing the orchestra from the keyboard and playing at sight from the score.

It was Neefe who arranged for the publication of Beethoven's Variations for Piano on a March by Dressler, WoO 63 (1782). Other compositions created under the aegis of Neefe were: the three *Kurfürsten* Sonatas, WoO 47 (1783) — published with a dedication to Maximilian Friedrich; the Piano Concerto in E-flat major, WoO 4 (1784); the three Piano Quartets, WoO, 36 (1785); the Rondos in C major, WoO 48 and in A major, WoO 49 (between 1782–85); and — in the same key as the Piano Concerto — the Minuet WoO 82. Beethoven's first major commission though at this period was the Cantata on the Death of the Emperor Joseph II, WoO 87 (1790). In its intensity of feeling it is prophetic of the later Beethoven — and remarkable testimony to the composer's formative years spent as an orchestral player. Although it was intended to be performed at a memorial service, the orchestration proved too challenging for the players and the work was not premiered until 1884. Its sombre tones, however, found expression some years later in the darker passages of the composer's Opera *Leonora / Fidelio.*

For Beethoven, as for Mozart, it was the piano concerto *par excellence* that served as the dramatic musical genre by means of which, in the role of soloist, he could give expression to his formidable talent. In 1781, and possibly again in 1783, Beethoven visited the Netherlands (Rotterdam) with his mother and 'played a great deal in houses'. In 1791 he performed in Mergentheim with other Court musicians and improvised at the piano in private gatherings. It is thought by some authorities Beethoven may have played his Concerto in E-flat major at the Bonn Court — although evidence for this is slight.[8]

In 1791, Carl Ludwig Junker heard Beethoven improvise at the keyboard. Junker had some standing as a dilettante composer and musical pedagogue and served as Chaplain to Prince Hohenlohe at his residence at Kirchberg. He relates:

> 'I heard ... one of the greatest pianists — the dear, good Bethofen [sic] ... I heard him extemporize in private ... I was even invited to propose a theme for him to vary. The greatness of this amiable, light-hearted man, as a virtuoso, may in my opinion be safely estimated from his almost inexhaustible wealth of ideas, the altogether characteristic style of expression in his playing, and the great execution which he displays ... His style of treatment of his instrument is so different from that usually adopted, that it impresses one with the idea, that by a path of his own discovery he has attained that height of excellence whereon he now stands.'[9]

Neefe wrote the first public notice about Beethoven that was published in the 2 March 1783 issue of Cramer's *Magazin der Musik*. He introduces Beethoven as a boy of 'the most promising talent' — giving himself mention as well! Neefe continues:

> 'He plays the clavier very skilfully and with power, reads at sight very well ... plays chiefly *The Well Tempered Clavichord* of Sebastian Bach ... Whoever knows this collection of preludes and fugues in all keys ... will know what this means. So far as his duties permitted, Herr Neefe has also given him instruction in thoroughbass. He is now training him in composition ... The youthful genius is deserving of help to enable him to travel. He would surely become a second Wolfgang Amadeus Mozart were he to continue as he has begun.'[10]

When Beethoven eventually left Bonn for Vienna, to commence his studies with Haydn, he did not forget the debt he owed to his former teacher. On 26 October 1793 he found time to write:

> 'I thank you for the advice you have very often given me about making progress in my divine art. Should I ever become a great man, you too will have a share in my success.'[11]

A bifolium (a manuscript page of double-leaf format) survives from around 1790 that indicates Beethoven's early propensity for elaborating his musical thoughts in sketch form — what he was later to describe as his 'bad habit'. The pages are heavily annotated down to the margins of the paper — not a square centimeter is wasted. At the top of the second leaf Beethoven wrote: 'Rondo zum Concert in es mit Triolen' — 'A rondo for the Concerto in E-flat major with triplets.' Although Beethoven's youthful Piano Concerto WoO 4 is in this key, there is some uncertainty whether these sketches actually belong to this work.[12] Other sketch leaves from this period, however, reveal Beethoven exploring ideas conjectured by musicologist Porter Johnson to be possibly part of a concerto.[13] Interestingly, Beethoven would revisit the key of E-flat major in his last completed Piano Concerto *The Emperor*.

Barry Cooper suggests Beethoven's youthful E-flat major Concerto may have been composed in response to Neefe's own Piano Concerto in G that was published in 1782.[14] From the time of Vivaldi, three movements had become the norm for a concerto. Accordingly, Beethoven designated his three movements: Allegro moderato, Larghetto, and Rondo. As remarked, only the piano part survives intact. This appears to be the work of a copyist but bears alterations by the composer. The Library of the Staatsbibliothek Preussischer Kulturbesitz holds an autograph copy of the composition that once was in the possession of the music publisher Domenico Artaria. He acquired a number of Beethoven's papers and sketches, following the composer's death, at the auction of his effects in November 1827. The Autograph is inscribed: 'Un Concert / pour le clavecin ou Forte-piano / Composé par / Louis van Beethoven / agé de douze ans.' Whilst the solo part is complete, the tutti sections of the orchestral part are only suggested in piano score. These, however, provide some instrumental cues that have enabled the orchestral part to be reconstructed.[15] In his writing out of the piano part, Beethoven was clearly determined to give expression to his command of his instrument. As Barry Cooper observes:

8

'[In] the first movement Beethoven uses not just semiquaver runs but semiquavers in parallel thirds for the right hand alone ... and in the second movement ... the piano launches into extensive runs in demisemiquavers, hemidemisemiquavers and even semi- hemidemisemiquavers!'[16]

Musicologist John A Meyer writes: The piano writing in Beethoven's first three concertos is extremely brilliant; in the E flat Concerto it is already surprisingly assured and difficult for a thirteen-year old even with Beethoven's technical ability. The themes lack individuality, however, and undue attention is consequently directed to the extended sections of figuration, whereas the next two concertos strike a much more satisfactory balance between thematic content and technical display.'[17]

Beethoven was severely self-critical of his work all his life and constantly strove to improve it, resolving, as he did, 'never to repeat himself'. He evidently grew dissatisfied with the Piano Concerto in E-flat major WoO 4 and appears never to have offered it for publication. The Swiss musicologist Willy Hess published a reconstruction of WoO 4 that was premiered by Edwin Fischer at Potsdam in 1943.[18] The text was duly published in 1961.

Perhaps one reason why Beethoven did not seek to publish his E-flat major Concerto was the dawning realization that he was capable of greater things in the concerto genre. It is to these that we next direct our attention.

[1] For a fuller account of Beethoven's youth and progress with his musical studies, see: Oscar G. Sonneck, 1927, pp. 3–10 and Peter Clive, 2001, p. 111.

[2] Beethoven House, Digital Archives, Library Document, Wegeler, W 171.

[3] Neesen's silhouette is reproduced in the prefatory pages to H. C. Robbins

Landon, 1992. Silhouettes of the von Breuning family can be seen by accessing the Beethoven House website, Older members of the family are depicted taking tea whilst younger members practice the violin.

[4] See: Beethoven House, *Beethoven Gallery*.

[5] Elliot Forbes editor, *Thayer's Life of Beethoven*, 1967 pp. 95–96.

[6] Leon Plantinga, 1999, pp. 1–10.

[7] Michael Steinberg, 1998, p. 50.

[8] Leon Plantinga, 1999, pp. 1–10.

[9] Elliot Forbes editor, *Thayer's Life of Beethoven*, 1967 pp. 104–05.

[10] The principal source for this quotation is once more Elliot Forbes editor, pp. 65–66. See also, for example: Oscar George Theodore Sonneck, *Beethoven: Impressions of Contemporaries*, 1927, p. 10 and Maynard Solomon, 1977, p. 27.

[11] Emily Anderson, editor and translator, 1961, Vol. 1, Letter No. 6, p. 9.

[12] See: Beethoven House, Digital Archives, Library Document, Sammlung Wegeler, W 3.

[13] *Ibid*, Library Document, HCB Bsk 17/65c.

[14] Barry Cooper, 2000, pp. 15–16.

[15] Leon Plantinga, 1999, pp. 305–06 and Michael Broyles, 1987, p. 179.

[16] Barry Cooper, 2000, p. 15.

[17] John A. Meyer, *The Concerto* in: Gerald Abraham, editor, *The Age of Beethoven, 1790-1830*, 1982, p. 223.

[18] Denis Matthews, 1985, p. 172.

PIANO CONCERTO NO. 1 C MAJOR, OP. 15

The composer, conductor and writer on music Ignaz von Seyfried was a close friend of Beethoven and has left the following account when he assisted him during the performance of one his piano concertos — most probably Op. 15:

'He invited me to turn over for him when he played one of his concertos; but, good heavens! that was more easily said than done; I saw nothing but blank leaves, with a few utterly incomprehensible Egyptian hieroglyphics, which served him as guides, for he played nearly the whole solo part from memory, as it generally happened that he had not had time to write it out in full. So, he always gave me a secret sign when he was at the end of one of these unintelligible passages.'

As recalled by Ludwig Nohl in, *Beethoven Depicted by his Contemporaries*, 1880, pp. 52–53.

> 'Beethoven's works ... are written for good, and cultivated pianists; that is, for those who, by the study of many other good works, have already acquired all that relates to mechanical facility and good performance in general ... The general character of Beethoven's works is fervent, grand, energetic, noble, and replete with feeling; often also humorous and sportive, occasionally even eccentric, but always intellectual; and though sometimes gloomy, yet never effeminately elegant, or whiningly sentimental.'

Carl Czerny published his guidance on 'the proper performance' of Beethoven's compositions for piano in 1846, from which the foregoing text is derived — in English translation, see: Paul Badura-Skoda, Carl Czerny: *On the Proper Performance of all Beethoven's Works for the Piano*, 1970, p. 31.

> 'The C major contains already the Beethoven-esque robust and joyous rhythms, in spite of being naïve. Already in the C major, there come some moments in which one would like all performers to play without breathing and the conductor to hold the work together without moving his baton ... Yes, the C major is a great little concerto in spite of its A flat movement not being one of Beethoven's greatest inspirations.'

Fanny Davies, *The Pianoforte Concertos* in: *Musical Times, Special Issue*, edited by John A. Fuller-Maitland, Vol. VIII, No. 2, 1927, p. 225.

'The Concerto [Op. 15] I only value at ten ducats, because ... I do not give it out as one of my best.' [Beethoven to the publisher Franz Hoffmeister] Beethoven was perfectly right. The Concerto [Op. 15], though elegant, is indeterminate ... It marks some advance, even if the material of the first movement is in the manner of Mozart. The *Largo* in A-flat major is modelled on Italian cantilena, and the lively Rondo is a good example of a type prevalent.'

Marion M. Scott, *Beethoven, The Master Musicians,* 1940, p. 181.

Sergei Rachmaninoff was engaged to play at a series of London concerts. After years of capitulation to concert managers, who demanded he should perform his own concertos, on this occasion he insisted upon playing a Beethoven concerto. Informing his friend that he was to play Beethoven's First Piano Concerto, he described it as 'that heavenly music'.

Victor I. Seroff, *Rachmaninoff,* 1951, pp. 196–97. See also Sergei Bertensson, *Sergei Rachmaninoff: A Lifetime in Music,* 1965, pp. 330–31.

'The C major Concerto was composed before the C minor Sonata (*Pathétique*), the First Symphony, and the String Quartets, Op. 18. Formally and technically, Beethoven followed the road Mozart had laid out in his Viennese concertos, that is to say, he fully embraced the concept that saw the concerto as a symphonic commonwealth in which the clavier appears not as a ruling member but a prominent one with a special task. He adopted the three-movement structure and formal designs Mozart applied to the individual movements.'

Joseph Braunstein, *Musica Aterna, Program Notes for 1971–1976, Vol. 2*, 1978, pp. 19–20.

'The greater importance of the Concerto No. 1 in C, Op. 15, is marked by an increase in the size of the orchestra: two clarinets, two trumpets and timpani are added.'

Basil Deane, *The Concertos* in: Denis Arnold and Nigel Fortune editors, *The Beethoven Companion*, 1973, p. 321.

'In spite of his disparaging remarks to Breitkopf and Härtell, Beethoven in fact had nothing to be ashamed of in the C major Concerto. It is a work of outstanding freshness of inspiration and beauty of melody, most effectively written for the soloist and splendidly orchestrated.'

R. Kinloch Anderson, *Liner notes to EMI, Classics for Pleasure, Beethoven, Piano Concerto No. 1*, 1977.

'By the time Beethoven came to write the C major Concerto in 1797–98, his perception of the possibilities had considerably sharpened ... Although he was undoubtedly too harsh towards the [B-flat major Concerto], we can easily see that the muscular compactness of the C major Concerto must have been preferred by him as more obviously expressing the confidence of a young master in his own strength; he had found a discipline holding the seeds of a new power, a kind of severity and rigour that became fully exerted only later. No early work shows more clearly what crisp and potent use he could make of mere formulae.'

Robert Simpson, *Beethoven and the Concerto*, in: Robert Layton editor, *A Guide to the Concerto*, 1996, p. 105.

'Brilliant concertos were a likely road to success, and in this work, with its grand scale — it would have been the longest concerto his audience had ever heard — its splendid orchestral style, and its difficult *and* impressive piano writing, Beethoven gave the Viennese a humdinger, something to make them sit up and take notice.'

Michael Steinberg, *The Concerto: A Listener's Guide*, 1998, p. 52.

'[A] capacity for self-criticism appeared early in Beethoven's career and was manifestly built into the history of the Concerto in B flat. The various versions of the piece articulate various stages of youthfulness — all seemingly exuberant. The Concerto in C by comparison, chronologically largely of a piece, reflects a certain consolidation, a settlement in style and expression wherein risks are calculated and enthusiasms controlled ... [In] 1795, the C major Concerto probably looked to be a more mature piece than the B flat Concerto did in 1798.'

Leon Plantinga, *Beethoven's Concertos: History, Style, Performance*, 1999, p. 4 and p. 66.

> 'The C major Concerto builds on some of the ideas of No. 2, while introducing new features and possessing a rather different, more military character emphasized by the use of trumpets and drums, which were absent in its predecessor.'

> 'In the C major Concerto, Op. 15, Beethoven retains the general formal outlines of the preceding work [Op. 19], with an *Allegro con brio* and a high-spirited rondo finale enclosing a thoughtful slow movement: a spacious, decorative, almost hymn-like *Largo* in A-flat major.'

Barry Cooper, Beethoven, The Master Musicians, 2000, p. 2000, p. 54.

William Kinderman, *The Concertos* in: Glenn Stanley editor, *The Cambridge Companion to Beethoven*, 2000, p. 108.

> The opus numbers to Beethoven's compositions usually reflect the date of their publication, not their composition, and in this regard — although with some exceptions — they are generally held to be reliable. This has a bearing on the opus numbers assigned to Beethoven's C major and B-flat major Concertos. The C major Concerto was published in March 1801 by Tranquillo Mollo and the B-flat major Concerto — although composed *earlier* — was not published until December 1801 by Hoffmeister and Kühnel of

Leipzig. Thereby, the C major Concerto acquired the designation Op. 15 and the B-flat major Concerto that of Op. 19. Setting aside this confusion, the C major Concerto is held in regard for being 'the more ambitious, brilliant, and impressive of the two'.[1]

From the foregoing it follows that the B-flat major Piano Concerto, Op. 19 was the one that immediately succeeded the youthful E-flat major Concerto, WoO 4. The reader wishing, therefore, to trace Beethoven's progress from that work should first consult the text to the Op. 19 Concerto.

Beethoven's five piano concertos, bearing opus numbers, are widely admired and occupy a prominent place in today's concert repertoire. Beethoven had a rich inheritance at his disposal from which to draw inspiration. A generation before him, Mozart had elevated the discourse between the piano and the orchestra in his great series of 27 piano concertos. Moreover, he had revealed how the soloist could embrace the genre as a vehicle for instrumental display and personal virtuosity. In due course, the concerto provided Beethoven with a platform to showcase his own powers as a keyboard virtuoso, and also to serve him as a compositional form by means of which he could give expression to some of his 'most noble, profound, beautiful and at times witty and playful thoughts'.[2]

Beethoven never held an official court position in Vienna or that of director of music. It may surprise some Beethovenians – given the composer's legendary independence of mind – that he cherished the post of kapellmeister right up to his middle age, by which time he realised it was beyond his reach – as was his hope of finding contentment in marriage. His success, most notably in the early years following his arrival in Europe's musical capital between

1782–85, was reliant upon the patronage he enjoyed through several noble benefactors. These included: Count Karl von Lichnowsky; Baron van Swieten; the Count and Countess von Browne; Prince Lobkowitz; Prince Johann Joseph von Schwarzenberg – in whose residence Beethoven's celebrated Septet Op. 20 was first heard; Prince Johann Joseph von Liechtenstein – to whose wife Beethoven dedicated the Piano Sonata Op. 27, No. 1 – *Quasi una fantasia*; Prince Kinsky; and, as we shall in due course relate, the composer's patron-pupil Anna Luisa Barbara (Babette) Scalchi, née Countess von Keglevics de Buzin – to whom he dedicated among other things, the subject of our narrative the Piano Concerto in C major, Op. 15. When Beethoven threatened to leave Vienna – at the invitation of Jérôme Bonaparte – the Archduke Rudolph, Prince Ferdinand Kinsky, and Count Franz Joseph Lobkow-itz united to deter Beethoven by pledging to secure his finances; they collectively agreed to settle upon him an annuity of 4000 gulden / florins – the equivalent offered to him by Jérôme Bonaparte.

Beethoven was accepted as Lichnowsky's guest. It was at his Friday morning concerts that such leading composers of the day as Haydn and Salieri gathered to hear the young composer's latest compositions – works that have been described as marking Beethoven's 'first maturity'. But it was his prowess at the keyboard that most captivated the audiences gathered in the salons of Vienna's nobility. From Beethoven's most celebrated piano pupil Carl Czerny – he of the thousand-and-more finger-dexterity studies – we learn:

'No one matched him in the speed of his scales, double trills, leaps, etc. (not even [Johann Nep-omuk] Hummel). His posture while playing was ideally calm, noble and good to look at, without the slightest grimace (though he did begin to bend forward as his deafness increased). His fingers were very powerful, not long, and flattened at the tips by much playing; because, as he told me, he had practiced prodigiously as a youngster, usually until well after midnight'.[3]

Further testimony to Beethoven's pianistic ability is conveyed in a letter August von Schall wrote to the Elector Maximilian Franz on 6 May 1796 having heard Beethoven perform; Schall was an official at the Elector's Court and had been aware of Beethoven's keyboard virtuosity from his days in Bonn. He writes:

'Beethoven was here [Dresden] for about eight days. Everyone who heard him play on the clavier was delighted. With the Elector of Saxony, who is a connoisseur of music, Beethoven had the privilege of playing accompaniments for one and a half hours.'

The Elector afterwards presented the composer with a gold snuffbox filled with Louis d'ors. Beethoven was given to declaring it was no ordinary snuffbox but such a one as might have been given to an ambassador. His improvisations at the keyboard thrilled and enchanted audiences, who found them 'rich in fantasy' with 'striking changes from adagio to allegro' — hallmarks of Beethoven's piano playing that would soon find a place in his piano-sonata and piano-concerto compositions.

Such was Beethoven's growing celebrity in musical circles that he was mentioned in Johann Ferdinand Ritter von Schönfeld's *Jahrbuch der Tonkunst von Wien und Prag*

— 'Yearbook for the art of tone in Vienna and Prague'. This listed musicians in alphabetical order. Beethoven is described as

> 'a musical genius who has lived in Vienna for two years. He is generally admired for his outstanding velocity and the great ease with which he performs extraordinary difficulties'.[4]

Although the piano — more correctly pianoforte — had benefitted from a number of developments since the death of Mozart, it was not yet, at the period under consideration, the powerful and sonorous instrument of Beethoven's maturity. Viennese makers were striving to extend the range of their instruments and make them more capable of dynamic gradations. In this context, mention should be made of parallel developments being undertaken in London, in response to such keyboard innovators as Muzio Clementi and Johann Baptist Cramer.

We detect something of Beethoven's disaffection with the instruments available to him from letters he wrote to the Vienna-based piano maker Andreas Streicher. Writing to him on 23 November 1796, when he was on a concert tour in Pressburg, he initially enthused: 'I received ... your fortepiano, which is really an excellent instrument ... Anyone else would try to keep it for himself.' However, he could not refrain from pointing out to Streicher what he considered to be its limitations: 'It robs me of the freedom to produce my own tone.' But, he added good-naturedly: 'This must not deter you from making all your fortepianos in the same way.' The reason for his reservations is revealing. He states: '[No] doubt there are few people who cherish such whims as mine' — by which he really meant make such demands of the instrument. A few weeks later, on his return to Vienna, he wrote once more to Streicher complaining the pianoforte is 'the least studied of all instruments'; he goes on to say that it is like 'merely listening to a harp'. He looked forward to the time 'when the harp and the pianoforte will be treated as two entirely different instruments'.[5]

Gerhard von Breuning, the son of Beethoven's friend Stephan, inherited the composer's pianoforte made by the Viennese piano-maker Joseph Brodmann. Writing about this in his *Memories of Beethoven* (1874) he states:

> 'When one looks at the Brodmann grand piano (still in my possession) considered one of the best makes at that time, with its tiny tone and mere five and a half octaves, one finds it hard to conceive how it could have been adequate for Beethoven's tempestuous improvisations ... [It] was as a consequence of Beethoven's sonatas that the piano was altered and strengthened into its present state, indeed it had to be almost made afresh.'[6]

Commenting on the lack of availability to Beethoven of the very highest notes on the early piano, Charles Rosen makes the interesting observation: 'The existence of these notes is *implied* in the music.' [italics added] In defence of this assertion he cites what he describes as 'an irritating or piquant wrong note' in the first movement of Beethoven's First Piano Concerto. This is a reference to the high F natural where 'the melody obviously calls for F sharp' – then not available on the keyboard at the period when Beethoven conceived the work. The more expanded compass came into being only some years later when Beethoven composed the most elaborate cadenza for the work (see later). With regard to this, and taking a dig at the more extreme dogma of the *Early Movement* enthusiasts, Rosen asserts: '[To] employ an instrument contemporary with the work would mean not only playing an evidently wrong note but even renouncing the best cadenza.'[7]

As the enlarged keyboard became available, Czerny had words of caution for those virtuosi tempted, as he saw it, to take liberties with Beethoven's score. He pronounced:

> 'In those pianoforte pieces ... which were written for the five-octave instruments of former times, the attempt to employ the sixth octave, by means of additions, is always unfavourable; and all embellishments, turns, shakes, etc. which the author himself has not indicated, justly appear superfluous, however tasteful they may be in themselves.'[8]

Years later, recalling his own youthful indiscretions, Czerny conceded that he did not always follow his own strictures and once yielded to the temptation of taking liberties with Beethoven's score. On 20 September 1845, he recalled the following incident in the *Wiener musikalische Zeitung*:

> 'In 1812 I played the Quintet for Piano and Winds [Op. 16] at one of Schuppanzigh's concerts; with the frivolity of youth, I took the liberty of complicating passage work, of using the higher octaves, etc. Beethoven rightly reproached me for it, in front of Schuppanzigh, Linke and the other players.'[9]

The next day, Czerny received a letter from Beethoven. He first apologised for rebuking Czerny but justified himself: 'You must forgive a composer who would rather have heard his work performed exactly as it was written, however beautifully you played it in other respects.'[10]

An anecdote from the recollections of Ferdinand Ries, another of Beethoven's piano pupils, suggests Beethoven very occasionally set aside his own self-imposed rules. He relates:

> 'I remember only two occasions where Beethoven instructed me to add a few notes to his compositions – once in the *Rondo* of the *Sonate Pathétique* (Op. 13), and again in the theme of the *Rondo* of his First Concerto in C major, where he specified several doublings to make it more brilliant.'

Of the interpretation of his own works, more generally, Czerny adds:

> 'In playing he would give now the right, now the left hand of a particular passage, a beautiful but nonetheless inimitable expression only in extremely rare cases would he add notes or ornamental decoration.'

Concerning the rendering of the *Rondo* to the Concerto Op. 15, Ries states:

> 'He performed this particular *Rondo* with a very special expressiveness. In general, he played his own compositions most capriciously, though he kept a very steady rhythm and only occasionally, indeed very rarely, speeded up the tempo somewhat. At times he restrained the tempo in his crescendo with a ritardando, which had a beautiful and most striking effect.'[11]

Although Beethoven had established a reputation in the salons of Vienna's nobility, by performing his sonata compositions and thrilling audiences with his improvisations, he still had to reach the wider music public through the medium of the piano concerto. Mozart had pioneered the way by playing his own works, and Beethoven had ambitions to do the same. In the eighteenth century the most wealthy, princely aristocrats maintained their own orchestras that had, in some measure, provided an outlet for Mozart and Haydn to showcase their orchestral works. We recall, for example, Haydn's relationship with Prince Esterházy held him captive at his summer residence at Eisenstadt — prompting his artful hint to his employer in the incident of *The Farewell* Symphony.

A letter of Mozart's is of interest here. When, for reasons of financial expediency, he was obliged to sell his Piano Concertos K. 451, K. 459 and K. 488 to Prince Joseph Wenzel zu Fürstenberg, he sent a revealing covering note:

> 'The compositions I keep to myself and a small circle of music lovers and connoisseurs (who promise not to let them out of their hands) ... I have the honour of sending them to His Highness ... [but] I must ask His Highness not to let them out of *his* hands.'[12]

Mozart's concerns were twofold. In the late eighteenth century, and extending into the early nineteenth, there was little or no copyright protection for a composer; pirate editions, and unauthorised transcriptions of a celebrated composer's works, were rife. Moreover, these deprived a composer from enjoying the celebrity of performing his own works. We shall see, notably in our study of the B-flat major Concerto, these circumstances disposed Beethoven to hold back the publication of this composition for a long time, and in some measure that also of the C major Concerto, Op. 15.

1795 was an auspicious year for Beethoven. It was when he made his public debut as a concert pianist. In March, the annual concerts in the Burgtheater were announced for the benefit of the Widows of the Tonkünstler-Gesellschaft/Societät — 'the Society of Musicians'. Two concerts were advertised for the evenings of the 29th and 30th of the month at which 'a concerto by Beethoven', then a pupil of Antonio Salieri, was promised. Whether Beethoven performed the B-flat Concerto or the C major Concerto on the 29 March is somewhat open to question — see our text to Op. 19.[13] At the 30 March concert, Beethoven contributed an improvisation. On 31 March, Mozart's widow arranged for a performance of *La Clemenza di Tito* to take place in the Burgtheater. This time the advertisement announced: 'Herr. Ludwig van Beethoven will play a concerto of Mozart's composition.' It is thought the work in question was the Concerto in D minor, K. 466 that Beethoven is known to have held in high regard and for which he wrote cadenzas. On the 16 December 1795, the *Wiener Zeitung* announced a further concert:

'Next Friday, the 18th, Herr Kapellmeister Haydn will give a grand musical concert in the Redoutensaal ... Herr van Beethoven will play a concerto of his composing'.

Beethoven's biographer Alexander Thayer remarks: 'One would gladly know what concerto was played.' Most authorities believe that it was at this concert that Beethoven premiered the C major Concerto.[14]

In 1796, Beethoven made his first concert tour in his

dual capacity as pianist-composer. There is no record of him having performed either of his new Concertos, Op. 15 or Op. 19, but his playing helped to establish his growing fame as both a virtuoso pianist and composer of striking originality. He undertook the tour between the months of February and July calling at Prague, Dresden, Leipzig and Berlin. He was well received and wrote to his brother Nikolaus Johann that he was earning 'a good deal of money'.[15] August von Schall, an official at the Court of the Elector Maximilian Franz, having heard Beethoven perform wrote to Franz in the following terms:

> 'Beethoven was here [Dresden] for about eight days. Everyone who heard him play on the clavier was delighted. With the Elector of Saxony, who is a connoisseur of music, Beethoven had the privilege of playing accompaniments for one and a half hours.'[16]

An indication of Beethoven's acceptance into Vienna's wider musical circle is evident from a letter he received on 10 February 1797 from his former teacher Antonio Salieri and Paul Wranitzky. They were respectively Vice President and Secretary to the Viennese Tonkünstier-Sozietät – Society of Musicians – to which we have made reference. Wranitzky also held the post of Music Director to Count Johann Esterhazy. At a meeting of the Society, it was resolved

> '[Those] famous musicians who had afforded the Society great services, or might serve the Society in some manner in the future, should be given free entrance tickets for all future Society academies [benefit concerts] and that these should be

> accompanied by a polite letter *ad captandum benevolentiam* ['to win over good will'].'

Beethoven was one of the Society's chosen musicians, and in their letter to him they expressed the hope that he would 'be so kind, in the future as in the past, to support the Widows and Orphans of the Society through your excellent talents'.[17]

Salieri and Wranitzky did not have to wait long for their expectations to be fulfilled. On 5 November 1797, *The Society of Plastic and Graphic Artists* (sculptors and painters) announced a forthcoming Masked Ball in aid of its Pension Fund. The programme promised 'the beloved Minuets and German Dances of Herr von [sic] Beethoven'.[18] At the start of Beethoven's career, the prefix *van* in his name was frequently misrepresented as the German *von* – an indication of noble birth. It has even been suggested Beethoven's ready acceptance into the salons of the Austro-Hungarian aristocracy may, in part, have been due to the fact that its members may have considered *van*, in his name, to be the equivalent of *von* in theirs, as remarked, an indicator of distinction and nobility. Notwithstanding Beethoven's unorthodox demeanour and unkempt appearance, he was, in effect, regarded as sharing their aristocratic kinship.[19]

In due course, Beethoven contributed on many charitable musical-occasions. Indeed, such was his generosity that towards the end of his life he was honoured in the form of a fulsome letter signed by twenty-four admirers of his art. They expressed their esteem of him, his works, and his charitable inclinations. The signatories included: Artaria & Co., (one of the composer's first music publishers); Carl Czerny (Beethoven's piano pupil and pianistic pedagogue); Anton Diabelli (composer and music publisher); and Prince

Eduard and Count Moritz Lichnowsky (respectively nephew and brother of Prince Carl Lichnowsky). Beethoven's devotees remarked:

> 'Out of the wide circle of reverent admirers that surround your genius in your native city, a small number of disciples and lovers of art approach you today to express long felt wishes.'[20]

During October 1798, Beethoven made a second concert-tour to Prague, once more in the capacity of pianist. He gave two public concerts. At the first he played the C major Concerto with two movements of the second Piano Sonata from his Op. 2 set — that Donald Francis Tovey once described as being 'flawless in execution and entirely beyond the range of Haydn and Mozart in harmonic language, except in the finale'.[21] At the second concert, he played the B-flat major Concerto incorporating one of his many revisions to the score.[22] Wenzel Johann Tomaschek, the Bohemian pianist, teacher and composer, was a close contemporary of Beethoven and heard him improvise at this concert on a theme of Mozart's. Recalling the occasion, he relates:

> 'Beethoven's magnificent playing, and particularly the daring flights in his improvisations, stirred me strangely to the depths of my soul: indeed, I found myself so profoundly bowed down that I did not touch the pianoforte for several days.'[23]

In 1845 the *Allgemeine musikalische Zeitung* published an extensive article from Tomaschek's recently published *Autobiography*. In this, Tomaschek appears to have considered aspects of Beethoven's improvisations in a more critical light. He states: 'To be sure I admired his strong and sparkling playing, but I did not fail to note his more frequent bold leaps from one motive to another.' Tomaschek then makes the generalization that was shared by many of Beethoven's contemporaries: 'Such drawbacks often weaken his most splendid works of music, which he created with overly exuberant inspiration.'[24]

On 2 April 1800, Beethoven may be said to have truly arrived in Vienna. This was the date of his first benefit concert – an *akademie* – at which works wholly of his composition were performed. He would henceforth stand alongside Haydn, not merely as his pupil, but as a composer of equal distinction. The forthcoming concert was announced in the *Wiener Zeitung* and stated:

'Wird Herr von [sic] Beethoven ein concert auf dem fortepiano spielen von seiner eigenen kom-position' – 'a new piano concerto by van Beethoven – together with other compositions.'[25]

In passing, it will be noted from the announcement's wording that Beethoven was still, after six years' residence in Vienna, being referred to as Herr *von* Beethoven.

Beethoven secured the Burgtheater – Vienna's most prestigious concert-venue – and the Burgtheater's orchestra. As was the custom of the period, Beethoven had to defray all the expenses himself. Perhaps for this reason the better seats were sold by him from his own apartment; others were available, in the normal fashion, at the box office.[26] Alongside the 'the new piano concerto', the composer's Symphony No. 1 in C major, Op. 21 was premiered. Beethoven dedicated the work to Baron Gottfried van Swieten, an early patron of the composer – and who, co-incidentally, shared the same prefix to his name. The *AmZ* review of the

Symphony was brief. The critic acknowledged the work possessed 'much art, novelty, and richness of ideas' but he protested, that Beethoven used the wind instruments 'far too much, so that it was more band music than true orchestral music'. More suited to the critic's taste was the composer's Septet in E-flat major, Op. 20, then newly composed. He regarded it as having been written 'with a great deal of taste and feeling'. The score contains the notation, 'Der Kaiserin Maria Theresia gewidmet' — 'Dedicated to the Empress Marie Therese' that, as H. C. Robbins Landon remarks, 'established [Beethoven's] connection, albeit a tenuous one, with the Royal and Imperial House'.[27]

The *AmZ* critic was charitable towards Beethoven, personally stating that he 'improvised masterfully'. He added, with tantalising ambiguity, that he performed 'a grand concerto on the pianoforte of his own composition'.[28] Which concerto was performed has been the subject of conjecture. Early Beethoven biographers, such as Anton Schindler, debated whether the concerto in question was Op.15 or even Op. 19 — now too-long established, though, in the repertoire to fit the description of 'a new concerto'.

Modern-day musicology favours the C major Piano Concerto as the likely candidate, particularly in view of the fact that Beethoven had revised the work and amended the score — just as he would have with performance in mind. Some authorities suggest Beethoven had intended to perform the C minor Piano Concerto, Op. 37. It is known he was working on this at the time, but it was not yet ready to be presented at the April 1800 concert.[29] Beethoven's revisions to the C major Concerto are today preserved in full score in Berlin.[30]

For the 1800 concert, it is thought Beethoven made use of an autograph from around 1798 — now lost — leaving the solo part, in some measure, to be improvised. He subsequently wrote out a new autograph, revising the orchestration and with the piano part in full score. As Leon Plantinga remarks, the 2 April presentation of the C major Concerto had served its purpose 'as his own performance vehicle'.[31]

It appears, from the review of the concert, that the Burgtheater orchestra played in slovenly fashion:

> 'In accompanying they did not even take the trouble to pay attention to the solo player; thus, there was no delicacy in the accompaniment, or any compliance with the progression of the soloist's feelings, and the like.'[32]

Perhaps, in mitigation, the players found the composer's new music too challenging.

Despite the *AmZ's* critical reservations about Beethoven's First Symphony, it was soon added to the repertory of the Gewandhuas Orchestra at Leipzig. In the years following its premier, in 1800, it was performed at Berlin, Breslau, Brunswick, Dresden, Frankfurt-am-Main, and Munich. Two performance of the Symphony also took place in England between 1804–05, news of which gave Beethoven particular pleasure.[33] It has been suggested he was so impressed by the early English reception of his music that it was this that disposed him, by way of an expression of gratitude, to write his Variations on *God Save the King*, WoO 78 and *Rule Britannia*, WoO 79.[34] The Septet was performed several times following the April 1800 concert; such was to become its popularity that, in later years, Beethoven had cause to wish he had never composed the work — for the reason he considered it distracted attention from his later creations that possessed greater merit.

Reflecting on Beethoven's growing celebrity at this period, Thayer remarks:

'Beethoven ... though almost unknown personally beyond the limits of a few Austrian cities ... had, in the short space of eight years, by simple force of his genius as manifested in his published works, placed himself at the head of all writers for the pianoforte ... The unknown student who had entered Vienna in 1792, was now in 1804 a recognised member of the great triumvirate, Haydn, Mozart and Beethoven.'[35]

In 1804 the pianist A. F. Wustrow performed the C major Concerto, Op. 15. Wustrow is one of the minor figures in Beethoven musicology; he is perhaps best remembered today for his Piano Trio version of Beethoven's Wind Sextet Op 71. Of the Concerto, the *AmZ*'s music critic acknowledged that Wustrow played 'the very difficult solo part with much skill' — notwithstanding what he considered to be music over-provided 'with chromatic passages and enharmonic changes, occasionally to the point of bizarrerie'. More generally, however, the critic seemed pleased with the work:

'The first movement was splendidly worked out, but the modulations were far too excessive; the *Adagio* in A-flat major was an extremely pleasant piece, richly melodic, and was greatly embellished by the obbligato clarinet. The last movement, *All' Inglese* [in an English country-dance idiom] distinguished itself by its unusual rhythms and also was well executed.'[36]

Between 12 November 1807 and 27 March 1808, the *Gesellschaft für Musikfreunde*, and other musical societies, gave some twenty concerts in Vienna. Ten of these included works by Beethoven, a number of which featured the First Piano Concerto and the First Symphony.[37] In the same concert season, we encounter Franz Joseph Clement, known to Beethovenians for his premiering of the composer's Violin Concerto, Op. 61 in 1806.[38] Clement was also an accomplished orchestral conductor and held the post of *Musikdirektor* at the Theater an der Wien. Clement directed a series of concerts in Vienna for the 1807–08 concert season. Among the music performed was the First Piano Concerto. Perhaps, for reasons of his encroaching deafness, Beethoven was not the soloist; the work was performed by Johann Baptist Steiner von Felsburg, whose name today is associated with the first performance of the composer's Piano Sonata in E minor, Op. 90.

Beethoven subsequently revised the Concerto's cadenzas. He appears to have made mention of this, sometime in January 1808, to Count Moritz von Dietrichstein – a founder member of the *Gesellschaft für Musikfreunde*. He stated he had written the cadenza in anticipation of his forthcoming so-called *Liebhaber-Concerte* to be held on 31 January 1808. On this occasion the pianist was to have once more been Johann von Felsburg. However, Beethoven appears to have mistrusted Felsburg's abilities; he considered he lacked the dexterity to do justice to the cadenza he had written, exclaiming 'as soon as he could play the Concerto better he would be allowed to perform it'. Today, the autograph of the cadenza in question exists as a fragment only of some sixty bars.[39]

Towards the end of Beethoven's life, the C major Piano Concerto was well established in the pianist's repertoire. We infer this from the occasion when, in September 1825, the Czech composer-pianist Wenzel (Wilhelm) Würfel made Beethoven's acquaintance; he greatly admired his compositions. Würfel is now remembered for being the teacher of

Chopin but in his day was celebrated as a concert pianist. According to the account of his meeting with Beethoven, he made it known to him that he had performed his First Piano Concerto 'to large audiences' and gave the composer his undertaking to always play his works authentically 'as they had been written'.[40]

From Carl Czerny we learn, at the period when Beethoven's hearing was unimpaired, that he would try out a passage at the keyboard until he was satisfied. His friend Ignaz von Seyfried, whom we have introduced in our prefatory quotations, remarks in similar fashion:

> 'He used to play over to me on the piano, as soon as it was finished, every portion [of his] compositions, which are now recognised as masterpieces by the whole world. Without giving me time to reflect, he immediately demanded my opinion, which I was able to give frankly, without any fear of offending that false pride from which he was entirely free.'[41]

The C major Piano Concerto reached its final form only after much gestation and exploration in sketch form — an enduring characteristic of Beethoven's approach to composition. We discuss this more fully in our commentary to the B-flat major Concerto. Suffice it here to quote Donald Tovey:

> 'The immense labour shown in Beethoven's innumerable sketches for all manner of works, from the greatest to the slightest, is mainly devoted to giving the written work the rhetorical perfection of an extemporization.'[42]

When indoors, Beethoven did much of his composition at

his writing desk. This was surprisingly small, given the proliferation of sketches he needed to consult, and took the form of a walnut bureau with a fold-down top.[43]

About two hundred loose sheets of sketches date back to Beethoven's days in Bonn, from about 1790 or even earlier. These have subsequently been assembled into two large gatherings, the larger of which is now preserved in the British Library and is known as the 'Kafka Sketchbook' (more correctly Kafka 'Miscellany') — taking its name from its one-time owner the collector of manuscripts Johann Nepomuk Kafaka. It has since been established that the Kafka Miscellany was used by Beethoven as a source for the Op. 15 Concerto.[44] Drafts for the first two movements are included alongside other pieces. These include the popular *Rondo quasi un capriccio* in G major, Op. 129.[45] Its late opus number is explained by the fact that it was left incomplete by Beethoven and was not finished until after his death by Anton Diabelli. Its popular name — *Rage over a Lost Penny* — is thought to have been provided by Anton Schindler. Several of Beethoven's original sketches are also preserved in the Fischhof Miscellany — a collation of single manuscript leaves representing Beethoven's compositional drafts for the period 1790—99.[46] The name of the collection derives from the pianist and music historian Joseph Fischhof who acquired an extensive library of Beethoven's printed and manuscript scores and sketches.

During Beethoven's early years in Vienna, his sketching had become so elaborate that by 1798 he found it more convenient to work with a ready-made manuscript sketch-book, in preference to loose, single-sheets. The first such book is known as Grasnick 1 and dates from about late summer 1798 to early 1799. The sketchbook originally had 48 leaves — a standard size in Beethoven's time. However, its first nine leaves were removed probably before the collector of autograph scores, Friedrich August Grasnick, acquired it in the middle of the nineteenth century. Evidence of a cadenza (see later) for the C major Concerto is found in Grasnick 1.[47]

From the foregoing it can be inferred the C major Concerto had its sketch origins from the period 1794–95, most probably alongside revisions for the B-flat major Concerto that preoccupied the composer for a number of years (see our following account). The sketches reveal Beethoven exploring ideas for cadenzas. In recent years, conjectural restorations of these have been made by the Swiss musicologist Willy Hess, as found in: the Fischhof Miscellany (1795), p. 30; Kafka Miscellany (1795–99), p. 72; Kafka Miscellany (1796–98), p. 138; and the Grasnick Sketchbook 1 (mid-1798), p. 2.[48] Between 1796–98, Op. 15 appears to have found its final form. However, as we shall see, the opportunities (and temptation) for further enriching the score of this, and other of his piano concertos, with more elaborate cadenzas continued to be one of Beethoven's preoccupations.

The sketch sources to which we have referred reveal Beethoven simultaneously turning his powers of invention to other compositions than the Op. 15 and Op. 19 Concertos; it would be a lifelong characteristic of his working method to turn from one work to another – usually of disparate genres and moods. Compositions from the period in question include: three Trios for Violin and Cello, Op. 1; three Piano Sonatas, Op. 2; the String Trio, Op. 3; several sets of German dances; and song settings – notably *Adelaide*, Op. 46.[49] As Barry Cooper states,

> '[Beethoven's] intention was to bring to public notice several works in different genres – piano solo, piano with accompaniment, strings, song, and concerto – in quick succession ...'.[50]

The evolution and growing importance of the cadenza, within the framework of the piano concerto at the period under consideration, is worthy of particular mention; it left its mark on the C major Concerto that pianists still respect today – with occasional exceptions (see later). Tovey's ideal classical cadenza was one that approximated to an actual extemporization, 'by a player capable of using the composer's language'. He elaborated: 'No artist deserved the title of *virtuoso* unless his extemporisations could pass for written compositions.' He condemned the pianist who inserted a cadenza into a concerto that was out of character with the music or, as he put it, who could not resist 'the temptation to display anything so banal as *a review of the progress of music since the composer's date.*' [Tovey's italics] In the words of the music polymath Antony Hopkins – composer, pianist, conductor, author, and radio broadcaster:

> 'The cadenza presented an opportunity for the performer to display his skill, and while technical virtuosity was certainly called for, further development of the thematic material was important.'

As he further observes, most pianists would prepare their cadenzas in advance of a performance – in the process of learning the composition as a whole. His next observation calls to mind the many testimonies to Beethoven improvising:

> '[The] stimulus of an audience may well have provoked new flights of fancy, and most particularly the presence of other musicians in the surrounding orchestra would be likely to encourage the performer to new invention.'[51]

37

A musically-minded audience, of the time of Mozart and Haydn through to Beethoven, would be alert to the arrival of the cadenza and, equally to its drawing to a close, by a sustained trill on the piano. The trill would summon the other players to attention to resume their role in the orchestral tutti – to be anticipated by both the players and the audience alike. In the days when he performed his own concerti, Beethoven took delight in sounding *false* trill entries – to the consternation of the players but to the amusement of the audience. Remarking on this, the respected Beethoven interpreter Alfred Brendel comments:

> 'Beethoven, one of the supreme musical archi-tects, wrote cadenzas that make Mozart's look like models of restraint. In the marathon cadenza for his own C major Concerto, the trill is espe-cially the target of his mockery. It never happens as it should. After some hundred bars, that run amok through various keys and wreck classical conventions right and left, the cadenza appears to come to an end ... [We] are in an area of ambiguity.'[52]

Elsewhere he writes:

> 'Beethoven's way with cadenzas was very different to that of Mozart who never exploded the struc-ture of a piece ... With Beethoven it is quite different, He clearly wishes to shock the listener, selecting the remotest keys and almost taking pleasure in flying in the face of the piece's basic character.'[53]

An anecdote from the *Autobiography* of Charles Hallé

has relevance to our discussion. In February 1862 he attended a concert in which the Hungarian pianist, teacher and composer Stephen Heller played a Mozart Concerto. In Hallé's estimation, Heller had admirably fulfilled his own ideals as to the role of a cadenza in a piano concerto; we recall that at the period in question, Hallé was himself a pianist of considerable renown. The music critic of the concert in question, though, appears to have upset Hallé by suggesting that the inclusion of a cadenza was *optional* with the performer. Hallé maintained, the cadenza was an integral part of the composition that could not be dispensed with without destroying the symmetry of the work. He elaborated that the role of the cadenza, at the conclusion of a movement, was to recapitulate the principal ideas that had gone before — 'to condense them, present them in a new form, and, in short, to give a *resumé* of the whole work'.[54]

Our reference to Hallé brings us closer to our own time. Such have been the liberties taken by some pianists that the cadenza has been described by some wit as 'the appendicitis of the concerto'. We catch a flavour of this in a review of a concert in which the ardent Beethovenian Leonard Bernstein was both soloist and conductor. In the Carnegie Hall concert-season 1960–61, Bernstein performed Beethoven's First Piano Concerto — directing the orchestra from the piano. The music critic of the *New York Herald Tribune*, Paul Henry Lang, was not enamoured of the liberties he considered Bernstein took with the music:

> 'In the cadenza, Bernstein sounded like a frustrated pianist ... With foot on the pedal, he whaled away at the keyboard, piling sonority on sonority. The results were disproportionate to say the least.'[55]

Glen Gould was a pianist who did not shrink from superimposing his own personality on a composer's music. In defence of writing cadenzas for the C major Concerto he once remarked: 'I can scarcely hope to conceal the fact that my cadenzas to the first and last movements of the Beethoven Concerto in C are hardly pure Beethoven style.' He defended his approach stating:

'In writing these cadenzas I had in mind a potpourri of motives which was possible only in an idiom considerably more chromatic than that of early Beethoven.'[56]

Gould's words prompt a personal recollection. The present writer remembers the occasion, more than fifty years ago, when the he heard the youthful Daniel Barenboim perform the C major Concerto at the Edinburgh International Festival. When it came to the cadenza, Barenboim — with the prerogative of youth — and with consummate mastery — set aside Beethoven's cadenza and substituted it for a paraphrase of melodies from the closing movement of the contemporaneous Piano Sonata in A major, Op. 2, No.2.

Beethoven composed the C major piano Concerto with the five-octave keyboard in mind. In the years following the work's first performance, the range of the keyboard was expanded. Beethoven took advantage of this by writing cadenzas for each of his Concertos Op. 15, Op. 19, Op. 37, and Op. 58; the cadenza for the Op. 73 Concerto forms a fully composed, integral part of the composition. The stimulus to write these cadenzas was, in part, to take advantage of the possibilities that the new-style keyboard presented but also to serve as vehicles for his pupil, the Archduke Rudolph. It is a tribute to Rudolph's pianistic attainments — particularly given the demands on his time arising from in his vocational obligations as Cardinal-Arch-bishop — that Beethoven considered his pupil could rise to the challenge of his new music's running-passages and rhetorical expression.[57] Of related interest is that the manu-script of the cadenza bears the Archduke's Library Cata-logue 'No. 50', the same as that for his copy of the C major Concerto; the inference being the cadenza had been com-bined, for completeness, with the original piano score.[58]

Beethoven completed two cadenzas for the opening Allegro of the Op. 15 Concerto. The longer of the two is widely admired and still performed. Tovey considered it to be a masterpiece among the composer's cadenzas: 'It is one of the most splendid in recording the style of an extempori-zation.' He praised it for raising piano-writing to the level of the *Waldstein* Piano Sonata, disposing him to conclude: 'I should never dream of writing another cadenza to Beethoven's C major Concerto!' Being the Beethoven enthusiast that he was, he could not resist adding:

> 'I cannot help wondering whether Beethoven could not have made something almost as great out of his first cadenza, which he left unfinished, just after it had developed [in a manner] calculated to bring certain discursive passages of the tutti into closer organic connection with the whole.'[59]

Interestingly, in his recording of the C major Concerto, Claudio Arrau performs his completion of the unfinished cadenza.[60]

Tovey is not alone in his admiration for the cadenza to the Op. 15 Concerto. Michael Steinberg writes:

> '[It] is as fantastical as it is immense. It revisits much of the music we have heard in the previous

fifteen minutes or so, and one of its finest and subtlest touches is the reappearance of the lyric E-flat major theme.'[61]

Denis Mathews enthuses:

'The largest of the two completed cadenzas is in a post-*Waldstein* style, like that of the B flat; and though it storms away for five minutes and tails off into a "joke" ending, it offers a splendid example of Beethoven's improvising manner and the Concerto is robust enough to take it.'[62]

Antony Hopkins believed the C major Concerto to be 'heroic' and anticipates that of the *Emperor* Concerto, composed between 1809–11, bearing a dedication to the Archduke Rudolph.[63]

Towards the end of his life, Beethoven was given to complain that much of his music was neglected. For example, it is thought that only one of his piano sonatas received public performance in his lifetime. We detect the extent of the neglect of the composer's works from a review of 15 July 1826 in the *Allgemeine musikalische Zeitung*. The Journal's music critic complained: 'Might it please maestro Beethoven to write cadenzas for his fortepiano concertos.' Perhaps the critic can be excused his lack of awareness of the existence of the composer's cadenzas since, consistent with performance-practice of the period, Beethoven's cadenzas were not published as part of the score in the first editions. In Beethoven's case, those for Opp. 15, 19, 37, and 58 did not appear as such until 1864. The *AmZ* critic reflected, more generally, in a manner that recognised the composer's virtuosity — at least as it was when he was at the height of his powers:

'One stumbling block that explains why Beethoven's fortepiano concertos are preformed so rarely is the fact that it is not everyone's business to create a cadenza that is comparable with Beethoven's muse.'

When other pianists played their own cadenzas, they clearly failed to meet the *AmZ* reviewer's expectations since he likened the experience of hearing them 'as if one were wearing a velvet evening dress'. Presumably he meant effeminately and lacking Beethovenian vigour.[64]

Beethoven continued to make revisions to the autograph score of the C major Concerto through 1800 to prepare it for publication; he may even have had a performance in mind for December of that year. He left the piano staves blank – to be supplied in performance according to his powers of improvisation.[65] The final movement underwent revisions as is evident in the so-called Autograph 19e. This was once owned by Arturo Toscanini and later by Vladimir Horowitz; it is now a prized possession of the Prussian State Library – Staatsbibliothek Preussischer Kulturbesitz, Berlin.[66]

On 15 December 1800 Beethoven wrote to the Leipzig music publisher Franz Anton Hoffmeister, who had earlier approached him with a view to publishing a selection of his works. Beethoven responded to Hoffmeister in his characteristically fulsome manner, addressing him as 'Most beloved and worthy brother' – a style he reserved for fellow composers, musicians, poets, artists and, occasionally, the more worthy music publishers. Beethoven offered Hoffmeister his Septet Op. 20 that he described as having become 'very popular'. The other works he offered Hoffmeister included 'a grand symphony' (First Symphony Op.

21) and 'a grand solo sonata' (Piano Sonata Op. 22). He invited Hoffmeister to fix the prices himself. Next, Beethoven offered 'a concerto for pianoforte' — taken to be a reference to the B-flat Concerto, Op. 19. He acknowledged: 'I do not make out to be one of my best.' He makes reference to another concerto 'which is to be published here [Vienna] by Mollo'. Tranquillo Mollo was a partner in the distinguished publishing firm Artaria & Co. The concerto referred to was the C major, Op. 15. Beethoven adds, in a somewhat conspiratorial manner: 'I am telling you this so that you may inform the Leipzig reviewers, because *I am still keeping back the better ones until I myself undertake a journey*'. [Beethoven's italics] From this, we can infer Beethoven was contemplating undertaking another concert tour; in the event, this did not take place. He could not resist adding: 'At the same time it would not disgrace you to engrave this Concerto' [Op. 15].[67]

Mollo subsequently made progress with the publication of the C major Concerto and announced its forthcoming appearance on 21 March 1801. In due course, Mollo contributed generously to Beethoven's early progress as a composer by publishing first editions of several of his works. These included the Piano Sonatas Op. 14, the Piano Quintet, Op. 16, and the String Quartets, Op. 18.[68] Maynard Solomon makes an interesting observation bearing on the publication of Beethoven's Op. 15 — to which he refers to as 'the sparkling Concerto No. 1'. He suggests, that in an effort to forestall negative criticism in Breitkopf & Härtel's *Allgemeine musikalische Zeitung*, Beethoven forewarned the Leipzig publisher that neither of his Piano Concertos Op. 15 and Op.19 'were among his better compositions in the form'.[69]

The Title Page of Mollo's edition of the C major Concerto proclaimed:

'Grande Concert pour le Forte Piano avec deux Violons, deux Alto, Basso et Violoncelle, deux, Flütes, deux Oboe, deux Clarinettes, deux Bassons, deux Trompettes et Timballes, composé et dedié à Son Altesse Madame la Princesse Odescalchi née Comtesse Keglevicz par Louis van Beethoven, Oeuvre 15 à Vienne chez T. Mollo et Comp.'[70]

The dedicatee, Countess Anna Luise Barbara von Keglevics, is worthy of mention; she was one of the most distinguished amateur pianists of her day. In fact, she must have been formidably gifted since she was just seventeen when Beethoven dedicated to her his new Piano Sonata Op. 7. She died aged just thirty-three but not before Beethoven had bestowed upon her the further dedications to his Ten Variations in B-flat, on the duet *La stessa, la stessissima,* from Salieri's Opera *Falstaff* (WoO 73, 1799), and the celebrated Six Variations Op. 34 of 1803. In 1801 Babette, whose full name was Anna Luisa Barbara Keglevics [Keglevich] von Buzin, married Prince Odescalchi. He was an imperial chamberlain at one of whose musical soirées Beethoven's popular Septet Op. 20 was performed. Count von Keglevics, Babette's nephew, has left a charming anecdote. At the time Beethoven was writing his new Sonata, Beethoven lived near to his youthful pupil's Vienna apartments — the precise details of Beethoven's residence are not known. It was apparently her master's habit to give her lessons attired in his morning gown, complete with slippers and a tasselled nightcap![71] This may, however, be an exaggerated family story. Of related interest is a reminiscence of Carl Czerny — who himself started to have lessons with Beethoven a few years after Babette. Czerny records,

Beethoven had considerable affection for Babette and may possibly have been in love with her.[72] Czerny even suggests that the sobriquet *Appassionata* should have been conferred on the Piano Sonata Op. 7 and not upon the celebrated Piano Sonata Op. 57. Whatever the circumstances, he informs us how Beethoven's Op. 7 was composed 'in a very impassioned mood'.[73]

Following Beethoven's death, various editions of the Concerto Op. 15 appeared. In 1834 the Frankfurt-am-Main publisher F. P. Dunst brought out an edition to be followed shortly afterwards by one from Tobias Haslinger of Vienna. Other full scores appeared in the Peters' Edition of Leipzig (1861) and in Breitkopf & Härtel's Complete Edition of the composer's works (1861). Publication in full miniature score had to await the Ernst Eulenberg edition of 1922.[74]

Charles Neate gave the first known public performance of the C major Concerto in England on 8 May 1820.[75] Neate was a fine pianist, cellist and composer who studied piano with John Field. Later, he became a founder member of the (Royal) Philharmonic Society. He met Beethoven in Vienna in 1815 and persuaded the composer to look through some of his compositions. Beethoven remarked on them favourably and appears to have held Neate in high regard. In 1861 Neate, who lived to the great age of 93, shared his impressions of Beethoven with the composer's biographer Alexander Wheelock Thayer. He remarked he had never met a man who so enjoyed nature, who 'took delight in flowers in the clouds ... nature was like food to him, he really seemed to live in it'. On Neate's return to England, Beethoven made him a parting gift of a manuscript copy of his Violin Concerto.[76]

A further connection of early performances of the C major Concerto, in England, relates to the London-born composer, pianist and teacher Cipriani Potter— alongside Neate, a founder member of the Philharmonic Society. He met Beethoven in 1817 when the two developed a firm friendship. Writing to Ferdinand Ries on 5 March 1818, Beethoven described Potter as 'a good fellow [with] a talent for composition'.[77] Potter performed the Op. 15 Concerto in London on 15 May 1822. His recollections of Beethoven derive from an article he published in 1836 in *The Musical Times*.[78]

By the close of the nineteenth century, the C major Concerto was well established in the concert repertoire in England. By way of illustration, on 25 June 1887 Sir Arthur Sullivan conducted a performance of the work given by the precociously gifted Joseph Hofmann — then age eleven.[79] The fortunes of the Op. 15 and Op. 19 Concertos in Vienna, however, appear to have been less favourable — at least according to the recollections of Artur Schnabel. Between 1891 and 1897 he studied piano in Vienna with the great Theodor Leschetizky. He recollects, at this period in Vienna the C major Concerto 'was played only be <u>debutantes'</u> and the B-flat major Concerto 'was simply unknown'.[80]

We draw our discussion of Beethoven's Piano Concerto No.1 in C major, Op. 15 to a close in the form of a documentary-style collection of texts. These are derived from the writings of musicologists and performing artists bearing on the musicology of the Op. 15 Concerto.

We commence with words of caution from Carl Czerny to the would-be performer of Beethoven's works for the keyboard:

'Each of [Beethoven's] pieces expresses some particular and well-supported idea or object, to which, even in the smallest embellishment, he always remains true. The melody everywhere pervades ... all rapid passages and figures are only employed as a *means*, never as an *end*; and if (particularly in his earlier works) many passages are found which demand the so-called *brilliant* style of playing, this must never be rendered principal. He who should only display his agility of finger therein, would entirely miss the intellectual and aesthetic, and prove that he did not understand these works.'

Turning to the C major Concerto Czerny adds — writing in 1846:

'With the present perfection of the pianoforte, which, in power and fullness of tone vies with the instruments of the orchestra, the performer of a concerto is more easy and grateful, than at a time when Beethoven himself played this First Concerto at the Kärntnerthor Theatre in Vienna (in 1801). We can now produce effects of which he had then no idea; and, in reference to the expression, we can now also reckon on a much more accurate accompaniment on the part of the orchestra than was the case at that period.'

Carl Czerny *On the Proper Performance of all Beethoven's Works for the Piano.* As translated, with annotations, in: Paul Badura-Skoda, 1970, p. 31 and p. 93.

The texts that follow are presented in the chronological order of their publication.

FIRST MOVEMENT
ALLEGRO CON BRIO
'The first movement of the present Concerto must be played in a rapid and fiery manner, and

the passages, which in themselves are not difficult, must acquire an appearance of bravura through a brilliant style of playing ... but they must never be rendered dragging, as the character of the whole is decidedly lively ... In quiet passages the player must not forget that some of the orchestral instruments are mostly employed, which either accompany, or perform a melody. In performance, therefore, we must not allow ourselves any humorous discretion, as in playing a solo piece, and, at the rehearsal, all that is necessary in this respect must, in every case, be fully determined on.'

Carl Czerny, *On the Proper Performance of all Beethoven's Works for the Piano*. As translated, with annotations, in: Paul Badura-Skoda, 1970, pp. 93–94.

'The basic mood is one of energy and vigour; it is determined by the march-like main idea, which opens the long orchestral exposition, but, curiously enough, is never assigned to the piano. The solo instrument enters with a new idea of rather gentle quality. The piano tenderly alludes to the main idea only rhythmically in the passages that precede the recapitulation, while in the recapitulation the orchestra states the main idea forcefully,'

Joseph Braunstein, *Musica Aeterna, Program Notes for 1971–1976, Vol. 2*, 1978, p. 20.

'The opening of the first movement, *Allegro con brio*, shows how Beethoven has learned how to tailor convention to his own ends. The first paragraph is a regular statement in *ceremonial* C major style ... The breadth of his formal conception is seen in the relationship of the main sections. After the active exposition, the middle section is relaxed and the *ff* return to the home key, preceded by a long but quiet dominant preparation, forms the climax of the movement.'

Basil Deane, *The Concertos* in: Denis Arnold and Nigel Fortune editors, *The Beethoven Companion*, 1973, p. 321.

'The opening tutti, having offered its martial first subject in both *p* and *f,* makes an original departure in presenting the second subject's initial phrase in a sequence of foreign keys to be duly completed and extended in the usual dominant after the solo's entry. There is also a march-like cadence-theme that forms an important sequel, but the very opening with its octave leap provides the dominating figure. Much of the solo writing is based on elementary patterns with a touch of caricature, owing more to Clementi than to Mozart, but there are already foreshadowings of the *Emperor* in the left-hand triplets and the veiled right-hand chromatics.'

Denis Matthews, *Beethoven, Master Musicians,* 1985, p. 174.

'Most of the themes of the first movement are made from tags that mean little in themselves. It is the force that infuses them that brings them to life. Beethoven's already remarkable power of momentum — so finely articulated is his progression from one theme, one sentence, one paragraph to another, that we are carried on an irresistible current. Passage-work that might have been by Czerny is swept into the general momentum by a continuously and perfectly defined sense of reassurance. In many ways, the first movement of this Concerto anticipates its much greater counterpart in the so-called *Emperor* — there are figurations that eventually generated vaster paragraphs in the later work.'

Robert Simpson, *Beethoven and the Concerto*, in: Robert Layton editor, *A Guide to the Concerto*, 1996, pp. 105–06.

'[Beethoven] scored the work in the festive trumpet-and-drums mode of Mozart's C major Concertos, and the first movement shares something of the march-like character of these works. Beethoven thinks and plans broadly and his initial exposition for the orchestra covers an astonishing lot of territory .... The development itself is one of Beethoven's most magical chapters ... with its descending parallel chords and scales, it is a kind of dream interlude, undisturbed by ghostly visitations of the movement's opening theme, many of them involving the same dissonantly overlapping semitones that initiated the piece.'

Michael Steinberg, *The Concerto: A Listener's Guide*, 1998, pp. 52–53.

'In its brilliance and grandeur, the first movement is somewhat reminiscent of Mozart's
Concerto K. 503, in the same key ... But
perhaps the funniest idea in the entire Concerto
is found near the end of the longest of the three
solo cadenzas for the first movement that
Beethoven wrote out in 1809. He indulges here
in a trick he employed in his solo performances. After twice sounding the trills that would
normally signal the end of the cadenza, and
imminent re-entrance of the orchestra,
Beethoven mischievously continues with the
lengthy cadenza.'

William Kinderman in: Glenn Stanley editor, *The Cambridge Companion to Beethoven*, 2000, p. 108.

'The First Concerto opens quietly, with a rising
octave figure — seemingly simple, but ripe for
development at points throughout the first
movement. Beethoven combines the symphonic inevitability innate to his own style with
movements of Mozart's opera buffa style.
Indeed, the precedent for the movement seems
to be Mozart's antepenultimate Piano Concerto, K. 503 in C major — complete with a
martial theme in the trumpets and horns ...
reminiscent of the Marseillaise-like theme in
the Mozart.'

David A. Thresher, Text to: *BBC Radio Three, Beethoven
Experience*, June, 2005.

SECOND MOVEMENT
LARGO

'This Largo is *alla breve* and must consequently be played tranquil *andante*. The noble melody must be performed softly, but with the most *cantabile* expression, and the simplicity of the passages must rise above the accompanying orchestra by means of refined tone and elegant delivery. The subsequent variation-theme must be well observed ... The character of this piece is a holy calm, and an elevation of the soul to the most noble sentiments, expressed by the purist harmonies and by the most feeling melody, which the player must always bear in mind during the performance.'

Carl Czerny, *On the Proper Performance of all Beethoven's Works for the Piano.* As translated, with annotations, in: Paul Badura-Skoda, 1970, p. 94.

'The slow movement (Largo, A-flat major, 4—4 time) expresses none but thoroughly approved sentiments; but this in such a way as to reveal them as true and sound.'

Donald Nivison Ferguson, *Masterworks of the Orchestral Repertoire: A Guide for Listeners*, 1954, p. 101.

'In the slow movement (Largo A-flat major), Beethoven followed Mozart's practice in excluding the trumpets and kettledrums. He also silenced the flute and oboes to achieve tender sonorities and to avoid bright colours.'

Joseph Braunstein, *Musica Aeterna, Program Notes for 1971–1976, Vol. 2*, 1978, p. 20.

'The Largo in A flat has the intimacy of a chamber-music composition, with the clarinet matching and answering the cantabile phrases of the piano.'

Basil Deane, *The Concertos* in: Denis Arnold and Nigel Fortune editors, *The Beethoven Companion*, 1973, p. 321.

'The slow movement follows the Mozartian pattern closely, treating the piano as a surrogate soprano with an exceptional technique and range. The conception is essentially vocal, even though it frequently goes beyond the compass of any mere mortal. One phrase especially, played as single unaccompanied notes, is lifted almost identically from the sublime *Et incarnatus est* in Mozart's Mass in C minor.'

Antony Hopkins, *The Concertgoer's Companion*, 1984, p. 83.

'The slow movement, though hardly more expressive than the B flat's, is far more extended, and the dialogue between the piano and the coda resolves into an eloquent dialogue between the piano and the first clarinet.'

Denis Matthews, *Beethoven, Master Musicians,* 1985, p. 174.

'Distinguished though it is by beautiful clarinet

writing, the slow movement (*Largo*) is surpassed by its more nearly sublime counterpart in the B flat Concerto. The solo part is elegant and decorative, and the orchestration translucent, with the clarinet a ready foil to the piano.'

Robert Simpson, *Beethoven and the Concerto*, in: Robert Layton editor, *A Guide to the Concerto*, 1996, p. 108.

'The A-flat major slow movement, strikingly, omits the flutes and oboes (as well as the trumpets and drums), giving much of the melodic interplay to the piano and the clarinet; interestingly, the luscious effect of combined clarinets, bassoons and horns in flat keys was one of which Mozart was especially fond.'

David A. Thresher, Text to: *BBC Radio Three, Beethoven Experience,* June, 2005.

THIRD MOVEMENT
ALLEGRO SCHERZANDO

'This finale is extremely gay, lively and sportive, and must always preserve this character in a rapid motion. The middle section ... must be played very *staccato* and humorous, and thus be energetically marked. The concluding passages with great ardour ...'.

Carl Czerny, *On the Proper Performance of all Beethoven's Works for the Piano.* As translated, with annotations, in: Paul Badura-Skoda, 1970, pp. 94–95.

'Beethoven never wrote a wittier paragraph

with more Haydnesque irregularity of rhythm than the main theme of the Rondo of this Concerto.'

Donald Francis Tovey, *Essays in Musical Analysis*, Vol. 3, 1935–41, p. 68.

'The larger-scale [found in the slow movement] also applies in the finale, which bristles with wit and vitality: in the length and capricious phrasing of the rondo-theme, the cross-accents and modulating sequel in the first episode, and the irresistible abandon of the second, all typifying the composer-pianist's growing confidence.'

Denis Matthews, *Beethoven, Master Musicians,* 1985, p. 174.

'The finale – a touch of polka here? – is full of rambunctious humour just on the edge of acceptable manners. The central episode is an irresistible bit of country-dance music – probably most listeners' favourite moment in this movement – and Beethoven is nicely generous in letting us enjoy our fill of it.'

Michael Steinberg, *The Concerto: A Listener's Guide*, 1998, p. 55.

'As in the B flat Concerto, Beethoven's humour is most obvious in the finale, especially in the colourful subordinate theme in A minor, with the insistent accented turns and staccato bass.'

William Kinderman in: Glenn Stanley editor, *The Cambridge Companion to Beethoven*, 2000, p. 108.

'The finale is a spirited, humorous rondo; some of its music is developed from an unpublished piano trio Beethoven had composed in 1791. The fecundity of invention in its bouncing themes is matched by the skilful harmonic hoops through which they are made to jump. The movement is ingeniously extended — never breathless, and always renewing itself where a lesser composer might have ended it; never outstaying its welcome.'

David A. Thresher, Text to: *BBC Radio Three, Beethoven Experience*, June, 2005.

[1] Michael Steinberg, 1998, p. 56.
[2] Liner notes to EMI, *Beethoven Concerto No. 1*, anon, 1998.
[3] Carl Czerny, *On the Proper Performance of all Beethoven's Works for Piano*, edited with commentary by Paul Badura-Skoda, 1970, p. 15.
[4] Cited by Eva Badura-Skoda, *Performance Conventions in: Beethoven's Early Works* in: Robert Winter editor, *Beethoven, Performers, and Critics: the International Beethoven Congress, Detroit, 1977*, 1980, pp. 32–33.
[5] Emily Anderson editor and translator, 1961, 1961, Vol. 1, Letters No. 17 and 18, pp. 24–6.
[6] Gerhard von Breuning, *Memories of Beethoven*, edited by Maynard Solomon, 1992, p. 38.
[7] Charles Rosen, 2000, p. 209.
[8] Carl Czerny, *On the Proper Performance of all Beethoven's Works for Piano*, edited with commentary by Paul Badura-Skoda, 1970, p. 32.
[9] Ignaz Schuppanzigh was a celebrated violinist who premiered a number of Beethoven's late string quartets. Joseph Linke was the cellist-member of Schuppanzigh's String Quartet.
[10] Emily Anderson editor and translator, 1961, Vol. 1, Letter No. 610, pp. 560–61.
[11] Franz Wegeler, *Remembering Beethoven: The Biographical Notes of Franz Wegeler and Ferdinand Ries*, 1988, p. 94. Paul Badura-Skoda (see above) also cites this anecdote, quoting Wegeler-Ries at pp. 106–07.
[12] Emily Anderson editor, *The Letters of Mozart and his Family*, Vol. 1, Letter No. 30, 1786, 1962–75.

[13] Barry Cooper suggests since the B flat Concerto was not 'entirely new' in March 1795, the evidence is in favour of Op. 15 being the work performed. Barry Copper, 2000 p. 53.

[14] Elliot Forbes editor, *Thayer's Life of Beethoven*, 1967 p. 178. Footnote 32 suggests the Concerto in B-flat major but Barry Cooper (2000) and H. C. Robbins Landon (1992) suggest it may have been the C major Concerto.

[15] Emily Anderson, editor and translator, 1961, Vol. 1 Letter No. 16, p. 22.

[16] Cited in H. C. Robbins Landon, p. 54.

[17] For a facsimile reproduction of this letter, together with the German text, see: Beethoven House, Digital Archives, Library Document, BH 194. For a translation of the text, with commentaries, see: Theodore Albrecht editor and translator, 1996, Vol. 1, Letter No. 24, pp. 46—47.

[18] Theodore Albrecht editor and translator, 1996, Vol. 1, Letter No. 27, pp. 50—51

[19] H. C. Robbins Landon, 1992, p. 79.

[20] Quoted in: Theodore Albrecht, editor and translator, 1996, Vol. 3, Document No. 344, pp. 4—11.

[21] Donald Francis Tovey, *Ludwig van Beethoven* in: *The Classics of Music*, Michael Tilmouth, editor, 2001, pp. 317-22.

[22] For some discussion of Beethoven's second Prague concert tour see: H. C. Robbins Landon, 1992, pp. 80—81 and Barry Cooper, 2000, p. 75.

[23] As recalled in: Elliot Forbes editor, *Thayer's Life of Beethoven*, 1967 p. 207. The theme on which Beethoven improvised is that known as *Ah vous dirai-je Maman* — not strictly Mozart's own.

[24] As recounted in: Wayne M. Senner, Robin Wallace and William Meredith editors, *The Critical Reception of Beethoven's Compositions by his German Contemporaries*, 1999, Vol. 1, pp. 56—57.

[25] Quoted in: H. C. Robbins Landon, 1977, pp. 129—30.

[26] For a commentary to Beethoven's concert on 2 April 1800 see: Leon Plantinga Beethoven's Concertos: History, Style, Performance, 1999, pp. 4-6.

[27] H. C. Robbins Landon, 1992, pp. 83-84.

[28] Recounted in: Anton Felix Schindler, Beethoven as I knew Him, edited by Donald W. MacArdle and translated by Constance S. Jolly from the German edition of 1860, 1966, pp. 72-73. Baron Gottfried van Swieten held the position of Imperial and Court Librarian. He was also a composer and patron of music who recognised Beethoven's gifts and welcomed him into his home where he was encouraged to improvise and play Bach fugues. It was Swieten who urged Beethoven to acquire a more thorough command of counterpoint than he had gained in his days in Bonn. See: Peter Clive, 2001, pp. 361-62.

[29] See, for example, Barry Cooper, 2000, pp. 89—90 and Leon Plantinga, 1999, pp. 4—6.

[30] See: Wayne M. Senner, Robin Wallace and William Meredith, editors, *The Critical Reception of Beethoven's Compositions by his German Contemporaries,* Lincoln: University of Nebraska Press, in association with the American Beethoven Society and the Ira F. Brilliant Center for Beethoven Studies, San José State University, 1999, pp. 162—63. The authors provide a translation of the review of the April 1800 concert and affirm their belief that Beethoven had planned to perform the Third Piano Concerto.

[31] Leon Plantinga, 1999, pp. 65–66.

[32] Quoted in Leon Plantinga, 1999, pp. 4–6.

[33] For a comprehensive study of the reception of Beethoven's compositions in England, see: Pamela J. Willetts, *Beethoven and England: An Account of Sources in the British Museum,* 1970.

[34] Maynard Solomon, 1997, p. 128.

[35] Elliot Forbes editor, *Thayer's Life of Beethoven,* 1967 pp. 361–62.

[36] Wayne M. Senner, Robin Wallace and William Meredith editors, 1999, Vol. 1, p. 149.

[37] Adapted from Theodore Albrecht, editor and translator, 1996, Vol. 1, Letter No. 128, pp. 197–99, footnote 7.

[38] Clement was born in Vienna in 1780 and was soon recognised for his remarkable aptitude for violin playing. He was also blessed with a remarkable memory; it is on record that he could recall whole passages of music after but a single hearing. To showcase his talent, he went on tour with his father, much as Mozart had done years before. At the age of ten he toured Germany, Belgium and England and when in London he performed a concerto of his own composition at the Hanover Square Rooms. This was so-well received that he gave a second performance of the work in Oxford on the occasion (July 1791) when Haydn was honoured with the degree of Doctor of Music.

[39] See text accompanying Beethoven House, Digital Archives, Library Document, HCB Mh 10. The manuscript was listed as Lot 161 at the auction of Beethoven's possessions.

[40] *Ibid,* p. 403.

[41] As recalled by Ludwig Nohl, *Beethoven Depicted by his Contemporaries,* 1880, pp. 52–53. Von Seyfried studied piano with Mozart and became acquainted with Beethoven in 1803. He enjoyed a lasting personal relationship with the composer and rendered the ultimate service to him by being a pall-bearer at his funeral.

[42] Donald Francis Tovey, 1949, p. 316.

[43] See Beethoven House website, *Beethoven's Possessions.* His bureau was one of the few pieces of furniture he possessed.

[44] Barry Cooper, 1991, p. 185.

[45] Leon Plantinga, 1999, p. 62.

[46] Barry Cooper, 1991, p. 185.

[47] Douglas Porter Johnson editor, 1985, p. 82. Grasnick 1 is today preserved in the *Staatsbibliothek zu Berlin Preussischer Kulturbesitz.* Most of the leaves that were removed from Grasnick 1 have subsequently been traced and identified. Two of these sketch leaves are illustrated as: Beethoven House, Digital Archives, Document, Sammlung H. C. Bodmer. HCB Mh 64. Other sketches are contained on leaves that did not belong to larger sketchbooks. Specimens are now held in the Bibliothèque National as MS 71 and MS 89. Additional sources are known as Bonn Mh 64 and Mth 65. See: Douglas Porter Johnson, editor, 1985, p. 72 and p. 78 and William Kinderman, editor, 2005, pp. 323–4.

[48] See, *The Unheard Beethoven: Sketch Sources for Cadenza to Piano Concerto Op. 15,* Hess 76.

49 Elliot Forbes editor, *Thayer's Life of Beethoven*, 1967 p. 123.

50 Barry Cooper, 2000, pp.52–53

51 Antony Hopkins, 1996, p. 6.

52 Alfred Brendel, *Must Classical Music be Entirely Serious?* in: *Alfred Brendel on Music: Collected Essays*, 2001, pp. 99–100.

53 Alfred Brendel, *The Veil of Order: Alfred Brendel in Conversation with Martin Meyer*, 2002, p. 116.

54 The original source was a letter to a Manchester paper (unspecified) and reproduced in: C. E. Hallé, *Life and Letters of Sir Charles Hallé: Being an Autobiography (1819–1860) with Correspondence and Diaries*, 1896.

55 As recorded in Joan Peyser, *Bernstein: A Biography: Revised & Updated*, 1998.

56 As recollected by Tim Page editor, *The Glenn Gould Reader*, 1987, p. 69.

57 Elliot Forbes editor, *Thayer's Life of Beethoven*, 1967 p. 478.

58 Beethoven House, Digital Archives, Library Document, HCB Mh 11 and HCB Mh 12.

59 Donald Francis Tovey, Vol. III *Essays in Musical Analysis*, London, 1936, p. 63 and p. 65. See also Edward T. Cone, *A Cadenza for Op. 15* in: Lewis Lockwood editor, *Beethoven Essays: Studies in Honour of Elliot Forbes*, 1984.

60 As referred to by Robert Simpson, *Beethoven and the Concerto*, in: Robert Layton, editor, *A Guide to the Concerto*, 1996, p. 108.

61 Michael Steinberg, 1998, p. 54.

62 Denis Matthews, 1985, p. 174.

63 Antony Hopkins, 1984, p. 80.

64 *Allgemeine musikalische Zeitung*, 15 July 1826, cited in Wayne M. Senner, Robin Wallace and William Meredith editors, *The Critical Reception of Beethoven's Compositions by his German Contemporaries*, 1999, Vol. 1, p. 37.

65 See Leon Plantinga, 1999, p. 289 and Barry Cooper, 1991, p. 221.

66 Leon Plantinga, 1999, p. 289 and Douglas Porter Johnson editor, 1985, p. 93.

67 Emily Anderson editor and translator, Letter No. 41, pp. 42–43, Vol. 1, 1961. For a facsimile reproduction of this letter, together with a transcription of Beethoven's text, see: Beethoven House, Digital Archives, Library Document, Bonn NE 181.

68 For a fuller account of Mollo's contribution to music publishing see: Peter Clive, 2001, pp. 236–37.

69 Maynard Solomon, 1997, pp. 102–03.

70 See Beethoven House, Digital Archives, Library Document, C major Piano Concerto.

71 The story has its origins in a letter written by Count von Keglevics. See: Thayer-Forbes, 1967, p. 198.

72 *Ibid*, 1967, p. 292.

73 The anecdote is recalled in William Newman, 1963, p. 512 and Paul Badura-Skoda, editor, 1970, p.12. See also: Peter Clive, 2001, p. 250.

74 Wilhelm Altman, *Foreword to Concerto No. 1*, Eulenberg Miniature Score, 1935.

[75] Cyril Ehrlich, *First Philharmonic: A History of the Royal Philharmonic Society*, 1995, p. 46.

[76] For a full account of Neate's relationship with Beethoven see: Elliot Forbes editor, *Thayer's Life of Beethoven*, 1967 pp. 619–20 and elsewhere in the Chapter *The Year 1815*. See also: Peter Clive, 2001, pp. 245–46.

[77] Emily Anderson editor and translator, 1961, Vol. 1, Letter No. 895, pp. 759–80.

[78] Peter Clive, 2001, pp. 269–70.

[79] Arthur Jacobs, *Arthur Sullivan: A Victorian musician*, 1992.

[80] Artur Schnabel, 1961, p. 26.

PIANO CONCERTO NO. 2, B-FLAT MAJOR, OP. 19 BEETHOVEN AND VIENNA

'It would be hard to refute Beethoven's own view that the B flat concerto *"is not one of my best compositions"* [Beethoven to Breitkopf & Härtel on 22 April 1801]. The influence of Mozart is strong and not entirely digested; it is apparent in all the overall forms, in the melodic figuration and often in the phrase structure. In other ways, however, Beethoven impresses his own personality on the material; so there is a stylistic conflict which remains unresolved.'

Basil Deane *The Concertos* in: Denis Arnold and Nigel Fortune editors, *The Beethoven Companion*, 1973, p. 320.

'Beethoven's first "mature" piano concerto was the B flat (1795), known as "No. 2" because of its delayed publication. Although he described it as "not one of my best" its freshness of spirit and invention have kept it firmly in the repertory. If the main subjects have Mozartian traits, their treatment is less poised but more robust, wilful and explosive, in fact more Beethovenish.'

Denis Matthews, *Beethoven, Master Musicians*, 1985, p. 172.

'The B-flat major Concerto is without doubt the most unjustly maligned of Beethoven's orchestral compositions. Until very recently it has been reserved for occasional appearance as a curiosity piece, and it is still greeted more often than not with critical reserve ... It is, of course, his first major orchestral composition (It antedates the C major Concerto, Op. 15, by several years), and it was written at a time when Beethoven's prowess as a solo pianist might well have prompted him to mould a showpiece for his own exhibition. Yet his concern for this work seems to have long outlived his personal need for it, for he not only set about revising it in 1800, at a time when the concertos in C major and C minor were extant, but provided a cadenza for the first movement (much the finest cadenza he ever wrote, too) in an idiom of such rugged motivic sculpture that it can scarcely have been written before 1815 ... All in all, a work which does not need the consideration of historical precedence to deserve the epithet "remarkable".'

Glenn Gould, *Liner Notes* to Columbia ML 5211 and Ml

5298, 1957 and 1958. Reproduced in: Tim Page editor, *The Glenn Gould Reader*, 1987, pp. 61–62.

> 'The B flat Concerto follows Mozart's lead with respect to formal outlines, balance between soloist and orchestra, and the basic style of piano writing. This concerto even shares the same key and scoring (no clarinets, trumpets, or timpani) with Mozart's last piano concerto, K. 595. Some strikingly different stylistic features are present, however, so that a careful listener is not likely to confuse Beethoven's concerto with that of Mozart.'

Michael Thomas Roeder, *A History of the Concerto*, 1994, p. 180.

> 'Any young man can scarcely be blamed for taking models, and since Mozart might be said to have mastered the keyboard as musical form, it was to Mozart that Beethoven turned, not in person of course but as a spiritual ancestor.'

Antony Hopkins, *The Seven Concertos of Beethoven*, 1996, p. 22.

> 'Modest it may be both in dimensions and demeanour when we compare it to the expansive and original Concerto in C, but the B flat Concerto is a joy nonetheless, fresh, personal, and crackling with invention. The young Beethoven is one of the most undervalued composers we have. Of charm and good humour there is no lack in the Concerto No. 2.'

Michael Steinberg, *The Concerto: A Listener's Guide*, 1998, p. 56.

> 'It is easy to imagine the young virtuoso delighting his new audiences in Vienna with the Concerto in B flat finishing with this Rondo [WoO 6]. True to the spirit of the Classical rondo, this exuberant piece has a bantering air that plays elaborately with the listener's expectations ... Beethoven's modest assessment of his composition has not met with widespread disagreement. And the piece itself may be called modest. Its orchestra is small, with no clarinets or trumpets or drums, and the writing for instruments is little more than routine: the winds almost always play together as a choir, often simply doubling the appropriate strings, the latter also seen in conventional roles. The first two piano concertos, we should remember, are among Beethoven's first large-scale essays in writing for orchestra; the later triumphs in this music for this grandest of instruments remain, for now, in the future.'

Leon Plantinga, *Beethoven's Concertos: History, Style, Performance*, 1999, p.56 and p. 67.

> 'No 2 is today regarded as conventional and relatively weak, at least compared with Beethoven's later concertos, but in 1795 it must have seemed bold and striking, with many unorthodox ideas. The first movement shows a much clearer organization of thematic material than his previous concerto (WoO 4 in E flat) ... The second movement is a wonderfully profound

adagio. Beginning very simply it makes great use
of dynamic contrasts and Mozartian expressive
appoggiaturas.'

Barry Cooper, *Beethoven, Master Musicians*, 2000, p. 53.

'Despite [Beethoven's] reservations, the B flat
Concerto is an attractive and subtle work. The
opening *Allegro con* brio opens with a dualistic
gesture: an assertion of the tonic chord *forte*,
spelled out in energetic dotted rhythm, followed
by lyrical legato phrases played *piano* ... The
reflective, hymn-like character of the *Adagio*
harbours surprising intensity and a compelling
rhetorical expression ... The rondo, in 6/8 time,
is characterised by immense vitality and humorous wit.'

William Kinderman, *The Concertos*, in: Glenn Stanley
editor, *The Cambridge Companion to Beethoven*, 2000, p.
107.

'Beethoven's Piano Concerto No. 2 in B flat, Op.
19, begun *c.*1788, written and revised over the
next ten years and No. 1 in C, Op. 15, written in,
and revised in 1800, preserve much of the spirit
of Mozart's concertos but also point in new
aesthetic directions.'

Simon P. Keefe, *The Cambridge Companion to the Concerto*, 2005, p. 84.

In our introduction to the Piano Concerto in C major,
Op, 15, we have remarked that the Piano Concerto in

B-flat Major, Op. 19 was the first of Beethoven's five piano concertos, bearing opus numbers, to be composed. With that in mind, the remarks that follow take up the account of Beethoven's writing for the genre of the piano concerto, as provided to the text accompanying the composer's youthful piano concerto in E-flat major designated WoO 4.

This text is in effect in two parts. We initially trace Beethoven's arrival in Vienna following his departure from his hometown Bonn. We consider aspects of his relationship with his teachers, notably, Joseph Haydn, his prowess as a virtuoso pianist, and impressions of him as recorded by his contemporaries. The piano was central to Beethoven's life and work and he followed its development throughout his career with keen interest. We therefore devote some of our opening remarks to this instrument and Beethoven's relationship with it. Having established these contextual matters, we devote our attention to our subject matter proper which is the creation origins of the B-flat major Concerto. In so doing, we consider the record of his endeavours, as extant in the composer's sketches, his negotiations with publishers, and the protracted composition-history of the Concerto that extended over a period of no less than twenty years. We close our account with a documentary-style summation of the work's merits as expressed in the words of selected musicologists and performing artists.

Having been granted leave of absence from his duties in his hometown of Bonn, by the Elector Maximilian Franz, Beethoven took up residence in Vienna, in November 1792, in order to continue his studies in Europe's musical capital with Joseph Haydn. He had already spent a short time in Vienna in 1787 and had received some instruction from Mozart. News that his mother (Maria Magdalena) — to whom he was closely attached — was terminally ill put an end to his studies and precipitated his return to Bonn; Maria died soon afterwards of consumption.[1]

We have seen (Concerto WoO 4) Beethoven's first musical appointment was that of Court Organist at the Bonn Court of the Elector Maximilian Franz. He soon recognised his youthful employee's talent and sponsored Beethoven's visit to Vienna so that he could study with Haydn and, thereby, perfect his skills. For his part, Beethoven was conscious of his lack of formal training and readily agreed to participate in the venture, even though it entailed departing from his hometown and circle of friends. Haydn, in his capacity as Kapellmeister to Prince Nicholas Esterhazy, had commended Beethoven warmly to the Elector. He had been introduced to the little known, but brilliantly gifted young composer, when coming home from his first London tour. Haydn had seen Beethoven's Cantata, written to commemorate the death of Joseph II, and immediately accepted him as his pupil.[2] He later planned to take Beethoven with him to London, on his return there for the summer season, but the political situation in Europe conspired against this. Instead, Haydn agreed to give Beethoven lessons in Vienna where he was acknowledged as the leading composer of the day.

Beethoven arrived in Vienna to find the city still sorrowing from the death of Mozart who had died there in straitened circumstances in December 1791. This is recalled in the following incident. Before leaving for Vienna, on 29 October 1792, Beethoven invited several close friends to a farewell meal at which they each inscribed his *Stammbuch* (family album) with a dedicatory message. Amongst the contributors was Count Ferdinand von Waldstein, whose name we associate today with the Piano Sonata in C major, Op. 53 – *The Waldstein* – of which he was the dedicatee. He sent Beethoven on his way with the often-quoted words:

'You are now going to Vienna in fulfilment of your long-frustrated wishes. Mozart's genius still mourns and is weeping over the death of its pupil ... Through uninterrupted diligence, you shall receive *Mozart's spirit from Haydn's hands.*'[3]

Waldstein was eight years older than Beethoven. The two men became acquaintances from about 1788 when Waldstein had been summoned to Bonn to perform official diplomatic duties by Maximilian Franz – the Grand Master of the *Teutonic Order*, of which Waldstein himself was a knight. Beethoven's early biographer Franz Gerhard Wegeler describes Waldstein as being 'the first person to recognize Beethoven's great talent' and it is probable he may have rendered discrete financial support, and related assistance, to the young composer. Waldstein had a genuine love of music and for the *Carnival Sunday* of 6 March 1791, the two young men collaborated in writing the music required for the spring aristocratic festivities – a masked ball known as the *Ritterballet* or 'Knight's Ballet' for which the participants dressed in old-style German costume.[4]

Often overlooked in Beethoven musicology are other farewell-signatories to Beethoven's album. We supply the names of a selection of these; their aristocratic and social standing is a measure of the esteem already felt for the young composer. They included Eleonore von Breuning – for whom Beethoven had written the twelve Piano and Violin Variations WoO 64. She wrote in verse: 'Oh, may your good fortune / Be exactly as I wish for you! / Then, this year, it will / Reach its highest goal.' Johann Joseph Eichoff, the Mayor of Bonn, wrote: 'So travel forth fine youth! And God's blessing go before you! For my dear Beethoven, with wishes for a prosperous journey, from his loving best friend.'

Johann Martin Degenhart, a lawyer-friend and dedicatee of the composer's Duet for two Flutes, WoO 26 wrote: 'Yea, I always think / Of you dearest one, with ardour! / Sometimes, as you coax love, anger and subtle jokes, / Mighty Master of Music!'. Heinrich Struve, an official in the Russian Imperial Service, encouraged Beethoven: 'In the purpose of mankind — To discern *Wisdom*, to love *Beauty*, / To desire *Good*, to do the *Best.*' These lines are believed to derive from the writings of the philosopher Moses Mendelsohn, grandfather of the composer Felix. Finally, from a long list of well-wishers, is an entry from Dr. J. H. Crevelt, a physician and an active member in Bonn's intellectual circle. Together with Waldstein he invoked the spirit of Mozart:

> 'Friend, in sometime at quiet midnight, / Far from us the magic power of music / Sinks you into gentle fantasies, / And exultation pulses through your whole being, / Mozart's genius hovers over you / And smiling at you, lends its approbation.'[5]

When the Elector Maximilian granted Beethoven leave of absence from his duties in Bonn, he conferred on him an allowance of 100 Viennese thalers (about 150 florins) to cover his basic living expenses. This was about the sum he had been paid in his capacity as assistant organist to Neefe.[6] In Vienna, the cost of living was high. For example, a bachelor living in central Vienna needed an income of at least 960 florins to cover his basic needs and 1200 florins to allow for luxuries and entertainment.[7] Anxious to secure further financial support, on 23 November 1793 Beethoven wrote a supplicatory letter to Maximilian Franz in which he stated:

'My sole endeavour is to render myself absolutely worthy of your Electoral Excellency's highest favour. With this in view I have employed this year all the powers of my soul for the benefit of music in order to be able, during the coming year, to send to your Electoral Excellency something that will reflect your magnanimous treatment of me.'

Beethoven is referring here to works that his teacher Haydn was about to send to Maximilian Franz as testimonies to the progress his pupil had been making in the art of composition.[8]

On the same day, 23 November, Haydn did indeed write a long letter to the Elector on behalf of his pupil. He listed several compositions, composed by Beethoven, and offered them as proof of his diligence and application to his studies. Haydn said, prophetically:

'On the basis of these pieces, expert and amateur alike cannot but admit that Beethoven will in time become one of the greatest musical artists in Europe, and I shall be proud to call myself his teacher.'

He also expressed regret that Beethoven would not remain his pupil for much longer; Haydn departed Vienna for his second concert tour to London on 19 January 1794. He stressed the need for his pupil to receive financial support, asking the Elector if he would allocate him an allowance of 1000 florins to provide for his subsistence and to enable him to continue with his music studies.[9]

A month later the Elector responded curtly and dismissively. He rejected Haydn's testimony that the compositions he had received were adequate evidence of Beethoven's progress on the grounds that he considered most of the compositions had been undertaken when Beethoven was still resident in Bonn. He concluded:

> 'I wonder, therefore, whether he should not begin his return journey here ... for I doubt he will have made any important progress in composition and taste during his present stay.'[10]

Beethoven's response to the Elector was characteristically defiant. He resolved to make his own way in the world by the fruits of his labours. Moreover, he remained in Vienna and never again set eyes on his native hometown.

When settled in Vienna, Beethoven did not forget the debt he owed to his former teacher Christian Gottlob Neefe (see WoO 4). On 26 October 1793, he found time to write to him:

> 'I thank you for the advice you have very often given me about making progress in my divine art. Should I ever become a great man, you too will have a share in my success.'[11]

In Vienna, Beethoven's initial position as 'pupil of Haydn' differed little from the experience of others in similar pupil-teacher relationships. As Tia de Nora remarks:

> 'In 1793 Beethoven was a young and, in Vienna, relatively unknown musician who had achieved some amount of distinction in a culturally important but distant north-German town.'[12]

For his part, Haydn, with the recent death of Mozart, was

increasingly recognised for being not only a popular composer (consider his many string quartets and symphonies) but also a generous contributor to charity concerts. His renown would be further increased with the performance and publication of his large-scale oratorios *The Creation* (1797–98) and *The Seasons* (1801).

In due course, Beethoven became dissatisfied with Haydn's instruction. He admired the older composer, who was then at the height of his powers and was in demand both in Vienna and London. Testimony to his respect is that over the years Beethoven acquired many of Haydn's works, including the autograph of *The London Symphony* that came into his possession after Haydn's death in 1809.[13] It appears, though, that Haydn was too pre-occupied with his own compositions to give Beethoven's studies the time and attention Beethoven expected; his exercises were returned, supposedly corrected, but with numerous errors overlooked.

Evidence of Haydn's pre-occupation with his own work comes indirectly from a letter that Albrechtsberger wrote to Beethoven on 15 December 1796. He invited Beethoven to pay him a visit and bring along the score of one of his trios – probably from the Op. 9 set on which he was then at work. Significantly, he adds: 'Haydn was here yesterday; he is preoccupied with the idea for a grand oratorio ... and hopes to have it finished soon'. This is thought to be a reference to *The Creation*.[14]

However, as remarked, Beethoven respected his elderly teacher. For example, when his Piano Sonatas Op. 2 were announced on 9 March 1796, in the *Wiener Zeitung*) ('Vienna Journal'), it was made public they were dedicated to Joseph Haydn – the only professional composer ever to receive such a dedication from Beethoven with the exception of Antonio Salieri. This was despite the tension that existed between master and pupil. Beethoven had resented

73

Haydn's suggestion that he should hold back publication of the third of his Piano Trios Op. 1 — the one he cherished the most. Beethoven duly acknowledged he had received instruction from Haydn but was given to saying 'he had learned little from him'.[15] In later years he renounced these headstrong views and even spoke of his mentor with respect and affection. There was the occasion, for example, when the composer and publisher Anton Diabelli called on Beethoven to present him with a lithograph of Haydn's rather modest birthplace — in the village of Rohrau in Lower Austria. It gave Beethoven much pleasure prompting him to remark: 'Just see the little house, and such a great man was born in it.'[16]

Beethoven's circumstances came to the attention of the composer and music teacher Johann Baptist Schenk. He made Beethoven's acquaintance in 1792 and in his *Autobiography* he writes:

> 'I saw the composer, now so famous, for the first time and heard him play ... He offered to improvise on the pianoforte. Having struck a few chords and tossed off a few figures, as if they were of no significance, the creative genius gradually unveiled his profound psychological pictures. My ear was continually charmed by the beauty of the many varied motives which he wove with wonderful clarity and loveliness into each other.'

Schenk became aware that Beethoven had been studying counterpoint with Haydn for some six months and that he was dissatisfied with his studies. He agreed to give Beethoven additional instruction on the grounds that his collaboration should not be made known to Haydn. He states: 'I gave him the familiar textbook of Joseph Fux, *Gradus ad Parnassum*, and asked him to look at the exercises that followed.' Schenk relates, his instruction commenced in August 1792 and lasted until May 1793. He generously exonerated Haydn's lax supervision on the grounds that when he returned to Vienna, from London,

> 'He was intent on utilizing his muse in the composition of large masterworks, and, thus laudably occupied, could not well devote himself to the rules of grammar'.[17]

Further testimony to Beethoven's need for formal instruction is his relationship at this period with Antonio Salieri. He was no less celebrated than Haydn as a composer and teacher and was a dominant figure in Vienna's musical scene. Beethoven turned to Salieri for instruction in vocal composition and the setting of Italian texts. His debt to Salieri is reflected in his later dedication to him of his Violin Sonatas Op. 12 and the set of Variations *La stessa, la stessima* (WoO 73) derived from Salieri's opera *Falstaff*.[18]

When Haydn departed Vienna, for his second visit to London in mid-January 1794, Beethoven turned to the greatly admired theorist and master of counterpoint Johann Georg Albrechtsberger. He was organist and *Kapellmeister* at Saint Stephan's Cathedral and was much sought after by young composers. Although Albrechtsberger was something of a dry, painstaking theorist, many of Beethoven's studies with him, of the old-fashioned contrapuntal curriculum, still survive — evidence of both his diligence and respect for the learned pedagogue.[19]

The recollections of the pianist and composer Ferdinand Ries are relevant to this part of our narrative. Sometime in late 1801, or early 1802, Ries commenced piano lessons with Beethoven and soon became a trusted companion to the composer. Beethoven relied upon Ries to copy out his scores and to perform various secretarial duties. Reflecting on his master's relationships with his teachers, Ries writes:

'I knew them all well; all three [Haydn, Albrechtsberger and Salieri] valued Beethoven highly, but were of one-mind touching his habits of study. All of them said Beethoven was so headstrong and self-sufficient that he had much to learn through harsh experience which he had refused to accept when it was presented to him as a subject of study.'

He adds: 'Beethoven found Albrechtsberger's "dry rules" irksome and was not readily disposed to Salieri's, Italianate school of dramatic composition that was then in vogue — although he did value Antonio Salieri's advice regarding the setting of Italian words.'[20] Beethoven's eminent biographer Alexander Thayer, with his wider perspective of the composer's life and work, observes: 'It is now known that the "dry rules" of Albrechtsberger could make a strong appeal to Beethoven as appertaining to theoretical study, and that the old method of composition, to which he remained true all his life, always had a singular charm for him as a subject of study and investigation.'[21]

We have a description of Beethoven at the period under consideration from a remarkably gifted young pianist, Elisabeth von Kissow — known in Beethoven musicology as Frau von Bernhard. When a mere twelve years old her father sent her from her native Augsburg to Vienna to study piano with Johann Andreas Streicher — celebrated for not only being a teacher of piano but an accomplished keyboard instrument maker (see later). Elisabeth had a number of occasions to observe Beethoven and indeed to perform in his company in the salon of the composer's patron Prince Lichnowsky's. Beethoven so prized her talent that for the next few years he sent her a copy of his newest pieces, usually accompanied with a typical Beethovenian jocular note.[22] Later in life, Elisabeth, as Frau von Bernhard, recalled her musical impressions of the time when she received her instruction from the composer:

> 'I still remember clearly both Haydn and Salieri sitting on a sofa on one side of the small music-room, both carefully dressed in the old-fashioned way with perruque [periwig], shoes and silk hose, whereas, even here, Beethoven would come dressed in the informal fashion of the other side of the Rhine, almost ill-dressed.'[23]

Beethoven's connection with Eleonore von Breuning is also relevant here; she was the wife of Franz Gerhard Wegeler, Beethoven's close friend from his youthful days in Bonn. On 2 November 1793, Beethoven wrote a long letter to Eleonore in which he remarks: 'I have been almost a whole year in this capital.' He informed her of the dedication she was to receive of his Variations for Piano and Violin, WoO 40. He did not think too highly of 'this little work' and wanted her to be the recipient of 'a work more worthy', but, he explained, 'people in Vienna have been pestering me to publish this little work'. On more sartorial matters he adds: 'I still have the waistcoat you kindly gave me ... But it is now so out of fashion that I can only keep it in my wardrobe as a very precious token from you.'[24] During his early years in Vienna, there is evidence Beethoven made serious attempts to overcome his social and sartorial deficiencies. Entries from an account book, of his personal income, reveal he acquired black silk stockings, boots, and incurred expenses for a wig maker and a dancing master – although, with regard to the latter, his piano pupil Ferdinand Ries recalls: 'He could never learn to dance in time, and his clumsy movements lacked all charm.'[25]

We have remarked Beethoven was sent on his way to Vienna with words of encouragement from Ferdinand von Waldstein, the son of a count and princess and a knight member of the Teutonic Order. This association with the aristocracy doubtless benefitted Beethoven's entry into Vienna's aristocratic circle. It has been suggested his acceptance into the salons of the Austro-Hungarian aristocracy may, in part, have also been due to the fact that its members may have considered *van*, in his name, to be the equivalent of *von* in theirs – a mark of distinction and nobility. Notwithstanding Beethoven's unorthodox demeanour and unkempt appearance, he was, in effect, regarded as being 'one of theirs'.[26]

Regarding Vienna's nobility, It has been estimated that at the time of Beethoven's arrival in the city, in December 1792, there were then resident there three princes and princess, nineteen counts and countesses, and nine barons and baronesses – compared with the more modestly ranked sixty-four musicians. Those with whom Beethoven would, in due course, associate include: Count Anton Appony, Count Moritz Lichnowsky, Baron Peter Braun, Countess Josephine Deym, Count Palfy von Erdödy, Count Johann Esterhazy, Count Moritz Fries (his music collection contained sixteen-hundred volumes), Count Galitzin (later a prince), Prince Ferdinand Kinsky, Prince Karl Lichnowsky, Prince Joseph von Lobkowitz, and Baron Gottfried van Swieten.[27] By the time of his death, in 1827, Beethoven's standing had transcended all of Vienna's nobility such that an estimated 10,000 people are believed to have followed his funeral cortege.

Beethoven initially secured his reputation in Vienna as

a virtuoso pianist possessed of extraordinary powers of improvisation. He gave evidence of these in the great salons of Vienna's nobility and, more widely, through the publication of sets of piano variations. At this period he composed several such sets including: WoO, 67 (1794); WoO 69 (1795); WoO 71 (1796); and WoO 73 (1799). His preoccupation with this genre of compositions is, in part, explained in a letter he wrote in June 1794 to Eleonore von Breuning to whom we have just referred. He sent her a set of his variations with the remark:

> 'I should never have written down this kind of piece had I not already noticed fairly often how some people in Vienna [his pianistic rivals] after hearing me extemporize of an evening would note down on the following day several peculiarities of my style.'

Beethoven resolved to forestall his rivals, whom he describes as 'his sworn enemies' and 'to take revenge on them in this way'. Mindful of his own prowess, at the keyboard, he added:

> 'I wanted to revenge myself on them in this way, because I knew beforehand that my variations would here and there be put before the said gentlemen and that they would cut a very sorry figure with them.'[28]

As themes for his piano variations, Beethoven would often adapt melodies derived from popular operas of the day. In the context of Beethoven's writing for the keyboard, and his relationship with distinguished women, mention may be made here of Count Lichnowsky's first wife, Princess Marie

Lichnowsky. She was one of Beethoven's most ardent early admirers and had a close friendship with Beethoven. In recognition of her untiring efforts on his behalf he inscribed to her the piano score of his ballet *The Creatures of Prometheus.*

At the same period when Beethoven was demonstrating his pianistic prowess, his fame as a composer was also becoming known more widely. His piano sonatas, sets of piano variations and other instrumental works were being published in Vienna and he achieved wider recognition when on a concert tour in Dresden, Berlin and other of Europe's capital cities. On this occasion he wrote to his younger brother Nikolaus Johann in the following terms: 'My art is winning me friends and renown, and ... this time I shall make a good deal of money.'[29] We make further reference to Beethoven's concert tour in due course.

Beethoven wrote to his close friend Karl Amenda in terms of similar self-confidence. He told Amenda that he had been invited to visit Poland where, he jests, 'I can amuse myself quite well ... and there is plenty of money to be made there too!' Amenda was a clergyman and violinist; he was sufficiently accomplished to perform with Beethoven and to be tutor to the children of Prince Lobkowitz - as we have seen, one of Beethoven's noble patrons. The visit to Poland though, like so many of Beethoven's planned excursions to other countries (notably England), never took place. However, Amenda responded to Beethoven with an affectionate letter of his own that is typical of the kind the composer received from close friends who were aware of his developing fame and emerging genius: 'You are responsible not only to yourself ... but indeed to the general progress of your art.'[30]

Between 1793–95, Beethoven composed the Piano Trios Op. 1 dedicated to Prince Karl Lichnowsky — a pupil of Mozart. The subscription list to these works bears testimony to the composer's growing fame. Ferdinand Ries recalls how the three Trios Op. 1 were to be performed for the first time 'before the art-world at a soirée given by Prince Lichnowsky'. He states:

> 'The majority of artists and music-lovers had been invited, in particular Haydn. The Trios were played and immediately aroused great interest. Haydn, too, said many good things about them, but advised Beethoven not to publish the third Trio in C minor. This surprised Beethoven very much inasmuch he considered it the best ... Haydn's remark made a bad impression on Beethoven.'[31]

Beethoven's first biographer Johann Schlosser, writing shortly after the composer's death, felt obliged to express his reservations concerning the innovative nature of Beethoven's compositions. He writes:

> 'Beethoven's genius first manifested itself in three trios for piano, violin and cello. They display extraordinary deep sentiments which have not yet found their true outlet. This has caused some to complain of disorder in these and some subsequent compositions, and not without reason. In these, and some later works, Beethoven reveals his heart in a great surge of feeling. With this music, we enter a new world which he was to conquer triumphantly. At this early stage his nature could express itself only in grand proportions, not always clearly realized but already sharply distinctive.'[32]

We consider for a moment Beethoven the pianist. His pupil Carl Czerny, who learned several of the composer's piano sonatas under his direction, has left several accounts of Beethoven's style of playing – more correctly his command of the keyboard. Czerny describes Beethoven's manner as being possessed of 'passionate strength' that alternated 'with all the charms of a smooth *cantabile*'. For him, this was its most outstanding feature. He refers to Beethoven's capacity to draw from the fortepiano 'new and daring passages', of his use of the pedal and a capacity to draw from the instrument 'a new type of singing tone and many other unimagined effects'. Czerny acknowledged Beethoven's playing did not possess 'that clean and brilliant elegance of certain other pianists'. On the other hand, he characterised Beethoven's playing as 'spirited, grandiose' and 'very full of feeling and romantic'.[33]

Comparing Beethoven's style with that of other pianists and piano schools of Czerny's acquaintance, he has this to say:

> 'Muzio Clementi's manner is distinguished by the regular position of the hands, a firm touch and tone, clear fluent execution and a correct declamation, and also in part by great velocity of the fingers.'

In the case of the style of performance of Beethoven's contemporaries Johann Baptist Cramer andJan Ladislav Dussek, Czerny considered they were characterised

> 'by a beautiful *cantabile*, avoidance of all coarse effects and a surprising smoothness in the runs and passages'. Czerny thought Mozart's school of playing to be 'clear and markedly brilliant' a

style of playing 'based more on staccato than legato [with] the pedal rarely used'.[34]

The Czech composer and pianist Johann (Jan) Tomaschek heard Beethoven perform the adagio and rondo from his Op. 2 Piano Sonata at a concert in which he also played the B-flat major Concerto. Tomaschek later recalled how Beethoven's playing stirred him strangely 'to the depths of his soul' to such an extent that he left off from playing the piano for several days.[35] Tomaschek also recalls a later occasion when Beethoven performed privately in the home of Count Clam-Gallas, a member of a noble Prague family well-known for its love of music. It was for the daughter of the family, Josephine, that Beethoven composed his scena *Ah! perfido*, Op. 65. Beethoven improvised on the theme to the word-setting 'Ah! vous dirai-je Maman'. This time, Tomaschek listened to Beethoven's playing 'with more composure'. He relates:

'I admired his powerful and brilliant playing, but his frequent daring deviations from one to another whereby the organic connection, the gradual development of the idea was broken up, did not escape me.'

These observations disposed Tomaschek to remark more generally: 'Evils of this nature frequently weaken his greatest conceptions, those which sprang from a too exuberant conception.' Notwithstanding these reservations, in later years, by which time he had heard all the great pianistic virtuosi of his day, Tomaschek was given to remark that Beethoven remained for him 'the lord of pianoforte players' and 'the giant among pianoforte players'.[36]

We recall once more Beethoven's friend from his Bonn

days Franz Gerhard Wegeler. He reports Beethoven's playing was initially considered by some to be 'rude and hard' but how a formative influence appears to have come about when Beethoven heard Johann Franz Sterkel perform, sometime in 1791. Wegeler describes Sterkel as being regarded as one of the finest pianists in the whole of Germany whose playing was 'refined and elevated to the utmost ... graceful and pleasing'. Sterkel, through his many piano sonatas, is acknowledged for having contributed to the development of a new pianistic idiom. According to Wegeler, when Beethoven heard Sterkel play: '[He] stood with attention ... for this grace and delicacy, if not power of execution, were a new revelation to him.' This anecdote reminds us that, independent-minded as he was, Beethoven was prepared to learn from fellow musicians and to absorb whatever they had to offer into his own manner.[37]

As we draw our prefatory remarks to a close, bearing upon Beethoven and his arrival in Vienna, we quote from Beethoven authority Barry Cooper:

> 'In terms of compositional craft, the period 1796–98 was one of consolidation for Beethoven. Having made his major impact in Vienna in 1795, he branched out into several related genres, writing works in which he continued gradually developing his own idiosyncratic brand of the high Classical style. Each work showed him to be a master of the conventional idiom, while being far from conventional in detail.'[38]

Compositions that Beethoven considered worthy of opus numbers for 1796–97 included: Scene and Aria, *Ah perfido!,* Op. 65; Piano Sonatas Op. 7, and Op. 49, No. 2;

Rondo for Piano, Op. 51, No. 1; Sextet, Op. 71; and Two Sonatas for Piano and Cello, Op. 5. Works published in 1796–97 included: Quintet, Op. 4 (a revision of the Septet, Op. 103); Three Piano Sonatas, Op. 2 (dedicated to Haydn); String Trio, Op. 3; Piano Sonata, Op. 7; and Two Sonatas for Piano and Cello, Op. 5 (dedicated to King Friedrich II of Prussia). Compositions for 1798–99 included: Piano Sonatas Op. 10, Op, 14 and Op. 49, No. 1; Three String Trios, Op. 9; and Piano Concerto No. 1, Op. 15. The most significant publication of 1799 was the Grand Sonata *Pathétique*, Op. 13.[39]

Before we direct our remarks to the origins of the Piano concerto, Op. 19, it is only fitting we should consider Beethoven in the context of the keyboard instruments available to him at the period under consideration.

We have remarked how closely Beethoven followed the technical development of the pianoforte. In his Bonn days he would be familiar with the five-octave keyboard typical of the period, and, later, of the emerging extension of the compass of the instrument accompanied by such other features as an increase in sonority and capacity for more expressive tone-colour. These changing circumstances had significant compositional implications for Beethoven. Most significantly, at the period in question, he was frequently constrained by the upper limits of the available keyboard, rewriting the transposition of parallel passages so as to keep within the prescribed keyboard limits. As keyboards expanded, especially in the treble, he was able to venture into the pianistic realms that would be further explored by such younger composers as Schubert and Weber.[40] These considerations also raise present-day related challenges concerning the 'authentic' interpretation of his piano music.[41] As Edwin Fischer's observes:

'There are still many passages where transfer to the now customary higher register may mean sacrificing beauties which arose from Beethoven having made a virtue of necessity.'[42]

The importance of the piano to Beethoven as an aid to composition — before the onset of his deafness — is worthy of mention. Czerny recalls in his reminiscences: 'Beethoven was accustomed to composing everything with the aid of the piano, and would try out a given passage countless times.'[43] Progressive deafness impelled him to torment his instruments severely in his efforts to capture their sound and would eventually isolate him from the keyboard altogether. These are circumstances we reserve for later discussion. For the present, we comment briefly on the composer's concert tour of 1796 and his growing enthusiasm for the pianofortes of Streicher's manufacture.

Streicher's instruments were considered by some to be the equal of, and possibly even superior to, the pianoforte of the Viennese maker Anton Walter. Beethoven possessed such an instrument (dating from around 1785) that had a range of five octaves and two notes — from the third F, below middle C, to the third G above. The Streicher manufacturer was a partnership between Nanette Stein and Johann Streicher who had moved to Vienna in 1794, shortly after which the two became acquainted with Beethoven. As a child, Nanette had been hailed as a prodigy and once performed for Mozart. However, more relevant to our narrative, as the daughter of Johann Stein — the celebrated builder of organs and pianofortes — she had learned the business of pianoforte manufacture and its technical intricacies and thereby — which is remarkable for the period in question — was 'the guiding spirit of the firm'. Her husband Johann, who was also an accomplished pianist, looked after the firm's business affairs. It is with him, that Beethoven transacted a spirited correspondence at various times throughout his life on the subject of the pianoforte and how it might be improved. In the composer's declining years, Nanette was of considerable assistance to Beethoven with regard to the management of his household affairs – concerning which, he was almost incapable.

The Streichers became important figures in Vienna's musical society. Their salon, in which their finest instruments were on display, became a venue for the great and the good in Vienna's musical society; distinguished guests, for example, included Beethoven's only composition pupil, and accomplished pianist, the Archduke Rudolph – youngest son of the Emperor Leopold II. Busts of celebrated composers adorned their salon including, eventually, that of Beethoven – commissioned by the Streichers from the sculptor Franz Klein.[44] Such was the social-standing of the Streichers' salon that it became a sort of

> 'testing-ground [and] whoever wanted to give a public concert [in Vienna] was obliged to perform first in the Streichers' salon before an invited audience'.[45]

On one occasion, Nanette and Johann themselves performed, giving a rendering of Carl Czerny's two-piano arrangement of Beethoven's *Pastoral Symphony,* prompting some members of the audience to cast their gaze admiringly at Klein's rendering of Beethoven's countenance that was by then on display.[46]

On the occasion when Beethoven made a concert tour to Prague, he wrote to Andreas Streicher on 19 November enthusing: 'I received ... your fortepiano, which is really an excellent instrument ... Anyone else would try to keep it for himself.' However, he could not refrain from pointing out to Streicher what he considered to be its limitations. 'It robs me of the freedom to produce my own tone.' But he adds, good-naturedly: 'This must not deter you from making all your fortepianos in the same way.' The reason for Beethoven's reservations is revealing. He remarks: '[No] doubt there are few people [fellow pianists] who cherish such whims as mine' — by which he really meant who make such demands of the instrument.[47] A few weeks later he wrote once more to Streicher complaining that the pianoforte is 'the least studied of all instruments' and went on to say that it is like 'merely listening to a harp'. He looked forward to the time 'when the harp and the pianoforte will be treated as two entirely different instruments'.[48]

A Streicher fortepiano from this period cost about 66 ducats (about thirty pounds sterling) whereas a Walter fortepiano could be had for 50 ducats (about twenty-three pounds sterling). Moreover, although the Streichers were innovative pianoforte builders, their predilection was in favour of the lighter-sounding instrument.[49] This is evident from a pamphlet the Streichers published, sometime around 1801, titled *Notes on the Playing, Tuning and Maintenance of the Fortepiano'.* This was issued on the sale of each of their instruments to ensure its proper care and maintenance. From it can be inferred the accepted fortepiano sound of the period. Streicher (it was probably Andreas who wrote the pamphlet) advocates the then current Viennese ideal of 'light playing and *pearly* passage work' in which flowing sequences of notes could be compared to 'matched pearls'. A restrained pianistic approach to playing was advocated with no 'pounding' and 'torturing the instrument'. Streicher had no time for the showy performer: 'By moving his body, arms and hands

88

he seems to want to show how difficult the labour under-taken by him is.' He gave the following advice:

> 'All musical instruments, *even the human voice*, have their own range of expression, which cannot be transgressed without making a bad impression on the listener, or provoking reproaches from the *connoisseur.*'[50]

Tia de Nora remarks, on the basis of her study of Beethoven's compositional procedures in the context of Streicher's system of piano aesthetics, that Streicher's precepts militated against Beethoven's 'tendency towards the strenuous and the dramatic, as opposed to the conventionally lighter and cleaner style'.[51]

We can appreciate how champions of such a style of playing, as the Streichers' were advocating, would find favour with a Viennese audience seated of an evening in their salon. However, the Streichers would, in due course, improve their fortepianos in response to the growing demand for a sturdier instrument and one with a greater compass. Such developments were due, in no small part, to Beethoven's encouragement and the new style of pianoforte sound he was promoting in such works as his Piano Sonatas Op. 2.

On his tour of Vienna, in 1809, the German composer and music critic Johann Reichardt became acquainted with Beethoven's piano music and recalled:

> 'Streicher has been persuaded away from the compliant ... musical characteristics of other Viennese instruments. On Beethoven's insistence he has given his instruments more resistance and elasticity. A forceful performer thus has a greater basic and continuous control over the instrument

... He has given his instrument a greater and more diverse character.'[52]

Later still (about 1816) Nanette Streicher patented an even more fully developed fortepiano with a compass of six and a half octaves and a *una corda* action foot pedal to allow the performer to depress a chord or to achieve a swell or diminuendo.[53] It was probably this instrument that, as his hearing deteriorated, Beethoven requested the Streichers to adapt so that he could capture more of its sound. It is believed they attached a form of acoustic hood above the keyboard of one of his instruments so as to reflect back more of the sound. No details, though, of this adaptation appear to have survived.[54] Beethoven's need for such a facility is poignantly revealed in a letter from the period in question when he wrote to Nanette Streicher referring to the benefits of his ear trumpet. This had been adapted for him by its inventor Johann Maelzel.[55]

On 6 August 1803, Beethoven received a splendid, state-of-the-art piano from the French manufacturer Sébastien Érard.[56] His instruments incorporated several innovations such as foot pedals that replaced the cumbersome knee-action lever-arrangement typical of instruments of the time. Érard's pianos were sturdily constructed and offered greater sonority than most other fortepianos pianos of the day — characteristics particularly valued by Beethoven in his quest for an evermore resonant keyboard sound. The gift was in recognition of Érard's esteem of Beethoven and of his growing reputation abroad as a pianist. Other distinguished musicians of the day, who owned an Érard piano, included Beethoven's teacher Haydn and fellow pianist Ignaz Moscheles.

In 1818 the English maker John Broadwood & Sons presented Beethoven with an even more magnificent instrument. Broadwood himself selected from his warehouse a six-octave Grand Piano, No. 7362 that was carefully packed in a deal case with a waterproof lining of tin foil. This was then delivered to a Mr. Farlowe of London ready for shipment to Trieste. The choice of particular instrument was, in part, made by a small group of distinguished musicians of the day. As a measure of their respect and esteem for the recipient, they test-played and signed the piano before it was sent away. The musicians involved in the enterprise were John Baptiste Cramer, Jaques Godfroi, Friedrich Kalkbrenner, Charles Knyvett, and Ferdinand Ries. They each inscribed the piano with their signatures alongside the inscription: *Hoc Instrumentum est Thomae Broadwood (Londrini) donum propter ingenium illustrissime Beethoven* – 'This instrument is a proper gift from Thomas Broadwood to the great Beethoven.' Broadwood's own, more prosaic, inscription reads: 'John Broadwood & Sons, Makers of Instruments to His Majesty and the Princesses. Great Pulteney Street, Golden Square, London.'[57] When Beethoven died the piano was purchased by the dealer Carl Anton Spina. In 1845 he gave it to Franz Liszt who in turn made a gift of it to the Hungarian National Museum, Budapest where it still remains.[58]

With these remarks concerning Beethoven and the piano, we now return to our discussion of the composition-origins of the Piano Concerto in B-flat major, Op. 19.

We recall Ferdinand Waldstein's farewell greetings to Beethoven on his departure to Vienna when he trusted that Beethoven, 'through uninterrupted diligence' would receive Mozart's spirit. It is open to question whether or not Beethoven perceived himself as Mozart's heir. Following Beethoven's meeting with Mozart, in 1787 – terminated, as we have seen, by news of his mother's serious illness – Cooper poses the intriguing question: 'Did he resolve to write a grand symphony, a new piano concerto ... ?'[59] What is known is Beethoven's admiration for Mozart's piano concertos. If Haydn was the father of the string quartet, Mozart may be regarded as the master of the piano concerto having composed no fewer than twenty-seven works in the genre. More generally, it is known Beethoven admired Mozart profoundly. He recognised him as one of music's 'great men' and once remarked: 'I have always counted myself amongst the greatest admirers of Mozart and shall remain so until my last breath.' After a performance of Mozart's Piano Concerto, K. 491, Beethoven is alleged to have said, to fellow pianist-composer Johann Baptist Cramer, 'We shall never be able to do anything like that' — or words to that effect.[60] Some authorities, however, suggest the anecdote should be treated with caution.[61]

On 31 March 1795, Beethoven performed a concerto by Mozart at a concert in Vienna for the benefit of Mozart's widow Constanza. Moreover, it is known he held Mozart's Piano Concerto, K. 466 in high regard, disposing him to write out cadenzas for its first and third movements. As Simon Keefe remarks, the themes may be Mozart's 'but the touch, the rhetoric is emphatically Beethoven's'.[62] Keefe is of course referring to Beethoven's expressive musicality. Beethoven's 'touch' and 'rhetoric' of a more physical kind, are recalled by Beethoven's friend the Czech-born composer Anton Reicha. He has left a memorable account of an occasion when he was required to turn the pages for Beethoven during a performance of a Mozart piano concerto. He relates: 'I was mostly occupied in wrenching out the strings of the piano, which snapped while the hammers stuck among the broken strings.'[63]

Performers and musicologists agree it is Mozart's presence that is felt in both of Beethoven's Piano Concertos Op. 15 and Op.19 although with reservations. In these early concertos, Beethoven assimilated and built upon Mozart's structure but allied to it his own powers of expression — that foreshadows what was to find even fuller expression in his later compositions.[64]

Op. 19 is laid out in three movements: Allegro con brio (4/4); Adagio (E flat, 3/4); and Rondo Molto (Allegro 6/8). Collectively, they have a playing time of about thirty minutes in an expansive performance. Beethoven's orchestration parallels that of Mozart's Concertos: B flat, K. 450; G major, K. 453; B flat, K. 456; and F major, K. 459. The wind section requires only one flute with pairs of oboes, bassoons and horns. A measure of Beethoven's expansion of the genre is evident in his next work. The C major Concerto comprises a full orchestra with clarinets, trumpets and kettledrums.

The creation origins of the Piano Concerto in B-flat major, Op. 19 extended over a period of some twenty years, when account is taken of its first gestation in the 1780s until the period of its final conception in 1809. This is explained, in part, when we recall Beethoven wrote his early piano concertos — at the period in his life when his hearing was intact — as vehicles to display his prowess at the keyboard in public performance. Later, his loss of hearing made this well-nigh impossible. His first attempts in the genre of concerto-composition, therefor, enabled him to reveal both his creative abilities, as a composer, and also to demonstrate his powers as a virtuoso-pianist. In an era of intense pianistic rivalry, amongst Vienna's 'lions of the keyboard', it was, as Cooper remarks, 'better that the concertos remained unpublished so that rival pianists would not be able to use them'.[65] Beethoven expressed such views in a letter to the Leipzig publisher Breitkopf & Härtel on 22 April 1801. He first makes known his intention that Anton Hoffmeister, in Leipzig, was about to publish the B flat Concerto, Op. 19

and that Tranquillo Mollo, in Vienna, would shortly follow with the publication of his C major concerto, Op. 15. He then explains:

> 'Musical policy [the twofold threat of nefarious pianistic-rivalry and the threat of publication-piracy] demands that one should keep one's finest concertos to oneself for a time.'[66]

In this respect, Beethoven was following Mozart's lead. Only about half a dozen or so of his keyboard concertos were published during his lifetime — notably the earlier ones. Otherwise, as Plantinga remarks: 'He was usually in no hurry to see them in print.'[67] Delaying publication, however, was not without its problems. As Beethoven periodically reflected on the score of Op. 19, with performance in mind, he had cause to make revisions in response to his developing thoughts about writing in the concerto-genre. We next trace the chronology of these creative thoughts, as evident in the work's sketches and sketchbook origins, and the preparation undertaken for scheduled public performance.

H. C. Robbins Landon has observed:

> 'Unlike Mozart, who was born with a mercurial temperament and a Mendelsohnian facility, Beethoven had to work extremely hard at his compositions, sketching and polishing his works over and over again until he considered them finished; this was a trait of Beethoven's entire career.'[68]

In similar vein Barry Cooper contends: 'Beethoven's overriding desire was ... not just to create music, but to create music of the highest worth, and it is this that necessitated all the sketching and labour. The sketches reveal a constant striving for perfection ...'.[69]

One of the principal reasons why the autographs of the Op. 19 Concerto underwent so many changes — over time — is the textual distinction Beethoven made in the writing out of the orchestral parts and that for the solo piano. The former were required to be clearly written out so that they could be copied in preparation for performance. Beethoven, like Mozart before him, could rely upon his powers of memory and capacity for improvisation to supply the solo part — almost *a prima vista* or from a mere sketch-outline. Leon Plantinga states:

> 'Getting all the details of a score fixed, that is making a final text, was associated not with performance but with publication. So, when the concerto was a vital instrument of the composer's own music-making, there was not yet a full score, and the solo part could [and in the case of Op. 19 clearly did] undergo radical alteration from one performance to the next.'[70]

About two-hundred loose sheets of sketches date back to Beethoven's days in Bonn, from about 1790 or even earlier. These have subsequently been assembled into two large gatherings, the larger of which is now preserved in the British Library and is known as the 'Kafka Sketchbook' (more correctly Kafka 'miscellany') — taking its name from its one-time owner the collector of manuscripts Johann Nepomuk Kafaka. Beethoven later systematised his sketching procedure by binding together bundles of pocket-sized sheets that he could take with him on his much-loved strolls in the country; later still, he made use of ready-bound sketchbooks.[71] These provided him with the means of not only sketching more systematically but also more extensively, particularly as his compositions grew in scale and complexity — posing related challenges in solving large-scale problems of musical continuity and construction. Today, the sketchbooks that have survived have, like the Kafka Sketchbook, acquired the names of their various owners — to which we make occasional reference in our subsequent commentaries to other of the composer's piano concertos.[72] Of Beethoven's predisposition to set his thoughts down in draft form, Joseph Kerman suggests:

> 'Beethoven seems to have experienced a compulsion to get things down on paper — not only musical monographs, but also drafts of all kinds — he had a veritable commitment to the graphic act.'[73]

Beethoven set down ideas for a new work, starting on a fresh page, frequently noting ideas for different movements alongside each other. As his powers of invention took hold, he would insert further thoughts, cramming them into any available space or even going back to make use of pages previously left blank. As a consequence, sketches for different compositions co-exist side-by-side, many to be discarded but others to be fully worked into the compositions we know and cherish today. In his lecture 'Questions about music' Roger Sessions, in his role as Charles Eliot Norton Professor, remarked:

> 'Beethoven could have made a great deal out of any one of the earlier versions [of his sketches] ... Obviously, it would have been a different piece, and since that piece is not in existence, we can never know what it would have been like.'[74]

Gustav Nottebohm, a pioneer in the study and decipherment of Beethoven's sketchbooks, has this to say:

> '[In] spite of this unsystematic procedure it is evident that, as a rule, Beethoven was clear about his objectives from the start; he remained true to his original conceptions, and once an idea was grasped, he carried it through to the end ... We may seek [in the sketchbooks] the artist himself, in the unity of his whole character and spirit, and in the harmony of his inner powers.'[75]

In his scholarly commentary to Beethoven's sketchbooks, Alan Tyson suggests they may have 'performed a special function for him in maintaining his morale as well as in facilitating his creative processes'. They did indeed become indispensable to him and at times, when his working method came up in conversation, he was given to quoting from Schiller's *Joan of Arc*: 'Without my banner I dare not come.'[76]

Sketches for the B-flat major Piano Concerto date from Beethoven's time in Bonn – perhaps from as early as 1787–89. A single leaf reveals figuration for the piano in the same key as Op. 19. Cooper conjectures:

> 'Whatever the relationship of the fragment to Op. 19, its crucial significance is that it demonstrates unequivocally that Beethoven was composing a new piano concerto at some point during the period 1787–89, to follow the one in E flat of 1784, and that he reached at least as far as the end of the exposition in full-score format, with the leaf in question being replaced by a revised version before the orchestral parts could be inserted.'[77]

It is assumed that, amongst the compositions Beethoven took with him to Vienna from Bonn, they included a version of the B flat Concerto. In 1793 he undertook adaptations of the work, perhaps with a projected performance in mind. Autograph score fragments and sketches for a cadenza exist from this period suggesting Beethoven made extensive revisions to his first thoughts.[78] These include a rondo that is thought may have been composed to replace an earlier final movement to Op. 19. Alternatively, the rondo may have been supplied to replace a finale hitherto only lightly sketched. That it was intended for the B flat Concerto is evident in the writing. It is in the same key of B flat and its orchestration (strings plus one flute, pairs of oboes, bassoons, and horns) also matches that of the Concerto. Moreover, Beethoven did not assign an independent title to the composition, suggesting he did not regard it as being an independent work. It is, however, today regarded as such — namely as Rondo WoO 6.

Rondo WoO 6 has a history somewhat independent of that of the Concerto. It was discovered among the composer's papers at the auction of Beethoven's *Nachlass* (estate) of November 1827, when it was described as a 'Rondo mit Orchester fürs Pianoforte, unbekannt'. The autograph was bought by Carl Anton Spina, who arranged for its publication in 1829 by Anton Diabelli (of *Diabelli Variations* fame). By then, almost thirty years had elapsed and the style of the work no longer reflected that of Beethoven's later compositions. In addition, the range of the keyboard had expanded beyond that of the five-octave instrument for which the Rondo had been conceived. Carl Czerny was therefore asked to elaborate the piano writing by exploiting the enlarged compass of the newer instruments with additional virtuoso passagework.

Throughout the nineteenth century the autograph was

considered lost and the Rondo was known only in Czerny's later arrangement. In 1863 it was listed as such when it was included in the *Gesamtausgabe* (complete edition) of Beethoven's works that was published by Breitkopf & Härtel between 1862 and 1865, with a supplementary volume appearing in 1888. The musicologist Carl Roland discovered the autograph in the Peterskirche in Vienna. It later became the property of the Gesellschaft der Musikfreunde. In 1960 the Swiss musicologist and Beethoven scholar Willy Hess conferred the independent status on the Rondo by assigning it his catalogue the designation WoO 6.[79]

It is open to question whether Beethoven would have approved of his former pupil's arrangement. As the composer's biographer Thayer remarks:

> 'The use of the high registers of the pianoforte, which Czerny employs somewhat too freely in view of the simple character of the piece, was not contemplated by Beethoven, who once remarked: "He uses the piccolo too much for me".'[80]

Beethoven drafted cadenza sketches for the B flat Concerto that are preserved in the Kafka Sketchbook (ff. 46 and 89); these are thought to date from around 1794.[81] They suggest Beethoven had performance in mind – albeit with the Concerto still in an early form. In support of this contention is the realization that Beethoven, the virtuoso pianist, had by now gained access to the salons of several of Vienna's aristocracy, a number of whom retained small private orchestras for their summer entertainment – the ideal setting for a young composer to give further evidence of his gifts.[82]

In 1794–95 Beethoven further revised ·Op, 19. He provided a new finale – to replace the Rondo (the pre-

Czerny version of WoO 6) and reworked the Adagio. Cadenza sketches further suggest Beethoven had performance in mind. He may have tried out the Concerto at a concert held on 2 March 1795 in the salon of his patron Prince Franz Lobkowitz. A diary entry of one of the participants (Count Johann Zindzendorf) reads 'un nommé de Bon [sic]'[83] had played and evidently 'touched everybody'.[84]

On 18 March 1795, the *Weiner Zeitung* announced forthcoming concerts to be held in Vienna's Burgtheater. It was here that three of Mozart's operas had been recently premiered: *Die Entführung aus dem Serail* (1782), *Le nozze di Figaro* (1786), and *Così fan tutte* (1790). Over time, annual concerts were held in the Burgtheater for the benefit of the Widows of *The Society of Musicians*. Although Beethoven's works were performed by the Society, Beethoven was never enrolled as a member. He was, however, honored for his services with a free pass to its concerts. Two such concerts were announced for 29 and 30 March 1795. At the first of these, Beethoven made his début appearance in public as both a virtuoso of the keyboard and as a composer. Selected for performance was 'a Concerto for Pianoforte and Orchestra, composed and played by Ludwig van Beethoven'. At this period concerts, in support of 'Widows and Orphans', were frequently held under the direction of Antonio Salieri, then at the height of his fame as a composer of opera. Thayer observes, it is tempting to think that Salieri 'may have indulged a pardonable vanity' in bringing forward his gifted pupil. He adds:

'By 1795, Beethoven had established himself in several of the private musical salons, but beyond these his exceptional powers were known only by report.'[85]

Thayer, drawing on the recollections of Beethoven's childhood friend Franz Gerhard Wegeler, relates the following. It was not until the afternoon of the second day before the concert, that was to take place, that Beethoven wrote the new Rondo. He was apparently suffering from an attack of colic, the debilitating abominable illness that recurred throughout his life. Wegeler, who had studied medicine, relieved the pain as best he could with simple remedies. Notwithstanding his discomfort, Wegeler relates: 'In the anteroom sat four copyists to whom [Beethoven] handed sheet after sheet as soon as it was finished.' Rehearsal of the Concerto took place the next day in Beethoven's apartment. To add to his tribulations, the pianoforte at his disposal was out of tune, being half a tone lower than the wind instruments. According to Thayer: 'Without a moment's delay Beethoven had the wind-instruments and the others tune to B flat instead of A and played his part in C sharp.'[86] [87]

Thayer was convinced Beethoven had performed the B-flat major Concerto at the 29 March Burgtheater concert. Subsequent authorities make out a case for Beethoven perhaps having played the C major Concerto.[88] What is known is that at the 30 March concert Beethoven improvised at the piano. The following day, Mozart's widow arranged for a performance of *La Clemenza di Tito* to be held in the Burgtheater. The concert announcement stated: 'After the first part Herr Ludwig van Beethoven will play a Concerto of Mozart's composition on the Pianoforte.'[89] This is assumed to have been K. 466 in D minor that, as we have remarked, Beethoven is known to have admired and for which he had written cadenzas.

Whichever of his concertos Beethoven performed at the Burgtheater, his playing clearly made a favourable impression as the reviewer of the concert made known in the April issue of the *Wiener Zeitung*.

'As an intermezzo, on the first evening [29 March], the celebrated Herr Ludwig van Beethoven reaped the unanimous applause of the audience for his performance on the pianoforte of a completely new Concerto composed by him.'[90]

Later in the year, the *Wiener Zeitung* announced that a further concert would take place on 18 December in Vienna's Redoutensaal. The announcement proclaimed:

'Next Friday, the 18th [of this month], Herr Kapellmeister Haydn will give a grand musical concert in the small Redoutensaal ... Herr Beethoven will play a Concerto of his composing on the pianoforte and three grand symphonies, not yet heard here, which the Kapellmeister composed during his last sojourn in London, will be performed.'

This would be Beethoven's second public appearance in public as a concert pianist. Thayer, whose words we have just quoted, further remarks: 'We would gladly know what concerto was played.' His editor (Elliot Forbes) was convinced it was the B-flat major, Op. 19.[91]

In the New Year of 1796, Beethoven appeared once more at a concert, this time given in the Redoutensaal; it was presented under the auspices of his teacher Haydn. We learn only that Beethoven 'played a piano concerto'[92] that, nonetheless, some authorities take to be a reference to Op. 19.[93]

1796 was an auspicious year for Beethoven; it was the year he made his first concert tour. Whilst no account is recorded of Beethoven having performed either of his new Concertos, Op. 15 or Op. 19, we learn of his growing fame as both a composer and pianist. He undertook the tour between the months of February and July calling at Prague, Dresden, Leipzig and Berlin. He was well-received and, as we have seen from his letter to his brother Nikolaus Johann, he earned 'a good deal of money'.[94] In Berlin, Beethoven met the distinguished pianist Freidrich Himmel and performed for Friedrich Wilhelm II, King of Prussia. In Dresden, he played accompaniments for one and a half hours to the delight of the Elector of Saxony who afterwards presented the composer with a gold snuffbox filled with Louis d'ors. Beethoven was given to declaring that it was no ordinary snuffbox, but such a one 'as might have been given to an ambassador'. His improvisations at the keyboard thrilled and enchanted audiences who found them 'rich in fantasy' with 'striking changes from adagio to allegro' — hallmarks of Beethoven's piano playing that would soon find a place in his piano-sonata writing.[95]

In 1798 Beethoven undertook a second concert tour, this time to Prague. For this, he revised the B flat Concerto once more. Evidence of his work is found in the so-called Grasnick 1 sketchbook that derives its name from its one-time owner, the manuscript collector Friedrich Grasnick. On his death it was purchased by the Berlin Royal Library — the Staatsbibliothek Preussischer Kulturbesitz, Berlin. Amongst its pages are revisions of Op. 19 — all three movements — alongside ideas for his first set of String Quartets, Op. 18.[96] On this occasion it is fairly certain that the version of the B flat Concerto that Beethoven performed incorporated the revised finale in place of the Rondo WoO 6. By way of evidence, Beethoven's revised autograph score dates from this period. He wrote out the orchestral parts but he only lightly indicated the piano part, leaving its realisation in performance to his acknowledged power of extemporization.

The Concerto was now close to its final version but Beethoven still held it back from publication; the reason, as we have stated, was to enable him to retain the exclusive right to its performance. To trace the work's eventual publication, we have to consider Beethoven's negotiations with various publishers.

In the autumn (or thereabouts) of 1800 Beethoven received a request for publications from the music publisher and composer Franz Anton Hoffmeister. His name is known today to Mozartians through association with the *Hoffmeister Quartet* (K. 499). In 1800, Hoffmeister established a publishing house in Leipzig with his colleague Ambros [Ambrosius] Kühnel, an organist in the employ at the Electoral Saxon Court Chapel. The two transacted business under the name Bureau de Musique, in Leipzig, and Hoffmeister and Kühnel in Vienna. Beethoven already had dealings with Hoffmeister; the year previously he had published the composer's celebrated *Sonate Pathétique*. It is not surprising, therefore, that Hoffmeister, having published the works of Albrechtsberger, Dittersdorf, Mozart, and Pleyel, should want to establish a relationship with Beethoven – a rising star in Vienna's musical firmament. Thayer writes, in his characteristically fulsome manner:

> 'Knowing Beethoven personally, and so intimately, it is alike creditable, to the talents of the one and the taste and appreciation of the other, that Hoffmeister, immediately upon organising his new publishing house, should have asked [Beethoven] for manuscripts.'[97]

On 15 December 1800, Beethoven responded to Hoffmeister's request. He initially addresses Hoffmeister, 'Most beloved and worthy brother' — terms of endearment the composer reserved when corresponding with fellow musicians, poets, artists, and (the more worthy) publishers. Beethoven offered Hoffmeister his Septet Op. 20, that he describes as having become 'very popular', 'a grand symphony' [First Symphony Op. 21] and 'a grand solo sonata' [Piano Sonata Op. 22]. He invited Hoffmeister to fix the prices himself. Next, Beethoven offered 'a concerto for pianoforte' — taken to be a reference to the B flat Concerto, Op. 19. He acknowledged: 'I do not make out to be one of my best.' He makes reference to another concerto 'which is to be published here [Vienna] by Mollo.'

Tranquillo Mollo was a partner in the distinguished publishing firm Artaria & Co. The concerto referred to was the C major, Op. 15. Beethoven adds, in a somewhat conspiratorial manner: 'I am telling you this so that you may inform the Leipzig reviewers, because *I am still keeping back the better ones until I myself undertake a journey'.* [Beethoven's italics] From this, we can infer Beethoven was contemplating undertaking other concert tours — in the event these did not take place. He could not resist adding: 'At the same time it would not disgrace you to engrave this Concerto [Op. 15].'[98]

Musicologist have censured Beethoven for writing as he did to Hoffmeister, suggesting the C major Concerto was available for publication when, as we have just seen, he had already pledged it to Mollo. It would not be the last time in his business dealings that Beethoven would play one publisher off against another. He may be exonerated, though, when it is remembered that piracy was rife at the period in question and threatened to undermine his livelihood. Beethoven, acutely aware of this, was doubtless seeking to forestall the nefarious publication of his new concertos by wanting to have them published simultaneously in two of Europe's musical centres. To illustrate the point, an unauthorised arrangement of the Septet Op. 20, offered to Hoffmeister, appeared as a string-quintet arrangement that was published shortly after the appearance of Beethoven's original composition. This prompted Beethoven to write a letter of protest, dated October 20 1802, to the *Wiener Zeitung*. He wished to make it known that the arrangement was not his nor had it been sanctioned by him. Beethoven accepted that the making of such transcriptions was widespread in what he described as 'our prolific age of transcriptions'. However, he demanded that publishers, of such transcriptions, should make due acknowledgement, on the title page, so that 'his honour as a composer may not be infringed nor the public deceived'. Moreover, he took the opportunity to state that his own original Quintet in C major, Op. 29 would soon be published by Breitkopf and Härtel at Leipzig. Op. 29 duly appeared in December 1802.[99]

Beethoven responded to Hoffmeister's letter of 15 December 1800 on 15 January 1801 — or thereabouts; Beethoven did not always date his correspondence with due care. He expressed, in fulsome terms, his wish to contribute to the endeavours of his 'fellow brothers in art' and trusted that their works will profit 'the lot of the true and genuine artists'. Turning to business matters, he offered Hoffmeister the following works: Septet Op. 20 (20 ducats) — Beethoven suggests this could be arranged for piano 'with a view to its wider distribution and to our greater profit'; Symphony No. 1, Op. 21 (20 ducats); Piano Concerto No. 2, Op. 19 (10 ducats); and Piano Sonata Op. 22 (20 ducats) — Beethoven describes this as 'a first-rate composition, most beloved and worthy brother'. In the following passage, he explains his estimation of the relative value of the works in question:

'I make no distinction between Sonata, Septet and Symphony. The reason is that I find a septet or a symphony does not sell as well as a sonata. That is the reason why I do this, although a symphony should undoubtedly be worth more.'

With reference to the B flat Concerto Beethoven adds: 'I am valuing the Concerto at only 10 ducats because, as I have already told you, I do not consider it to be one of my best concertos.' He explains: 'I have endeavoured to make the prices as moderate for you as possible.' Acknowledging his limitations, in business matters, he states:

'The only currency I can cope with is Viennese ducats. How much that sum amounts to in your thalers and gulden does not concern me, because I am really an incompetent business man who is bad at arithmetic.'

In releasing the Op. 19 Concerto to Hoffmeister, in the form in which it then existed, Michael Steinberg suggests Beethoven had something of a dilemma. He explains: It is as if he felt caught between the desire to make improvements on the basis of his rapidly growing experience and skill, on the other hand, some unease at the thought of moving too far from his original concept. Not entirely convinced by the outcome, he let the publisher, Hoffmeister, have [the Concerto] for only half the price.'[100]

Beethoven closed his letter to Hoffmeister: 'Well that tiresome business has now been settled', by which he means the complex and time-consuming procedures he had to transact with Hoffmeister to see his works in print. Beethoven calls it tiresome because, as he remarks, 'he should like such matters to be differently ordered in this world'. He goes on to say:

> 'There ought to be in the world *a market for art* [Beethoven's italics] where the artist would only have to bring his works and take as much money as he needed.'

He laments, how he had to be both an artist and 'to be to a certain extent a business man as well, and how can he manage to be that — Good Heavens!' Worthy of note is that Beethoven's gifted contemporary Franz Schubert, in the years of his maturity, gave expression to just such frustrated sentiments as those expressed by Beethoven in his letter to Hoffmeister.

Beethoven briefly mentions the adverse reviews of his works expressed by the Leipzig music critics of the *Allgemeine musikalische Zeitung*. He remarked that he did not take them seriously — but they had clearly annoyed him. He protested: 'Just let them talk, they will never be immortal nor would they be able to take immortality away from anyone upon whom Apollo had bestowed it.' Beethoven clearly considered himself to be one of Apollo's chosen ones!

On 22 April 1801, Beethoven wrote once more to Hoffmeister in Leipzig. He apologised for his failure to uphold his expressed obligations and his apparent tardiness. He exonerated himself on the grounds that he had been unwell and was very busy. He had in fact been hard at work completing the music for the Ballet *Die Geschöpfe des Prometheus — The Creatures of Prometheus*, Op. 43. He remarked, 'perhaps the only touch of genius which I possess is that things are not always in very good order'. He adds, 'Yet no one but myself is able to deal with them'; at this stage in his career Beethoven did not have the benefit of a secretary-amanuensis as was the case later in life.

Regarding the Concerto Op. 19, he states:

> 'As usual with me, the pianoforte part of the *Concerto* was not written out in the score. I have only written it out now, so that, as I am in a hurry, you will receive that part in my own not very legible handwriting.'

Beethoven urged Hoffmeister to publish his compositions in their correct opus-number sequence, namely: Piano Concerto, Op. 19; Septet, Op. 20; First Symphony, Op. 21; and Piano Sonata, Op. 22. He complimented Hoffmeister on his recently published arrangement of Mozart's sonatas for string quartets. This was unusual since Beethoven did not generally approve of such transcriptions. He sent 'all kind wishes' to Hoffmeister's partner Kühnel and expressed the hope that their business transactions would go well in the future.[101]

That Beethoven acted on this occasion as his own copyist is an indication he did not want to delay publication of Op. 19 any longer than necessary. Ordinarily, when Beethoven sent off a work for publication, the publisher would expect to receive a clean, legible handwritten copy of the work in question, so as to minimise the likelihood of errors. This was the so-called engraver's model (*stichvolagen*) that was used to produce the copper printing-plates.[102] Beethoven would usually have recourse to a professional copyist. In later years, his favourite copyist was Wenzel Schlemmer who worked for the composer until his death in 1823. He was one of the few copyists who could fulfil Beethoven's exacting demands and accurately decipher his manuscripts. Schlemmer charged the composer about twelve Kreutzer per sheet. In the money values of the period, this worked out at about five sheets of copying for two English shillings — but out of this sum Schlemmer also had to pay his assistants.[103]

When Beethoven revised the score of Op. 19, to meet Hoffmeister's urgent need for it, he felt impelled to make yet further changes. As Cooper remarks: 'Artistic progress was not ... for [Beethoven] a smooth continuum.' With the composer's self-deprecatory remarks in mind, concerning his low estimation of his Op. 19, Cooper adds:

> '[Not] every work surpassed its immediate pred-
> ecessor, as [Beethoven] was well aware, and
> sometimes a great work was followed by compo-
> sitions of less significance before the next major
> leap forward.'[104]

Beethoven made changes to the Concerto's score, notably the tutti to the first movement; for clarity he used a distinctive grey ink. However, not all the amendments were incorpo-rated. To quote Cooper once more: 'Beethoven compro-mised his artistic goals and sent off the parts unaltered to save time.' Cooper has identified some fourteen passages where the amendments were required to be incorporated.[105] Consequently, when Hoffmeister eventually published the B-flat major Piano Concerto, Op. 19, later in December, it did not strictly accord with Beethoven's intentions. Indeed, until relatively recently, the 'grey ink' amendments have not been included in standard performing editions. This circum-stance is, however, being corrected with the growing aware-ness of Beethoven's hasty transactions in the spring of 1801.[106]

We have already seen that on 22 April 1801, Beethoven wrote to the music publisher Breitkopf & Härtel, like Hoffmeister, based in Leipzig. This was the first of many such letters he sent to this famous publishing house — a correspondence he maintained until 1816. Härtel, like Hoffmeister, appears to have approached Beethoven with a view to publishing some of the composer's compositions. Beethoven opened his letter by saying:

> 'I am very sorry not to be able to accept [your proposal] at the moment. But please be so kind just to inform me what kind of compositions you would like to have from me, namely symphonies, quartets, sonatas and so forth, so that I may be guided by your wishes and, should I happen to have the works you require or desire, be able to supply them.'

He explained: 'Mollo here [in Vienna] is going to publish, with my consent, seven or eight works; and Hoffmeister in Leipzig is also publishing four works.' He elaborated: 'Hoffmeister is publishing one of *my first concertos*, which, of course, is not *one of my best compositions*. [Beethoven's italics]' He is referring, as we have noted, to Op. 19. He adds: 'Mollo is also publishing a concerto which was written later, it is true, but which is also not one of my best compositions of this type.' This is a reference to Op. 15 that, although the second of his compositions in the concerto genre, Beethoven clearly did not hold in the highest regard.

Beethoven had words of censure for Härtel's publishing house. He had received an adverse review of his works in the *Allgemeine musikalische Zeitung* – published by Härtel. This prompted him to rebuke him: 'Advise your reviewers to be more circumspect and intelligent, particularly in regard to the productions of younger composers.' On this occasion, however, he characteristically dismissed the reviewers on the grounds: 'They don't know anything about music.' He further observed:

'And indeed, what made it easier for me to keep calm was that I noticed how much certain people were being praised to the skies who, in Vienna, had very little standing among the best local composers.'[107]

On 21 June, Beethoven had occasion to write a letter of reassurance to Hoffmeister. Word, it would seem, had been circulating amidst Leipzig's musical fraternity that a new concerto of Beethoven's was soon to be published. Hoffmeister was concerned that Beethoven was collaborating with other publishers regarding the publication of works for which he alone had transacted payment. His remarks prompted Beethoven to respond: 'I am really a little surprised at the message you sent me through your business agent in Vienna.' He sought to reassure Hoffmeister:

'I give you herewith my written assurance that I have sold the Septet, the Concerto [Op. 19], the Symphony, and the Sonata to nobody else in the world but to yourselves, Herren Hoffmeister & Kühnel, and that you may certainly regard those works as your property; and on that I stake my honour.' [Beethoven's italics]

At the same time, Beethoven provided Hoffmeister with the name of the dedicatee of the Concerto, together with details of the composition's orchestration:

'Concert pour le pianoforte avec deux Violons, viole, basse et violoncelle, un flute, deux oboes, deux cors, deux fagots, composé et dédié à Monsieur Charles Nikl noble de Nihctsberg,

112

Conseiller aulique de sa Majesté Impériale et
Royal, par Louis van Beethoven , Oeuvre 19.'[108]

Little is known of the Concerto's dedicatee Carl (Charles)
Nicklas von Nickelsberg beyond that he came from a
musical family and was Senior Court Secretary in the
Austrian Imperial Commerce Department.[109] The Title Page
of the Concerto duly announced the work in accordance
with Beethoven's directions:

> 'CONCERT / pour le / PIANOFORTE / *avec
> deux Violons, Viole, Violoncelle et Basse* / *une
> Fluite, 2 Oboes, 2 Cors et 2 Bassons* / *Composé
> et dédié* / *à Monsieur* / *Charles Nikl* / *Noble de
> Nihctsberg, Conseiller aulique* / *de sa Majesté
> Impériale et Royal* / *par* / LOUIS van
> BEETHOVEN / Oeuvre XIX.'

Facsimile reproductions of the Title Pages to first
editions of the B-flat major Concerto, Op. 19, by the
publishing houses of Hoffmeister and Peters, are reproduced on the Beethoven House, Digital Archives website.[110]
An English edition, edited by J. Moscheles, was entered at
Stationers Hall, London with the Title Page:

> 'BEETHOVEN'S WORKS / Edited by / J.
> MOSCHELES / Complete Edition / No. 2 /
> GRAND CONCERTOS / FOR THE / PIANO
> – FORTE / With Accompaniments / ad lib /
> Composed by / LOUIS VAN BEETHOVEN /
> Op. 19 / LONDON / *Published by Cramer,
> Addison & Beale* ...'.

A footnote to the Title Page reads:

'NB: The tuttis of these Concertos have been adapted from the score and small notes added to the Solos by Mr. Moscheles so that they may be performed with or without accompaniments: when the full orchestra is employed the small notes in the stringed instrument parts must be omitted. The flute part, which has been expressly arranged for this edition, is only to be used when unaccompanied by other wind instruments.'
[original italics]

In England, at this time, the Law of Copyright required eleven copies of newly printed works to be deposited at Stationers Hall, the London home of the Worshipful Company of Stationers and Newspaper Makers; a Livery Company that regulated the affairs of the printing and publishing industry. On receipt of new works, the Company then passed these to the eleven libraries that were privileged to exercise their right of demand to receive new works – the equivalent of today's system of Legal Deposit. As Pamela Willets explains in her study of *Beethoven and England*:

'This is the principal source of the collections of the English, Beethoven [first] editions preserved in the British Museum, the Bodleian Library at Oxford, [and] the University Library at Cambridge.'[111]

On 13 March 1802, the *Zeitung für die elegante Welt* made the following public announcement:

'The *Bureau de Musique* in Vienna and Leipzig has recently published in a splendid engraving: A

114

beautiful but rather difficult fortepiano concerto in B-flat major, written with much art, which is the most recent by this ingenious composer and greatest fortepianist in Vienna, Louis van Beethoven.'

The following year, on 8 February 1803, the same journal made a further announcement: 'This Concerto [Op. 19] is very brilliant, diligently composed, and full of beautiful ideas.' At the same time the journal's reviewer remarked on the appearance of Beethoven's First Symphony, Op. 21 that is described as being 'A very originally composed, beautiful symphony that is very effective'. Symphony No. 1 had been published in December 1801, together with the Concerto Op. 19, by Hoffmeister in Vienna and by the Bureau de Musique in Leipzig. It is described as a 'Grande Symphonie' on the Title Page.[112]

In 1809, fully twenty years after Beethoven had begun work on the B-flat major Concerto, he once more turned his attention to the composition. His incentive to do so was to provide his pupil, the Archduke Rudolph, with additional elaboration of the piano part in the form of a cadenza-model for the first movement. Rudolph was Beethoven's only composition pupil and, notwithstanding his religious vocation and attachment to church affairs, was an accomplished pianist. Such was Beethoven's diligence towards his pupil that he also wrote out cadenzas for the C major Concerto, Op. 15, the C minor Concerto, Op. 37, and the G major Concerto, Op. 58. When he came to compose the Concerto in E-flat major, Op. 78 (1809–10), he incorporated cadenza passage-work in the score from the outset.[113]

In 1820 a sensation occurred in Vienna's musical circles. The circumstance relates to Marie Leopoldine Pachler (née Koschak), described as 'one of the finest women pianists of the day'. She was a youthful Beethoven enthusiast from Graz who, when only eight-years old, gave a performance of the B flat Concerto on 4 April.[114] With Beethoven's encouragement she later performed the piano part to his *Choral Fantasia*. More than this, Leopoldine was possessed of exceptional beauty. Such was her pulchritude that the poet Anselm Hüttenbrenner was disposed to describe her as 'the most beautiful girl ... the most beautiful woman in Graz ... the daughter of heaven'.[115]

We draw our discussion of Beethoven's Piano Concerto No. 2 in B-flat major, Op. 19 to a close in the form of a documentary-style collection of texts. These are derived from the writings of musicologists and performing artists bearing on the musicology of the Op. 19 Concerto.

It is perhaps fitting we should preface these texts with the guidance Beethoven's pupil Carl Czerny has for the would-be performer of the Piano Concerto in B-flat major, Op. 19:

FIRST MOVEMENT

'To be performed in the same gay and lively style as the first movement of the foregoing Concerto [Op. 15]. Though rather slower.'

SECOND MOVEMENT

'[The] bass must be marked with particular energy. Subsequently, the right hand in a similar manner. At the end, a cadence must likewise be extemporised. This *Adagio* may be compared to a dramatic vocal scene, in which the most heart-felt sensibility manifests itself, and the performance must be in perfect accordance with the frequently concerted orchestra.'

THIRD MOVEMENT

'Very gay, light and brilliant.' Czerny adds: 'Naturally, one will not "improvise" a cadenza today, but will play Beethoven's own magnificent cadenza.'

Carl Czerny: *On the Proper Performance of all Beethoven's Works for the Piano*, as reproduced, with commentaries, in: Paul Badura-Skoda, 1970, pp. 106–07.

The texts that follow are presented in the chronological order of their publication.

FIRST MOVEMENT
ALLEGRO CON BRIO

'In Beethoven's first two Concertos, in C major, Op. 15 and B flat, Op. 19, he had not made his opening tutti so dangerously like a symphonic opening; but he had produced a mass of delightful discursiveness as if the orchestra were extemporising ... The pianoforte can release itself from paraphrasing the opening tutti and can expand and expatiate as a solo part as it should.'

Donald Francis Tovey, *Beethoven*, 1944, p. 116.

'The only original cadenza for the first movement [of Op. 19] is in a later style but, like the longest of those for the C major Concerto, too good to miss. Its recurring fugato reminds one that B flat was to become Beethoven's fugal key (Op. 106, Op. 133) and the fact that it dwarfs the orchestra's modest cadence-theme might be justified as a ripe example of Beethovenish humour.'

Denis Matthews, *Beethoven, Master Musicians,* 1985, p. 173.

Glen Gould describes the cadenza in the B flat Concerto as 'that imaginative ... quasi-fugal reflection upon the themes of his youthful essay'. He also observes:

'In recent years it has become the commendable practice of musicians to contribute cadenzas which observe an idiomatic identification with the concerto subject.'

He adds that such an attachment to historical authenticity has not always prevailed. He cites the prevalence, amongst many nineteenth-century composers, including for example Brahms, who, Gould states, 'undertook to produce cadenzas of various older works without foregoing their customary [musical] vocabulary'. This observation calls to mind the waggish observation that misconceived cadenzas are 'the appendicitis of the concerto'.

John P. L. Roberts and Ghyslaine Guertin editors, *Glenn Gould: Selected letters*, 1992, p. 245.

'At the time Beethoven published his early concertos, cadenzas were still expected to be improvised by the performer, so printed scores contained no written-out cadenzas. Beethoven later came to a different point of view, including cadenzas in his scores and even composing several cadenzas for his earlier concertos ... The popular cadenza for the first movement of Op. 19 was composed in 1808 or 1809, [and is] a product of Beethoven's middle period (1802–16)

... The substantial cadenza opens with a fugal setting of a variation of the Concerto's fanfare opening and continues with other themes from the first movement ... Not only is this cadenza typical of Beethoven's later style but it was written for a newer form of piano with a greater range in the upper-register than had been the case before 1804.'

Michael Thomas Roeder, *A History of the Concerto*, 1994, p. 181.

'A formula often used by Mozart (and for that matter a number of eighteenth-century composers) was an alternation between quasi-heroic ideas that established the tonic or "home" key and more gentle responses. Beethoven unashamedly copies his predecessors in this respect, and the Concerto begins with the full orchestra declaiming the notes that comprise the chord of B-flat major ... When at last the soloist enters the fray it is in a manner that Beethoven had clearly learnt from Mozart; no attempt is made to dominate or rival the orchestra in any way. Rather, it is with a completely new theme that remains the exclusive property of the pianist.'

Antony Hopkins, *The Concertgoer's Companion*, 1996, p. 22 and p. 25.

'The opening tutti is eventful and, for a cheery comedy, surprisingly full of minor harmonies. The piano enters with something new and lyric that, with a delightful sense of leisure, initiates a

119

transition to the return of the orchestra's alert opening theme ... Just before the end of the first movement, in accordance to custom, Beethoven allows space for a cadenza, which he would have improvised in his own performances. Some years after the composition of this concerto, however, he wrote out a cadenza that both in compositional style and pianistic manner goes far beyond the movement into which it is placed. It is hugely irruptive, forward-looking even for its presumed date of 1809 or so, and wonderful. Beethoven was utterly free of scruples when it came to mixing vintages.'

Michael Steinberg, *The Concerto: A Listener's Guide*, 1998, pp. 56–57.

'The formal shape of this movement, broadly considered, is about what one expects in the first movement of a Classical concerto: the three sections in which the soloist participates correspond roughly to the exposition, development, and recapitulation of a sonata-allegro form; these alternate with four tuttis, the last of them interrupted by the soloist's cadenza ... The basic language of Beethoven's Concerto is one he shared with Western Europe as a whole.'

Leon Plantinga, *Beethoven's Concertos: History, Style, Performance*, 1999, p. 68 and p. 87.

Notwithstanding the many expressed attestations to the influence of Mozart ... that of Haydn is also considered by some authorities to be evident in Beethoven's Op. 19: '[Its] simple themes and the way in which they are treated suggest the influence of Beethoven's teacher Haydn: Roger Fiske, in his *BBC Music Guide* to Beethoven's concertos and overtures, even calls [Op. 19] "arguably the most Haydn-esque work he ever wrote".'

Anthony Burton, *Piano Concerto in B-flat major, The BBC 3 Beethoven Experience*, June 2005.

'The piano's arpeggios contrast thematically with the quaver figures in the winds, but also act as a bridge between the strings (with which it plays) and the winds (with which it alternates), beginning and ending on or close to the lowest note in the strings and the highest in the wind. Clearly, this is not a grand confrontation along the lines of those in [Mozart's] K.449/I. and K.491/1. By demonstrating collaborative intent, instead, this interaction brings contrast into the realm of intimate grandeur.'

Simon P. Keefe, *The Cambridge Companion to the Concerto*, 2005, p. 84.

'Some of the first movement, and much of the last, is in the language of the *opera buffa* and uses those delightful, cheerful formulas which had been part of comic opera for decades. The elaborate passage-work for the piano, especially in the slow movement, is more decorative than expressive or atmospheric ... But there are of course many touches which are typical of Beethoven.'

Liner notes to EMI, *Beethoven: Piano Concerto Nos. 2 & 4*. [undated and anonymous]

SECOND MOVEMENT
ADAGIO
'The slow movement, with its noble melodic line and its purposeful decorations in the solo part, is of a higher order.'

Denis Matthews, *Beethoven, Master Musicians,* 1985, p. 173.

'The Adagio in E flat is filled with carefully thought-out ornamentation, paradoxically creating the feeling of an improvisation. The little "cadenza" near the end of the movement consists of a most unusual single line of broken phrases in the solo instrument in dialogue with the strings. The piano part here is a fascinating experiment of a highly expressive nature that points toward much later developments in Beethoven's piano writing.'

Michael Thomas Roeder, *A History of the Concerto*, 1994, p. 180.

'The slow movement, if not directly influenced by Mozart, could be regarded as the sort of music he might have written if he had lived to be fifty — an extension of his idiom rather than a direct copy ... The orchestral opening sets a very slow tempo, a real adagio, and it might almost be taken from a religious work.'

Antony Hopkins, *The Concertgoer's Companion*, 1996, p. 27.

'Beethoven's pupil Carl Czerny, he of the thousand finger-exercises, wrote an illuminating and authoritative book on the performance of his teacher's piano music ['*On the Proper Performance of all Beethoven's Works for the Piano*'], and of the deeply plumbing slow movement of the Second Concerto he says it might be compared to a dramatic vocal scene. Here is music that offers us a glimpse of Beethoven the great *adagio* player. The orchestra leads off with music whose meditative lyricism is soon ruptured by impassioned outbursts, and it is at the height of one of these that the piano enters with an unforgettably eloquent gesture ... The pianist is the principal singer; nonetheless, the movement as a whole is an intense dialogue between piano and orchestra. Beethoven's new and original voice is everywhere manifest: nowhere in Mozart, for example, will you find anything like the passage in which, against pizzicato strings, woodwinds carry the melody while the piano adds a rapid flicker of thirty-second triplets.'

Michael Steinberg, *The Concerto: A Listener's Guide,* 1998, p. 58.

'The *Adagio* of Op. 19, a movement that first shows up in the revisions of 1794–95, is a contemplative, serious piece. Like slow movements of many concertos, it might remind us of an aria sung by a character recently embroiled in high drama, but now pausing for introspection and reflection. The reflection here is not of Beethoven's most pessimistic sort. The triple meter alone sets it apart from the high pathos, for example, of the adagio from the slightly later Sonata Op. 10, No. 3.'

Leon Plantinga, *Beethoven's Concertos: History, Style, Performance*, 1999, p. 76.

'The second movement is a wonderfully profound adagio. Beginning very simply it makes great use of dynamic contrasts and Mozartian expressive appoggiaturas. The piano part becomes increasingly decorative, again in a Mozartian manner, but in the recapitulation the decoration is so elaborate that it far surpasses anything in Mozart's concertos.'

Barry Cooper, *Beethoven, Master Musicians,* 2000, p. 44.

'The second movement is "an air with variations":
... The tonality of E-flat major remains firm throughout.'

Nicolas Slonimsky, *The Great Composers and their Works*, 2000, p. 141.

'The slow movement is an adagio in E-flat major, with a serene main theme which, as in many of Beethoven's early works with piano, is encrusted with increasing amounts of virtuoso decoration on its later reappearances. Unexpectedly, though, at the point towards the end of the movement where the orchestra pauses for a cadenza, what follows is more decorative glitter, but a simple unsupported melodic line, marked "with greater expression", which continues in recitative-like dialogue with the strings.'

Anthony Burton, *Piano Concerto in B-flat major, The BBC 3 Beethoven Experience,* June 2005. Burton's text was one of several written to accompany the occasion in June 2005 when all of Beethoven's compositions were played in a single week.

THIRD MOVEMENT
RONDO; MOLTO ALLEGRO
'The finale, with its syncopated rondo theme, much mulled over in the sketches, replaced an earlier movement with an andante middle section (WoO 6) and has greatly helped the work's popularity.'

Denis Matthews, *Beethoven, Master Musicians,* 1985, p. 172.

'In nearly all Beethoven's works there is an unprecedented dynamism. The main theme of the finale of the Piano Concerto No. 2 shows this element to have been important from the outset.'

Barry Cooper, *The Beethoven Compendium: A Guide to Beethoven's Life and Music,* 1991, p.218.

'[The] rondo is clearly derived from eighteenth-century sensibilities. Its playful, tuneful nature is reminiscent of Mozart and Haydn. The piano writing is nothing but brilliant with frequent broken octaves and double thirds.'

Michael Thomas Roeder, *A History of the Concerto*, 1994, p. 180.

'Beethoven begins the last movement with eight bars of solo piano ... The theme is joyous, even a little frivolous, and if this is music that he penned hastily from his sick-bed it says a lot for the power of the mind over physical frailty ... Historically, the impression we have of Beethoven is usually one of a rather solemn, severe character. Nothing could do more to dispel that image than this movement, bubbling over with musical high spirits and humour from start to finish.'

Antony Hopkins, *The Concertgoer's Companion*, 1996, p 28 and p. 30.

'The brilliant final rondo is one of the most delightful of Beethoven's early finales, effervescent and zestful in a way difficult to reconcile with the story that he was suffering a severe attack of colic while composing it.

Robert Layton, *A Guide to the Concerto*, 1996, p. 105.

'[The] finale is probably a substitute for the Rondo in B flat (WoO 6, *c.*1795) which may at first have been intended for this Concerto, and which now exists only in a somewhat adulterated edition by Carl Czerny ... At the last moment, this time clearly taking a leaf out of Mozart's book, Beethoven treats us to a graceful and entirely new phrase as well as concocting something quire special by way of a neat exit for the soloist.'

Michael Steinberg, *The Concerto: A Listener's Guide,* 1998, pp. 58–59.

'It starts brilliantly in piano solo ... with strong off-accents [which] the orchestra picks up while the piano provides a background in bravura passages ... The conclusion is terse and vigorous.'

Nicolas Slonimsky, *The Great Composers and their Works,* 2000, p. 141.

[1] For an account of Beethoven, in the context of his family life in Bonn, see: Elliot Forbes editor, *Thayer's Life of Beethoven,* 1967 p. 207; The years 1787-88, 1967, pp. 86-99.

[2] For a fuller documentary account see: H. C. Robbins Landon, pp. 53–54.

[3] Theodore Albrecht editor and translator, 1996 Vol. 1, Document No. 13g, pp. 22–3. For a reproduction of Beethoven's Album, open at the pages showing Waldstein's text together with his silhouette, see: Hans Conrad Fischer, and Erich Kock, 1972, p. 107.

[4] For an account of Ferdinand Waldstein and his relationship with Beethoven, see: Elliot Forbes editor, *Thayer's Life of Beethoven,* 1967, pp. 91–2 and p. 351; Peter Clive, 2001, pp. 385–7; and Eric Blom, 1938, p. 148.

[5] All the signatories who signed Beethoven's *Stammbuch,* together with other expressions of affection and esteem for Beethoven, are quoted in full by Theodore Albrecht, 1996, Vol. 1, pp. 10–29.

[6] See: Beethoven-Haus, Bonn, website.

[7] Barry Cooper, 1991, p. 69.

[8] Emily Anderson, editor and translator, 1961, Vol. 1, Letter No. 8, p. 12.

[9] Thayer-Forbes, 1967, p. 144 and Theodore Albrecht, translator and editor, 1996, Vol. 1 Letter No. 16, pp. 32–4. For a commentary on this extended and eloquent letter, with remarks concerning the compositions mentioned therein, see also: H. C. Robbins Landon 1959, pp. 141–2.

[10] Theodore Albrecht, editor and translator, 1996, Vol. 1 Letter No. 17, pp. 34–5.

[11] Emily Anderson, editor and translator, 1961, Vol. 1, Letter No. 6, p. 9.

[12] Tia de Nora, 1997, pp. 99.

[13] For a discussion of these circumstances see: Beethoven House, Digital Archives,

Document, Sammlung H. C. Bodmer. HCB Mh 42.

14 Theodore Albrecht editor and translator, 1996, Vol. 1, Letter No. 21, pp. 41–42.

15 Franz Wegeler, 1838, English edition, 1988, p. 75.

16 Gerhard von Breuning, 1874, English edition, 1992, pp. 98-9. Diabelli made the gift of the lithograph of Haydn's birthplace when Beethoven was in his last illness. Gerhard von Breuning was a frequent visitor to Beethoven at this time and helped to have the lithograph framed.

17 Johann Baptist Schenk, as recorded by Oscar George Theodore Sonneck, *Beethoven: Impressions of Contemporaries*, 1927, pp. 15–16.

18 Peter Clive, 2001, p. 302.

19 Joseph Kerman, 1967, pp. 4–5.

20 The original account is given by Ferdinand Ries: *Impressions of Beethoven*, in: Oscar George Theodore Sonneck, 1927, p. 49.

21 Elliot Forbes, editor, 1967, *Thayer's Life of Beethoven*, 1967, pp. 149–50. See also: Philip G. Downs, 1992, pp. 559–60 and Barry Cooper, 2000, pp. 78–9.

22 The reminiscences of Fräulein von Kissow, as Frau von Bernhard, are told in: Oscar G. Sonneck, 1927 pp. 19–20.

23 As recounted in *Vienna and its Musical Life* in: *Haydn: The Years of the Creation*, H. C. Robbins Landon, 1977, p. 25.

24 Emily Anderson editor and translator, 1961, Vol. 1, Letter No. 7, pp. 9–11.

25 Hans Conrad Fischer and Erich Kock, *Ludwig van Beethoven: A study in Text and Pictures*, 1972, pp. 29–30.

26 H. C. Robbins Landon, 1992, p. 79.

27 Tia De Nora, 1997, p. 19.

28 Emily Anderson, editor and translator, 1961, Vol. 1, Letter No. 9, pp. 13–15.

29 Letter of 19 February 1796. See: Emily Anderson, 1961, Vol. 1 Letter No. 16, p. 22.

30 Theodore Albrecht, editor and translator, 1996, Vol. 1, Letter No. 31, p. 56.

31 H. C. Robbins Landon, 1992, p. 61.

32 Johann Schlosser, *Beethoven: the First Biography, 1827* edited by Barry Cooper, 1996, pp. 135–36. Schlosser's book is dated 1828 but it is thought to have appeared in 1827, the year of Beethoven's death.

33 Derived, with adaptations, from: H. C. Robbins Landon, *Essays on the Viennese Classical Style: Gluck, Haydn, Mozart, Beethoven*, 1970, p. 44 and *Beethoven: His Life, Work and World*, 1992, p. 60.

34 *Ibid.*

35 Elliot Forbes editor, *Thayer' Life of Beethoven*, 1967 p. 207.

36 H. C. Robbins Landon, 1992, p. 81. Tomaschek's impressions of Beethoven improvising are also recounted in Oscar. G. Sonneck, 1927, p. 22. Drawing on the accounts of others, he reports that Beethoven's 'frequent daring deviations from one motive to another' disturbed the music's 'organic connection' and 'sprang from a too exuberant conception'. See also: Elliot Forbes editor, *Thayer's Life of Beethoven*, 1967 p. 208.

37 Wegeler's account is recalled in Elliot Forbes editor, *Thayer's Life of Beethoven*, 1967, p. 103. See also: Franz Wegeler, 1838, English edition: 1988, p. 113. For engraved portraits of Wegeler, with brief biographical

details, see: Beethoven House Bonn, Digital Archives, and Library Document W 162.

[38] Barry Cooper, 2000, pp. 75–76.

[39] For a more comprehensive list of Beethoven's compositions, for the period mentioned, including many vocal works and lesser compositions now designated with WoO numbers, see: Elliot Forbes editor, *Thayer's Life of Beethoven*, 1967 pp. 201–02.

[40] See, for example: *Instruments, Temperaments, and Tempos* in: Leon Plantinga, 1999, p. 293.

[41] The implications for interpreting Beethoven's early compositions, particularly the piano sonatas – in the context of different keyboards and sonorities – is discussed in *Historical Problems in Beethoven Performance* in: *Beethoven Performers and Critics,* Robert Winter, editor, 1977, pp. 41-51.

[42] *Beethoven's Instruments* in: Edwin Fischer, 1959, p. 83.

[43] For the recollections of Carl Czerny see: Paul Badura-Skoda, editor, 1970, p. 13. Czerny also states (p. 6) that his own performance of Beethoven's works did not always go down well. He comments 'the pianoforte had not yet begun to have the splendid effect it does now'.

[44] This is the bust that is frequently reproduced as a frontispiece in works celebrating Beethoven's life and work. It was derived from a facial likeness of the composer taken by Franz Klein, a professor of sculpture, in 1812. The likeness was later adapted by the sculptor Kaspar Zumbusch for his monumental seated sculpture of Beethoven that now adorns Vienna's *Beethovenplatz*.

[45] For an illustration of Streichers' pianoforte showroom see: Hans Conrad Fischer and Erich Kock, 1972, p. 23.

[46] Peter Clive, 2001, pp. 357–9.

[47] Emily Anderson, editor and translator, 1961, Vol. 1, Letter No. 17, pp. 24–5. For a facsimile reproduction of this letter see: Beethoven House, Digital Archives, Library Document NE 94.

[48] *Ibid* 1961, Vol. 1, Letter No. 18, pp. 25–6.

[49] The Streicher fortepiano of this period was of relatively lightweight construction with a five-octave range of F – F. For an illustration of such a fortepiano, from 1814, see: Edwin Marshall Good, 1982, p. 78 and fig. 3.2.

[50] As quoted by Tilman Skowroneck, *The Keyboard Instruments of the Young Beethoven*, in: Scott G. Burnham, and Michael P. Steinberg, editors, 2000, pp. 167–68.

[51] Tia de Nora, 1997, p. 175.

[52] Cited in: Hans Conrad Fischer and Erich Kock, 1972, p. 13. See also: Edwin Marshall Good, 1982, p. 71 and Tia de Nora, 1970, p. 179.

[53] A copy of Nanette Streicher's fortepiano of 1816 is preserved in the Yale Collection of Musical Instruments. See Website: *Ludwig van Beethoven, Beethoven's Pianos.*

[54] A tantalising inference may be drawn from a letter Beethoven wrote to Nanette Streicher on 26 August 1817 when he remarks: 'I have long desired to make its [the piano in question?] acquaintance. See Emily Anderson, editor and translator, 1961, Vol. 2, Letter No. 844, pp. 726–7.

⁵⁵ Emily Anderson, editor and translator, 1961, Vol. 2, Letter No. 844, p. 726. For an illustration of the various ear trumpets Beethoven used, see: Derek Melville, 1973, Plate 8. Images of these poignant contrivances can also be viewed by accessing the Beethoven House Digital Archives.

⁵⁶ This is the date Érard despatched the piano to Beethoven; he may not have received it, however, until sometime later.

⁵⁷ See: David Wainright, *Broadwood by Appointment*, The Book Service, 1982 and Reginald Gerig, *Famous Pianists and their Technique*, Washington: R. B. Luce, 1974, p. 44. See also: Derek Melville, *Beethoven's Pianos* (Plate 4a) in: Denis Arnold and Nigel Fortune, editors, *The Beethoven Companion,* 1973.

⁵⁸ After years of neglect, Beethoven's Broadwood piano was restored in 1991 by the piano maker and restorer David Winston. The sound of the instrument can be appreciated on Melvin Tan's recording on EMI Classics: *The Beethoven Broadwood Fortepiano*, CDC 7 54526 2.

⁵⁹ Barry Cooper, 2000, p. 22.

⁶⁰ The quotation cited exists in a number of versions. Ours is derived from: Simon P. Keefe, *The Cambridge Companion to the Concerto*, 2005, pp. 83–84.

⁶¹ See, for example, Barry Cooper who remarks: 'The anecdote was related only years later by Cramer's widow, who was not present at the concert, and the identity of the concerto was not the central part of the story.' Barry Cooper, 2000, p. 125 and footnote 6.

⁶² Simon P. Keefe, 2005, pp. 83–84.

⁶³ *Ibid.*

⁶⁴ For some discussion of this kind, see: Elizabeth Schwarm Glasner, *Beethoven's Piano Concerto, Op. 19*, website text.

⁶⁵ Barry Cooper, 1990, p. 183.

⁶⁶ Emily Anderson editor and translator, 1961, Vol. 1, Letter No. 48, pp. 52–53.

⁶⁷ Leon Plantinga, 1999, p. 286.

⁶⁸ H. C. Robbins Landon, 1970, p. 32.

⁶⁹ Barry Cooper, 1909, p. 21.

⁷⁰ Leon Plantinga, 1999, p. 58.

⁷¹ The artist Donna Dralle has created an imaginary study in pencil and watercolour titled *Beethoven Stitching a Notebook.* See: http//www.graphixnow.com/fine_art/images/fine_art_pgs/lvbsew.jpg

⁷² See: Joseph Kerman, *Beethoven's Early Sketches* in: Paul Henry Lang, editor, 1971, pp. 13–36. Kerman, quoting Dr. Hans Schmidt of the Beethoven Archive, Bonn, suggests nearly 400 sketch-sources of various kinds have been identified, to date, consisting variously of single sheets, bifolia (double sheets), bound sketchbooks and miscellaneous gatherings.

⁷³ Joseph Kerman, *Write all these down: Essays on Music*, 1994. For a facsimile illustration of a typical two-page bifolium, of the kind Beethoven carried around with him, see: Beethoven House, Digital Archives, Library Document, Sammlung H. C. Bodmer, HCB BSK 16/24.

⁷⁴ Edward T. Cone, editor, *Roger Sessions on Music: Collected Essays*, 1979, p. 45.

⁷⁵ Gustav Nottebohm, *Two Beethoven Sketchbooks: A Description with Musical Extracts,* 1979, pp. 4–7.

[76] Alan Tyson, *Sketches and Autographs*, in: Denis Arnold, and Nigel Fortune, editors, *The Beethoven Companion*, 1973, pp. 443– 58.

[77] Barry Cooper, 2000, pp. 23–25. See also: Beethoven House, Digital Archives, Library Document, BH 121. The sketch illustrated is very tidy, typical of Beethoven's youthful manuscripts that became progressively more illegible over time. The supporting text reads: 'Since Beethoven performed his own concertos, a complete notation of the solo part would therefore not have been necessary'. The inference is Beethoven used the leaf as an aid to memory. For related discussion see: Leon Plantinga, 1999, pp. 305–06.

[78] Barry Cooper, 2000, p. 46. An autograph score fragment, from the development section of the first movement, is preserved in the Bibliothèque Nationale, Paris, as MS. 61, fol. 2v, from c.1790–92. See: Leon Plantinga, 1999, pp. 305–06. See also: Maynard Solomon, 1997, p. 70.

[79] With acknowledgement to Leon Plantinga, 1999, pp, 56–57. See also: Barry Cooper, 1991, p.220. H. C. Robbins Landon, 1970, p. 45, illustrates a sketch for a passage intended for the Rondo for the B-flat major Piano Concerto. Its many crossings-out bear testimony to the composer's search for a satisfactory final form. Some of the background history to the sketches, and revisions for the Rondo of the Concerto in B-flat major, are discussed by Douglas Porter Johnson editor, *The Beethoven Sketchbooks: History, Reconstruction, Inventory*, 1985 p. 514. Czerny's role is mentioned by Peter Clive, 2001, p. 90.

[80] Thayer's further remarks are of interest here. He comments, there is no authentic record of the time of the Rondo's original composition. He cites the musicologist Otto Jahn who surmised it was designed for the Concerto in B flat and that its contents indicate an early period. Thayer also cites the musicologist Eusebius Mandyczewski who compared Beethoven's original manuscript with Czerny's printed version. Mandyczewski concluded the original plan of the Rondo and *motivi* were Beethoven's but that he had only indicated the cadenzas. As remarked in the main text, Czerny added these and extended the pianoforte passages that Beethoven had only indicated 'making them more effective and brilliant'. See: Elliot Forbes, editor, *Thayer's Life of Beethoven*, 1967 pp. 174–75.

[81] Leon Plantinga, 1999, pp. 60–61.

[82] Barry Cooper, 1990 pp. 284–85. Cooper provides a chronological table tracing the sketch origins of Op. 19 together with references to known performances.

[83] Peter Clive, 2001, p. 213.

[84] Barry Cooper, 2000, p. 53.

[85] Elliot Forbes editor, *Thayer's Life of Beethoven*, 1967, pp. 173–74.

[86] Ibid.

[87] It is on record that Beethoven experienced severe diarrhoea as early as 1789; he was confined to his sick bed and was attended by Wegeler who had just finished his medical studies. Wegeler records that Beethoven fell ill again with intestinal complaints in 1795 and 1796. Drawing on the available medical knowledge of the period, he believed this may have had a bearing on his later loss of hearing. Anton Neumayr suggests the composer's acute paroxysmal abdominal pains and intense abdominal colic may have been

the result of chronic pancreatitis. See: Anton Neumayr, Music and Medicine, 1994-1997, pp. 324-25. On the occasion of his illness, Beethoven wrote to Wegeler in the most affectionate terms recalling their time together in Bonn and of his longing to be once more 'amongst the beautiful country where I first opened my eyes to the light'. However, he soon reveals to Wegeler his poor health and how his abdominal condition 'wretched even before I left Bonn ... has become worse in Vienna where I have been suffering in consequence'. He explains that Dr. Johann Frank — Director of the General Hospital and Professor of Medicine at Vienna University — had tried to relieve his condition 'with strengthening medicine' but to no effect. He adds: 'Such was my condition until the autumn of last year; and sometimes I gave way to despair.' He eventually found relief from his abdominal condition after being prescribed — by a different physician — to bathe in the tepid baths of the Danube. Recourse to hydrotherapy would be a lasting feature of Beethoven's continuing search for improved health. See: Emily Anderson editor and translator, 1961, Vol. 1, Letter No. 51, pp. 57- 62.

[88] See, for example, the discussion of Op. 19 in: Barry Cooper, 1990 pp. 283–303.

[89] Elliot Forbes editor, *Thayer's Life of Beethoven*, 1967, p. 175.

[90] H. C. Robbins Landon 1970, p. 44.

[91] Elliot Forbes editor, *Thayer's Life of Beethoven*, 1967, pp. 177–78 and footnote 32.

[92] *Ibid*, p. 182.

[93] H. C. Robbins Landon states: 'It is assumed, and probably correctly, that Beethoven will have once again played his B-flat major Concerto, Op. 19.' H. C. Robbins Landon, 1977, p. 93.

[94] Letter of 19 February 1796. See: Emily Anderson, editor and translator, 1961, Vol. 1 Letter No. 16, p. 22.

[95] For an extensive account of Beethoven's first concert tour see: Elliot Forbes editor, *Thayer's Life of Beethoven*, 1967, *The years 1796 and 1797*. For a documentary study of Beethoven's concert tour, see: H. C. Robbins Landon, 1992, pp. 53–4.

[96] Douglas Porter Johnson editor, *The Beethoven Sketchbooks: History, Reconstruction, Inventory*, 1985, p. 72. See also: Barry Cooper, 2000, p. 76.

[97] Elliot Forbes editor, *Thayer's Life of Beethoven*, 1967, pp. 259–60. With acknowledgment also to Peter Clive, 2001, pp. 166–67.

[98] Emily Anderson editor and translator, Letter No. 41, pp. 42–43, Vol. 1, 1961. For a facsimile reproduction of this letter, together with a transcription of Beethoven's text, see: Beethoven House, Digital Archives, Library Document, Bonn NE 181.

[99] Emily Anderson editor and translator, Appendix H, p. 1434, Vol. 3, 1961.

[100] Michael Steinberg, 1998, p. 56.

[101] Emily Anderson editor and translator, Letter No. 47, pp. 50–52, Vol. 1, 1961. See also: Elliot Forbes editor, *Thayer's Life of Beethoven*, 1967 p. 273.

[102] Beethoven House, Digital Archives, Library Document, HCB Mh 4.

[103] For details of the life and work of Wenzel Schlemmer, see: Peter Clive, 2001, pp. 315–16. See also: Beethoven House Digital Archives, Library Document

Sammlung H. C. Bodmer HCB Br 64 and Emily Anderson, editor and translator, 1961, Vol. 1, Letter No. 108, p. 129.

[104] Barry Cooper, 1991, p. 159–60.

[105] Barry Cooper 2000, pp. 104–05.

[106] For example, Glenn Gould has recorded the B-flat major Concerto with the Leningrad Conservatoire Orchestra, conducted by Vladimir Slovák, from an edition that incorporates all of Beethoven's amendments.

[107] Emily Anderson, editor and translator, 1961, Vol. I, Letter No. 48, pp. 52– 3.

[108] *Ibid*, Vol. I, Letter No. 50, pp. 55–57. For a facsimile reproduction of this letter, together with a transcription of Beethoven's text see: Beethoven House, Digital Archives, Library Document HCB BBr 33.

[109] Peter Clive, 2000, pp. 248–9.

[110] Beethoven House, Digital Archives, Library Documents: HCB C Op. 19 (Hoffmeister); and HCB C Md 53, 11(Peters).

[111] Pamela J. Willetts, 1970, pp. 27–31.

[112] Wayne M. Senner, Robin Wallace and William Meredith editors, 1999, Vol. 1, pp. 158–59.

[113] A cadenza sketch intended for the Archduke Rudolph is in the possession of the Beethoven House, Bonn. It is laid out in Beethoven's most legible script – a measure of the care he took with his distinguished pupil. The manuscript bears the reference number '74', indicating that it once belonged to Rudolph's music library. See: Beethoven House, Digital Archives, Library Document, HCB Mh 13.

[114] Thayer-Forbes, 1967, p. 771.

[115] H. C. Robbins Landon, 1992, p. 185 and *Marie Leopoldine Pachler* in: Peter Clive, 2001, pp. 253–4. See also, editor's note 79 (III) at pp. 189–90 in: Anton Schindler, 1860, English edition, Donald Macardle, 1966. Marie's portrait was painted by the artist Josef Abel and is reproduced in facsimile in the Beethoven House Digital Archive, Library Document B 497/b. This does, indeed, reveal a young woman of exceptional beauty. Marie is depicted holding a lyre, rather than being seated at the keyboard. A later copy, as depicted in Library Document B 2350, is inferior. Marie met Beethoven and, according to the composer's biographer Anton Schindler, she became his 'autumn love'; this assertion has since however been discredited, not least on the grounds that by then Marie had relinquished her short career as a concert pianist for married life. Hüttenbrenner is known to Schubertians; it was from him the manuscript of the much-loved *Unfinished Symphony* was rescued from possible oblivion in 1817.

PIANO CONCERTO NO. 3, C MINOR, OP. 37

'The present grand concerto belongs to the most significant works that have appeared from this ingenious master for several years, and in several respects it might distinguish itself from all the rest to its advantage. In addition to such a total sum of beautiful and noble ideas, the reviewer finds, at the very least, in none of his newest works such a thorough working out, yet without becoming turgid or overly learned, a character so solidly maintained without excess, and such unity in workmanship. It will and must have the greatest and most beautiful effect everywhere that it can be well performed.'

The music critic of the *Allgemeine musikalische Zeitung* for 10 April 1805, as translated in: Wayne M. Senner, Robin Wallace and William Meredith editors, *The Critical Reception of Beethoven's Compositions by his German Contemporaries*, 1999, Vol. 1, p. 205.

'The style and character of this Concerto are much more grand and fervent than in the two former.'

Carl Czerny, *On the Proper Performance of all Beethoven's Works for Piano*, 1846, edited with commentary by Paul Badura-Skoda, 1970, p. 97.

'The C minor, a great concerto, is a glorious link between the early Beethoven and the later. The very first theme of the *tutti* is cast in Beethoven's heroic mould. The writing is still mostly that of the earlier concertos, the solo standing against the orchestra, rather than working in with it, but there are moments when it breaks away from this.'

Fanny Davies, *The Pianoforte Concertos* in: *The Musical Times, Special Issue* edited by John A. Fuller-Maitland, Vol. VIII, No. 2, 1927, p. 225.

'Beethoven's Third Piano Concerto was projected at the same time as his First and Second; neither of which, as he openly avowed, was so important as this for which he was reserving his best efforts. It is one of the works in which we most clearly see the style of his first period preparing to develop into that of his second ... It is the C minor Concerto that has ever since been taken as the normal classical example, and not the G major and E flat Concertos, which are supposed to introduce bold innovations.'

Donald Francis Tovey, *Essays in Musical Analysis*, Vol. 3, 1935–41, pp. 69–70 and p. 71.

> 'With the Concerto No. 3, in C minor, Op. 37 (composed in 1800) we reach Beethoven the tone-poet. Conventional elements are still retained in the disposition of the orchestral *tutti,* and the cadenza for the piano, etc., and even in the idiom of the subject, the impassioned quietude of the *Largo*, the biting brilliance of the *Rondo* and the subtle key-scheme underlying the whole work are pure Beethoven. Indeed, I sometimes think this whole Concerto is as much a self-portrait of Beethoven at thirty as the *Eroica* is of Beethoven at thirty-three.'

Marion M. Scott, *Beethoven, The Master Musicians*, 1940, p. 182.

> 'The key of C minor was for Beethoven filled with implications of high import. *Pathos*, in the sense of profound feeling, had already found expression in the Trio, Op. 1, No. 3, in the *Sonata Pathétique* (so named by him); and in the great Violin Sonata, Op. 30, No. 2; and it was to find even intenser utterance in the Fifth Symphony [Op. 67], the Thirty-two Variations [WoO 80], and the last Piano Sonata, Op. 111. Here, as in Piano Sonata, Op. 10, No. 1, the probe does not go so deep: but it touches the same vein, nevertheless.'

Donald Nivison Ferguson, *Masterworks of the Orchestral Repertoire: A Guide for Listeners.* 1954, p. 103.

'The Third Concerto, in C minor, Op. 37, is at once more ambitious and more problematic than its predecessors. The minor tonality presented Beethoven with both opportunity and a challenge: opportunity to express the turbulent, darker side of his personality, and a challenge to solve in the concerto-context the special structural problems inherent in the minor mode. Of the strength of impulse behind the Concerto there can be no doubt.'

Basil Deane, *The Concertos* in: Denis Arnold and Nigel Fortune editors, *The Beethoven Companion*, 1973.

'The Concerto No. 3, Op. 37, which was completed in 1800, represents a marked advance over its predecessors, and it became an established model of Classic Romantic concerto-form for the nineteenth century. Where the First Concerto has elements of what Tovey calls the Classic "comedy of manners", and the Second reveals a more intimate, if not fully realized, chamber-music quality, the Third represents Beethoven's first effort in this genre to record something far beyond merely exterior wit or refinement, and to move toward dramatic oratory.'

Maynard Solomon, *Beethoven*, 1977, p. 103.

'In Beethoven's artistic development the Concerto in C minor occupies a position similar to that of the Second Symphony. Requiring the classical standard symphony orchestra with pairs of flutes, oboes, clarinets, bassoons, horns, trumpets and kettledrums, it effected the transition from Beethoven's earlier concertos, in B-flat major (Op. 19, 1794—95) and C major (Op. 15, 1795—96), to the great creations in G major (1806) and E-flat major (1809).'

Joseph Braunstein, *Musica Aeterna: Program Notes for 1971—1976*, Vol. 3, 1978, p. 31.

'The Third Piano Concerto is as decisive a landmark in its way as the Third Symphony; both works show the composer widening his musical horizon and stretching established forms in a way that his predecessors had never envisaged. The first two concertos are clearly influenced by Mozart, and do not really extend the demands made on the soloist by all that much. But in this work, written in 1800, one feels that Beethoven is turning his back on the past and looking positively and with new authority into the century that lay ahead.'

Antony Hopkins, *The Concertgoer's Companion*, 1984, p. 86.

'With the Third Concerto (1800) we approach the middle period manner, and in its final form (1803) Beethoven utilised the new keyboard extension, adding brilliance to some of the passage-work and length to the downward swooping scales. The key of C minor already had its Beethovenish associations and a minor-key concerto offered its own dramatic possibilities, with Mozart's D minor and C minor as admired precedents.'

Denis Matthews, *Beethoven, The Master Musicians*, 1985, pp. 174–75.

'[Op. 37] is a work of deathless genius and an original achievement beyond all the highest powers ... [It] is a cumulative work, the climax of an unorthodox process started with the two previous concertos. It does not restate their mistakes – it advances on their discoveries.'

Robert Simpson, *Beethoven and the Concerto* in: Robert Layton editor, *A Guide to the Concerto*, 1996, p. 109.

'The opus number of the Concerto in C minor – 37 – reflects the date of publication, which was 1804, the year in which Beethoven completed the *Waldstein* Sonata as well as the short and ever-astounding Sonata in F major, Op. 54, and in which he began the *Appassionata*. The Concerto itself belongs more to the world of the Op. 18 String Quartets, the Septet, and the Symphony No. 1 ... The C minor Concerto is, and feels, light compared to its expansive predecessor in C major. Lean and spare, it has moments of severity that sometimes bring Gluck to mind.'

Michael Steinberg, *The Concerto: A Listener's Guide*, 1998, pp. 60–61.

'The piano writing of the Concerto represents a transition between the facile virtuosity of the era of Mozart and Haydn and the dramatic, massive style of the mature Beethoven. The nature of melody and harmony is also indicative of this transition. Time and again, in the midst of a hedonistic development, there is a glimpse of the sombre image of Beethoven of his future tragic years.'

Nicolas Slonimsky, *The Great Composers and their Works*, edited by Electra Slonimsky Yourke, Vol. 1, 2000, p. 142.

'In his previous piano concertos, Beethoven had increasingly sought to create themes which were simply in outline but suitable for thorough development, and in the C minor Concerto this trend is fully exploited.'

Terry Barfoot, *Piano Concerto No. 3, Radio 3, Beethoven Experience*, 8 June, 2005.

In his *The Seven Concertos of Beethoven*, the musical polymath Antony Hopkins writes: 'In this Concerto Beethoven seems to have "come of age" as a composer of works for soloist and orchestra.' He acknowledges that whilst the presence of Mozart can still be felt – notably the C minor Concerto, K. 491 and the D minor Concerto, K. 466 – in his C minor Concerto, Op. 37, Beethoven 'shows a new mastery of material and a far greater individuality in all aspects'. Much of the music was composed around 1800 – with Beethoven approaching his thirtieth year. It is tempting, thereby, to think of him emboldened, with the prospect of a new century, to turn away from classical procedures. To quote Hopkins once more:

'The work is essentially forward-looking, and it might be said to have laid the foundation on which great romantic concertos of the nineteenth century were ultimately to be built.'[1]

Whilst his hearing was still intact, the piano concerto was a genre to which Beethoven returned at intervals and endowed with fresh vitality and originality. We have seen that his earliest essay in the medium dates from his time in Bonn and commenced a series that would extend throughout the first decade of the nineteenth century. In Kinloch Anderson's words:

> 'The [piano] concerto provided a form in which Beethoven found fulfilment, no less complete than in the symphony for the expression of his most noble, profound, beautiful and, at times, witty and playful thoughts.'[2]

On a personal level, the C minor Concerto was conceived during the happiest and most successful period in Beethoven's life. He had found fame in the musical salons of the nobility, where he was recognised for being one of the most daring of keyboard virtuosi, he went on concert tours where he was celebrated and found favour with the great and the good, and he was making his way in the world as an independent composer. Indeed, such was his success that he could write to his younger brother Johann: 'My art is winning me friends and renown, and what more do I want? ... I shall make a good deal of money.'[3]

When the C minor Concerto was reviewed in the *Allgemeine musikalische Zeitung* of 10 April 1805, the journal's music correspondent recognised Beethoven had set new standards:

> 'The Concerto demands an orchestra that is

capable of much, wants the best, and, in order also to accomplish that truly, understands what it plays. It also demands a capable soloist, who, in addition to all that is customarily called virtuosity, also has knowledge in his head and a heart in his breast.'[4]

The piano writing in this Concerto is technically more difficult than that in the earlier Concertos Op. 15 and Op. 19, with its challenging cadenza passages set in hemidemisemiquavers and much else besides.

Beethoven's Op. 37 is his only piano concerto in a minor key and his choice of C minor is significant. This key was for Beethoven 'filled with implications of high import [and] pathos, in the sense of profound feeling'.[5] Beethoven had already given expression to the key of C minor in what Barry Cooper has described as his 'C minor phase'.[6] By way of illustration, we may cite the following compositions: Piano Trio, Op.1, No. 3 (1795); Piano Sonata, Op. 10, No. 1 (1798); Piano Sonata, Op. 13, *Pathétique* (1798); String Trio, Op. 9 (1798); and String Quartet, Op. 18, No. 4 (1799). He soon gave further expression to C minor in such works as: Violin Sonata, Op. 30, No. 2 (1803); *Eroica* Symphony — funeral march (1803–04); and Overture *Coriolan*, Op. 62 (1807). C minor would become Beethoven's *heroic* key in other works for piano such as the Thirty-Two Variations, WoO 80, (1806) and would reach a point of consummation in the Fifth Symphony, Op. 67, (1808). Towards the end his life he returned to C minor for his final great Piano Sonata, Op. 111 (1822).

The C minor Piano Concerto has symphonic proportions with a playing time of about thirty-five minutes. The opening orchestral exposition, in particular, is expansive as it outlines the themes that the piano will, in due course, adopt. Originality abounds in the orchestral writing as, for example, in the thematic use of the timpani in the first movement. William Kinderman characterises this as being 'noteworthy' for the manner in which 'the drum passage takes on a mysterious intensity in association with the solo cadenza' and, more generally, for the manner in which Beethoven's use of the timpani anticipates his later practice in other works:

> 'One thinks of the drum taps in the Violin Concerto, or the transition to the finale in the Fifth Symphony, not to mention the prominent timpani in the Seventh Symphony or the scherzo of the Ninth.'[7]

To Kinderman's formulation, from which we have just quoted, we may add Beethoven's innovative use of the tympani in the transcription of the Violin Concerto for piano, Op. 61a, and the closing pages of the Piano Concerto No. 5 in E-flat major, Op. 73 (*The Emperor*).

'So where does the C minor Concerto stand?' – asks the American musicologist Leon Plantinga. Does it belong to the composer's professed 'new path' of 1802, and the years following, 'or does it fit with the First Symphony and the String Quartets, Op. 18?' In support of the view that the composition is a forward-looking work, he cites the daring manner in which Beethoven juxtaposes unorthodox key relationships (C minor to E major) that Plantinga describes as 'straying well outside the ordinary boundaries of the genre'.[8] Donald Francis Tovey reasons as follows:

> 'The first three pianoforte concertos of Beethoven show, in the opening tuttis of their first movements, a phenomenon almost unique in his works. In other branches of music, we may find

signs of struggle with stubborn material and Beethoven himself sometimes admitted that for this or that problem of vocal and dramatic music he had "not studied enough". But in the first two pianoforte concertos all is facile and spacious, while in the third, in C minor, which he declared, before he wrote it, "will be the best of the three", he not only made a great stride in the direction of his *second style,* [Tovey's emphasis] but set the model for the orthodox concerto-form of his younger contemporaries and later theorists.'[9]

Having opened our account of the C minor Piano Concerto with the foregoing remarks, we now proceed to the principal themes of our narrative. In this part of our study of Beethoven's five piano concertos, bearing opus numbers, we consider the following: references to Beethoven the man, as revealed in recollections and portraits of the composer; the piano as a developing instrument — in which Beethoven took a keen interest all his adult life; Beethoven's powers of improvisation; contemporary money-values and their financial considerations; the composition chronology of the C minor Concerto; the onset of Beethoven's deafness; sketchbook sources; publication; contemporary performances of Op. 37 and their reception; nineteenth-century reception and reception nearer to our own time; and, to close, a documentary study of the C minor Concerto, as expressed in selected writings of musicologists and performing artists.

On 21 May 1801, the Leipzig music publisher Gottfried Christoph Härtel wrote to Beethoven in encouraging terms. He stated how pleased his publishing house would be 'to do everything that circumstances allow' to further the composer's compositions, especially 'piano sonatas without accompaniment, or with the accompaniment of violin, or of violin and violincello'. Härtel adds, with a touch of flattery, doubtless to secure the composer's commissions: 'The fame of your talents is established firmly enough.'[10] Härtel concluded by requesting where Beethoven's portrait may be seen so that a likeness could be taken for its publication alongside his series of 'the most prominent composers'.

An engraving of Beethoven duly appeared in Volume 6 of the *Allgemeine musikalische Zeitung* (October 1803 – September 1804). Johann Neidl created this from a drawing by the artist Gandolph von Stainhauser, made sometime in 1800, and later reproduced by the Viennese music publisher Giovanni Cappi (who subsequently published the composer's three Piano Sonatas, Op. 26 and the two Piano Sonatas, Op. 27). The artist C. F. Riedl also made an engraving from Stainhauser's drawing that was published by Anton Hoffmeister at the Bureau de Musique, Leipzig. These near identical studies are the first of Beethoven's portraits since the early likenesses that had been taken of him in his Bonn days.

Beethoven appears to have been satisfied by the outcome since he mentioned his new portrait in a letter of 16 November 1801 to his Bonn friend Franz Gerhard Wegeler – although the subject proper of this poignant letter was the revelation of his encroaching deafness (see later). The Stainhauser–Neidl– Riedl likenesses depict Beethoven well-dressed and elegant, as he might have appeared as a lion of the keyboard in the glittering salons of the Viennese aristocracy and, indeed, how he may have appeared before the public on the occasion when he premiered the C minor Concerto – to which we make reference in due course. The likeness, in question, serves also to remind us that Beethoven, 'the colossus', was in fact a relatively slight figure of about 1.62 m. – much the same as Mozart.[11]

From 1803, we have a miniature portrait of the composer, set on ivory, created by the Danish artist Christian

Horneman. This depicts Beethoven elegantly attired with fashionable stylish sideburns. Beethoven gave the miniature as a keepsake to his friend Stephan von Breuning, with whose descendants it remained for a hundred years before eventually finding a home in the Beethoven House in Bonn — via the famous collector of Beethoven memorabilia Dr H. C. Bodmer. A facsimile reproduction can be seen, with a later portrait of the composer, in the Beethoven House Digital Archives (Library Documents B 7 and HCB Bi 1). A copy of the portrait hangs in the New York Public Library.

For his portrait Beethoven wore a blue tailcoat and white neckerchief, then both fashionable. His short hairstyle, created after the model of antique standards, also corresponds with the fashion of the time.

> 'It can be assumed that this is a good painting of Beethoven's physiognomy and expression, and that the painter has captured a lot of Beethoven's character while he was young and expressed it very well through this vivid expression and the concentrated look.'[12]

A measure of Beethoven's growing fame at this period is further indicated by the circumstance of him being persuaded to have his portrait painted by Joseph Mähler — a personal friend of the composer In this he is portrayed in an Arcadian setting striking a lyre, in the background is a temple of Apollo. Although this portrait situates Beethoven in a somewhat idealised pastoral setting, the artist is not considered to have sacrificed his appearance in striving for Romantic effect.[13]

The piano was Beethoven's instrument. We recall from his Bonn days (see text to WoO 4) that by the early 1780s piano makers (more correctly pianoforte makers) were extending the standard five-octave keyboard (F1 to f3) in the upper range. The mechanics of the instrument were also undergoing change. However, in the case of the older-style instruments, tone was modified through the action of knee and foot operated devices. Barry Cooper explains:

> 'These could variously raise the dampers, providing a sustained tone (sometimes the two halves of the keyboard could be affected separately); shift the action sideways, enabling *una corda* and / or *due corda* effects; dampen the tone, by sliding material between the strings and the hammers; or produce special effects, such as lute or percussion.'[14]

As in his early concertos Beethoven only ever used two functions — the damper-raising and action-shifting devices. From the early 1800s the knee-action device began to be replaced by the foot pedal. In his directions to the performer, Beethoven indicated raised dampers by the term 'senza sordino' (remove or play without the mute) and cancelled it with 'con sordino' (play with the mute).[15] The C minor Concerto was the last time, in such a major work, that Beethoven used these designations. Thereafter, he used the term 'Ped', for raising the dampers, by depressing the foot pedal, and the companion term 'O' for restoring them — by releasing it.[16] In his efforts to coax greater sonority from the limited pianoforte instruments then available to him, Beethoven's piano pupil Carl Czerny relates how he would frequently hold down the sustaining pedal for long passages. This would, of course, on a modern-day instrument, produce an unacceptable blurring of sound.

Later in life, Beethoven contemplated revising many of

his keyboard works and, with a complete edition of them in mind, he even thought of composing new works to fill in the gaps where he considered further compositions were required. Nothing, however, came of this although, as we shall see, he did make revisions to the cadenza for the C minor Concerto in 1809 to exploit the newly expanded keyboard.[17]

Another circumstance is relevant to our discussion and may have had some bearing on the writing of the solo part of the C minor Concerto. On 6 August 1803, Beethoven received the gift of a splendid, state-of-the-art piano from the French manufacturer Sébastien Érard. The date given is believed to be that when Érard despatched the piano to Beethoven from Paris but Beethoven may not have received it until sometime later. The gift was in recognition of Érard's esteem of Beethoven and of his growing reputation abroad as a pianist. Doubtless, also, it was good for his business to have it known that a composer of such celebrity as Beethoven owned one of his instruments. Years later, the English piano maker John Broadwood made a similar gesture by presenting Beethoven with an even more resourceful instrument.[18]

Beethoven's Érard, which is preserved today in Vienna's *Kunsthistoriches Museum*, is triple-strung and equipped with four foot-pedals, namely, a lute stop, sustaining pedal, *sourdine* (mute) and *una corda* (soft pedal).[19] Of significance to Beethoven was the innovation of an enlarged compass; Érard's piano extended the upper register to high C offering the composer new expressive possibilities. It is open to question though as to how much the Érard piano influenced Beethoven's rewriting the piano part of his Third Concerto. H. C. Robbins Landon suggests the extended upper register of the French instrument may, indeed, have stimulated him to revise some of the higher piano writing.

Notwithstanding his initial enthusiasm for his new instrument, Beethoven apparently found its action somewhat heavy He considered it lacked the light touch of the Viennese instruments, such as those by Walter and Streicher with which he was familiar and found more congenial to his dextrous style of playing. As Landon further remarks, 'what Beethoven wanted was an instrument that combined the silvery tone of a Walter or Streicher but with the strength of the Érard Piano'.[20]

In our previous studies (Op.15 and Op. 19) we have encountered Beethoven the master of keyboard improvisation. Bearing in mind the bravura pianistic challenges that confront the soloist in the C minor Concerto ('hemidemisemiquavers and much else besides') it is only fitting that we pay further tribute to Beethoven the virtuoso when he was at the height of his powers, before deafness would progressively isolate him, as a virtuoso, from the keyboard forever.

We have remarked, Beethoven was a slight figure and had correspondingly small hands — he could only just span a tenth. Stephan von Breuning, the son of Beethoven's lifelong friend Gerhard von Breuning, has left the following description of the composer's hand position at the keyboard:

'He held his fingers very curved, so much so that they were completely hidden by the hand, what is called *the old position,* in brief, as contrasted to the present way in which the fingers are characteristically more extended.'

We recall (from Op. 15) that it was Stephan who inherited Beethoven's Brodmann pianoforte, considered to be one of the best makes at the time. Contemplating it later in life, its modest proportions disposed Stephan to remark:

'[With] its tiny tone and mere five and a half octaves, one finds it hard to conceive how it could have been adequate for Beethoven's tempestuous improvisations ... [It] was as a consequence of Beethoven's sonatas that the piano was altered and strengthened into its present state, indeed it had to be almost made afresh.'[21]

A measure of Beethoven's pre-eminence amongst even the most accomplished pianists of the day, is conveyed in an anecdote told to the father of Carl Czerny by the keyboard virtuoso, and would-be rival of Beethoven, Joseph Gelinek. Inspired by Gelinek's account of Beethoven's playing, Czerny's father was motivated to seek out Beethoven and persuade him to give lessons to his then ten-year old son Carl. He thereby initiated a pupil-teacher relationship that would permanently enrich Beethoven musicology. Concerning Gelinek, his prowess at improvisation had impressed even Mozart and, later in his career, Carl Maria von Weber was so taken by Gelinek's playing that he wrote an epigram in celebration of his powers.[22]

On being invited to take part in a pianistic contest with Beethoven, Gelinek rashly boasted: 'We are going to thrash him soundly! I'll work him over!' A few days later, quite dejected, he bemoaned: 'That young man is possessed of the devil. Never have I heard such playing! He will play me and all of us to death! And how he improvised!' Beethoven had apparently improvised on a theme of Gelinek's choosing and then performed compositions of his own (unspecified) that Gelinek regarded as 'wonderful and grandiose to the highest degree'. He adds how Beethoven achieved effects 'such as we have never even dreamed of'.[23] Gelinek appears to have swallowed his pride since he went on to create a piano arrangement of Beethoven's First Symphony and later composed a set of variations on the *Allegretto* of the Seventh Symphony.

Johann Schenk provides further testimony to Beethoven's powers of improvisation. He gave instruction to Beethoven in counterpoint in 1793 and was immensely impressed by his pupil's technical virtuosity:

> 'My ear was continually charmed by the beauty of the many varied motives which he wove with wonderful clarity and loveliness into each other, and I surrendered my heart to the impressions made upon it.'[24]

Until Beethoven's hearing deteriorated, his powers of improvisation were generally regarded as being without equal. However, one evening in 1804 Beethoven took part in a pianistic contest with Georg Joseph Vogler, in which he may not have emerged the victor. Vogler was a theorist, organist, pianist and composer and improvised on a theme given to him by Beethoven who in turn improvised on a theme of Vogler's. A guest at the event later recorded in his diary that although he was greatly impressed by Beethoven's improvisation, it had not aroused in him 'the enthusiasm inspired by Vogler's learned playing'. Doubtless Beethoven's flights of fancy and departures from pianistic convention had proved too much for the guest in question.[25]

In September 1799, the year of publication of the *Pathétique* Sonata, the celebrated English pianist Johann Baptist Cramer arrived in Vienna. He remained there through the following winter and, according to contemporary newspaper accounts, 'earned general and deserved applause for his playing'. He also developed a cordial relationship with Beethoven, to the benefit of his pianism. Writing of this, Beethoven's pioneering biographer Alexander Wheelock Thayer remarks upon the advantages to Beethoven of him enjoying the company of a pianist 'whose noblest characteristics were the same as Mozart's'.[26] Beethoven esteemed Cramer's *Grosse Pianoforteschule* – 'Instructions for the Pianoforte', published in 1815, and considered the study of them to be ideal preparation for the performance of his own piano compositions. Authorities consider he even absorbed some of Cramer's stylistic characteristics into his own keyboard idiom.

Earlier in the year, Beethoven had occasion to engage in friendly rivalry with a pianist of recognised formidable powers, namely the Austrian-born Joseph Johann Baptist Wölfl (Woelfl). He was more than six feet tall and, significantly, nature had conferred upon him enormous hands. As a consequence, he could span ten notes – and more – just as easily as others could span an octave, making it possible for him to perform continuous double-stopped passages 'as quick as lightening' and 'to overcome difficulties that for other pianists would be impossible'.[27] Thayer writes of Wölfl: 'It was no longer the case that Beethoven was without a rival as a pianoforte virtuoso. He had a competitor fully worthy of his powers.'[28]

Wölfl appears to have divided Vienna's musical circles equally for and against him. Although he is described as being trained in Mozart's school of piano playing, characterised by a clear, precise tone, his powers of virtuosity appear at times to have dominated his playing, prompting a reviewer of the *Allgemeine musikalische Zeitung* to record: 'Herr W's works ... have exaggerated difficulties for those who perform them, and are approached with a certain amount of circumspection.'[29]

Beethoven encountered Wölfl in the home of Baron

Raymond von Wetzlar, an accomplished musician who had himself been on familiar terms with Mozart. The composer Jan Tomaschek was present and has left an account of the meeting between the two virtuosi that was later recalled by Beethoven's close friend Ignaz von Seyfried:

> 'Each brought forward the latest product of his mind. Now one ... and the other gave free reign to his glowing fancy; sometimes they would seat themselves at two pianofortes and improvise alternately on themes they gave each other.'

Tomaschek concluded: 'It would have been difficult, perhaps impossible, to award the palm of victory to either one of the gladiators in respect of technical skill.'

It appears that Wölfl was the more popular for those present who preferred the more showy style of performance. However, it was Beethoven who won the day for the connoisseurs able to respond to what Tomaschek describes as, playing that was 'brilliant and powerful [if] not infrequently [disposed to] jolt the unsuspecting listener violently out of his state of joyful transports'.[30]

Writing of the contest between Beethoven and Wölfl, the music correspondent of the *Allgemeine musikalische Zeitung* reported:

> '[Beethoven] shows himself to the greatest advantage in improvisations, and here, indeed, it is most extraordinary with what lightness and yet firmness in the succession of ideas Beethoven not only varies a theme given to him on the spur of the moment by figuration ... but really develops it. Since the death of Mozart, who in this respect is for me still the *non plus ultra*, I have never

enjoyed this kind of pleasure in the degree in
which it is provided by Beethoven.'[31]

A further reference to one of Beethoven's contemporary
'lions of the keyboard' relates to an encounter the composer
had with the German-born pianist Daniel Steibelt; what
ensued amounted to a pianistic confrontation. Steibelt was
born in Berlin and toured as an accomplished soloist. It was
in this capacity when he arrived in Vienna on a concert tour
from Paris. His prowess at the keyboard had earned for him,
with the public at large, the reputation for being a formidable
virtuoso — although professional musicians were inclined to
dismiss him for being something of a showy charlatan.
Beethoven and Steibelt met at the house of Count Moritz
Fries for a pre-arranged pianistic *contest*. Fries was a wealthy
banker, a patron of the arts and a founder member of the
famed *Gesellschaft der Musikfreunde*. For his later generosity to Beethoven, he was rewarded with the dedication of
his Seventh Symphony.

On the evening in question, Steibelt performed a carefully
prepared *improvisation*, having provocatively chosen a theme
used by Beethoven in his then recently published Trio in
B-flat major, Op. 11. Ferdinand Ries, although not present
himself, relates how this 'outraged Beethoven's admirers as
well as Beethoven himself'. When it was Beethoven's turn to
improvise he went to the piano, turned upside down the copy
of Steibelt's music — a quintet of his own composition — and
'hammered out a theme from the first few bars with one
finger' and then 'improvised in such a manner that Steibelt
left the room before Beethoven had finished'. He shunned
Beethoven's company ever after.[32]

Czerny recalls making the acquaintance of the Austrian
pianist-composer Johann Nepomuk Hummel at a musical
soirée held at the residence of Mozart's widow. He was

initially unimpressed by the young man's appearance, describing him as looking vulgar and attired like a village schoolmaster. He noticed, though, that his fingers were covered with valuable rings — gift tokens from wealthy admirers after hearing him play. When Hummel was asked to perform, Czerny's attention was aroused. He recalls: 'I had never heard such exceeding brilliancy, purity of grace, and tenderness of execution, united with so much taste and fancy.' This is praise indeed, since Czerny was himself a pianist possessed of exceptional keyboard prowess that would, over the years, find expression in a vast number of finger-dexterity studies.

Comparing the styles of Hummel and Beethoven, Czerny remarks:

'If Beethoven's playing was distinguished by immense power, characteristic expression, unparalleled bravura and fluency, Hummel's was a model of the utmost purity, cleanness, elegance and tenderness; and had the combined characteristics of Mozart's style with the judicious principles of the Clementi school; his execution always excited admiration.'[33]

The Austrian-born, French composer and piano builder Ignaz Pleyel founded his celebrated firm in Paris in 1795 — that was to become one of the world's oldest makers of keyboard instruments. Pleyel's pianos were so admired that by 1834 his firm employed some 250 workers. The firm's instruments were showcased at the Salle Pleyel in Paris where Chopin performed both his first and last Paris concerts. Pleyel travelled to Vienna to promote his instruments and subsequently met Beethoven at the palace of Prince Lobkowitz where one of his string quartets was performed. Czerny was present and recalls Beethoven was persuaded to improvise which he did selecting a theme from one of Pleyel's string-quartet movements.

According to Czerny, Pleyel was so moved by Beethoven's extemporization that at its conclusion he kissed his hands in admiration. Later, Pleyel wrote to his family of his experience of hearing Beethoven playing but, it seems, after mature reflection he could not refrain from expressing his reservations:

> 'He has great execution but ... his execution has no finish, that is, his playing is not clean. He has much fire but he pounds a bit too much. He overcomes diabolical difficulties but he does not do them quite neatly. Nevertheless, his improvising gave me much pleasure ... He plays anything that comes into his head and there is nothing he does not dare.'

Pleyel concluded his letter with an interesting generalisation — doubtless prompted by the realization that Beethoven devoted his primary energies to composition, to the neglect of maintaining his keyboard technique. He states: '[Beethoven] should not be regarded as a pianist because it is very difficult to be a composer at the same time.'[34]

Pleyel's observation is a timely reminder that it was as a composer that Beethoven earned his living, albeit that he also received financial support from a small circle of devoted patron-admirers. These included Prince Karl Lichnowsky, a competent pianist who had studied with Mozart and who, shortly after Beethoven's arrival in Vienna, was one of the first to recognise the young composer's gifts. In recognition of his rising accomplishments, and his growing admiration of him, in 1800 Lichnowsky conferred on his protégée an annuity, in effect a stipend, of 600 florins – about sixty pounds sterling in early nineteenth-century values.

The Prince's intention was to provide Beethoven with some financial security. His payments continued for several years until Beethoven received a more secure annuity in 1809 from three of Vienna's most notable citizens, namely, the Archduke Rudolph (Beethoven's only composition pupil), Prince Kinsky and Prince Lobkowitz. Writing of Lobkowitz's support, Beethoven's early biographer Anton Schindler remarks: 'The great love this princely family felt for Beethoven was constant and unwavering.' He adds: 'In fact, for ten to twelve years, nearly all Beethoven's works were first tried out in the music circle of Count Lobkowitz.'[35]

An article published in a contemporary issue of the *Allgemeine musikalische Zeitung* places Beethoven's annuity in its contemporary context – and also reveals how little the average musician received for his labours. It reveals that a player in an orchestra could expect to earn from 200 to 300 gulden (about 20–30 pounds sterling). In the Austro-Hungarian Empire at this time the gulden was a standard unit of currency and was the equivalent of the Austrian silver florin (about two English shillings or a half-crown depending on currency values). Violinists were in the worst position because, the article states, 'they are expected to play for nothing since ten dilettante can readily be found who will do so with great pleasure'. A teacher of pianoforte could earn a decent living but 'must possess enough self-denial to serve willingly the houses that support him' and, furthermore, 'to give lessons 'morning, noon and night'. On a more positive note, the article concludes: 'But as there are exceptions ... amongst musicians, so there are worthy houses to which the above complaints do not apply.'[36]

By way of further illustration of money values, at the period when Lichnowsky conferred his 600 florins on

Beethoven, the following are typical: A clerk working for a nobleman could earn 550 florins in 1821, rising to 2,000 florins after twenty years' of service. A teacher could earn as much as 700. A postal worker received 400 and a senior civil servant, with the title of secretary, 2,500 florins. The concertmaster (conductor) of the opera received 2,400 florins.

Inflation progressively reduced the value of these sums. In later life, Beethoven paid his female servants around 130 florins a year. In comparison, a count had an income from 30,000 to 100,000 florins a year. In 1824, Beethoven offered the publisher Schott's & Sons the Ninth Symphony for 1,000 florins and the String Quartet Op. 127 for 125 florins.

A concert ticket cost about 1 florin. An entire opera score typically cost 11 florins. String quartet-parts were available on loan from music libraries for a relatively small charge.[37] The cost of living for a typical unmarried, middle-class gentleman in Vienna in 1793 – at about the time when Beethoven arrived in the city – was 775 florins per year but by 1804 this had risen to some 900 florins. Lichnowsky's contribution to Beethoven's income enabled him, as we have remarked, to dress fashionably, to purchase the quite expensive hand-made manuscript paper he required, and to furnish his modest library. Beethoven owned very few valuable possessions.[38]

We have seen (Op. 15 and Op. 19) Beethoven made his public debut as a concert pianist in Vienna in March 1795. This was at one of the annual concerts in the Burgtheater for the benefit of the Widows of the Tonkün-stler-Gesellschaft / Societät – 'The Society of Musicians'. We have also remarked, it is open to question as to which whether Beethoven performed the B flat Concerto or the C major Concerto. In common with these two works, the Third Piano Concerto had an extended compositional genesis. Beethoven may have noted down the first ideas for the C minor Concerto during his extended concert tour of 1796 — perhaps following his recital at the Berlin Court in May or June.

His musical thoughts for this period are contained in the miscellaneous collection of sketches known as the Kafka Miscellany, named after its one-time owner Johann Nepomuk Kafaka that are preserved today in the British Library, London. From these many sketches, a performing version of some thirty-two bars has been reconstructed from the Kafka Miscellany to yield a pr-1800 concept of the Rondo for the C minor Concerto.[39] Beethoven clearly had innovative orchestration in mind since in the marginalia of a sketch leaf he wrote 'Zum Concert aus C moll puake bej der Cadent' — 'To the Concerto in C minor kettledrum at the Cadenza'. This idea persisted since further wording in a later draft reads 'im Concert bej der Cadenza' — 'in the Concerto at the Cadenza'.[40] Commenting on this text, Barry Cooper describes Beethoven's thematic use of the timpani to be 'one of the most original ideas in the Concerto' and 'remarkable for being one of [the composer's] earliest ideas'.[41]

Drums do in fact feature at the close of the first movement and impart a militaristic character to the music; could Beethoven perhaps have been recalling Mozart's Piano Concerto K. 415? Writing of the sketch-origins of Op. 37, Thayer states:

> 'Sketches for the first movement of the Third Sonata [Op. 2, No. 3] are found among notes for the Sextet for Wind Instruments [Op. 74] (composed about 1796) and also for the Concerto in C minor, which, therefore, was begun thus early.'[42]

From 1798, Beethoven started to make use of bound sketchbooks with ruled pages to replace blank, loose leaves, the order of which could become confused. The earliest of these, known as Grasnick 1, set the pattern for many other such sketchbooks. It consists of forty-eight leaves sewn together in notebook form that served the composer from mid-1798 to early 1799. As we have seen (Op. 19) this sketchbook includes revisions for the Prague concert-tour performance of the B-flat major Piano Concerto. Later on, Beethoven often resorted to binding miscellaneous leaves together himself. As Cooper remarks:

> '[The] sketchbooks greatly enhanced [Beethoven's] ability to think on paper, on a much larger and more complex scale, and may also have partly compensated for his growing deafness in later years.'[43]

The care Beethoven expended, to give musical expression to the forms and ideas for which he was striving, is evident in the many erasures and transformations that are evident in the sketches.[44]

That so few sketches survive for the Third Piano Concerto suggests Beethoven worked with a sketchbook sometime after 1796 that has subsequently been lost His second sketchbook, Grasnick 2, dates from 1799 — leaving an uncharacteristic, sketchbook-free gap of three years. The presumed lost sketchbook presents a challenge to tracing the progress of the creation origins of the C minor Concerto, as it does for other works of the period, on which Beethoven is known to have been working. These include the String Quartet, Op. 18, No. 4, the Septet, Op. 20 and the First Symphony, Op. 21.[45] To quote Thayer once more:

'The sketches for the last movement of [Concerto] No. 3 are associated with sketches for a cadenza for the C major Concerto which Beethoven played in Prague in 1798, and may therefore be placed in this year.'[46]

More generally, authorities agree Beethoven composed much of the Op. 37 Concerto during the years 1799–1800 when he was free to do so following his return from his concert tour. With characteristic eloquence Thayer writes:

'Throughout this period of Beethoven's life, each summer is distinguished by some noble composition, completed, or nearly so, so that on his return to society, his time was his own; his fancy was quickened, his inspiration strengthened, in field and forest labour was his delight.'

Beethoven's friend Ignaz von Seyfried writes of this period in a similarly florid style:

'Every year Beethoven spent the summer months in the country, where under the skies of azure blue he liked to compose ... So a four-horse wagon was freighted with a few articles of his furniture and a tremendous amount of music; the tower-like machine slowly got underway, and the owner of its treasures marched along ahead of it as happy as could be, per pedes apostolorum – "by means of the feet of the apostles".'[47]

Thayer gives the date of 1800 as representing the culminating point of the writing out of the C minor Concerto. This contention has held sway in Beethoven musicology for over a century — as evidenced in several of our opening quotations. However, modern-day re-dating of Beethoven's autograph score to the C minor Concerto, by such Beethoven authorities as Karl-Heinz Köhler, Alan Tyson, and Leon Plantinga, affirm that completion of the C minor Concerto belongs more closely to 1803. Although such considerations mean little to the typical music lover, as Plantinga observes:

'The chronological position of a composition, within any major composer's oeuvre, must affect our perception of it, the way we listen to it, and think about it ... In the present case a difference between 1800 and 1803 determines whether we group the Third Concerto with the Fourth Symphony, the Septet, the String Quartets Op. 18, and the Horn Sonata, Op. 17, or, alternatively, with that very different and altogether remarkable series of pieces that stood on the threshold of the *Eroica*: the Second Symphony, the *Kreutzer* Sonata, the Piano Sonatas Op. 3, and the Variations Opp. 34 and 35 ... The years in question were ones of rapid stylistic change for Beethoven as he moved into what is sometimes called his *heroic* period.'[48]

That Beethoven continued to work intermittently on the C minor Concerto over the period 1800–03 is evident from modern-day study of the sketches that have survived. From December 1801 to July 1802, Beethoven made use of the so-called Kessler Sketchbook. It takes its name from the composer and pianist Joseph Christoph Kessler (1800–72) to whom it was given by Carl Andreas Stein, a member of the Vienna family of piano manufacturers, and was subsequently acquired by the Gesellschaft der Musikfreunde. This sketchbook is almost unique in having survived with its 96 leaves intact.[49] The Kessler Sketchbook testifies to Beethoven's efforts to provide compositions for a concert of 1802, that in the event did not take place (see later).

The sketches reveal the composer working on a *rondo moderato* and a companion movement in the key of C major. Also included are sketches for a concertante in D major for piano, violin, cello and orchestra — considered as a possible precursor of the Triple Concerto, Op. 56.[50] Between the autumn of 1802 and May 1803, Beethoven used the Wielhorsky sketchbook that today consists of 87 leaves. Its name derives from its one-time owner, the Russian Count Mikhail Wielhorsky. Its present location is the Glinka Museum — State Central Museum of Music Culture, Moscow.[51] Four loose leaves — bifolia (eight sides) — are today in possession of the Beethoven House, Bonn. These include sketches for the Cadenza to the Third Piano Concerto alongside thoughts for the Oratorio *Christ on the Mount of Olives*, Op. 85.[52]

The Autograph of the C minor Concerto disappeared following the Second World War and was thought to be lost until it reappeared in Poland in 1977; it was later returned to the Staatsbibliothek Preussischer Kulturbesitz, Berlin. Its rediscovery led to a re-evaluation of the text and to its re-dating to 1803. Beethoven's (typically) heavily revised emendations bear testimony to his thoroughgoing compositional changes to the score. In William Kinderman's words: 'Beethoven subjects his own style to incisive critique.' The autograph indicates the full orchestral parts but solo the piano-writing [that] sometimes degenerates into unresolved sketchy alternative readings ... showing nothing for the keyboard player to do in the tuttis'.[53] In this form It was essentially a personal document, rather than one intended as an aid to performance by others, and, as such, could be realised only by Beethoven himself – drawing on his powers of improvisation.

Based on his study of the manuscript, former Yale musicologist Leon Plantinga writes: 'The beginning of the recapitulation, with its exquisite exchanges between piano and orchestra, cost Beethoven great effort. The pages of the Autograph became so cluttered with second and third thoughts that he resorted to the addition of a fresh bifolium (between the present folios 67 and 70), sewing the new paper over the pages they replaced.' He further remarks: 'Beethoven's main indecision was about the distribution of music between piano and orchestra, by slow stages, he approached the happy solution of giving the orchestra the lion's share of thematic matter ... with ever more intricate piano commentary in its long Interstices.'[54]

In his decipherment of the composer's changes and adjustments to the score, Kinderman further comments: 'The solo part was left in an unfinished state in the autograph score. The earlier layer of writing in the score, in brown ink, shows the rondo theme of the Finale with syncopated chords in the left hand in place of the melodic accents of the finished work; the sixteenth-note figuration in the left hand was not originally part of Beethoven's conception at all.' Kinderman makes reference to revisions that 'supress gestures of an excessively showy pianistic virtuosity in favour of a more organic and logical development of the musical material'.[55]

We have remarked (text to Op. 15) that Beethoven gave his first public concert in Vienna on Tuesday, 2 April 1800, having secured Vienna's most prestigious concert venue, the Burgtheater (Royal Imperial Court Theatre). We briefly recall the circumstances.

This was the occasion of Beethoven's first benefit

concert — an *akademie* — at which works wholly of his composition were performed. He premiered his Symphony No. 1 in C, 'a grand Concerto for the pianoforte' (unidentified) and improvised at the piano. The correspondent of the contemporary journal *Allgemeine musikalische Zeitung* considered the concert to be 'truly the most interesting for a long time'. He found in the Symphony 'considerable art, novelty and a wealth of ideas', the Piano Concerto to be 'written with a great deal of taste and feeling', and Beethoven's improvisation to be 'masterly'.[56]

Which concerto was performed has been the subject of conjecture. Early Beethoven biographers, such as Anton Schindler, debated whether the concerto in question was Op.15 or even Op. 19 — although by then both were too established in the repertoire to fit the description 'a new concerto'. Modern-day musicology favours the C major Piano Concerto as the likely candidate, particularly in view of the fact that Beethoven had revised the work and amended the score — just as he would have with performance in mind. Most authorities suggest Beethoven intended to perform the C minor Piano Concerto, Op. 37. As we have seen, he was working on this at the time but it was not yet ready to be presented at the April 1800 concert.[57]

We pause for a moment in our narrative, relating to the origins of the C minor Concerto, to consider an aspect of Beethoven's personal circumstances that would change his life forever. We refer to the *jealous demon* — Beethoven's expression — that was now haunting him and which was to transform both his future existence and his relationship with his art — namely, the onset of deafness. This was to initiate a period of what has been described as 'Crisis and Creativity'.[58]

Beethoven's hearing had begun to deteriorate significantly from about 1798, and by 1800 he was consciously avoiding social gatherings, 'fearing his disability would become common knowledge' (his words).[59] In his despair, he confided his circumstances to the physician Dr. (later Prof.) Franz Gerhard Wegeler, a close friend from his schooldays in Bonn. In a letter of 29 June 1801 – one of the most poignant in cultural history – he explained how for the last three years his hearing had become weaker and weaker and how his ears 'continue to hum and buzz day and night' (a characteristic of tinnitus – a disease of the inner ear). He confessed to leading a miserable life and could not bring himself to say to people, 'I am deaf'. He admits even to cursing his Creator and his very existence. But, with characteristic Beethovenian defiance, he resolved to accept his fate adding: 'I live entirely in my music; hardly have I completed one composition when I have already begun another.'[60]

A few days later (1 July1801) he wrote in similar terms, to those he had shared with Wegeler, this time to his close friend the theologian and amateur violinist Karl (Carl) Amenda. He told Amenda of the success he was having with his compositions, and of his relative financial security – the combined income from his works and the money from Prince Lichnowsky's annuity. He then disclosed the circumstances of his increasing deafness and the tribulations it was causing. He wrote:

'We must wait and see whether my hearing can be restored ... I must hope, but I hardly think it possible ... Oh, how happy should I be now if I had perfect hearing.'[61]

Later in the year (16 November) Beethoven wrote again to Wegeler asking if he considered if galvanism might benefit his hearing. Only ten years previously (1791) Luigi Galvani had published his treatise on what he termed 'biological electricity' with sensational claims of its alleged powers to animate the muscles of dead limbs — including those of human beings (derived from the corpses of criminals). The reader will recall this innovation was the genesis of Mary Shelly's *Frankenstein*. It is a measure of Beethoven's desperation, concerning his hearing, that he was prepared to contemplate such new and untested procedures. His letter to Wegeler, however, reveals how love and his indomitability of spirit were helping him to conquer his *jealous demon*. He told Wegeler that he was 'leading a slightly more pleasant life' and mixing more with his 'fellow creatures'. Hitherto, he explains, how his poor hearing had haunted him everywhere 'like a ghost' and had made him seem to be 'a misanthrope' which he insisted he was 'far from being'.

The more positive transformation in his life, and outlook, had been brought about by 'a dear charming girl' who, Beethoven revealed, 'loves me and whom I love'. Beethoven even contemplated marriage in the hope it might bring him further happiness. He recognized, however, this was impossible since, as he explained, 'unfortunately [the lady in question] is not of my class'. In any event, Beethoven concluded, he could not marry at the present moment on the grounds: 'For me there is no greater pleasure than to practice and exercise my art.' Beethoven concluded his letter by resolving 'to grasp fate by the throat' so that it would not completely bend him and 'to live life a thousand times'.[62]

The 'dear charming girl', to whom Beethoven makes reference, was Countess Gillette Guicciadi. She would eventually receive the dedication of the second of the Piano Sonatas Op. 27 — *The Moonlight*. It is possible the young countess may, for a while, have entertained romantic feelings towards Beethoven until her marriage in 1803.[63]

We sense, albeit Indirectly, Beethoven's despair at the realization of the loss of his hearing from the writings of

Gabriel Fauré. Like Beethoven he was similarly afflicted by deafness — although only towards the end of his life. Writing to his wife from Switzerland he lamented:

> 'I am so overwhelmed by this affliction that has struck me in what it is most important I should preserve intact ... I am weighed down by a frightful cloak of misery and discouragement.'[64]

In Electra Yourke's memorable phrase: 'The gate of music is the ear.' As she elucidates, our faculties of musical perception, and the ability to perform music, depend upon 'the perfection of our auditory apparatus'. It is to mankind's benefit that, by drawing upon his indomitability of spirit, Beethoven protected his creative imagination in the form of 'a dome of sound' such that, thereby, his inner ear remained intact. As Yourke states: '[Beethoven] no longer needed external stimuli to organize ... sounds into melodies or harmonies.'[65] Others have written in similar terms. Maynard Solomon remarks:

> 'Despite his initial fears ... his art actually became richer as his hearing declined ... One begins to suspect that Beethoven's crisis and his extraordinary creativity were somehow related, and even that the former may have been the necessary precondition of the latter.'[66]

Reflecting on Beethoven's response to deafness, musicologist Michael Thomas Roeder comments:

> 'Beethoven composed the [C minor] Concerto at the peak of his performing career, when he was widely regarded as the foremost pianist and

composer of piano music of the day. He used the piano in several seminal works in the few crucial years leading up to the famous *Heiligenstadt Testament* of October 1802.'[67]

Roeder considers: 'In the musical works [of the period in question] he stretched the traditional Classical forms to meet the expressive needs of his expanded musical vision.' He concludes:

> 'A growing sense of isolation, humiliation, and anxiety nearly led him to suicide. But a counter-vailing devotion to music, indeed a sense of calling, restored perspective, giving his music a greater urgency and becoming this deaf person's most effective means of communication.'[68]

During the winter of 1801–02, Beethoven resumed work on his Second Symphony, Op. 36 and the Triple Concerto, Op. 56. He also entertained hopes of appearing at one of Vienna's Lent concerts in the spring of 1802 for which Beethoven, the celebrated pianist, would be expected to present a piano concerto. Since the B-flat major and C major Concertos were by then in the public domain, a *new* concerto would be expected. As Plantinga states, '[Beethoven] laboured earnestly to produce such a piece' — reference to the C minor Concerto.[69]

That Beethoven was making progress with the Op. 37 Concerto is evident from a letter his brother Kaspar (Caspar) Karl (Carl) wrote, on the composer's behalf, on 22 April 1802, to the publisher Breitkopf and Härtel. This was in response to the request the Leipzig publishing house had made to Beethoven on 21 May 1801 (see above). They asked Beethoven for a selection of works with a view to their eventual publication. Carl, as we shall refer to him (to avoid confusion with his son who was named Karl) had relocated from Bonn to Vienna to be closer to his brother in order to assist him with his business affairs.

From 1800, Carl worked as a clerk in Vienna's Department of Finance, in which capacity he found time to correspond with publishers to offer his brother's works for sale and — importantly — to secure the best prices he could. Carl's letter enclosed a note from Beethoven stating how busy he was with composition but adding, reassuringly: '[You] can rely entirely on my brother who, in general, attends to my affairs.'[70] Whilst Carl promoted Beethoven's interests with determination, he appears to have lacked tact and made enemies. For example, Ferdinand Ries is on record as describing Carl as being 'the biggest skinflint in the world'.[71]

In his April letter, Carl apologised for the delay in giving Härtel a reply. He explained the reason was that the works he wanted to offer were still in fact in preparation. He therefore suggested the typical prices Beethoven would require for various types of composition; for example, he requested '50 ducats for a grand sonata' — the ducat being valued at about four-and-a-half florins. He also makes reference to 'a symphony and a concerto' — taken to be a reference to Symphony No. 2 and the Piano Concerto No. 3. He explained these works were not available at the moment since he anticipated they were required for performance at the concert that Beethoven had in mind.

Beethoven was probably planning to hold his concert either at the Kärntnerthor Theater or the Burgtheater where the Director, Baron Peter Anton Braun, had authority in his capacity as theatre manager. Braun played a prominent role in Vienna's cultural life especially when, in 1804, he purchased the Theater an der Wien. Beethoven's concert arrangements appear to have been undermined, though, by Braun's inept actions that prompted Carl to complain to Härtel:

'[The] Theater Director Baron von Braun, who is known to be a stupid and crude fellow, has refused him the Theater for his concert and has rented it to the most mediocre artists.'[72]

'The Baron's actions put an end, for the time being, to Beethoven's hopes of presenting his music to the Viennese public, including any new concerto that he might have contemplated.'[73]

On 10 June 1802, Gottfried Christoph Härtel, the active member of the publishing firm, replied to Carl van Beethoven's correspondence — in somewhat cautious terms. He explained how the problems of piracy were bearing down on his firm: '[In] Germany the profit from the publication of a significantly new original work benefits many publishers but not the rightful one.' He explained how the rightful publisher could not sell his work as cheaply as the pirate printer, 'since he [the rightful printer] had to bear the cost of the composer's fees.'

Beethoven new the value of his work and always demanded a high fee. To illustrate the problem Härtel had to confront, shortly after Beethoven's Piano Trios Op. 1 were published, by the Viennese firm Artaria, Simrock in Bonn, and some half-a-dozen Parisian publishers, brought out their own unauthorised editions. Consequently, Härtel felt obliged to inform Beethoven these circumstances constrained his publishing house from being able to remunerate him as they would wish. They were prepared to purchase the Symphony, Op. 36 and the Concerto Op. 37

but only for a smaller fee than Carl was endeavouring to secure on his brother's behalf. Härtel concluded by expressing the hope that his firm would in future be able to offer Beethoven more favourable terms, depending upon their 'mercantile success'.[74]

It is a measure of Beethoven's growing fame that at the close of the year he was approached by another music publisher. In November 1802 Beethoven received a letter from Johann Anton André, composer and founder-member of the publishing firm based at Offenbach, close to Frankfurt am Main. André is recognised in musicology for his negotiations with Constanza Mozart for the publication of many of the compositions left after Wolfgang's death. These included the scores of *The Marriage of Figaro*, *The Magic Flute*, and *Eine Kleine Nachtmusik*. Doubtless being aware of Beethoven's standing in music – now spreading beyond the confines of Vienna – he approached the composer expressing the wish to publish some of his works.

On 23 November 1802, Carl van Beethoven responded to André, once more on his brother's behalf. He offered the Second Symphony, Op. 36 and the C minor Piano Concert, Op. 37. He requested 300 florins for each composition together with eight printed copies of the engravings. Beethoven frequently made such a request of his music publishers so that he could give a copy of his most recent work to close friends and fellow musicians. It is indicative of Beethoven's productivity that Carl also offered André the two *Romances* for Violin and Orchestra, Op. 40 and Op. 50, and the Piano Sonatas, Op. 49.[75]

Carl's prices for his brother's compositions appear to have been too high though for André since no further negotiations appear to have taken place between the two parties.

In 1803, Caspar Carl acted once more as his brother's

amanuensis. On 22 January he wrote again to Gottfried Härtel. He explained he could offer 'a grand Symphony' [No. 2, Op. 36] and 'a grand Piano Concerto' [No. 3, Op. 37]. He continued: 'I believe if I allowed you to have both these works for 600 florins you would not be overcharged.' He emphasized, though, that he wished to see both compositions engraved 'by the end of May' — Beethoven wanted to see his works in print as soon as possible. As further inducements to Härtel, Carl also offered the Overture to the Ballet *The Creatures of Prometheus*, Op. 46 and the music to several of its scenes. He proudly remarked:

> '[These] have been received very often as concert pieces in the Augarten concerts here [in Vienna] with uncommon applause, an honour that has heretofore never been accorded to ballet music.'

Typical of Carl's entrepreneurial zeal, he offered 'three piano sonatas' — that were in fact not yet composed! [76]

The Augarten, to which Carl makes reference, was the venue for *Morgenkonzerte* — 'morning concerts' — that were held in the Augarten Saal (Concert Hall). This was situated within a pavilion-like building set amidst formal landscape gardens. Mozart performed his Piano Concerto No. 10 in the Saal on May 26 1782 and later gave a performance there of his *Paris* Symphony. Beethoven premiered his Violin Sonata No. 9, *The Kreutzer* at a Morgenkonzert in 1803 and in 1824 Schubert's song *The Nightingale* was heard in the Saal. Writing of his experience of an Augarten concert, in October 1800, a correspondent of the *Allgemeine musikalische Zeitung* enthused: 'The auditorium was very brilliant, and everything went off with decorum; everyone was glad to do their part in helping the organization.' Both amateur and professional musicians contributed to the orchestra and 'ladies of the highest nobility were to be heard'.

On 28 January 1803, Gottfried Härtel replied to Carl who, true to his nature, was again demanding high prices for his brother's compositions. Härtel once more expressed his uncertainty concerning 'the mercantile success' that his firm might expect from the sale of the works being offered. He stated he could offer only 500 florins for the Second Symphony and C minor Concerto combined – 100 florins less than the sum Carl was seeking.[77]

On 3 March, Härtel wrote to Carl urging him to confirm if his offer of 500 florins was acceptable. He was anxious to proceed with the engravings for the Symphony and the Concerto in order to have these ready for display at the Easter Leipzig Music Fair (Leipzig *Messe*).[78] Carl responded on 28 March, somewhat intemperately, insisting his request for 600 gulden (interchangeable with the florin) for the Symphony and Concerto was an 'exceptionally moderate' price and that he could not accept the 500 florins offered. He thereby terminated the planned transaction with the Leipzig publisher stating: 'I have sold these two works to one of your colleagues for 700 gulden.'

The 'colleagues' in question were the Kunst- und Industrie-Comptoir of Vienna who subsequently published the Symphony No. 2, Op. 36 and the C minor Concerto in March and summer 1804 respectively (see later). Mindful of Breitkopf and Härtel's standing in music publishing, Carl kept his future options open with the Leipzig firm by stating: 'In three or four weeks, I shall make you a few offers, which I hope you will honour better, because I wish very much to do business with you.'[79] Carl's demeanour, though, appears to have proved too abrasive for Härtel who did not transact any further business with Beethoven. Later on, Beethoven conducted his affairs directly with his Härtel. This came about as Caspar Carl's heath progressively deteriorated, obliging him to be less closely involved with his brother's affairs; Carl eventually died in 1815.

Härtel's expressed wish that his firm would, in future, be able to offer Beethoven 'more favourable terms' was amply fulfilled. Breitkopf and Härtel proved to be one of Beethoven's most supportive publishers. In 1808, Gottfried Härtel visited Vienna and reached an agreement with Beethoven to publish a number of his compositions. Between 1809–12, his firm printed first editions of several of the composer's major works including: the Fifth Symphony, Op. 67; the Sixth Symphony, Op. 68; the Cello Sonata Op. 69; the Piano Trios, Op. 70; the Sextet, Op. 71; the Fifth Piano Concerto, Op.73; the String Quartet, Op. 74; the Piano Sonata, Op. 78; the *Choral Fantasia*, Op. 80; the Piano Sonata, Op. 81a; and the Mass in C minor.[80]

Not only is this list of works testimony to Beethoven's remarkable creativity and powers of invention, by implication it is indicative also of the many demands made on his time in transacting the business formalities necessary to see his works in print. Little wonder that his surviving correspondence, much of it to do with business affairs, consists of almost 1,600 letters and related documents.[81]

On 13 June 1803, the Theater an der Wien opened. This has a bearing on the next part of our narrative and progress with the C minor Concerto. The theatre's champion and instigator was the theatrical impresario Emanuel Schikaneder — best known today, perhaps, as Mozart's librettist and collaborator with him for the Opera *The Magic Flute* (1791). The Theater an der Wien would play a significant role in Beethoven's developing musical career and on him becoming established in Vienna's musical circle. It was here he conducted a performance of the *Eroica* Symphony (7 April 1805), where Franz Clement premiered the Violin Concerto (23 December 1806), and where *Fidelio* received its first performance (20 November 1806). The *Allgemeine musikalische Zeitung* described the establishment in laudatory terms for being the 'most comfortable and satisfactory in the whole of Germany'.[82]

Schikaneder wasted no time in commissioning Beethoven to write an opera for his company to his libretto *Vestus Feuer* — 'The Vestal Flame'. An incentive to do so was the offer of free accommodation for the composer and his brother Carl in an apartment within the theatre complex. Beethoven appears, however, to have struggled with Schikaneder's text. On 4 January 1804, he expressed his disaffection to the theologian and writer Johann Friedrich Rochlitz:

> 'Just picture to yourself a Roman subject (of which I had been told neither the scheme nor anything else whatever) and language and verses such as could come out of the mouths of our Viennese apple-women [street vendors].'[83]

Beethoven eventually abandoned Schikaneder's libretto and commenced work on a new word-setting adapted from a French text — Jean-Nicolas Bouilly's *Leonore*. The time he spent on *Vestus Feuer* was not entirely wasted, though, since some of its music was absorbed into *Leonore* and thereby *Fidelio* — the most memorable of which being the celebrated Leonora-Florestan duet 'O namenlose Freunde!'

On 30 March 1803, the *Wiener Zeitung* contained the following announcement: 'On the 5 April, Herr Ludwig van Beethoven will produce a new Oratorio set to music by him, *Christus am Ölberge* [at the] Theater an der Wien.' Of interest is that this was his first public appearance as a dramatic vocal-composer. The announcement stated the other pieces to be performed would be displayed on the Theatre billboard. The most important of these were Beethoven's First and Second Symphonies and the C minor Piano Concerto. Thayer conjectured that other compositions may also have been played including the song-settings *Adelaide*, *Ah, perfido!* and *Tremate, empi tremati* – Beethoven always gave value for money at his major concerts![84]

Only the First Symphony had been heard before, and, consequently, considerable preparation was required at rehearsal for the players to familiarize themselves with so much new music. The rehearsal started at eight in the morning and continued without a break until half-past two in the afternoon, by which time the players were exhausted. As Thayer recounts, Beethoven's patron, Prince Karl Lichnowsky, helped revive the players' spirits: '[He] sent for bread and butter, cold meat and wine ... the result being good-nature was restored again.'[85]

The Oratorio proved to be so challenging that it took up much of the rehearsal time, to the neglect of the Piano Concerto. Moreover, the piano part was not yet fully written out – as Ignaz von Seyfried was to discover. Beethoven, who was to play the work, asked von Seyfried if he would be his page-turner. But, at the evening performance, von Seyfried realized Beethoven had merely noted down the ritornellos and first notes of the solo passages, as aids to his memory, and had left many bars only half-filled or quite blank. As he later recalled:

'Heaven help me! I saw nothing but empty pages; at most on one page or the other a few Egyptian Hieroglyphics wholly unintelligible to me scribbled down to serve as clues for [Beethoven] since he played nearly all the solo part from memory.'

Beethoven, anticipating the challenge the appearance his manuscript posed, had a prior arrangement with von Seyfried that he would indicate when he wanted a page turning. During the performance, however, Beethoven's sense of humour appears to have got the better of him since the hapless Seyfried recounts:

'Cheerful and alive to the enjoyment ... [he] could not deny himself the pleasure of putting me in a fidget and delaying the promised signal as long as possible.'

Seyfried later confessed he would have deserted his post 'had not the beauty of the music atoned for the composer's ill-timed pleasantry'.[86]

Reviews of the concert were indifferent, according to the account published in the Berlin journal *Der Freimüthige* ('Candid—Outspoken'). This was co-edited by the distinguished dramatist August von Kotzebue — with whom Beethoven later collaborated in the music dramas *The Ruins of Athens* and *King Stephen*. The music critic considered the Symphonies and single passages in the Oratorio to be 'very beautiful' but the Concerto received little acclaim and for once Beethoven's playing did not attract admiration. The reviewer of the sister music journal *Zeitung für die elegante Welt* ('Newspaper for the elegant World') felt similarly inclined to remark: 'Herr van Beethoven, otherwise known as an excellent pianist, performed not completely to the public's satisfaction.' We should bear in mind, as remarked, Beethoven performed with the solo part not fully written out — let alone practiced. Moreover, even his indomitability of spirit may have been taxed. It is on record that on the day of the concert he had to rise very early in the morning in order to write out the trombone parts for the Oratorio, from which the players performed shortly after – with the ink hardly dry. [87]

In his *Autobiography* (English translation 1865), the violinist, composer and conductor Louis Spohr describes an account he received from von Seyfried that authorities believe relates to the 1803 concert. Spohr writes:

> '*Beethoven* was playing a new Pianoforte-Concerto of his, but forgot at the first tutti, that he was a solo player and, springing up, began to direct in his usual way. At the first *sforzando* he threw out his arms so wide asunder, that he knocked both the lights off the piano onto the ground. The audience laughed, and *Beethoven* was so incensed at this disturbance that he made the orchestra cease playing and begin anew.'

Seyfried intervened and requested two chorus boys, from the Oratorio, to place themselves on either side of *Beethoven* and to hold the lights in their hands. However, such was Beethoven's loss of composure, it is alleged that at the first chords of the solo he pounded the keys so vehemently that several strings broke. [88]

Later in the year, on 24 May, the public had a further opportunity to witness Beethoven at the keyboard and to hear more of his new music. This was the occasion when he premiered his Violin Sonata, No. 9, Op. 47 – the so-called Kreutzer Sonata. The event in question took place in the Augarten Saal at the unlikely time of eight in the morning. It appears to have been a characteristically rushed Beethoven-style performance since the violinist had to sight-read his part from the composer's much-changed manuscript and without the benefit of a prior rehearsal. Beethoven's hapless partner was the Afro-European George

Bridgetower who, as his name suggests, had English connections. Unfortunately for Bridgetower, he later quarrelled with Beethoven who, thereby, denied him his intended dedication, conferring it instead on the French violinist Rudolph Kreutzer. Paradoxically, Kreutzer disliked the composition, considered it too difficult, and never performed the piece.

Following his performance of the C minor Concerto on 5 April, Beethoven made changes to the solo part. Later in June he wrote to his piano pupil Ferdinand Ries to check through his manuscript for errors, with a view to sending the work to the Bonn publisher Nikolaus Simrock with whom he was then conducting negotiations.[89] These eventually were not fulfilled and, as we shall see, the Concerto was eventually published by the Kunst- und Industrie-Comptoir known also by its French title as the Bureau des Arts et d'Industrie.

Since Ferdinand Ries features significantly in the next part of our account, he deserves a more rounded introduction. Like Beethoven he was born in Bonn and received musical instruction initially from his father; he may be considered to be Bonn's second most famous composer after Beethoven. He received instruction in piano from Beethoven soon after his arrival in Vienna, either late 1801 or early 1802. Despite Beethoven's pressing commitments, relating to his concerts and the demands made on his time composing, Beethoven did not neglect his pupil. On 6 May 1803, Ries wrote home enthusiastically to Nikolaus Simrock. He had been a horn player in the Bonn Electoral Court Orchestra, was a friend of Beethoven and from 1793 he transacted business in music publishing. In this capacity, he brought out the works of Haydn and later on some of Beethoven's compositions, including the Kreutzer Violin Sonata, Op. 47 and the two Cello Sonatas, Op. 102.

Ries informed Simrock:

'Beethoven takes more trouble with me than I could have believed. Each week I receive three lessons, usually from 10 o'clock to 2.30. I can almost play his Sonata *Pathétique*, which might give you pleasure, because the precision that he demands is hard to imagine. To hear him improvise, however, may not be imagined at all — I have already had this pleasure five times.'

Writing of Carl van Beethoven's business dealings on his brother's behalf he writes less enthusiastically:

'[Carl] is the biggest skinflint in the world — for a single ducat he would take back 50 words of promise and his good brother makes the greatest enemies because of him. For every note that Beethoven plays there is a corresponding base element in his brother's soul.'[90]

Beethoven came to rely on Ries as his unpaid secretary and in this capacity he assisted him with his letters to publishers and with other of his daily affairs. Although Ries was a prolific composer, much of his music in now neglected. He is perhaps best remembered, in Beethoven musicology, for being a founder member of the (Royal) Philharmonic Society, London and for his actions with the Society in the commissioning of the *Choral* Symphony. From a brief note Beethoven wrote to Ries, in early July 1804, we learn he was planning for his pupil to appear in public playing the C minor Concerto.[91] We recall how, in much the same manner, Antonio Salieri had presented Beethoven to the public some years before as his chosen pupil (see text to Op. 19). Ries himself records:

'Beethoven had given me his beautiful Concerto in C minor, Op. 37, in manuscript, so that I might make my first public appearance *as his pupil* with it [Ries's italics].'

With a touch of pride he adds: 'I am the only one who ever appeared as such while Beethoven was alive.'[92]

The concert in question was planned to take place on Thursday 19 July as part of the Augarten concert series. Beethoven himself was to conduct with Ignaz Schuppanzigh as leader of the orchestra. Schuppanzigh was an excellent violinist and had some responsibility for organizing the Augarten concerts. Beethoven held Schuppanzigh in high regard and maintained a close working relationship with him for the rest of his life.

On 14 July, Beethoven informed Ries of his intention to have the C minor Concerto rehearsed at Schuppanzigh's apartment. We have just seen that Ries was in possession of the manuscript copy of the Concerto but he requested a cadenza from Beethoven, since it was not yet written into the piano part. Beethoven refused, instructing Ries to compose one himself that he gave an undertaking to look through and, if necessary, correct. Ries duly obliged, apparently to the composer's satisfaction since Beethoven requested only a few changes. However, Ries — eager to display his burgeoning virtuosity — had incorporated what he describes as 'an extremely brilliant and very difficult passage' in his cadenza. Although Beethoven appreciated his pupil's efforts, he considered this part of his writing to be 'too venturesome' and requested something more restrained in its place.

A week before the concert, Ries ventured once more to play the technically challenging version of his cadenza, only to flounder at the obstacles he had set himself. This time, Beethoven 'a little ill-naturedly' insisted Ries should change the offending measures. Ries recalls: 'I did so, but the new passage did not satisfy me; I therefore studied the other, and zealously, but not quite sure of it.' He continues:

'When the cadenza was reached in the public concert Beethoven quietly sat down. I could not persuade myself to choose the easier one. When I boldly began the more difficult one, Beethoven jerked his chair; but the cadenza went through all right and Beethoven was so delighted that he shouted "Bravo" loudly. This electrified the entire audience and at once gave me a standing among artists. Afterwards, while expressing his satisfaction, Beethoven added: "But all the same you are wilful! If you had made a slip in the passage I would not have given you another lesson".'[93]

The correspondent to the *Allgemeine musikalische Zeitung* held the C minor Concerto in higher regard than his counterpart had done following the composition's premier in 1803. Writing in the 15 August 1804 issue he reported:

'This Concerto without doubt belongs among Beethoven's most beautiful compositions. It is worked out in a masterly fashion. Herr Ries, who took the solo part, is, at present, Beethoven's only pupil and his most fervent admirer. He had prepared the piece entirely under the direction of his teacher and gave proof of a very smooth expressive execution as well as unusual polish and sureness overcoming with ease the most extraordinary difficulties.'[94]

The following year, the *AmZ* remarked once more on the favourable reception the C minor Concerto had received in Vienna and Leipzig 'even to audiences accustomed to hearing the concertos of Mozart' — a form of words that implies the critic's recognition of the 'newness' in Beethoven's score. Writing in the 10 April 1805 issue of the same Journal, the critic wrote extensively of the work, combining his text with numerous musical quotations. Discussing Beethoven's craftsmanship, the reviewer drew attention to his use of modulations into distant keys. He likened these to spices that must be used in moderation. He accused Beethoven in the past of sometimes being guilty of this but here he enthused:

'He offers modulations ... but only rarely ... and precisely for this reason [they] have the proper effect.' He concluded: 'With regard to both spirit and effect [the Third Piano Concerto] is one of the most outstanding ever written.'⁹⁵

Two sets of recollections connect us with the Augarten concerts, the C minor Concerto, and two of Beethoven's celebrated contemporary composer-pianists. The first relates to the Prague born Ignaz Moscheles. On discovering Beethoven's piano sonatas, he became one of the composer's most ardent admirers. In the Preface to the English edition (London, 1841) of Anton Schindler's *Biographie von Ludwig van Beethoven*, he is quoted as stating:

'I longed to see and become acquainted with *that man* who had exercised so powerful an influence over my whole being; whom, though I scarcely understood, I blindly worshiped.'⁹⁶

The music publisher Domenico Artaria introduced Moscheles to Beethoven sometime in 1810; Artaria had recently published some of Moscheles's compositions. Moscheles relates:

'I never missed Schuppanzigh's quartets [quartet concerts], where Beethoven was often present, nor the delightful concerts in the Augarten where he conducted his own symphonies.'

He adds:

'I also heard him play a few times; this he did very rarely, sometimes in public, sometimes in private circles. The pieces I heard him play which made the most impression on me were the *Fantasia* with orchestral accompaniment and chorus, and the Concerto in C minor.'[97]

In 1814, by which time Moscheles was on more familiar terms with Beethoven, he entrusted him with the responsibility of preparing a piano reduction of the score of his Opera *Fidelio* – (which the present writer, in his school days, once attempted to play through – and failed miserably!).

Our second recollection concerns the Manheim-born, London-based Johann Baptiste Cramer – whose piano studies Beethoven admired. It derives from an account communicated by Cramer's widow to Beethoven's biographer Alexander Thayer. Thayer states:

'At an Augarten concert the two pianists [Beethoven and Cramer] were walking together and, hearing a performance of Mozart's pianoforte Concerto in C minor (K. 491), Beethoven suddenly stood still and, directing his companion's attention to the exceedingly simple, but equally beautiful motive which is first introduced towards the end of the piece, exclaimed: "Cramer! Cramer! We shall never be able to do anything like that!".'

Such was Beethoven's response to the music, it is alleged he swayed his body to and fro, marked the time, and 'in every possible manner manifested a delight rising to enthusiasm'.[98]

Beethoven's admiration for Mozart's Piano Concerto, K. 491 (and others) is not in question, but modern-day Beethoven musicology has cast doubt on how much trust can be placed on this story. The meeting between Beethoven and Cramer is supposed to have taken place sometime in 1799. However, authorities have found no record of a Mozart piano concerto being performed in that year and the Concerto K. 491 was not published until 1800. As remarked, it was not until years later that Cramer's widow recounted her story to Thayer. Since Cramer died in 1858 it is possible that by then his wife's recall of events had become confused with some other meeting and conversation with Beethoven.

Reflecting on the story, Cooper states:

'[Beethoven's C minor Concerto's] similarities with Mozart's C minor Piano Concerto, K. 491 — especially in the opening bars — has often been noted, and most writers have assumed that Mozart's work had a profound influence on Beethoven's. Yet it is doubtful whether Beethoven actually knew Mozart's Concerto when he was first sketching his own.'

*

As we have seen, by 1799—1800 Beethoven had made substantial progress with his own composition leading Cooper to conclude: 'More probably, Beethoven conceived his Concerto independently. Indeed, he might not have made parts of it so similar to K. 491 had he known it.'[99]

Plantinga expresses views similar to those of Cooper, although embracing a somewhat wider perspective. He first cites Carl Czerny's conviction: 'Individual traits of the C minor Concerto of Mozart encourage the presumption that Beethoven allowed himself to be influenced by this work.' Plantinga then urges caution in too-ready an acceptance of this. He acknowledges that only Mozart's K. 491 and Beethoven's Op. 37 Concertos adopt the key of C minor — which was rare for the period. He further observes that such composer-contemporaries as Dittersdorf, Haydn, and Pleyel did not use this key in a piano concerto — and that this enhances the likelihood of some connection between the Mozart and Beethoven compositions. Also relevant is his recognition that Beethoven's desire, as a young composer, was 'to match or exceed the artistic and popular triumphs of Mozart's concertos of the later 1780s' and of his readiness to adopt Mozart as his model. Plantinga further cites Beethoven contemplating a C minor concerto from the mid 1790s — as evidenced in his sketchbooks. Finally, he concludes:

> 'Perhaps an acquaintance with the Mozart concerto after it was published in 1800 — the only concerto on the landscape in C minor and one whose dark urgency of expression was akin to Beethoven's idea of that key — provided an impetus for him to work seriously on his own'.[100]

In the autumn of 1804, Beethoven sent a note to Ferdinand

Ries requesting him to check the proofs of the C minor Concerto in readiness for its November publication. He was too unwell to undertake the work himself – an endeavour that, in any event, he always found tiresome – and he wanted the proofs correcting 'without delay'.[101] Shortly after, the orchestral parts and separate piano part were sent to the Bureau des Arts et d'Industrie where they served as the engraver's model.[102]

Regrettably, these manuscripts have since been lost. It is known that after a composition of his had been published, Beethoven had little interest in the work's autograph. Ries tells us:

> 'Once they had been printed, they usually lay about in an adjoining room or scattered on the floor in the middle of his study with other pieces of music ... At any time I could have carried off all those originally autographed compositions that had been engraved already; he would almost likely have given them to me without hesitation had I asked him'.[103]

We may ruefully observe how even a few mere pages of the composer's heavily-worked manuscripts are treasured today by musicologists, for the insights they reveal into the composer's working process, and, as objects of veneration, they commend such fabulous prices at auction.

As remarked Beethoven's chosen publisher for the C minor Concerto was known variously as the Kunst- und Industrie-Comptoir and the Bureau des Arts et d'Industrie. This was a firm of music publishers and dealers in maps and prints. Founded in 1801; Beethoven was among their earliest composer-clients and remained his principal publisher from 1802 to 1808. Major works of his published by the consortium include: *Concertos*: Third and Fourth Piano Concertos, Triple Concerto, Violin Concerto, and Beethoven's arrangement of it for Piano Concerto (see later text); *Orchestral works*: Second and Third Symphonies, *Coriolan* Overture; *Piano and Chamber works*: Piano Sonata, Op. 28, *Waldstein* Piano Sonata, String Quartet arrangement of Piano Sonata Op. 14 — Beethoven's only example, and the *Razumovsky* String Quartets.[104]

The Bureau des Arts et d'Industrie duly announced the C minor Concerto with the following Title Page:

> 'GRAND CONCERTO / *par le* / Pianoforte / *Violons 2, Alto 2, Flutes 2, Hautbois 2, Clarinettes 2, Cors 2, Trompettes et Timbales, Violincelle et Basse* / *composé et dédié* / *À Son Altesse Royale Monseigneur le Prince* / LOUIS FERDINAND DE PEUSSE / *par* / *Louis van Beethoven* / Op. 37 / *À Vienne au Bureau des Arts et d'Industrie.*'

The price requested was four florins and thirty pfennigs — quite a large sum. In 1823 Steiner and Company purchased the Industrie Comptoir and secured the right to publish Beethoven's works either entirely or in parts. At this time they re-published an edition of the Op. 37 Concerto with the same Title Page as that just quoted but with the modified wording *Propriétes des Éditeurs*. The price of this edition had risen to six florins.[105]

The dedicatee, Prince Louis Ferdinand of Prussia, was the youngest brother of Frederick the Great. He was a talented composer and brilliant pianist — esteemed even by Beethoven. It is believed he owned more than a dozen pianofortes — little wonder that he has been described by some historians as 'the musical prince'. Beethoven met Louis

Ferdinand sometime in 1804 when he visited Vienna in connection with the manoeuvres of the Austrian army. Concerning which, even when on military exploits, he carried with him his treasured Cremona violin. Louis attended one of the early performances of the *Eroica* Symphony at the *Palais* of Prince Franz Joseph von Lobkowitz; it has been suggested, Beethoven originally may have intended to dedicate his Third Symphony to Louis Ferdinand. Regrettably, Lobkowitz encouraged Louis Ferdinand to confront the French (1806) to the subsequent loss of his life.[106]

In tracing the progress of the C minor Concerto we turn to 1808. Two concerts were held that year for the benefit of the Widows and Orphans Fund. The first of these took place on 22 December; this was the memorable concert at which Beethoven premiered several new compositions including the Fifth and Sixth Symphonies. The second concert on the 23 December was, in part, intended as an act of homage to the venerable Haydn — then age 76. Some of his vocal works were performed. For this concert, Beethoven requested Ferdinand Ries to play his then newly composed Piano Concerto No. 4, Op. 58. Ries, however, was unfamiliar with the work and, realizing how little time he had to learn it, declined. Endeavouring to accommodate Beethoven, he asked his permission to play the C minor Concerto instead. Beethoven, in a characteristic rage at Ries's refusal, approached the young pianist Carl Friedrich Stein, brother of Nanette Streicher — wife-member of the celebrated Viennese firm of piano manufacturers.

Stein initially agreed to play the new concerto but, realizing the challenge of the undertaking, he later declined and, like Ries, asked permission to play the C minor Concerto. With time so short, Beethoven had little option but to give his consent. Ries reports the Concerto 'made no effect' and that 'Beethoven was very angry'.[107] Ries did, however, derive some satisfaction from the incident. He relates how, at the close of the concert several members of the audience — familiar with Ries's earlier interpretation of the work — remarked: 'Why didn't you let Ries play it, since he had such a success with it?' Ries concluded his account: 'These remarks gave me a great deal of pleasure.'[108]

The following year Beethoven had cause once more to return to the C minor Concerto — a full ten years since he set down tentative ideas for the work. As with its predecessors, Op. 19 and Op. 15, the Op. 37 Concerto underwent a prolonged period of gestation before finding its final form. By now, Beethoven had composed the first four of his piano concertos, bearing opus numbers, and the piano transcription of the Violin Concerto (see our later text). He had also written out cadenzas for the first and third movements of Mozart's Piano Concerto in D minor, K. 466 — as a parting gift for Ferdinand Ries prior to his leaving Vienna.

The cadenza, we recall, is the term used to describe a characteristically brilliant solo passage in a concerto that serves as a vehicle for the pianist to display a command of the keyboard. In the eighteenth-century, it was almost *de rigueur* for performers of a concerto to demonstrate their virtuosity and powers of spontaneous creativity in the form of extempore variations, and in embellishing and ornamenting melodic lines and themes in repeats — in all of which Beethoven, at the height of his powers, was without equal.

In 1796, Johann Ferdinand von Schönfield published a treatise under the title *Jahrbuch der Tonkünst von Wien und Prag* — 'Yearbook for the art of tone in Vienna and Prague'. Concerning instrumental ornamentation, he states: 'There are places where it is advantageous to insert much ornamentation.' However, the author cautions: 'This ... must be done with care and consideration in such a way that the basic emotion does not suffer, but is enhanced.'[109]

Von Schönfield was aware of the temptation, on the part of the more showy virtuoso, to get carried away and over-ornament extemporary passages to the disfigurement of the whole. Such abuse, in the nineteenth century, led some wit to describe the cadenza as 'the appendicitis of the concerto'!

In 1809, Beethoven revisited the piano concertos Opp. 15, 19, 37 and 58, providing each with new, or revised, cadenzas: Op. 15, three cadenzas for the first movement; Op. 19, one for the first movement; Op. 37, one for the first movement (there is a sketch for another cadenza for this movement in the Bodmer Collection in the Beethovenhaus at Bonn); and Op. 58, two for the first movement and one for the third movement.[110] As we shall see (text to Op. 73) Beethoven incorporated cadenza-writing directly into the score of the *Emperor* Concerto. An incentive to write these cadenzas was to provide material for his pupil and patron the Archduke Rudolph, the youngest son of Emperor Leopold II. Rudolph was an accomplished pianist and started to receive instruction from Beethoven at this time; Rudolph also has the distinction of being the composer's only composition pupil.

Kinderman characterizes the cadenza for the C minor Concerto as possessing 'a vast architectural logic'. He also draws attention to Beethoven's use of the extended trill that he describes as an 'unmeasured pulsation'.[111] The trill held particular fascination for Beethoven, as found near the conclusion of the early Piano Sonata, Op. 2, No. 3 – also in C minor – and perhaps its ultimate consummation in the last movement of his last Piano Sonata, Op. 111.

Donald Tovey was uncharacteristically critical of Beethoven's writing in the Op. 37 cadenza. He considered the Third Piano Concerto was 'ill served' by the later cadenza. He regarded the piece as being 'perfunctory and dry' on the grounds: '[Beethoven] can never have extemporised as feebly as that ...'. He went so far as to suggest Beethoven's 'absurd anachronisms' were such as to 'lull the listener's critical faculty' — harsh words, indeed, from the former doyen of Beethoven musicology.[112]

We discuss the musicology of the C minor Concerto in greater detail in our closing remarks. As a footnote to our present observations, the following is of related interest. In 1989 the American musicologist Robert Freeman discovered a number of cadenzas to Beethoven's concertos that were preserved in the archives of the Benedictine Abbey of Melk, situated in Lower Austria. These have since been identified as copies of the cadenzas Beethoven wrote in 1809. It is believed they were transcribed by Father Robert Stipa (1781—1850), a virtuoso fortepiano-pianist who served as Musical Director of the Abbey from 1828 until 1833. Stipa inscribed on his texts that they were copied 'directly from Beethoven's handwriting' — that is from his original manuscripts.[113]

Towards the end of his life, Beethoven complained of the public neglect of many of his works. This appears to have been the fate of the concertos according to the composer's biographer Anton Schindler. He lamented: '[The] virtuosi of the time approached the Beethoven concertos with unconcealed reluctance, while the public showed no liking or very little of them.' He adds: 'The C minor Concerto and The *Choral Fantasy* were each performed perhaps twice in fifteen years, and the Violin Concerto was performed ... by Franz Clement in 1806 with no success at all.' He adds:

'The principal cause of this neglect was a change
in the style of piano playing introduced by
Hummel, Moscheles, Czerny, and others. This

new style was totally foreign to Beethoven's music, both in form and in material. Its salient characteristics — elegance, polish, and technical display — were inappropriate to Beethoven's piano compositions and failed to convey to audiences the profound spiritual nature of the concertos.'[114]

Despite what Schindler has to say, the concertos were not entirely neglected in the ensuing years. In 1812, the horn player and composer Friedrich Starke met Beethoven and established a friendly relationship with him. He is credited with possessing a thorough knowledge of wind and string instruments to which he gave expression in his many musical arrangements — for example he adapted Beethoven's Overture *Egmont*. Starke published a piano tutor — *Wiener Pianoforte-Schule* — for which he commissioned contributions from Vienna's leading composers. Beethoven contributed the five Bagatelles Op. 119, the *Andante* and *Rondo* from the Pastoral Sonata, some passages from the Piano Sonata in D minor, Op. 31, No. 2, and 'a free arrangement' of the Coda from the last movement of the Third Piano Concerto. Starke paid homage to Beethoven in his *Pianoforte-Schule* by describing him as 'a star of the first magnitude in the musical firmament'.[115]

The pianist, composer and music teacher Anton Halm was a Beethoven enthusiast and gave a performance of the C minor Concerto in Graz on 16 April 1814. In Vienna, he took part in performances of other of the composer's works. One such occasion was a concert in the Kärntnertor Theater on 15 November 1817. The *Choral Fantasia* was the main attraction with Halm at the piano. The performance failed to impress, though, due to Halm not maintaining the correct tempo — and incurring Beethoven's displeasure thereby. By 1826, Beethoven appears to have set the incident aside since he consented to Halm making a four-hand piano arrangement of the celebrated *Grosse Fuge*, from the String Quartet, Op. 133. This had been requested by the music publisher Artaria.

Halm appears to have applied himself diligently to his task and on 24 April he wrote to Beethoven: 'I have finished your Fugue which I have the honour of sending along, with the greatest possible diligence and care!'[116] He also shared his views on the keyboard-setting required for the four instrumental voices. Notwithstanding Halm's care, the resulting transcription was not to Beethoven's satisfaction; he considered Halm had divided the parts too much, so as to avoid the crossing of hands. He duly made his own transcription whilst on his deathbed.[117]

According to the recollections of Ignaz Schuppanzigh, the Irish pianist and composer John Field visited Beethoven sometime in 1822. Schuppanzigh makes reference to Field having performed the C minor Concerto 'in the most beautiful way'. This may have been at a private gathering. Authorities caution that Schuppanzigh's anecdote should be taken *cum grano salis* since Field is known to have had reservations about Beethoven's music.[118]

We extend our account of the C minor Piano Concerto with a selection of anecdotes and recollections drawn from various periods in the nineteenth century and closer to our time.

Following Beethoven's death, a memorial concert was held in his honour on 4 May 1827. This was organized by members of the Concerts Spirituels and took place in Vienna's Provincial Assembly Hall. The programme included the first movement of Beethoven's Violin Concerto − long neglected − and the first movement of the C minor Piano Concerto. The main work performed was the Fifth Symphony.[119]

In 1817 the composer-pianist Cipriani Potter made Beethoven's acquaintance in the hope of receiving composition lessons. Beethoven declined – as we have seen, the composer's only composition pupil was the Archduke Rudolph. On 29 April 1836, Potter recalled his meeting with Beethoven in an article for *The Musical Times* under the title *Recollections of Beethoven*. In this he sought to dispel the then popular view of the composer as being 'a morose and ill-tempered man'. He insisted: 'This opinion is perfectly erroneous.' Potter acknowledged Beethoven could be irritable, passionate, and sometimes of a melancholy mind but all of which affectations he believed arose from his deafness. Regarding Beethoven the composer, Potter stated: 'The most prominent feature in Beethoven's music is the *originality* of his ideas.' With Beethoven's growing fame, and deepening understanding of his music, Potter's article was republished in *The Musical Times* on 1 December 1861 – the year of the London Great Exhibition. This may not be entirely co-incidental, since several of Beethoven's works were subsequently performed at its venue in the Crystal Palace.

We have remarked that Potter performed the Piano Concerto, Op. 15 for the first time in England on 15 May 1822. He also has the added distinction of performing the C minor Concerto in England for the first time. This took place on 6 March 1824 as part of the London concert season of the (Royal) Philharmonic Society – of which Potter was a founder-member. Of related interest is that the conductor for the occasion was Sir George Smart. Smart, like Potter, was personally acquainted with Beethoven – the two met in 1825 – and he too was a founder member of the Philharmonic Society. Smart continued to conduct the concerts of the Philharmonic Society until 1841. Writing about Beethoven in *The Musical times* of 29 April 1836, he remarked: The most prominent feature in Beethoven's music is the *originality* of his ideas, even in his mode of treating a subject, and in the conduct throughout of a composition. No author is so free from the charge of *mannerism* than Beethoven.'[120]

Heinrich Adami, a contributor to the *Wiener Allgemeine Theaterzeitung*, writes of Franz Liszt's performances in Vienna in 1839. He relates:

'The enthusiasm which this great virtuoso is exciting cannot be described ... Not since Paganini has an artist made such a magical impression on the Viennese public.'

On 4 December 1839, Liszt performed the *Appassionata* Sonata that disposed Adami to enthuse:

'For younger listeners ... who never had the opportunity of hearing Beethoven himself play his piano sonatas and concertos, Liszt's renderings are of exceptional interest, and from them they are best able to study these works.'[121]

In his maturity, Liszt wrote transcriptions of all five Beethoven concertos for two pianos, giving the orchestral tutti to one instrument and reserving the piano part for the other. These were subsequently published by the publishing house founded by Johann Georg Cotta.[122]

The Franco-German romantic author and historian Comtesse Marie d'Agoult lived openly with Franz Liszt between the years 1836–39, despite being married with two children. On 6 December 1839 Liszt – then age 28 – wrote to Marie of the progress of the series of concerts he was then giving in Vienna. Such was his popularity that a single concert earned for him 1,700 florins (about 4,000 francs). He complained the dinners and banquettes in his honour 'were killing him'. He informed Marie how he had to learn the C minor Concerto in just twenty-four hours and improvised a cadenza 'with the most unheard success'.[123]

Many authorities consider Camille Saint-Saëns to be one of the most remarkable musical child-prodigies in history. On 6 May 1846, when only ten years of age, he made his official public debut at the Salle Pleyel, Paris. He opened his concert with Mozart's B flat Piano Concerto, K. 450. It is reported: 'From this moment on his audience listened in fascination.' Following this, he played a number of solos including a sonata by Hummel and a prelude and fugue by Bach. At the close of the concert he was rejoined by the orchestra in Beethoven's C minor Concerto. In quiet passages the audience admired 'the softness and delicacy of his touch' and when the piano was challenged by the orchestra 'they were astonished at the power that seemed to flow so easily from his fingers'. What is all the more remarkable is that Saint-Saëns played all these works from memory and, at the close of the concert, he offered to play any one of Beethoven's piano sonatas – also from memory!

Apocryphal as the foregoing may seem, this testimony to the youthful Saint Saëns's musical memory is well substantiated. Moreover, critics praised the young Camille for his restrained style of playing remarking: '[There] were no writhings at the keyboard, no tossing around of the hair, in fact, nothing of the *enfant terrible*.'[124]

The reader will recall Anton Schindler had cause to regret how, during Beethoven's lifetime, much of his piano music – notably the sonatas and concertos – were neglected. When writing his Beethoven *Biography* in 1860, he felt able to revise this opinion:

'[Recent] times have expiated the sins of the past by retrieving these works from library dust and restoring them to their place: technique has assumed its proper relationship to genius, so that Beethoven's works now rightfully stand above all others.'[125]

Clara Schuman is regarded as one of the most distinguished pianists of the Romantic era. She exerted her influence over a 60-year concert career, changing the format and repertoire of the piano recital from displays of virtuosity to programmes of serious works. For example, in Vienna's music season of 1837–38, when Clara was just eighteen, she gave a series of recitals to packed audiences; her concerts typically included a number of piano sonatas by Beethoven. Franz Grillparzer — Austria's leading dramatic poet who had officiated at Beethoven's funeral ten years before — heard Clara perform and was so moved by her playing he composed a poem in her honour, adopting her maiden name, entitled *Clara Wieck and Beethoven*. When Frédérick Chopin heard Clara perform, he so fulsomely described her playing to Franz Liszt that he promptly attended one of her recitals and wrote a laudatory review for the Parisian *Revue Musicale*.

An entry in Clara's Diary, of November 1868, sheds light on music-making in parts of Germany at this time. After giving a concert tour — performing in Oldenburg, Bremen, and Berlin — she wrote: 'I played Beethoven's C minor Concerto for the first time [which seems hardly credible].' She adds: 'This Concerto was very hackneyed at one time, and that is why I did not study it; now one seldom hears it.' Notwithstanding her reservations, she concludes her entry with a touch of pride: 'I made a cadenza for it which I really do not think is bad.'[126]

By a rather remarkable coincidence, we have a similar

diary entry from the following year. Gabriel Fauré studied piano with Camille Saint-Saëns for whom he was given to express his admiration and unceasing gratitude. A diary entry for 1869 – when he was age 24 – records that he composed a cadenza for the C minor Concerto.[127]

The Austrian composer Hugo Wolf is known and admired for his contribution to nineteenth-century German lied, but he also left a considerable body of music criticism; in 1883 he was appointed music critic of the Wiener Salonblatt. His weekly reviews are valued for the insights they provide into the Viennese music-making of his day. He could be unsparing – excoriating – in his criticism as we discern from the 27 February 1887 issue of the Wiener Salonblatt:

> 'Fräulein Marie Pohl [a young pianist] who now abused Beethoven's Piano Concerto in C minor was ill-advised to poke her nose into matters becoming solely and exclusively to that avenging angel Hans von Bülow.'

Bülow is remembered today as an eminent conductor but in his own time was recognised as a virtuoso pianist. Perhaps there was too much, though, of the titan of the keyboard for Wolf, in Bülow's style of interpreting Beethoven, as is implied in the rest of Wolf's review: '[Bülow], at least, kills Beethoven with respect and good manners, rather systematically, and that, too, is an art.' Returning to Fräulein Pohl's interpretation of the C minor Concerto, Wolf railed:

> 'But to fall blindly upon the Titan [Beethoven] as upon a finger exercise by Czerny is going too far. Respect for genius! Beethoven is no children's playground, his spirit no proper nourish-

ment for the immature impulses of adolescent females. He is not the composer for kindergartens and nurseries.'[128]

The American composer Amy Beach is acknowledged for being a pioneering female composer of large-scale orchestral works. She was also highly regarded as a concert pianist. On 21 April 1888, she performed Beethoven's Third Piano Concerto with the Boston Symphony Orchestra. It is a measure of her indomitable spirit that she set aside Beethoven's cadenza for one of her own composition. By any measure, it was a major endeavour with a performing time of a third of the whole of the first movement. This disposed one critic to suggest her cadenza might benefit 'from some judicious cutting', but he pardoned Beach for basing her conception 'entirely — and correctly — on themes from the movement' that he considered, thereby, 'connected the cadenza seamlessly to the body of the movement'.

A review in the contemporary journal *The Beacon*, complemented Beach on her 'sustained and yet splendid style of playing' and also for her 'bold, large and shining cadenza'. The critic of the sister journal *The Home Journal* similarly enthused, describing the cadenza as being no less 'a masterpiece that is entitled to rank with some of the most important productions of its class'.[129]

George Bernhard Shaw is known and admired for being a dramatist and social reformer, but in his day he was also recognised as a respected music critic; his collected music criticism extends to three sturdy volumes.[130] From the accounts of his playing four-hand arrangements of Beethoven's symphonies, with his sister, we can also infer he was a capable pianist.

Shaw's version of the ideal music critic was not a mere passive reporter of musical events but rather 'a vital and initiating force within the music community'.[131] Shaw had no time for what we have earlier described as a 'showy style of performance' – the hallmarks of good performing style, for him, were authenticity and adherence to the composer's text. We detect this in a review of his from 28 January 1891, when he attended a London recital given by the nineteen-year old, German pianist Bernhard Stavenhagen – a pupil of Franz Liszt. Shaw writes:

> 'Stavenhagen played the C minor Concerto of Beethoven, but hardly succeeded in getting back to its date. The first movement, which made hardly any effect, is, when properly handled, grand in the old-fashioned way; and the *Largo* is anything but trivial, though it sounded a little so on Thursday.'

Shaw considered Stavenhagen's style was more suited to playing the music of his former teacher, however, he acknowledged the young man's strength, intelligence and skill and recognised 'more would be said of him in the future'. These words proved to be prophetic as Stavenhagen embarked on a highly successful ten-year series of concert-tours in Europe and North America.[132]

During the years 1891–97, the Austrian-American pianist-composer-pedagogue Artur Schnabel studied piano in Vienna with the celebrated titan of the keyboard Theodor Leschetitzky. Schnabel was the first pianist to record the entire cycle of the Beethoven piano sonatas; such was his devotion to Beethoven's piano works that the music critic Harold C. Schonberg once described Schnabel as 'the man who invented Beethoven'.[133] Schnabel is also respected for championing the once neglected piano sonatas of Franz Schubert. Recalling his student days in Vienna, what Schnabel has to say, regarding the C minor Concerto, appears to confirm Clara Schuman's remarks — 'now one seldom hears it'. He recalls: 'In Vienna the C minor Concerto was only played in conservatories by the lower grades.'[134]

We associate Sir Charles Hallé's name with that of the Hallé Orchestra that he founded. In his early years, however, he was celebrated as an accomplished pianist who, when in Paris, enjoyed the company of Chopin and Liszt. English audiences owed much to Hallé; for example, he was the first pianist in England to perform the entire cycle of Beethoven's piano sonatas — first in London, on several occasions, and later in Manchester.

Hallé agreed to participate in the 1895 Manchester concert season. On the night of 25 October, whilst practising the C minor Concerto, he was taken ill and died shortly afterwards of a cerebral haemorrhage. The *Guardian* newspaper reflected: 'He never failed to impress those who came under his influence.' George Bernhard Shaw praised Hallé for his restrained style of playing Beethoven, remarking, with a touch of his characteristic wit: 'He gave you more of Beethoven and less of Hallé.'[135]

The Australian pianist, composer and arranger of folk music Percy Grainger gave his first public recital in Melbourne at the age of twelve — including works by Beethoven. In 1903, Grainger studied with the eminent pianist Ferruccio Busoni. Later, when performing in London, The Times critic reported how Grainger's playing 'revealed rare intelligence and a good deal of artistic insight'. On 1 January 1897, he wrote to Dr. Henry O'Hara — an acquaintance in his hometown of Melbourne: 'I am now practising the first movement of Beethoven's Concerto in C minor, a very difficult thing and beyond me in technique — but a splendid piece.' Grainger was then just fifteen years old. He enthused to Dr. O'Hara: 'Concertos are lovely things to practice and

Beethoven was such a master of them, for instance his glorious E-flat major is a real masterpiece.'[136]

For many music lovers the Polish-American classical pianist Arthur Rubinstein is inseparably associated with the music of Chopin. This is, however, to the detriment of the international acclaim he received for his performances of music written by a variety of composers. From his Autobiography, *My Many Years*, Rubinstein recalls the occasion, sometime in the mid 1920s, when he performed at a concert in Rome's Augusto Concert Hall. This was the first time he had played Beethoven's C minor Concerto in public and he relates: 'I remember this concert particularly well because I feel a special love for this Concerto and had, at last, the chance to play with a fine orchestra.'

The pianist and music teacher Heinrich Barth had recommended he should play the cadenza by Clara Schuman (see above) but apparently it was not to Rubinstein's liking. Concerning the cadenzas provided by the composer, Rubinstein comments: 'The original cadenzas by Beethoven were discarded by all the pianists in those times and these wonderful originals came into their own only many years later.' Of his performance he states: '[My] happiness in playing this work must have been so great that it reached the audience; it turned out to be one of my best concerts in Rome.'[137]

In the autumn of 1944, Rubinstein received an invitation from Arturo Toscanini — then head of the NBC Orchestra — to take part in a series of Beethoven concerts that included his five piano concertos. Toscanini invited different pianists to participate, and selected Rubinstein to play the C minor Concerto. Rubenstein records how he was 'thrilled to have the chance to make music with the great conductor and ... was also fascinated to meet him at last'. To his surprise, Rubinstein discovered it was the first time Toscanini had conducted the work and was, therefore, uncharacteristically nervous. Rubinstein was also nervous — being mindful of the maestro's fiery temper. However, according to his account, the subsequent performance was a success.

Rubinstein recalls:

'The tempo was right ... and the tutti sounded with all the nuances required. Toscanini did not miss one tiny detail. He was right there, and we finished every phrase beautifully together. He respected all my dynamics, held up the orchestra where I made the tiniest rubato, came in after the cadenza on the dot, and we finished ... with a flourish.'

The performance, which had been recorded, was later released by the RCA recording company. What is more remarkable is that, just one hour later, Rubinstein gave a Chopin recital at the Carnage Hall — 'to rapturous acclaim'.[138]

The English pianist and musicologist Dennis Matthews, writing of his student days, recalls having to give his first performance of the C minor Concerto: 'It was somewhat alarming for a novice to find himself about to play the Beethoven C minor Concerto'. He adds, with an entertaining sustained metaphor:

'I am relieved to recall that I did not drown on my maiden voyage with the Beethoven C minor: as for "sinking or swimming," I remember falling overboard halfway through the finale, but I had by then acquired sufficient confidence for my fingers to tread water, as it were, until my mind was able to rescue them!'

Reflecting on the period in question – the late 1930s – he remarks more generally:

> 'According to box-office statistics, the concerto is still the most popular of all serious musical forms: it is perhaps doubly satisfying to hear and see a soloist, in a glamorous orchestral setting, fighting a battle of brain and brawn against odds of sixty-or-more to one.'

Later in his career, Mathews performed the C minor Concerto on a number of occasions. One of these took place in Brighton where the Op. 37 was the centrepiece of the concert. Mathews suggested to the concert manager that the programme should state that the cadenza to be played was Beethoven's own, that Matthews describes as Beethoven's 'grandest and longest'. A misunderstanding appears to have ensued since the review of the concert, in the following morning's newspaper, stated: 'With the audacity and pre-sumption of youth, Mr. Matthews interpolated a massive cadenza of his own invention.' Mathews reflected: 'I was naturally flattered to have been thought capable of compos-ing it myself.' He initially considered phoning the music critic, adopting the guise of the composer, and saying: 'This is Beethoven speaking. I wrote the cadenza!'[139]

The Canadian pianist Glen Gould recalls an exchange of badinage with the celebrated conductor Leopold Stokowski. In 1977, it chanced that both of them were due to perform at the Vienna Festival. Gould proudly informed Stokowski that he was programmed to perform 'the Beethoven Third' under the direction of Herbert von Karajan. According to Gould, Stokowski counterfeited ignorance of the Op. 37 Concerto, remaking: 'Is that not the lovely Concerto in G major?' Gould knew well that he was being teased and recalled:

'[Stokowski] was not in awe of the *Generalmusik-direktor* [Karajan] of Europe, [and] that soloists, as a breed, were to be shunned on principle, and that concertos, as a symphonic sub-species, were quite beneath his notice.'[140]

The American pianist, author and teacher David Dubal interviewed several distinguished concert pianists including the Chilean-born Claudio Arrau. Arrau recollected his youthful days in Berlin where he heard such legends of the keyboard as Eugene d'Albert and Ferruccio Busoni. This was the era of monumental piano-playing concerts. Arrau, for example, recalls the occasion when Busoni once performed no fewer than nine Mozart concertos in a single evening! In the same spirit, the Venezuelan virtuoso pianist Teresa Carreño — coincidentally the wife of d'Albert — performed Beethoven's Third, Fourth and Fifth Concertos in a single programme. Legend has it that she kept a revolver by her piano to intimidate anyone who threatened to disrupt her practicing! [141]

We draw our discussion of Beethoven's Piano Concerto No.3 in C minor, Op. 37 to a close in the form of a documentary-style collection of texts. These are derived from the writings of musicologists and performing artists bearing on the musicology of the Op. 37 Concerto. For a moment, though, we may imagine we are in the presence of the composer himself whilst he was performing — as was his pupil Carl Czerny on so-many occasions. Czerny recalls: 'Beethoven played with rounded fingers that constantly touched the keys in a gliding manner suggestive of a largo style ... He used a lot of pedal — much more than indicated in his works.'[142]

The texts that follow are presented in the chronological order of their publication.

FIRST MOVEMENT
ALLEGRO CON BRIO

'After the long pause at the end of the *tutti,* begins
the solo in a steady, but not too rapid time, [to be
played] with energy and decision.'

Carl Czerny, *On the Proper Performance of all Beethoven's
Works for Piano,* 1846, edited, with commentary, by Paul
Badura-Skoda, 1970, p. 97.

'The last C minor bars of the first movement,
leading us straight into E major (second movement), produces at once the later Beethoven, that
is, the lifting us at once into another sphere, or,
so-to-say, on another star.'

Fanny Davies, *The Pianoforte Concertos* in: *The Musical
Times, Special Issue* edited by John A. Fuller-Maitland, Vol.
VIII, No. 2, 1927, p. 226.

'Now comes a turning point in the history of the
classical concerto. The opening orchestral ritornello of the first movement in the concerto form
had been developed by Mozart on a scale that has
not to this day been surpassed; with the result that
the entry of the solo instrument must, if it means
anything at all, mean an event impressive because
long delayed ... The main theme is a group of
pregnant figures which nobody but Beethoven
could have invented. They would rank as important themes in his latest works; but he here states
them, quite successfully and unselfconsciously, in
the tonic and-dominant symmetries that still interested him for their own sake in his first period.'

Donald Francis Tovey, *Essays in Musical Analysis*, Vol. 3, 1935–41, p. 70.

> 'Strings alone announce quietly the first strain of the main subject ... this is answered, a step higher, by the winds and is completed by a descending phrase, still within the compass of a fifth, derivable from the main theme and accompanied by a bass derived from the first bar ... The solo, leading off with the main theme, now presents a far more colourful version of the expository tutti than was given in the First Concerto. Energetic left-hand passages, in particular, give much weight to the closing section. The background of the passages is derived from the main theme.'

Donald Nivison Ferguson, *Masterworks of the Orchestral Repertoire: A Guide for Listeners,* 1954, p. 103.

> 'The opening sixteen-bar paragraph, with its direct, unadorned thematic statement, rhythmic emphasis, and hammered *ff* cadence, conveys both energy and structural force. But the intensity of impact is lessened in the following passage by the immediate modulation to the relative-major key and the subsequent move to C major. From then onwards, the interplay of major and minor modes is the distinctive factor in the tonal structure.'

Basil Deane, *The Concertos* in: Denis Arnold and Nigel Fortune, editors, *The Beethoven Companion*, 1973.

> 'During the opening ritornello of Beethoven's

Third Concerto, not only is the piano waiting for its moment to enter, but the orchestra is determining the moment.'

Edward T. Cone, *Ernst Block Lectures*, 1972, published later as: *The Composer's Voice*, 1974.

'While one might argue with some conviction that both the opening theme and the closing pages of the first movement show some indebtedness to Mozart's great C minor Concerto, the scale of the work is substantially larger. Here, for the first time, we find the soloist beginning to assume the *heroic* role that was to become the hallmark of the virtuoso concertos of Chopin, Liszt, Brahms or Rachmaninoff. The instrument for which Beethoven was writing was not yet capable of the physical domination that we find in the *Emperor* Concerto, some ten years, later but the aspiration to such dominance is certainly there ...Veiled arpeggios from the piano add moonlight glitter to the scene. Almost imperceptibly a sense of urgency creeps in until a sudden outburst from the full orchestra elicits a torrent of notes from the keyboard culminating in rising scales through four octaves, an extension of the initial rhetorical gesture that is perfectly placed.'

Antony Hopkins, *The Concertgoer's Companion*, 1984, p. 86 and p. 89.

'The two Piano Concertos in C minor (Mozart's K. 491 and Beethoven's No. 3) are particularly close, both opening in a similar way with a unison theme initially stated *piano* but later *forte*. Beethoven's Concerto is also his first to feature the piano in the first-movement coda – a further feature adapted from K. 491, the only Mozart concerto where this happens ... [The] soloist's entry is noteworthy in that it is particularly dramatic in order to counterbalance the orchestral opening. The piano opens with three imposing scale passages which lead to a four-octave presentation of the principal theme. This flourish immediately attracts the listener's attention, and it establishes the virtuoso role of the piano.'

Barry Cooper, *The Beethoven Compendium: A Guide to Beethoven's Life and Music*, 1991, p. 83 and p. 218.

'The opening theme in C minor is typical of this period. It is compact and made up of very simple materials, which are amenable to intense development while passing through various keys.'

Michael Thomas Roeder, *A History of the Concerto*, 1994, p. 183.

'[Three] scales, uncompromisingly marked *forte*, lead to the opening themes in octaves, both hands, a statement of a boldness that, so far as I know, had never been known before. In order to make absolutely sure of his intentions, Beethoven not only repeats the *forte* injunction but even adds a *sf* (strong accent) on the top of the phrase.'

Antony Hopkins, *The Seven Concertos of Beethoven*, 1996, pp. 34–35.

'The ensuing entrance of the solo piano is forti-
fied by ascending scales leading to the principal
subject boldly proclaimed in octaves ...
Beethoven's treatment of his main theme in the
solo cadenza is especially original and displays a
vast architectural logic ... [He] dwells at length on
the interval of a rising third from its first bar, as
brilliant arpeggiations carry on the music into
distant regions ... Strictly considered, the cadenza
embraces not only the solo but also the timpani
statements.'

William Kinderman, *Beethoven*, 1997, p. 109.

'For this movement, as for the first movements
of the two preceding concertos, we have a
cadenza by Beethoven, but from a later date,
possibly 1809, and an assertive and pianistically
brilliant affair it is. Even more remarkable is
Beethoven's way of bringing the orchestra back
in after the cadenza: here we sense one of his
periodic stirrings to question the conventional
ways of handling major points of demarcation ...
In the C minor Concerto, in lieu of the normal
cadenza-ending with a trill on the dominant and
a *forte* orchestral entry, he gives us something
mysterious and tension-laden which, in a completely unexpected way, also at last brings together
the [previously heard] timpani figure with the
timpani themselves.'

Michael Steinberg, *The Concerto: A Listener's Guide*, 1998,
pp. 56–57.

'The orchestral exposition, as in virtually all his previous concertos ... spends much time away from the home key, before returning to it towards the end. The initial unison phrase for the strings is full of possibilities for development, which are exploited in the rest of the movement ...'.

Barry Cooper, *Beethoven, The Master Musicians*, 2000, p. 125.

'There is a lengthy orchestral introduction, which summarizes, like an overture to an opera, the entire content of the first movement, *Allegro con brio*. Both principal subjects, the dramatic first theme in C minor and the romantic contrasting subject in E-flat major, are explicitly stated.'

Nicolas Slonimsky, *The Great Composers and their Works: edited by Electra Slonimsky Yourke*, 2000, p. 142.

SECOND MOVEMENT
LARGO

By way of introduction, we recall Carl Czerny's recollection once more that Beethoven used the soft pedal more than indicted in his published scores. It is from Czerny we learn 'he performed the entire *Largo* with his foot on the pedal'.[143] Writing of what he describes as the 'notorious pedal indications' at the opening of the slow movement, Charles Rosen asserts:

'[It] is not the sustaining of the bass that is essential but the richness of the sonority ... What is significant in this passage is not where the pedal is to be held down, but where it is to be released.'[144]

Ernest Newman reasons:

> 'Beethoven ... depressed the pedal throughout this theme, which worked very well on the weak-sounding pianos of the time ... But now, with a much stronger tone, we must advise that the damper pedal be reapplied with each significant change of harmony, yet so that no break in the tone can be noticed. For the whole theme must sound like a distant, holy, unearthly harmony'.[145]

Musicologists Eugene Wolf and Edward Roesner suggest a compromise:

> 'It is hardly necessary to repeat that Beethoven's pedal marks must be obeyed to the letter, at least in using half pedal. We may assume that audiences are no longer shocked by the blur effect which Beethoven intended in places. This applies particularly to the opening of the slow movement of the Concerto Op. 37 that Czerny heard Beethoven play ...'.[146]

> 'This is assuredly one of the most expressive and emotionally rich instrumental pieces that has ever been written, and if is well performed by the soloist and the entire orchestra (which, however, is of no little significance here) and does not create a sensation, the fault can only be with the audience ... Beethoven has brought into play here

all the means that this instrument possesses for
the expression of gentle feelings.'

Derived from the review in the *Allgemeine musikalische
Zeitung* of 10 April 1805, as recalled by Wayne M. Senner,
Robin Wallace and William Meredith, editors, *The Critical
Reception of Beethoven's Compositions by his German
Contemporaries*, 1999, Vol. 1, p. 206.

'The *Largo* is the most highly developed slow
movement in all Beethoven's concertos, and *a
fortiori* in any concerto. In his later concertos the
slow movements lead into the finales; gaining
thereby dramatic subtleties and depths by the
necessity of completing their own design. But in
the C minor Concerto we have one of the great
independent symphonic slow movements, reaching the climax of Beethoven's powers of solemn
expression in his first period, and indeed quite in
keeping with all that he found to say in his second.'

Donald Francis Tovey, *Essays in Musical Analysis*, Vol. 3,
1935–41, p. 73.

'The *Largo* speaks of an aspect of nobility which
the early nineteenth century, imbued with a good
deal of philosophy of the Revolution, by no
means disdained to contemplate; it speaks wor-
thily of that topic — which is not easy to do. To
make his message the more impressive,
Beethoven chose the very distant key of E major,
and allowed the solo instrument, quite unaccompanied, to set forth the essence of the thought.'

Donald Nivison Ferguson, *Masterworks of the Orchestral Repertoire: A Guide for Listeners*, 1954, p. 104.

> The *Largo* is in the distant key of E major. The contrast of tonality is striking even disjunctive. Rarely does Beethoven juxtapose two such unrelated keys ... E major strikes the ear without preparation ... The richly ornamented style of the solo writing is also in great contrast to the first movement.'

Basil Dean, *The Concertos* in: Denis Arnold and Nigel Fortune, editors, *The Beethoven Companion*, 1973, p. 322.

> 'Throughout, the writing for the piano is powerful, often brilliant and, in the slow movement (unusually, for a work in C minor, in E major), full of luxuriant decorative writing which shows Beethoven making full use of the increased compass and possibilities of the instrument.'

R. Kinloch Anderson, *Beethoven, Piano Concertos*, Liner notes to *Classics for Pleasure*, EMI, 1977.

> 'The *Largo* which follows is remarkable in many ways. First, the key (E major) is almost as remote from C minor as it is possible to be, instantly taking us into a different world; secondly, it begins with an extensive meditation for solo piano, a device that Beethoven uses in no other concerto; thirdly, the movement is complete in itself, whereas the slow movements of the Fourth and Fifth Concertos are linked by subtle means to the finales; lastly, not only is it the most highly

developed of all the concerto slow movements but it is also the most elaborate in ornamentation.'

Antony Hopkins, *The Concertgoer's Companion*, 1984, p. 89.

Hopkins returned once more to the C minor Concerto:

'The piano begins the movement, setting a tempo for the orchestra ... The theme contains a striking modulation into the key of G major ... [This] meditation is notable for two further points. One is a strange *tremolando* effect to be found in the left hand which would not surprise us in Liszt but is unusual in Beethoven; the other is the fact that this quite lengthy solo, at the beginning of the slow movement, is unique to this Concerto. In all other concertos of Beethoven, it is the orchestra that sets the mood with an introduction that may only be brief, but which is always significant.'

Antony Hopkins, *The Seven Concertos of Beethoven*, 1996, pp. 38–39.

'In the first movement, the note E natural (as opposed to E flat) has been emphasized by means of long-term strategy. It becomes the tonality of the beautiful E major *Largo*, the largest and noblest of Beethoven's early slow movements, its gravity worthy of Gluck and its depth purely its own. There is enormous breadth and calm, a profound, unusually sustained maturity of feeling that Beethoven seems always to have possessed.'

Robert Simpson, *Beethoven and the Concerto* in: Robert Layton, editor, *A Guide to the Concerto*, 1996, p. 111.

'The slow movement is a reflective *Largo*, whose expressive contrast to the pathos of the outer movements is heightened by the brighter tonal colour of E major as the tonic key.'

William Kinderman, *Beethoven*, 1997, pp. 109–10.

'Beethoven sometimes set his slow movements in remote keys. Here he chooses E major, and the sound of that first hushed chord on the piano is a shock that does not lose its magic. This *Largo* is a movement of immeasurable depth, beautiful melodies, and wonderful sounds. The sheerly sensuous element is manifest with special magic in the quietly suspended transition passages in which the dialogue of flute and bassoon is accompanied by plucked strings and wide-ranging, delicate piano arpeggios.'

Michael Steinberg, *The Concerto: A Listener's Guide*, 1998, p. 63.

'The second movement is noteworthy for being in the key of E major — evoking a completely different world from C minor.'

Barry Cooper *Beethoven, The Master Musicians*, 2000, p. 125.

'The central *Largo* is among Beethoven's most exalted lyrical creations, featuring a piano part which demands great sensitivity in phrasing, and gloriously eloquent writing for strings. As the music proceeds, the florid decorations of the piano seem to anticipate the style of Chopin, while at the heart of the movement there is a quasi-operatic duet for bassoon and flute, set against impressionistic piano arpeggios.'

Terry Barfoot, *Piano Concerto No. 3, Radio 3, Beethoven Experience*, 8 June 2005.

THIRD MOVEMENT
RONDO — ALLEGRO SCHERZANDO
'The theme of this finale, though plaintive, must be performed with artless simplicity, without being spun out, except the last three bars, which are to be played *ritardando* and with humour.'

Carl Czerny, *On the Proper Performance of all Beethoven's Works for Piano*, 1846, edited with commentary by Paul Badura-Skoda, 1970, p. 98.

'This great *Rondo* is an admirable study in temper, worthy of the wisdom that inspired the tragic style of the other movements. Among the works with which this Concerto is always provoking comparison, by reason of its singularly direct influence on later composers, three finales are conspicuous — those of Joachim's *Hungarian* Concerto, Brahms's First Piano Concerto, and Mendelssohn's C minor Trio.'

Donald Francis Tovey, *Essays in Musical Analysis*, Vol. 3, 1935–41, p. 74.

'Certainly, the piano concerto as such could never be the same again after Beethoven had written his Third'.

R. Kinloch Anderson, *Beethoven; Piano Concertos*, Liner notes to *Classics for Pleasure*, EMI, 1977.

'A more-or-less conventional recapitulation follows leading to a brief cadenza which ends with the same joke that we find at the start of the finale of the First Symphony — a series of ascending scales, climbing a step further each time until, after a fraught pause, the music spills into a happily vivacious tune ... and the movement ends in a mood of wild exuberance, the notes spilling over each other like the champagne overflowing.'

Antony Hopkins, *The Concertgoer's Companion*, 1984, p. 91.

'The boisterous rondo-finale opens with a single G in the piano, providing some harmonic shock after the finale E major triad of the Largo. Beethoven exploits the conflict between G natural and C sharp at several places in the movement. He also includes his typical rondo episode in minor this time on the main theme in F minor.'

Michael Thomas Roeder, *A History of the Concerto*, 1994, p. 184.

'Beethoven liked to refer to his moments of good humour as his *unbuttoned* mood, and here he truly seems to have relaxed. After the rather sombre opening of the Concerto and the profound feelings expressed so eloquently in the slow movement, it is good that the clouds finally disperse in these eminently enjoyable final pages.

'The tune is taken over joyfully by violins and flute, eliciting a clatter of triplet semiquavers from the pianist which sound like the musical equivalent of peals of laughter. A few Scarlatti-like leaps of two octaves merely add to the fun, before the strings adopt a more sober note by introducing yet another element in smooth counterpoint. Indeed, after the high spirits of what has gone before it seems positively academic.'

Antony Hopkins, *The Seven Concertos of Beethoven*, 1996, pp. 40–42.

'So this is after all a great and deep masterwork, in no need to fear irrelevant comparison with Mozart or anybody else. None of its critics could have attempted anything like it, for Beethoven himself could not have achieved it without fully understanding what their misunderstanding suggested he did not know.'

Robert Simpson, *Beethoven and the Concerto* in: Robert Layton, editor, *A Guide to the Concerto*, 1996, p. 111.

'Beethoven's rondo design makes room for a dream-like recall of E major in the central section – a glimpse of the slow movement seen through the veil of the rondo theme ... The expressive atmosphere of the coda is unmistakably that of the *opera buffa* finale; comic wit and jubilation crown the denouement of this drama of tones.'

William Kinderman, *Beethoven*, 1997, p. 110.

'This movement ... has a cadenza near the end, and, like Mozart in *his* concerto in the same key, Beethoven has the music emerge from that cadenza with a rush to the finish in a new key (C major), a new meter (6/8), and a new tempo (*presto*).'

Michael Steinberg, *The Concerto: A Listener's Guide*, 1998, p. 63.

'The rondo finale is high spirited, but beneath the surface there seems to lurk a more intense emotional mood; this is soon confirmed at the first climax, when the trumpets and timpani hammer out the rhythm.'

Terry Barfoot, *Piano Concerto No. 3, Radio 3, Beethoven Experience*, 8 June 2005.

[1] Antony Hopkins, 1996, p. 31. Musicologist Michael Steinberg acknowledges Beethoven's debt to Mozart stating: 'In his C major Concerto, Op. 15, Beethoven had before him the C major models of Mozart's K. 415, K. 467, and K. 503 and in his C minor Concerto, Op. 37, that of Mozart's K. 491.' Michael Steinberg, 1998, p. 60.
[2] R. Kinloch Anderson, *Beethoven, Piano Concertos, Liner Notes to Classic for Pleasure*, EMI, 1977.
[3] Beethoven writing from Prague, on 19 February 1796, to his brother Johann in

Vienna. Emily Anderson editor and translator, 1961, Vol. 1, Letter No. 16, pp. 22–23.

4 Wayne M. Senner, Robin Wallace and William Meredith editors, *The Critical Reception of Beethoven's Compositions by his German Contemporaries*, 1999, Vol. 1, p. 213.

5 Donald Nivison Ferguson, 1954, p. 103.

6 Barry Cooper, 2000, p. 125 and elsewhere in other of Cooper's extensive Beethoven writings.

7 William Kinderman, 1997, pp. 64–65.

8 Leon Plantinga, 1999, p. 254.

9 Donald Francis Tovey, *Essays in Musical Analysis*, Vol.3, 1935–41, p. 64.

10 Theodore Albrecht, editor and translator, 1996, Vol. 1, Letter No. 34, pp. 63–4.

11 For a reproduction of the Neidl and Riedl studies of Beethoven see: H. C. Robbins Landon, 1992, plates 3 and 4.

12 Derived from the text to, Beethoven House Library Document HCB Bi 1. See also H. C. Robbins Landon, 1970, text to plate 5.

13 Beethoven House Digital Archives, *Beethoven Gallery* and Library Document B 2388. See also: H. C. Robbins Landon, 1992, plate 6.

14 'These devices could variously raise the dampers, providing a sustained tone (sometimes the two halves of the keyboard could be affected separately); shift the action sideways, enabling *una corda* and /or *due corda* effects; dampen the tone, by sliding material between the strings and the hammers; or produce special effects, such as lute or percussion.' Barry Cooper, 1991, p. 287.

15 *Ibid.*

16 *Ibid.*

17 To quote Cooper once more: 'Commentators today wonder why he did not amend his early piano works to take account of the enlarged compass of later pianos; the reason seems to be that he saw many other faults besides the awkward figuration that had sometimes resulted from a restricted compass,, and had he begun revising, the whole operation would have taken some considerable time and would really have necessitated a complete new edition of all his works.' Source, as given above.

18 On 27 December 1817, Broadwood selected from his warehouse a six-octave Grand Piano, No. 7362 that was carefully packed in a deal case with a waterproof lining of tin foil; this was then delivered to a Mr. Farlowe of London ready for shipment to Trieste. The choice of particular instrument was in part made by a small group of distinguished musicians of the day. As a measure of their respect and esteem for the recipient, they test-played and signed the piano before it was sent away. The musicians involved in the enterprise were John Baptiste Cramer, Jaques Godfroi, Friedrich Kalkbrenner, Charles Knyvett and Ferdinand Ries. They each inscribed the piano with their signatures alongside the inscription: *Hoc Instrumentum est Thomae Broadwood (Londrini) donum propter ingenium illustrissime Beethoven* – 'This instrument is a proper gift from Thomas Broadwood to the great Beethoven.' Broadwood's own, more prosaic,

223

inscription reads: 'John Broadwood & Sons, Makers of Instruments to His Majesty and the Princesses. Great Pulteney Street, Golden Square, London.See: Dieter Hildebrandt, 1988, p. 27.Beethoven's new Broadwood had a range of six octaves (from the third C below middle C to the third C above), a half octave less than the Streichers' latest instrument, which meant it was unsuitable for the performance of the *Hammerklavier* Piano Sonata. Its case was constructed from Spanish mahogany inlaid with marquetry. It was triple strung and was equipped with a *una chord* pedal enabling the action to move the keys to the right so that the hammers would strike one string only. The soundboard was thicker than that of equivalent Viennese instruments and the hammers were heavier. These gave the piano a more sonorous tone than its Viennese rivals but at the expense of a heavier action, making the performance of passages requiring great velocity more difficult.See: David Wainright, *Broadwood by appointment*, The Book Service, 1982 and Reginald Gerig, *Famous pianists and their technique*, Washington: R. B. Luce, 1974, p. 44. See also: Derek Melville, *Beethoven's Pianos* (Plate 4a) in: Denis Arnold and Nigel Fortune, editors, *The Beethoven Companion,* 1973.

[19] See: Derek Melville, *Beethoven's Pianos* in, Denis Arnold and Nigel Fortune, editors, 1973, pp. 50–1; Leon Plantinga, 1999, Plate 6; and Ernest Closson, *History of the Piano*, translated by Delano Ames and edited by Robin Golding, 1947, plate 27.

[20] H. C. Robbins Landon, 1977, p. 56.

[21] As recalled in: Gerhard von Breuning, *Memories of Beethoven*, edited by Maynard Solomon, 1992, p. 38 and p. 78.

[22] For a brief account of Joseph Gelinek and his relationship with Beethoven see: Peter Clive, 2001, pp. 124–5.

[23] From the recollections of Carl Czerny, see: Paul Badura-Skoda, editor, 1970, p. 4. Czerny conveyed his father's recollections of Gelineck to Beethoven's early biographer Otto Jahn.

[24] Johann Schenk, as recollected in: O. G. Sonneck, 1927, pp. 14-15. For an account of Gelineck's meeting with Beethoven, see: Thayer-Forbes, 1967, p. 139 and Ludwig Nohl, *Beethoven Depicted by his Contemporaries*, 1880, pp. 36–47.

[25] See: Beethoven House, Digital Archives, Library Document, B 937 and Peter Clive, 2001, pp. 381–2.

[26] Thayer-Forbes, 1967, p. 211. For a reproduction of Cramer's likeness, see: Beethoven House, Digital Archives, Library Document, B 1254.

[27] Hans Conrad Fischer and Erich Kock, 1972, p. 12.

[28] Thayer-Forbes, 1967, p. 204.

[29] Quoted by Tia de Nora, 1997, pp. 149–50. The story of Beethoven's encounter with Wölfl is also described in: H. C. Robbins Landon, 1976–80, p. 592. See also: Oscar George Theodore Sonneck, 1927, p. 36.

[30] Tomaschek's recollections, as recalled by Ignaz von Seyfried, are preserved in: Ludwig Nohl, 1880, pp. 35–7. For other accounts of the encounter between Wölfl and Beethoven see also: Thayer-Forbes, 1967, pp. 205–7 and Tia de Nora, 1997, pp. 152–4.

[31] Quoted in: Thayer-Forbes, 1967, p. 205.

[32] As recalled by Ferdinand Ries in: Franz Wegeler, 1838, English edition, 1988, p. 71. For a more extended account of Beethoven's pianistic confrontation with Steibelt, see: Thayer-Forbes, 1967, p. 257. See also: *Ferdinand Ries* in: Oscar George Theodore Sonneck, 1927, pp. 47–59.

[33] Czerny's recollections are recorded in Ludwig Nohl, 1880, pp. 44–45.

[34] H. C. Robbins Landon, 1992, p. 81 and Peter Clive, 2001, pp. 268–69.

[35] Anton Felix Schindler, *Beethoven as I Knew Him*, edited by Donald W. MacArdle and translated by Constance S. Jolly from the German edition of 1860, 1966, p. 50.

[36] Cited in: Piero Weiss and Richard Taruskin, 1984, p. 325. The quotations from the *AmZ* are derived from Wayne M. Senner, Robin Wallace and William Meredith, editors, *The Critical Reception of Beethoven's Compositions by his German Contemporaries*, 1999, Vol. 1.

[37] Derived from: Leon Botstein, *Music, Culture and Society in Beethoven's Vienna* in: Robert Winter and Robert Martin, editors, *The Beethoven Quartet Companion*, 1994, p. 86.

[38] Barry Cooper, 2000, p. 104. Beethoven's surviving personal possessions can be viewed on the Beethoven House website.

[39] The reconstruction has been recorded on *The Unheard Beethoven* website, Gaurdi 05.

[40] William Kinderman, 1997, p. 109.

[41] Barry Cooper, 2000, p. 125.

[42] Elliot Forbes editor, *Thayer's Life of Beethoven*, 1967 p. 213.

[43] Barry Cooper, 2000, pp. 76–77.

[44] See, for example, an illustration derived from the autograph of the second movement of the Third Piano Concerto reproduced as Plate 7 in: Leon Plantinga, 1999.

[45] Barry Cooper, 1990, p. 80 and p. 88 and 2000, pp. 92–93.

[46] Elliot Forbes editor, *Thayer's Life of Beethoven*, 1967 p. 213.

[47] Ignaz von Seyfried as recalled in: Oscar George Theodore Sonneck, *Beethoven: Impressions of Contemporaries*, 1927, pp. 56–57.

[48] Leon Plantinga, 1999, pp. 115–18

[49] A commentary on the sketchbook Beethoven used for the period 1801–2 (Kessler Sketchbook) is provided by Nottebohm, 1979, pp. 3–43.

[50] For a commentary on this aspect of the Kessler sketchbook, see: Leon Plantinga, 1999, pp. 113–134 and pp. 307–09.

[51] Douglas Porter Johnson editor, 1985, pp. 132–33.

[52] Beethoven House, Digital Archives, Library Document, HCB Mh 71.

[53] William Kinderman, 1997, p. 64. Kinderman's text incorporates a reproduction of a typical page from the composer's autograph that vividly illustrates his many revisions – see plate 5.

[54] Leon Plantinga, 1999, p. 246.

[55] William Kinderman, 1997, p. 64.

[56] Barry Cooper, 1999, pp. 254–5. Beethoven's growing reputation at this period is considered by, amongst others, Wilfrid Mellers, 1957, p. 11.

[57] See, for example: Barry Cooper, 1991, p. 15 and 2000, pp. 89-90; Leon

Plantinga, 1999, pp. 113–134; Hans-Werner Küthen, *Beethoven, Kla-vierkonzert , No. 3, Op. 37*, c. 1984; and William Kinderman, 1997, p. 109.

⁵⁸ Quoted from William Kinderman, 1997, p. 73.

⁵⁹ The bearing of these circumstances on Beethoven's frame of mind is discussed by many writers, see, for example, Wilfrid Mellers, 1957, p. 12.

⁶⁰ From a letter of Beethoven to Franz Gerhard Wegeler, in: Emily Anderson, editor and translator, 1961, Vol.1, Letter No, 51, p.57 and p.62. Later in life Wegeler became Rector of the University of Bonn, both Wegeler's and Beethoven's hometown. For a facsimile reproduction of this letter together with the original German text, see: Beethoven House, Digital Archives, Library Document, Wegeler, W 17.

⁶¹ From a letter of Beethoven to Karl [Carl] Amenda, in: Emily Anderson, editor and translator, 1961, Vol.1, Letter No. 53, pp. 63–5. For a facsimile of this letter see: Beethoven House Digital Archives Library Document, Bodmer HCB:BBr:1.

⁶² From a letter of Beethoven to Franz Gerhard Wegeler, in: Emily Anderson, editor and translator, 1961, Vol. 1 Letter No. 54, pp. 66–8. For a facsimile reproduction of Beethoven's letter to Wegeler see: Beethoven House, Digital Archives, Library Document, Wegeler, W 18.

⁶³ For a reproduction of Giulietta Guicciardi's likeness, see: Beethoven House, Digital Archives, Library Document, B. 489.

⁶⁴ Quoted in: Madeleine Goss, *Bolero: The Life of Maurice Ravel*, 1945, p. 51.

⁶⁵ Electra Yourke, 2003–5, Vol. 4, p. 150.

⁶⁶ Maynard Solomon (1977, p. 115) quoted by William Kinderman in: *Beethoven*, 1997, p. 61.

⁶⁷ The Heiligenstadt Testament is a highly personal document in the form of a letter that Beethoven wrote in October 1802 to his brothers Kaspar Anton Karl (1774-1815) and Nikolaus Johann (1776-1848). In it Beethoven confides his loss of hearing and his personal struggle to overcome his ensuing feelings of isolation. His indomitability of spirit ultimately prevailed through his commitment to his art and saved him from taking his life. Beethoven did not reveal the document to anyone and knowledge of it only came to light some twenty-five years later following his death.

⁶⁸ Michael Thomas Roeder, 1994, p. 183.

⁶⁹ Leon Plantinga, 1999, pp. 113–134. See also: Barry Cooper, 2000, pp. 112–13.

⁷⁰ Emily Anderson, editor and translator, 1961, Vol. 1, Letter No. 58, p. 74.

⁷¹ Theodore Albrecht, translator and editor, 1996, Vol. 1, Letter No. 58, pp. 100–1.

⁷² *Ibid*, Vol. 1, Letter No. 38, pp. 70–71.

⁷³ Leon Plantinga, 1999, pp. 113–134.

⁷⁴ Theodore Albrecht editor and translator, 1996, Vol. 1, Letter No. 42 and footnote 3, pp. 74–76.

⁷⁵ Theodore Albrecht editor and translator, 1996, Vol. 1, Letter No. 49, pp. 84–86. For a facsimile reproduction of this letter, together with the German text, see: Beethoven House, Digital Archives, Library Document, BH 147.

⁷⁶ *Ibid*, Vol. 1, Letter No. 52, pp. 90–92. For a facsimile reproduction of Carl's

letter, together with the German text, see: Beethoven House, Digital Archives, Library Document, HCB Br, 301.

77 Theodore Albrecht editor and translator, 1996, Vol. 1, Letter No. 53, pp. 92–94.

78 *Ibid*, Vol. 1, Letter No. 56, p. 98.

79 *Ibid*, Letter No. 57, pp. 99–100. For a facsimile reproduction of Carl's letter, together with the German text, see: Beethoven House, Digital Archives, Library Document, HCB Br, 303.

80 For a fuller account of Beethoven's working relationship with Breitkopf & Härtel, see Peter Clive, 2001, pp. 46–47.

81 For many years the three-volume survey of Beethoven's letters, translated and edited by Emily Anderson has served the English-language, Beethoven scholar-researcher. First published in 1961 it has been republished since in various formats including a hardback edition in 1986. Letters *to* Beethoven have been translated and edited by Theodore Albrecht in three volumes published in1996. Scholars at The Beethoven House, Bonn are currently working on a definitive, multiple-volume edition of Beethoven's correspondence that will encompass all known letters, written by or to Beethoven.

82 Theater an der Wien website.

83 Emily Anderson editor and translator, 1961, Vol. 1, Letter No. 87a, pp. 105–6.

84 Elliot Forbes editor, *Thayer's Life of Beethoven*, 1967 pp. 328–29.

37 *Ibid*.

86 As recollected by Ignaz von Seyfried, *Louis van Beethoven's Studies in Thorough-Bass, Counterpoint and the Art of Scientific Composition*, Leipzig; 1853. Seyfried's anecdote is recalled in several other more accessible accounts. See, for example, Barry Cooper, 2000 and H. C. Robbins Landon, 1992.

87 Quotations are derived from Leon Plantinga, 1999, p. 114.

88 The original source is: Louis Spohr's *Autobiography*, translated from the German, 1805, and recalled in Oscar George Theodore Sonneck, *Beethoven: Impressions of Contemporaries,* 1927, pp. 97–98.

89 Emily Anderson editor and translator, 1961, Vol. 1, Letter No. 76, p. 92.

90 Theodore Albrecht editor and translator, 1996, Vol. 1, Letter No. 58, pp. 100–01.

91 Emily Anderson editor and translator, 1961, Vol. 1, Letter No. 91, p. 110.

92 Elliot Forbes editor, *Thayer's Life of Beethoven*, 1967 p. 355. It is not clear here whether Ries is making explicit reference to a performance of the C minor Concerto. The point being that Beethoven's other piano pupil, Carl Czerny, rendered a similar service to that by Ries when he performed the Emperor Piano Concerto on 12 April 1818 – Beethoven being too deaf by then to play the work himself.

93 Elliot Forbes editor, *Thayer's Life of Beethoven*, 1967 pp. 354–55.

94 As recollected in: H. C. Robbins Landon, 1970, p. 74.

95 Wayne M. Senner, Robin Wallace and William Meredith, editors, *The Critical Reception of Beethoven's Compositions by his German Contemporaries*, 1999, p. 206 and p. 209.

[96] Peter Clive, 2001, pp. 237–40.

[97] H. C. Robbins Landon, 1992, pp. 65–66.

[98] Elliot Forbes editor, *Thayer's Life of Beethoven*, 1967 p. 209.

[99] Barry Cooper, 2000, p. 125 and footnote 6.

[100] Leon Plantinga, 1999, pp. 241–42.

[101] Emily Anderson editor and translator, 1961, Vol. 1, Letter No.100, p. 121.

[102] Han-Werner Küthen, *Beethoven, Klavierkonert, Nr. 3, Opus 37*, München, G. Henle Verlag, c. 1984.

[103] Franz Wegeler, *Remembering Beethoven: The Biographical Notes of Franz Wegeler and Ferdinand Ries*, 1988. See also: Barry Cooper, 1991, p. 188.

[104] For other evaluations of Beethoven's creative output, bearing on the period under consideration as expressed in relation to his negotiations with various publishers, see: Elliot Forbes, 1967, p. 362; Peter Clive, 2001, pp. 200–01; and Barry Cooper, 1991, p. 193.

[105] Beethoven House, Digital Archives, Library Document, HCB C. Op. 37.

[106] Peter Clive 2001, pp. 216–17.

[107] Elliot Forbes editor, *Thayer's Life of Beethoven*, 1967 pp. 449–50.

[108] As recalled in: Franz Wegeler, *Remembering Beethoven: The Biographical Notes of Franz Wegeler and Ferdinand Ries*, 1988, p. 103.

[109] Quoted by Eva Badura-Skoda, *Performance Conventions* in: Robert Winter editor, *Beethoven, Performers, and Critics*: The International Beethoven Congress, Detroit, 1977, 1980, pp. 57–58.

[110] Elliot Forbes editor, *Thayer's Life of Beethoven*, 1967, p. 478 and footnote 25.

[111] William Kinderman, 1997, pp. 66–67.

[112] Donald Francis Tovey, *Essays and Lectures on Music*, 1949 p. 317.

[113] Source: *The Unheard Beethoven, Cadenza to Piano Concerto No. 3, Op. 37.*

[114] Anton Felix Schindler, *Beethoven as I Knew Him* edited by Donald W. MacArdle and Translated by Constance S. Jolly from the German edition of 1860, 1966, pp. 161–62.

[115] Peter Clive, 2001, pp. 348–49.

[116] Theodore Albrecht, editor and translator, 1996, Vol. 2 Letter No. 431, pp. 137–8.

[117] For many years it was considered Beethoven's Autograph Score was lost. The only known surviving text was a fragment consisting of the last seventeen bars of the fugue. Authorities believed Beethoven may have removed this from the Autograph that he then replaced with an amended version before sending the final score to Artaria. (See text to: Beethoven House Digital Archives, Library Document H. C. Bodmer, HCB Mh 25) The manuscript was listed in an 1890 catalogue and sold at an auction in Berlin to William Howard Doane, a Cincinnati industrialist. In 1952 his daughter gave this, and other manuscripts, to the Palmer Theological Seminary. Beethoven's manuscript languished in the basement of the Seminary until its discovery in 2005 by the Seminary's Librarian Heather Carbo. It later sold at auction for £1,128,000.

[118] As recalled in: Patrick Piggott, *The Life and Music of John Field, 1782–1837: Creator of the Nocturne*, 1973, pp. 52–53.

[119] As recalled by Johann Schlosser in: *Beethoven: The First Biography, 1827*, edited by Barry Cooper, 1996, pp. 120–23.

[120] The foregoing is with acknowledgment to Peter Clive, 2001, pp. 269–70.

[121] Adrian Williams, *Portrait of Liszt: By Himself and His Contemporaries*, 1990, pp. 114–15.

[122] See: (La) Mara [pseudonym], *Letters of Franz Liszt*, London: H. Grevel & Co., Vol. 2 1894, p. 330.

[123] Recollected in: Adrian Williams, editor and translator, *Franz Liszt: Selected Letters*, 1998, pp. 118–19.

[124] James Harding, *Saint-Saëns and His Circle*, 1965, pp. 26–27. See also: Brian Rees, *Camille Saint-Saëns: a life*, 1999, pp. 36–37.

[125] Anton Felix Schindler, *Beethoven as I Knew Him*, edited by Donald W. MacArdle and translated by Constance S. Jolly from the German edition of 1860, 1966, pp. 161–62.

[126] Berthold Litzmann, editor, *Letters of Clara Schumann and Johannes Brahms, 1853–1896, Vol. 2*, 1971, p. 261.

[127] Jean Michel Nectoux, *Gabriel Fauré: A Musical Life*: translated by Roger Nichols. 1991, p. 303.

[128] As related in: Henry Pleasants, editor and translator, *The Music Criticism of Hugo Wolf*, 1978, pp. 262–63.

[129] Adrienne Fried Block, *Amy Beach, Passionate Victorian. The Life and Work of an American Composer, 1867–1944*, 1998, p. 59.

[130] See: Dan H. Laurence, editor, *Shaw's Music: The Complete Musical Criticism* (in three volumes), 1981.

[131] Eugene Gates, *The Journal of Aesthetic Education*, University of Illinois Press, 2001, Vol. 35, No. 3, pp. 63-71.

[132] Dan H. Laurence, Vol. 2, pp. 250–51. The review cited was originally published in *The World*, 28 January 1891.

[133] Harold C. Schonberg, *The Great Pianists*, 1987.

[134] Artur Schnabel, 1961, p. 26.

[135] Michael Kennedy, *Hallé Tradition: A Century of Music*, 1960, p. 93.

[136] Malcolm Gillies and David Pear, editors, *The All-Round Man: Selected Letters of Percy Grainger, 1914–1961*, 1994, p. 280.

[137] Arthur Rubinstein, 1980, p. 225.

[138] *Ibid*, pp. 504–07. For a listing of all of Toscanini's Beethoven recordings see: H. Frank Mortimer, *Arturo Toscanini: the NBC years*, 2002, pp. 120–23.

[139] Dennis Matthews, 1968, pp. 50–51 and p. 170.

[140] Originally published in *The Piano Quarterly*, 1977–78 and quoted in: Tim Page, editor, *The Glenn Gould Reader*, 1987, pp. 260–61.

[141] David Dubal, 1985, p. 23.

[142] Carl Czerny, edited with commentary by Paul Badura-Skoda, 1970, p. 22. This text, with other observations, is also quoted by Barry Cooper, 1991, pp. 287–88. Czerny's observations on Beethoven's use of the pedal may be interpreted as Beethoven's attempts to compensate for the limited sonority of the keyboard instruments available to him – at least in his early years in Vienna when he performed in the salons of the nobility.

[143] Carl Czerny, edited with commentary by Paul Badura-Skoda, 1970, p. 22.
[144] Charles Rosen, 1995, p. 19.
[145] Ernest Newman, 1988, pp. 247–48, as quoted, with adaptations, in: Barry Cooper, 1991, p. 288.
[146] Eugene K. Wolf and Edward H. Roesner, editors, 1990, p. 155.

PIANO CONCERTO
NO. 4 G MAJOR, OP. 58

'In speaking of Beethoven's piano concertos,
whose mind does not run at once to the G major
and the E flat, those greatest of all pianoforte
concertos? One does not try or wish to give the
palm to either the one or the other – the G major
of such wondrous lyrical beauty – the E flat in its
glorious majesty. Both are supreme, both give us
glimpses of another world, both are of the greatest
Beethoven.'

Fanny Davies, *The Pianoforte Concertos* in: *The Musical
Times. Special Issue*, editor John A. Fuller-Maitland, Vol.
VIII, No. 2, 1927, p. 21.

'All three movements of Beethoven's G major
Concerto demonstrate the aesthetic principles of

concerto form with extraordinary subtlety ... Beethoven has now well and truly laid the foundations of his concerto forms and is free to raise his edifice to heights undreamt of in earlier music.'

Donald Francis Tovey, *Essays in Musical Analysis, 1935–41*, Vol. 3, p. 76 and p. 78.

Later Tovey wrote:

'Nobody with a sense of style has the slightest doubt that Beethoven's three greatest concertos, the G major, Op. 58, and the E flat, Op. 73, for pianoforte, and the Violin Concerto, Op. 61, are among his grandest works. The orchestra is not only symphonic, but is enabled, by the very necessity of accompanying the solo lightly, to produce ethereal orchestral effects that are in a quite different category from anything in the symphonies. On the other hand, the solo part develops the technique of its instrument with a freedom and brilliance for which Beethoven has no leisure in sonatas and chamber music.'

Donald Francis Tovey, *Beethoven*, 1944, pp. 114–15.

Discussing the extraordinary creative period of the composition of the Fourth Piano Concerto, Donald Ferguson remarks:

'Spiritually ... these were for Beethoven *halcyon days*. That such a work as this could originate in mere aesthetic speculation is unthinkable. That it is the mere reflection of a particular experience is equally so. But that it is the product of an unusual state of calm and exaltation in a mind already deeply imbued with the implications of experience is indubitable.

Donald Nivison Ferguson, *Masterworks of the Orchestral Repertoire: A Guide for Listeners*, 1954, p. 105.

'The Fourth Piano Concerto is perhaps the greatest — and certainly the most perfectly formed — of all Beethoven's works in the genre. It was composed between 1805 and 1806 ... Beethoven himself played the premiere, but it was Mendelssohn's Leipzig performance (1836) that helped establish the Concerto's early reputation. Beethoven's G major is a predominantly lyrical composition. One of its most unusual features is that the first movement's principal theme is initially stated not by the orchestra, but by the soloist. Thereafter, lyricism and pearl-like keyboard runs predominate. There's a "Beauty and the Beast" slow movement that alternates bold orchestral entreaties with submissive piano responses, and a bustling final *Rondo* that features a chuckling, Keystone Cops-like cadenza. Robert Schumann claimed that the Fourth Concerto gave him "a joy such as I have never experienced before".'

Rob Cowan, *Liner Notes to: Beethoven, Piano Concerto, No. 4, Phillips Classics*, 1972.

'It would be difficult not to feel in the E minor *Andante con moto* the confrontation of two worlds, in which the aggressive rhythms of the unison orchestral strings are answered and finally overcome by the pleading phrases of the muted piano. Such confrontation is often implicit in Beethoven, but never elsewhere in the instrumental music is it so explicitly stated, and Liszt's view that the movement represents Orpheus taming the Furies is a creditable programmatic interpretation.'

Basil Deane, *The Concertos*, in: Denis Arnold and Nigel Fortune, editors, *The Beethoven Companion*, 1973, pp. 326–27.

'For some years this work was neglected in favour of the Fifth Concerto, popularly known as the *Emperor*, until a performance of the G major, during November 1836 by Felix Mendelssohn at a Gewandhaus concert in Leipzig, brought its exquisite beauties to light. Robert Schumann, eminent critic as well as composer, wrote as follows in his account of the occasion: "This day Mendelssohn played the G major Concerto of Beethoven with a power and finish that transported us all. I received a pleasure from it as I have never enjoyed; I sat in my place without moving a muscle or even breathing — afraid of making a noise!" '

Albert E. Wier, *The Piano Concertos of Bach, Beethoven, Brahms*, Foreword to *Miniature Score Series*, Belwin Mills, 1973.

'Small wonder ... that this Concerto, written at the full flowering of Beethoven's genius, should be a work of quite extraordinary qualities. In his three earlier piano concertos Beethoven had grappled with the form of the first movement. In the Triple Concerto, completed in 1804, he had found a solution, as had Mozart earlier, which prepared the listener to accept the initial orchestral *tutti* as a procession, a statement of themes, rather than as their dramatic presentation which must follow later from the solo and orchestra. By the time he came to write the Fourth Concerto the problem was behind him. He could compose with the greatest freedom knowing that he was master of himself.'

R. Kinloch Anderson, *Liner Notes to: Beethoven, Piano Concerto, No. 4,* EMI Classics for Pleasure, 1977.

'To turn from the Triple Concerto to the Fourth Piano Concerto in G major (1806) is to exchange an interesting and unjustly neglected work by a master for an undisputed masterpiece of the highest order ... The Concerto breathes warmth of heart and serenity, even in its rapid passage-work, much of it in triplet semiquavers.'

Denis Matthews, *Beethoven, Master Musicians,* 1985, pp. 176–77.

'With Beethoven the orchestra-solo relationship reached the peak of its development. It was with the Fourth Concerto in G major that the ultimate of condensation, of unity with the solo exposition, of imagination, and of discipline was attained.'

Tim Page, editor, *The Glenn Gould Reader,* 1987, p. 68.

'Within a short period Beethoven composed three large concertos, the Triple Concerto, Op. 56, the Fourth Piano Concerto, Op. 58, and the Violin Concerto, Op. 61, all of which refine and clarify the established structure ... The expanded dimensions — for these three works are all very big — are not so much achieved through the additive principle of the first Sonata, but by a developmental technique, in which a melodic fragment is enlarged in different ways. Perhaps most indicative of Beethoven's stylistic direction in these works is the enormous amplification of the key scheme and the way in which melodies themselves wander from key to key, which almost becomes a mannerism of his writing at this time.'

Philip G. Downs, *Classical Music: The Era of Haydn, Mozart, and Beethoven*, 1992, pp. 600–01.

'The Fourth Concerto is not only the most lyrical and poetic, it is in many respects his most unusual. It is the first following the *Heiligenstadt Testament* of October 1802 which marked a turn to new directions. The G major Concerto appeared in that highly productive and experimental period which saw the composition of the Fourth Symphony, the Violin Concerto, the quite original Op. 59 *Razumovsky* Quartets, and the Thirty-two Variations for Piano in C minor. The powerful and radically different *Eroica* Symphony and *Appassionata* Sonata had been completed a few years earlier. Throughout the early portion of this experimental period, the piano served as a major source of inspiration.'

Michael Thomas Roeder, *A History of the Concerto*, 1994, p. 185.

'It hard for us today to appreciate the full impact this work must have had on the listeners at its first performance in March 1807 ... A Beethoven première is always an occasion for the Viennese, and they are full of anticipation ... How will he begin the convention of an orchestral introduction — mysteriously, perhaps, on cellos and basses or with a blare of brass and tympani? And then this extraordinary and unprecedented happening ... It is the *soloist* who begins, and not even with a masterful cascade of notes but with a soft and gentle phrase that is far from what they expect.'

Antony Hopkins, *The Seven Concertos of Beethoven*, 1996, p. 43.

'Not many listeners ... stop to notice that the exquisitely gentle and sensitive main theme of the Fourth Piano Concerto is founded on the same rhythm as the fierce opening of the Fifth Symphony.'

Robert Simpson, *Beethoven and the Concerto* in: Robert Layton, editor, *A Guide to the Concerto*, 1996, pp. 116–17.

'Pieces like the G major Piano Concerto and the Violin Concerto, and to some extent the *Pastoral* Sonata, belong together; The idea of expressing tranquillity through motion. This plays a major part in the *epic* pieces of the later middle period ... They are like the female element, the *Shekinah* ['divine presence of God'].'

Theodor W. Adorno, *Beethoven: The Philosophy of Music; Fragments and Texts*, 1998, p. 88.

'The Fourth Piano Concerto is perhaps the most sublime work of this period, and hence of the entire concerto literature. Its second movement, stripped of abstract form to speak in its unbroken arc of poignancy and calamity, quickly became associated with Orpheus and the Furies ...'.

Robert Levin, *Liner Notes to Piano Concerto, No. 4*, Deutsche Grammophon, 1998.

'Beethoven made his last appearance as a concerto soloist in the first public performance of this work, which was the famous *Akademie* on 22 December 1808 in the Theater an der Wien ... when the Fifth and the *Pastoral* Symphonies and the *Choral Fantasy* also had their premieres along with the first hearings in Vienna of three movements of the Mass in C and the concert Aria *Ah! Perfido*, not to forget one of Beethoven's remarkable solo improvisations. Beethoven's student Carl Czerny tells us that his teacher's performance on this occasion was very playful (*muthwilligkeit*), and it seems very likely that it incorporated many of the virtuosic, capricious and sometimes witty variants he entered into the corrected copy of a professional copyist's manuscript score, but which have not yet found their way into any printed edition.'

Michael Steinberg, *The Concerto: A Listener's Guide,* 1998, p. 64.

'As Beethoven moved into the magnificent years of his middle period ... he seems to have thought of his compositions, including his concertos, less as grist for mills of performance than as *works,* as monuments to his artistry with a certain fixedness and durability ... [22 December 1808] was the last time, so far as we know, that Beethoven played a concerto in public [the G major, Op. 58]; burgeoning fame as a symphony composer (and local fame as a conductor of his own works), as well as international success in publishing his music, finally made concerto playing – that preferred means of putting his musical persona before audiences in the Bonn and early Vienna years – ever more dispensable.'

Leon Plantinga, *Beethoven's Concertos: History, Style, Performance*, 1999, p. 204 and p. 292.

'Many of the compositions of Beethoven's so-called middle period are famously dominated by the notion of heroic struggle, spawning the popular image of the fist-shaking, furrow-browed Titan. But that is far from the whole picture. And in other works, among them the *Pastoral* Symphony, the Violin Concerto, and the Fourth Piano Concerto, the expanded range and scale of Beethoven's symphonic thinking go hand in hand with an unprecedented lyric breadth. In particular the opening movements of all three works — all, significantly, marked *Allegro moderato ma non troppo* — have a sense of spaciousness, with moments of profound reflective stillness, that is in its way no less revolutionary and prophetic than the mighty strivings of the *Eroica* and Fifth Symphonies.'

Richard Wigmore, *Notes to the BBC Radio Beethoven Experience*, Friday 10 June 2005, www.bbc.co.uk/radio3/Beethoven

Beethoven composed his G major Piano Concerto No. 4, Op. 58 when he was in his mid-thirties. He was by then celebrated in Vienna as a virtuoso pianist and, despite the onset of deafness, was still able to perform in public. His fame as a composer — of daring and innovative works — was recognised at home and abroad and publishers were prepared to pay the high prices he demanded for his compositions. Notwithstanding his unconventional demeanour, his capacity for making acerbic remarks, and his pronounced Bonn accent, he had secured the attention, friendship and financial support of a number of Vienna's musically-minded aristocracy. At the close of the period under consideration, he would soon count no less than the Archduke Rudolph — the Emperor's son — as his composition pupil and who would, in due course, be the recipient of the dedication to many of Beethoven's greatest works.

Beethoven authority Maynard Solomon characterises the composer's creativity at the period we are about to consider as 'an explosive inauguration of [his] post-Heiligenstadt style'.[1] He is making reference here to the intensely personal document Beethoven set forth when living at Heiligenstadt — at the time a small village on the outskirts of Vienna — with the realization of his increasing deafness. He contemplated taking his life but found the resolve to overcome his physical and emotional impediments in fulfilment of his artistic destiny. The Austrian medically-qualified musicologist Anton Neumayr has considered the many illnesses that afflicted Beethoven throughout his adult life. Reflecting on his poor state of health, he describes the composer's musical output around the period of composition of the G major Piano Concerto 'as astonishing'.[2]

Beethoven was disposed to copy extracts from morally improving texts — as a means to self-exhortation and self-improvement. One such source was a copy of Christian Sturm's *Betrachtungen* ('Meditations'), a heavily annotated copy of which was found amongst the composer's possessions following his death. The writings of this German preacher influenced Beethoven's moral and philosophical outlook. One such text reads:

'Sickness and other misfortunes hast Thou inflicted upon me so that I might realize my transgressions ... I have but one prayer, O God: do not cease to work to make me better. Let me be fruitful only in the good works that Thou wouldst leave me to do.' Beethoven's biographer Alexander Thayer describes these words as being, fittingly, of 'great propriety and elegance'.[3]

In this part of our study of Beethoven's five piano concertos, bearing opus numbers, we consider the following: the creative context amidst which the G major Concerto was conceived and its composition chronology; Beethoven's personal circumstances; negotiations with publishers; contemporary performances; nineteenth-century and later reception; and, to close, a documentary study of the musicology of the G major Concerto, as expressed in selected writings of musicologists and performing artists.

We consider for a moment the creative and imaginative context amidst which the G major Concerto was conceived — Maynard Solomon's 'explosive inauguration'.

On 7 April 1805, the epochal *Eroica* Symphony was performed for the first time in public at the Theater an der Wien, and characteristically divided critical opinion — as evident in a review that appeared in the Journal *Der Freimüthige*. One party, comprising Beethoven's closest supporters, contended:

> '[This] particular Symphony is a masterpiece ... of the highest type and that if it does not please now it is because the public is not sufficiently cultivated in the arts to comprehend these higher spheres of beauty, but after a couple of thousand years its effect will not be lessened.' The other party found no artistic merit in the work claiming it revealed, 'the symptoms of an unbridled attempt at distinction and peculiarity' and that 'neither beauty, true sublimity nor power have anywhere been achieved'.[4]

The following compositions had their genesis around the period of composition of the G major Concerto and are illustrative of Beethoven's capacity, and predilection, for working on several works at the same time:

Two Sonatas for Piano, Op. 49, published in 1805; Piano Sonata, Op. 53, dedicated to Count Ferdinand von Waldstein; the Triple Concerto, Op. 56; Piano Sonata in F minor, Op. 57 — *Appassionata*; three *Razumovsky* String Quartets, Op. 59; work on the Fourth Symphony, Op. 60 — completed in 1806; Violin Concerto in D major, Op.61

— first performed in 1806; and *Ah! perfido,* for Soprano and Orchestra, Op. 65. In 1807 and 1808 he completed the Fifth Symphony in C minor, Op. 67 and the Sixth Symphony in F major, Op. 68 — the *Pastoral.* Mention may also be made of the following: the First and Second *Leonora* Overtures; the Andante in F major, for Piano, WoO57; and the Thirty-two Variations for Piano, WoO 80.

In the words of the Viennese-born musicologist Joseph Braunstein — who attained the great age of 104:

> 'Every work in this list ... is a seminal masterpiece, and everyone breaks new ground. The scale, scope and originality are unprecedented, constituting a miracle of despatch equal to the record-breaking feats of Mozart and Schubert, and surpassing them in density of thought.'[5]

The Scottish pianist-musicologist Ronald Kinloch Anderson succinctly concurred: 'Such a crop of masterpieces is rare in musical history. Beethoven had reached full maturity as an artist.'[6]

In his first three piano concertos, Beethoven had been largely content to follow Mozart's precedent of combing the piano with the orchestra as a corporate member of the *tutti* — one assigned a special, but not a dominating, role. In the G major Concerto, as we shall see, all that would change. American pianist-composer-musicologist Robert Levin declares:

> 'By this time, Beethoven's style had irrevocably transformed the language that he inherited into a highly wilful rhetoric of unprecedented power and immeasurably heightened personal intensity.'[7]

In his *The Concerto: a Listener's Guide*, Michael Steinberg considers the concerto-genre to be 'a form of theatre'. Surveying Beethoven's achievement he remarks:

'Commanding pianist and experienced performer that he was, Beethoven had a keen feeling for that [form of theatre], and his first three piano concertos ... and the Violin Concerto ... make something quite striking of the first solo entrance.'

He cites the manner in which the solo cello enters in the Triple Concerto, repeating the first theme and how, in the Violin Concerto, the solo 'rises spaciously from the receding orchestra with wonderful quiet authority'. In his final completed concerto, the *Emperor*, Steinberg cites the opening chords in the orchestra that provoke the soloist to discharge 'three grand fountains of arpeggios, trills, and scales'. Turning to the G major Concerto, however, he proposes: '[It] is here, in this most gently spoken and poetic of his concertos, that Beethoven offers his most radical response.'[8]

In his *In Pursuit of Music*, Dennis Matthews expresses similar thoughts to the foregoing: 'The] concerto is one of the most dramatic art-forms ever devised.' Reflecting on the manner of the opening of the typical concerto, of the Romantic era, he adds:

'This drama starts from the first note of the work, which usually happened to be the orchestra's note, until Beethoven *emancipated* [Matthews's emphasis] the soloist in his G major Concerto.'[9]

It is enlightening to compare the thoughts of Steinberg and Matthews, concerning the nature of the concerto, with the *music theory* as propounded by the contributor to the *Allgemeine musikalische Zeitung* – published at the period when Beethoven was composing the G major Concerto. He suggested there are three basic types of musical composition:

> 'First, the composer can represent ... something objective, an ideal world of tones, an organic structure of tones that pleases through its free regularity ... Second, the composer can represent the subjective ... the expression of sensations and emotions, effects and passions ... Third, music can unite feelings and their underlying causes in a representation that illustrates ... objects through which it is aroused and demonstrates stirrings of the soul.'

> 'The contributor in question considered the best recent music of his acquaintance to be that possessed of a 'sentimental' character, as found, he believed, in the works of 'Haydn, Mozart ... Beethoven, Cherubini, among other masters'.

Worthy of note is that the *AmZ* contributor considered the still relatively young Beethoven to be worthy of mention alongside Haydn and Mozart.[10]

Issue eight of the *AmZ* for 1805 sheds further light on the reception of Beethoven's music and his perceived standing amongst his musical contemporaries. Luigi Cherubini and Beethoven are together identified as 'following the master Mozart with distinguished talent and a great knowledge of art [music]'. Although Cherubini's star has waned in our own time, Beethoven himself regarded Cherubini as his greatest musical contemporary. The *AmZ* reviewer chastises both, though, for not subduing their nature and guarding against 'excesses of bombast'. Concerning Beethoven, however, he later relents:

> 'Nevertheless, whoever doesn't recognize — as even now some try to do — the exquisite artist, born particularly for the genre, in several of Beethoven's instrumental pieces, particularly in his symphonies and fortepiano concertos, and also in various of his quartets and sonatas, regardless of the abuses ... and many irregularities of details, such a person can only be pitied, not disputed.'[11]

The *AmZ's* contributor was evidently alert to the *newness* — departure from convention — that Beethoven was expressing in his music. As Michael Thomas Roeder states in his *A History of the Concerto*:

> 'The writing for the solo instrument is clearly beyond the world of Mozart's concertos, for Beethoven not only introduces virtuoso effects, rarely heard earlier, but also makes effective use of the new upper-reach of the instrument.'[12]

With regard to the G major Concerto, one of its most original features — to which we make reference in due course — is the manner in which Beethoven allows the solo instrument to open the music. All previous piano concertos had commenced with an extended orchestral *tutti* before the entrance of the soloist; we later acknowledge Mozart's precedent in his Concerto in E flat, K. 271.

Writing of Beethoven's innovation, Barry Cooper comments:

'It is as if Beethoven has deliberately set up an uncompromising opening, before using the rest of the movement to justify the unorthodoxy. The purpose of giving the opening to the piano proves to be that it heralds a new and closer relationship between piano and orchestra ...'.[13]

Some authorities propose the manner in which Beethoven allows the soloist to open his G major Concerto, was a source of inspiration to other composers. We may cite, as possible candidates, the following: Rachmaninoff's Piano Concerto, No.2 — whose opening is perhaps even more celebrated than Beethoven's G major Concerto; Bartok's First Violin Concerto; Prokofiev's Second Violin Concerto; Schoenberg's Violin Concerto; Schoenberg's Piano Concerto; and Shostakovich's Cello Concerto, No. 2.[14]

Concerning the originality to be found in Beethoven's G major Concerto, mention must be made of the Orpheus legend and the manner in which, to many ears, its influence may be detected in the work's second movement:

In 1985, the American musicologist and teacher Owen Jander wrote an article titled *Beethoven's Orpheus in Hades: The Andante con moto of the Fourth Concerto*. In this he advanced the thesis that the status of the music should be considered as 'Beethoven's most elaborate venture into the realm of programme music'. He went further — controversially to some — and proposed Beethoven's imagery to be 'the most totally programmatic piece of music — great art music — ever composed'.[15] In the same spirit, Michael Thomas Roeder enthuses:

'The *Andante con moto* second movement is surly one of Beethoven's most unusual creations.

It is in no set instrumental form and seems to have been conceived as a quasi-operatic scene.'[16]

The reader will recall that in classical mythology Apollo gave Orpheus a lyre with which he brought forth melodies of such enchantment that animals, and even trees, were moved − quite literally − by the power of his music. Orpheus was subsequently granted entrance to Hades to retrieve his beloved Euridice, his melodious powers overcoming the wiles of the furies. It is this part of the legend that captivated nineteenth-century musicologists and disposed them to find parallels with the manner in which the gentle tones of the piano, in the second movement of the G major Concerto, triumph over the assertive tones of the orchestra. In the classical legend, Orpheus is not so fortunate; he violates the stipulation that he should not look back and, when he does, forfeits his beloved Euridice.

Given that Beethoven began work on the G major Concerto at the period when the Viennese six-octave piano was now available to him, the American musicologist and music critic Michael Steinberg suggests the new instrument's upper range may have suggested to Beethoven the potential for evoking the plangent sounds of the harp − that is, the beguiling tones of Orpheus's lyre.[17]

Other composers had been drawn to the potentialities of setting the mythological Orpheus subject to music, notably Christoph Willibald Gluck in his *Orfeo ed Euridice − Orphée et Eurydice − Orpheus and Eurydice*. First performed in 1762, it became a source of influence on Mozart (*The Magic Flute*) and Beethoven (*Fidelio*) and Joseph Haydn conducted a performance of the music in 1776 at the Palace of Prince Nikolaus Esterházy. Of related interest is that the composer, poet, physician, and theologian Friedrich August Kanne composed an opera *Orpheus* that was produced at the Kärntnerthor Theater on November 1807 — contemporaneously with Beethoven's Concerto Op. 58. Kanne was known to Beethoven. Moreover, they shared the same patron, Prince Lobkowitz, and from Anton Schindler we learn the two of them discussed 'the psyche ... implicit within the scale of each key'.[18]

Musicological tradition maintains it was Franz Liszt who first promulgated the notion that a connection was to be found between the Orpheus tale and the G major Concerto. Although Liszt composed a Symphonic Poem *Orpheus*, with an appended prose introduction and essay on Gluck's *Orfeo ed Euridice*, no direct connection is in fact known associating Liszt with Beethoven's Concerto and the Orpheus legend. Donald Tovey, drawing on the evidence available to him, makes qualified reference to the then accepted view that it was indeed Liszt who first compared the character of the slow movement of the G major Concerto to Orpheus taming the furies with his music. He describes the comparison as being 'remarkably spiritual' but considers the music to be 'free from concrete externals'. He elaborates:

'In this *Andante* [second movement] the orchestra does not imitate wild beasts or nature, and the pianoforte does not imitate a lyre or a singer ... The orchestra ... is entirely in octaves, without a vestige of harmony, so long as it remains stubborn and rough in its share of the dialogue with the quiet veiled tones of the solos.'[19]

Before Franz Liszt, Carl Czerny was affected by the mood prevailing in Beethoven's *Andante con moto* disposing him to comment:

'In this movement — which, like the entire Concerto, belongs to the finest and most poetical of Beethoven's creations — one cannot help thinking of an antique tragic scene and the player must feel with what intense, pathetic expression his solo is performed, in order to contrast with the powerful and austere orchestral passages, which are, as it were, gradually withdrawn.'[20]

Another claimant to likening the music of the *Andante* to Orpheus's taming of the Furies is Beethoven's early biographer Adolf Bernhard Marx.[21]

In his summative overview concerning the atmosphere that pervades throughout the *Andante con moto*, Yale musicologist Leon Plantinga remarks:

'The truth is that we cannot have any clear idea about scenes or events Beethoven may have had in mind when he composed this movement; he did not tell us, and the music cannot. But we do know that in this riveting dialogue he decided to leave any dramatic personae unnamed, and what they said and did unspecified. He thus kept our imaginations unfettered, free to make our own constructs, or to ponder, perhaps, a more general idea of human conflict and concord within a genre of musical expression for which such matters stand at the very centre.'[22]

British musicologist and Beethoven authority Barry Cooper comments in a similarly measured fashion: 'The myth itself is archetypal and symbolic — wildness tamed through culture and art, demons overcome by the power of music.' He concludes:

'[It] is preferable to regard the concerto movement as reflecting all these stories and the universal idea of art overcoming barbarism, music dissolving, and gentleness pacifying anger ...'.[23]

We give the last words on this aspect of the *Andante con moto* to the musicological polymath Antony Hopkins — composer, pianist, conductor, writer, and radio broadcaster. Hopkins first recalls the *Heiligenstadt Testament* of 1802 in which Beethoven expressed the misery of his deafness and in which he makes reference to his enforced 'isolation' and 'solitude'. Hopkins posits:

'Is it not possible that this [second] movement symbolises [Beethoven's] isolation from the material world, which beats in vain about his now unhearing ears?'

He further proposes:

'Only when the orchestra has been reduced to silence does the pianist (i.e. Beethoven) allow himself to grieve openly in phrases whose emotional expressiveness is in striking contrast to the reticence of what has gone before.'

In further support of his contention, Hopkins draws a parallel with the piano's closing bars and Beethoven's moving last words in his *Testament*:

'Forgive me then, if you see me shrink away when I would fain mingle among you ... All alone ... I must live like an exile'.[24]

We pause for a moment here in our narrative, concerning

the origins of the G major Concerto, and turn our attention to a consideration of aspects of Beethoven's personal circumstances at the period in question. We reflect on his relationships, his growing reputation, health concerns, expressions of unrest, and his expressed resolve to leave Vienna.

On 1 January 1804, Beethoven sent a New Year's greeting card — as was the custom in Vienna — to Baroness Dorothea von Ertmann. The wording is simple: 'To the Baroness Ertmann, at New Year 1804, from her friend and admirer.'[25] This literary fragment serves to remind us that Beethoven was not an abstract master of tones but a warm-hearted, sentient human being. Dorothea was a pianist who performed the composer's piano sonatas to considerable acclaim. She received lessons from Beethoven and so earned his respect as to be known by him as 'Dorothea *Cecilia*' — Cecilia being, of course, the patron saint of music. In 1817, he dedicated to her his Piano Sonata in A major, Op. 101. The German composer and music critic Johann Friedrich Reichardt heard Dorothea perform Beethoven in the winter of 1808—09. He comments on her noble manner and her beautiful face 'full of deep feeling'. Regarding her interpretation, following a performance of 'a great Beethoven sonata' (he does not say which), Reichardt remarks: 'I have never seen such power and innermost tenderness combined in even the greatest virtuosi.'[26]

Later in the year, Beethoven had a lady visitor-admirer (unnamed) who requested the loan of his portrait to hang in her room during her stay in Vienna. The portrait in question was that painted by Joseph Mähler. It is a measure of Beethoven's growing fame, at this period, that he was persuaded (no easy matter) to have his portrait painted by Mähler. Perhaps Beethoven relented since he and the artist were on friendly terms. Mähler portrayed Beethoven in an Arcadian setting striking a lyre, in the background is a temple of Apollo. The painting remained in Beethoven's possession until his death. Regarding the request for the loan of his portrait, Beethoven sent a note to Mähler remarking: 'Who can resist such *charming advances?*' [Beethoven's emphasis][27]

Matters of a more musicological kind come to the fore next. On 10 June 1804, the Italian-born, London-based Muzio Clementi — composer, pianist, pedagogue, conductor, music publisher, editor, and piano manufacturer (!) — had occasion to write to the innovative London piano maker William Frederick Collard — recognised for his improvement of the working-action of the piano. Clementi entertained hopes that he would soon secure the publication rights of certain of Beethoven's works that were still in manuscript. He states how he hoped to secure the compositions 'at a tolerably easy rate'. He was aware that in his dealings with publishers, Beethoven could be 'very exorbitant'. This remark may be taken as referring indirectly to Beethoven's brother Caspar (Kaspar) Carl (Karl).

Carl, as we shall refer to him (to avoid confusion with his son who was named Karl) had relocated from Bonn to Vienna to be closer to his brother, in order to assist him with his business affairs. From 1800, Carl worked as a clerk in Vienna's Department of Finance, in which capacity he found time to correspond with publishers to offer his brother's works for sale and — importantly — to secure the best prices he could. Clementi concluded his letter to Collard: '[Beethoven] is well, by a miracle, for he quarrels with almost every living creature.'[28]

On 16 January 1805, Beethoven had occasion to write to the publishers Breitkopf and Härtel. He complained how the winter took its toll on his health: 'In the winter my health is usually weaker than in the summer.' As a consequence, he could not take on extra work so readily. In addition, his favourite copyist had fallen unwell and he was having to proofread his manuscripts himself, prompting him to remark '*checking* is often a real effort and is far-less enjoyable than just composing'. He took the opportunity to pay a compliment to his then patron, Prince Karl Lichnowsky, describing him as 'what is surely a rare specimen in the class to which he belongs — one of my most loyal friends and promoters of my art'. Alas, as we shall shortly relate, Beethoven's relationship with his patron would suffer irreparable harm.[29]

A letter Beethoven wrote later in the spring, to the Countess Josephine von Deym, reveals the difficulty he was experiencing in coming to terms with his deafness. Beethoven had a great affection for Josephine and several love letters survive bearing testimony to his feelings for her. The origins of their relationship began when she commenced piano lessons with him soon after her arrival in Vienna. It has been conjectured Josephine was the subject of Beethoven's impassioned *Immortal Beloved* letter dating from 1812.

It was never sent and was only discovered amongst Beethoven's possessions following his death. In music, Beethoven gave declaration to his feelings for Josephine in his *Andante favori* (WoO 57), thought by some to have been intended as the middle movement of the tempestuous *Waldstein* Piano Sonata, Op. 53. Concerning his affliction, he writes cryptically:

'[A] *private* grief robbed me for a long time of my usual intense energy ... As soon as we are together again ... you shall hear all about my real sorrows and struggle with myself between death and life, a struggle in which I engaged for some time ... a

254

certain event made me despair of ever achieving happiness *during my life on this earth.*'[30]

The following year Beethoven received a compliment, albeit somewhat indirectly, from the enterprise of his former piano pupil Ferdinand Ries. On 21 May 1806, the publisher Nikolaus Simrock wrote to the composer on learning that Ries had, 'by way of an experiment', arranged for piano trio one of Beethoven's String Quartets from his Op. 18 set. Simrock was so pleased with the result that he informed Beethoven he intended to publish all six quartets as his (Simrock's) Op. 60 – 'as a pleasant surprise for his friend'. Simrock new Beethoven from their days together in Bonn; he had played the horn in the Elector's orchestra. He added: 'If the works of Pleyel have been found worthy of so many variations, yours are truly a hundred times more deserving.' He justified himself saying:

> 'This is not merely my predilection for your compositions, but also [my] inner conviction to make the good taste of your excellent composi-tions more generally known, and to bring [them] to among a greatly expanded public.'[31]

A few weeks later Ries himself wrote to Beethoven with, in effect, another compliment. He informed his former teacher 'of the first fruits of his labours', a reference to his first compositions – the two Piano Sonatas, Op. 1. They were duly published in Bonn by Simrock bearing a dedication to Beethoven as Ries's tribute 'to so great a master'.[32]

Although Beethoven's Opera *Leonora / Fidelio* had troubled origins, and took some time to be assimilated into the repertoire, it also had its early admirers. Amongst these was Stephan von Breuning. He was one of Beethoven's closest friend's – despite their occasional differences of opinion – and was the dedicatee of the Violin Concerto, Op. Op. 61. Stephan had revised the original libretto to *Fidelio* for its performance on 29 March 1806 at the Theater an der Wien (repeated on 10 April). This disposed him to write on 2 June to Franz Gerhard Wegeler and his wife Eleonora (Stephan's sister) a long letter replete with extensive quotations from his lyrics that Beethoven had set to music. Of the latter, he remarked:

> 'The music is among the most beautiful and perfect that can be heard; the subject is interesting because it concerns the liberation of a prisoner through the loyalty and courage of his wife.'

Stephan added: 'For all this, however, probably nothing has caused Beethoven so much grief as this work, whose value will be fully appreciated only in the future.'[33]

Later in the year (autumn) Beethoven established what was to be a long and fruitful connection with the Scottish publisher George Thompson. His great passion was collecting and publishing folk songs. For some time Haydn had provided harmonized accompaniments to Scottish airs provided by Thomson. With the elderly composer's failing health, he wrote to Beethoven to solicit his support in his publishing enterprise, declaring: 'Of all composers now living [you are] the only one who occupies the same distinguished rank.'[34] Beethoven replied to Thompson on 1 November. His long letter, written in French by another hand, reveals Beethoven the businessman and the prices he demanded for his compositions. As requested, he offered to harmonize 'the little Scottish airs' and observed that 'Mr. Haydn was paid one-pound sterling for each song'.

For his part, Thomson requested settings 'that his young

ladies could manage to play' — he was mindful of Beethoven's challenging keyboard style. Beethoven responded, stating he would provide 'compositions easy and pleasing as far as I can' but insisted, they would be 'consistent with that elevation and originality of style that ... characterize my works and from which I shall never stoop'. In addition, he offered Thomson string trios, string quartets, string quintets, and piano sonatas. For such sets of works he requested 100 pounds sterling or 200 Vienna gold ducats — that Beethoven considered to be 'by no means excessive'. In the event, only the Scottish songs, though plentiful, were the outcome.[35]

We move forward in time to 1807. July of that year found Beethoven suffering from a persistent headache and he sought advice from Dr. Johann Schmidt. He was an ophthalmologist — of value to Beethoven who sometimes had to resort to spectacles for close work — a pharmacologist, and a surgeon. Beethoven turned to Schmidt when he learned he practiced *galvanism* — the newly introduced procedure of applying electrical current to the affected part of the body as propounded by the Italian physiologist Luigi Galvani. Beethoven hoped, unrealistically, this might restore, or at least alleviate, his hearing. This was also the era when physicians sought to restore the body's 'humours' by blood-letting' (we recall the last hours of Mozart). Schmidt, however, discouraged Beethoven from applying leaches since he considered 'nothing could be expected of them'. Instead, he encouraged his patient to 'take hearty walks, work little, and sleep; also eat well and drink spirits in moderation' — a modern-day sounding regimen![36]

Beethoven continued to consult Schmidt at different times for a number of years as he sought relief from his many ailments. As a token of appreciation, and as a gesture of friendship to his physician, he dedicated to him the Piano Trio, Op. 28 — an arrangement of the Septet, Op. 20. Doubtless Schmidt appreciated this since, alongside his attainments in medicine, he was a good amateur violinist and, moreover, had a daughter who played the piano proficiently.[37]

One of Beethoven's most generous patrons, in his early years in Vienna, was Prince Karl Lichnowsky. He had been a pupil and friend of Mozart and was a pianist of some ability. In recognition of his support for Beethoven, he received the dedications to the *Sonate Pathétique*, the Piano Sonata in A-flat major, Op. 26, and the Second Symphony. The composer's Piano Trios, Op. 1 were first performed at one of Lichnowsky's soirées in late 1793, or early 1794, and Beethoven later dedicated them also to him.

The Prince had in his service a quartet of young string players headed by Ignaz Schuppanzigh. A professional musician, he established a close relationship with Beethoven and remained devoted to him throughout his life. By way of illustration, Schuppanzigh's Quartet gave the first performances of the String Quartets, Op. 95 (*Quartetto Serioso*), Op. 127, Op. 130, and Op. 132.

We pause for a moment longer in our discussion of the Fourth Piano Concerto, to consider Beethoven's relationship with Prince Lichnowsky. In so doing we will illustrate how challenging it was, for even so noble-minded a patron as Lichnowsky, to retain an equable rapport with the temperamental composer. We also make reference to Beethoven's growing disenchantment and how he felt disposed to leave Vienna for good.

In addition to his soirées, Lichnowsky made his salon available for regular Friday morning concerts. We gain a glimpse into these musical and social events by calling to mind one of Beethoven's piano pupils at this period. She was a gifted young maiden by the name of Fräulein Elisabeth von Kissow. At an early age she showed pronounced musical talent, prompting her father to send her to Vienna to receive instruction. Such was her ability, she was invited to perform at Count Lichnowsky's musical entertainments. Later in life Elisabeth, as Frau von Bernhard, recalled her musical impressions of the time when she received instruction from the composer:

> 'I still remember clearly both Haydn and Salieri sitting on a sofa on one side of the small music room, both carefully dressed in the old-fashioned way with perruque [periwig], shoes and silk hose, whereas, even here Beethoven would come dressed in the informal fashion of the other side of the Rhine, almost ill-dressed.'[38]

During his early years in Vienna there is evidence, though, that Beethoven made attempts to overcome his social and sartorial deficiencies. Entries from an account book, recording his personal income, reveal he acquired black silk-stockings, boots, and incurred expenses for a wig maker and a dancing master! With regard to the latter, his piano pupil Ferdinand Ries recalls: 'He could never learn to dance in time, and his clumsy movements lacked all charm.'[39]

Beethoven's star was rising and publishers were eager to accept his works – largely on his own (and his brother's) financial terms. Doubtless, in recognition of the composer's rising accomplishments, and his growing admiration of him, Lichnowsky conferred on his protégée an annuity, in effect a stipend, of 600 florins – about sixty pounds sterling. The Prince's intention was to provide Beethoven with some financial security. The payments continued for several years until he received a more secure annuity in 1809 from three of Vienna's most notable citizens, namely, the Archduke Rudolph (Beethoven's only composition pupil), Prince Kinsky and Prince Lobkowitz.[40]

In the context of Beethoven's writing for the keyboard, and his relationship with women, mention may be made here of Count Lichnowsky's first wife, Princess Marie Lichnowsky. She was one of Beethoven's most ardent admirers and had a close friendship with Beethoven. In recognition of her untiring efforts on his behalf, he inscribed to her the piano score of his Ballet *The Creatures of Prometheus*.

We turn now to the circumstances that gave rise to a breach in Beethoven's relationship with his patron.

At this period, the invading French army still occupied Grätz and Prince Lichnowsky, perhaps for reasons of circumspection, or simply out of good-natured courtesy, invited a number of French officers to dine with him and his guests — including Beethoven. At some part in the proceedings, Lichnowsky asked Beethoven to play for the assembly; this was not a new experience for the composer as we learn from a recollection of Carl Czerny:

'In 1805, when the French occupied Vienna for the first time, [Beethoven] was on one occasion visited by several officers and generals who were musically inclined. He played them Gluck's *Iphigenie in Tauris* from the score, and they sang the aria and choruses not at all badly.'

Czerny's recollection is of further interest. He adds

'I asked [Beethoven] for the score and wrote out the piano arrangement at home, putting down, as exactly as possible, what I had heard him play

[Czerny was still only fourteen years old]. I still have my arrangement. My skill in arranging orchestral works dates from that time, and [Beethoven] was always completely satisfied with my transcriptions of his symphonies, etc.' [41]

Sometime later, Beethoven placed his trust in the youthful Czerny to make a piano transcription of the score to his opera *Fidelio* and, after the composer's death, Czerny brought out piano-duet arrangements of all nine symphonies.

The occasion of Prince Lichnowsky's dinner party, in the company of French officers, appears to have found Beethoven in an ill-humour and he resolutely declined to improvise at the piano despite the Prince's protestations. Perhaps Beethoven now felt some antipathy towards the French?

Since their occupation of Vienna, most of the nobility had fled the city, including the wealthy classes who were Beethoven's most loyal supporters and upon whom he depended, in part, for his income — for instance giving piano lessons. Moreover, things had gone badly for the first performances of his Opera *Leonora*, upon which he had expended so much effort. We learn the following from a letter the composer's friend Stephan von Breuning sent to their mutual friend Franz Gerhard Wegeler on 2 June 1806:

'Nothing has caused Beethoven so much grief as this work ... In the first place, it was performed seven days after entry of the French troops [13 November 1805], and thus at the most unfavourable time.' [42]

Elsewhere Breuning remarks:

'Beethoven is at present in Silesia with Prince Lichnowsky ... His circumstances are not of the best at present, since his Opera, owing to the cabals of his opponents [and the bad behaviour of some French officers], was performed seldom, and therefore yielded him nothing. His spirits are generally low, and to judge by his letters, the sojourn in the country has not cheered him.'[43]

Beethoven's unsettled nature at Lichnowsky's was made all the worse by the incautious behaviour of one of the French officers. From the recollections of Dr. Anton Weiser, a guest of Lichnowsky's and Director of the Troppau Hospital, we learn:

'In order to honour them [the French officers], it was promised that after dinner they would have the pleasure of hearing the famous Beethoven, who was then a guest at the castle, to play. One of the French staff officers unhappily asked Beethoven if he also knew the violin!'

Weiser saw at once how this outraged Beethoven who did not deign to answer his interlocutor. Another version of the story suggests one of the French officers jested they would have the composer arrested if he would not condescend to perform![44] The outcome was Beethoven left the company in a rage, packed his belongings, that included the autograph of the *Appassionata* Sonata, and departed, but not before leaving Prince Lichnowsky a note: 'There are many princes and noblemen. There is only one Beethoven!'

The foregoing anecdote has a sequel. Once back in Vienna, a plaster bust of Prince Lichnowsky became the victim of the composer's still simmering wrath — Beethoven dashed it to pieces on the floor. Furthermore, on the return journey the autograph of the Op. 57 Piano Sonata, locked away in a trunk, also became a victim; it was saturated in a thunderstorm. The surviving manuscript still bears traces of the downpour, showing dark blotches and stains along the edges of the manuscript.[45]

For many years after these incidents, Prince Lichnowsky sought reconciliation with Beethoven but to no avail. Later in life, his fortune and health much reduced, he occasionally attempted to hear Beethoven play — his admiration for the composer still intact — by surreptitiously sitting in a nearby anteroom, the composer's servant being told not to inform the composer of his presence.

Our reference to Carl Czerny and Beethoven's Opera *Fidelio*, calls to mind recollections left by the tenor Josef August Röckel. He sang the role of Florestan in the second version of the music — *Fidelio* — on 10 April 1806. Following the première of its original version — *Leonora* — on 20 November 1805, the composer's closest friends realized the necessity for changes — abridgements — to which Beethoven agreed, but only after many entreaties and supplications by his well-meaning friends.

Röckel called on Beethoven to receive his copy of the music and has left the following description:

> 'I entered the place consecrate to supreme genius. It was almost frugally simple and a sense of order appeared never to have visited it. In one corner was an open piano, loaded with music in the wildest confusion. Here, on a chair, reposed a fragment of the *Eroica*. The individual parts of the Opera, with which he was busy, lay, some on other chairs, others on, and under, a table which stood in the middle of the room. And, amid

263

chamber music compositions, piano trios and symphonic sketches, was placed the mighty bathing apparatus with which the Master was laving his powerful chest with the cold flood.'[46]

Beethoven continued to receive the annuity Prince Lichnowsky had generously conferred on him until about 1806; it is assumed the payments ceased following the quarrel between them. Anxious to secure his financial position, and status as an established composer, Beethoven wrote to the Directors of the Imperial and Royal Court Theatres seeking employment in the form of a contract. The Directors included the Princes Lobkowitz, Schwarzenberg and Esterhazy amongst others. Beethoven gave an undertaking to compose, each year, at least one grand opera, to subjects chosen by the Directors, and, in addition, a little operetta or a *divertissement.* He also requested the freedom to hold each year a benefit concert in one of the Court Theatres.

For these services and privileges, Beethoven requested a fixed annual income of 2,400 gulden, as well as all the takings from his benefit concerts. In considering his proposals Beethoven urged the Directors to bear in mind the time and mental energy demanded in composing an opera. The effort he had expended on *Leonora/Fidelio* once disposed him to exclaim: 'This Opera shall earn for me a martyr's crown!' He concluded by petitioning that if his proposals were not acceptable, then he should at least be granted access to one of the Court Theatres during the Christmas period. As far as is known, Beethoven did not receive a reply to his petition nor was he granted his wish to hold a benefit concert for the Christmas Season 1807.[47]

His rejection came as no surprise since earlier in the year (11 May), on learning that the Court Theatres were under new management, Beethoven had written to his friend, Count Franz Brunsvik: 'I shall never come to an arrangement with this tribe of princes connected with our theatres.'[48] A further disappointment to Beethoven was the failure of his Mass in C, Op. 86 to make a favourable impression.

The work had been commissioned by Prince Nikolaus Esterházy and was premiered on 13 September 1807 at the Prince's estate at Eisenstadt. Following the performance, it is alleged Esterházy turned to Beethoven and remarked: 'But, my dear Beethoven, what is this that you have done again?' Beethoven's indignation at these disparaging words was compounded by the ironic laughter of the Prince's Kapellmeister – who had overheard the remark. Thinking himself ridiculed, Beethoven left Eisenstadt in a state of anger.[49] On 12 September 1807, Esterházy confided his feelings about Beethoven's new Mass to his confident Countess Henriette von Zielinska: 'Beethoven's Mass is unbearably ridiculous and detestable, and I am not convinced that it can ever be performed properly. I am angry and mortified.'[50]

These experiences contributed to Beethoven's feelings of unrest and general disaffection that came to a head the following year. We learn something of this from a letter the pianist Wilhelm Karl Rust wrote to his sister on 9 July 1808. As a child, Rust had been hailed in the *Berliner musikalische Zeitung* as 'A new musical child prodigy', and his performances of Bach's preludes and fugues had impressed even Beethoven. In his impressions of Beethoven, Rust states: 'He is as original and singular as a man as are his compositions; usually serious, at times merry but always satirical and bitter.' He concluded: 'It is very probable Beethoven will leave Vienna; at any rate he has frequently spoken of doing so and said; "They are forcing me to do it".'[51] In similar vein, on 16 July, in the course of making negotiations with the publisher Breitkopf and Härtell, Beethoven complained: '[For] the last two years I have suffered a great many misfortunes, and, what is more, here in Vienna.'[52]

Later in the summer Beethoven sought to collaborate with the Austrian poet and dramatist Heinrich von Collin; in 1807 he had composed the Overture *Coriolan* to the author's tragic drama. Writing to Collin with the opening salutation 'brother of Apollo' — a form of address Beethoven frequently adopted when corresponding with fellow votaries of the arts — he expressed his interest in writing an opera to a libretto supplied by him, provided 'it was without dancing and recitatives'. He explained, however, that such an outcome would have to await what 'the high and mighty theatrical directors decreed'. He once more pessimistically reflected:

> 'I have so little reason to expect anything favour-
> able from them that the thought that I shall
> certainly have to leave Vienna and become a
> wanderer haunts me persistently'.[53]

Beethoven's unrest was heightened in the autumn when Napoleon's younger brother Jérôme — recently installed as the King of Westphalia — invited him, through the diplomatic offices of his High Chamberlain, to consider an offer of appointment as his Senior Kapellmeister in Kassel. Despite the somewhat archaic-sounding title, the post held distinct attractions for Beethoven. His duties would not be onerous; he would merely be required to play for Jérôme's personal pleasure and to conduct occasional concerts. Moreover, he was offered a salary of 600 gold ducats — the equivalent of about 4,000 gulden / florins or 200 pounds sterling — and an additional 150 ducats for travelling expenses.[54]

Denis Matthews makes the interesting observation that although the title of kapellmeister was becoming somewhat antiquated, in the first decade of the nineteenth century, it may have had a particular resonance for Beethoven. His grandfather had held such an appointment, and this, combined with childhood memories, may, Matthews suggests, have exerted an influence on his subconscious mind.[55]

Beethoven was immediately attracted by the invitation and was disposed to accept it. On 24 November he wrote in enthusiastic terms to his new confident and general factotum Baron Gleichenstein; an official in Vienna's War Department and a proficient cellist — he received the dedication to the composer's Cello Sonatas, Op. 69. This time he greeted his friend with the salutation 'Dissolute Baron' — a characteristic example of the word-play he inflicted on his close friends and associates. He informed Gleichenstein:

> 'I have received the offer of a fine appointment as Kapellmeister to the *King of Westphalia*. I am to be paid handsomely — I have been asked to state how *many ducats* I should like to have — and so forth.' He closed the letter by asking Gleichenstein for a meeting to seek his advice.[56]

Remarks by Carl Czerny shed light on Beethoven's feelings at this time and put them into perspective. He writes:

> 'It has often been said abroad that Beethoven was despised and repressed in Vienna. The truth is that even as a young man he received all possible support, attention and encouragement from our great aristocracy which could have been given to a young artist ... It is true that, as an artist, he had

to deal with intrigues, but the public were not to blame for that. He was always admired as an unusual character, and his greatness was assumed by everyone who didn't really know him.'[57]

In late November, Beethoven wrote once more to Gleichenstein regarding his offer of appointment from 'the Kingdom of Westphalia'; he confirmed he was indeed to receive a yearly salary 'of 600 gold ducats'. This appears to have been sufficient incentive to dispose him to accept the post. When news of the threat of Vienna losing its most celebrated composer became known to those of influence, they became alarmed. To invoke Thayer's characteristic eloquence: 'What an inexcusable, unpardonable disgrace to Vienna would be the departure of Beethoven under such circumstances!'[58]

Beethoven did not accept his lucrative offer of appointment at the Court of Jérôme Bonaparte — but only after the intervention of three of Vienna's most influential citizens — and soon-to-be the composer's beneficiaries. We discuss the financial arrangements (inducements) they ultimately conferred on Beethoven, to secure his continuing presence in Europe's musical capital, in the context of our following account of the *Emperor* Concerto.

The following year almost proved disastrous for Beethoven the virtuoso pianist. He nearly lost a finger because of a *panaritium* — a bacterial infection. In March 1808, Stephan von Breuning wrote to the medically qualified Gerhard Wegeler (he was professor of medicine at the University of Bonn) to reassure him that their mutual friend was 'completely well again'. His reassurance was, however, qualified: 'Thus, he escaped a great misfortune that, combined with the hardness of hearing, would have stifled any good humour, seldom as it appears now,'[59]

On 30 November, the German composer and music critic Johann Friedrich Reichardt was in Vienna; his reminiscences provide us with a brief pen-portrait of Beethoven at this time. Reichardt's visit was primarily to pay his respects to the elderly Haydn — then at the height of his fame. Earlier in the year (22 March) a performance of *The Creation* had been given in his honour; he was carried into the auditorium in an armchair to a fanfare of trumpets and drums and to be respectfully greeted by Beethoven — a moment in musical history captured by the water colourist Balthazar Wigard. Haydn was so emotionally exhausted by the experience he had to leave during the intermission; it is recorded Beethoven kissed his former teacher on his forehead and hands.[60]

On being received by the venerable composer, Reichardt found him 'seated very stiff and almost rigid ... not unlike a living wax-figure'. Haydn exclaimed to his visitor: 'Ah, I have strained my spirit too much; I'm already just a child.' The conversation then turned to his former pupil Beethoven who, Haydn believed, appeared 'to be withdrawing more from society'. This remark resolved Reichardt to visit the aging master's gifted, up-and-coming contemporary. He tells us:

'I have also sought out and visited the good Beethoven. People pay so little attention to him here no one could tell me where he lives, and it entailed quite a lot of trouble on my part to locate him.'

He eventually tracked down the composer in what he describes as a large, desolate and lonely apartment. Of his eventual meeting with Beethoven he writes:

'His is a powerful nature, like a Cyclops in appearance but at the same time very intimate, hearty and good ... But he has become quite estranged from Prince Lichnowsky who lives in the upper part of the same house, although some years ago they were on very intimate terms.'[61]

The reader will recall how Beethoven had left Prince Lichnowsky in a rage when asked to play for French officers.

On 3 December Reichardt had a further opportunity to meet Beethoven and hear him improvise. He informs: 'I was invited to [a] most agreeable dinner by means of a very friendly note from Beethoven.' The hostess was Countess Anna Maria Erdödy. She was an accomplished pianist who held musical soirées in her apartment. Beethoven was fond of Anna Maria and dedicated his two Piano Trios, Op. 70 to her. Reichardt recalls:

'[We] got the temperamental Beethoven to the fortepiano ... He improvised for a good hour from the depths of his artistic feelings, ranging from the highest heights to the depths of the celestial art, with mastery and versatility, so that ten times at least tears came to my eyes.'

Reichardt was so overcome with emotion that at the close of Beethoven's playing he embraced him 'like an ardently emotional child'.[62]

Concerning Reichardt's meeting with Haydn – If the two were under the impression that Beethoven was 'withdrawing more from society', a month later they would have received a quite different impression. On 22 December, Beethoven give the celebrated concert that has passed into musical legend. It was at this concert that the G major Piano

Concerto received its first public performance — we discuss this shortly.

A further recollection of Beethoven, from the time he was at work on the Op. 74 String Quartet, comes from an unlikely source in the guise of the French army officer Baron Louis-Philippe Trémont. He had been made a member of Napoleon's *Conseil d'État* and in this capacity was responsible for delivering the Council's despatches to Napoleon during the French invasion of Austria; Bonaparte had by then established his headquarters in Schönbrunn Palace.

Trémont called on Beethoven, sometime in 1809, and to his great surprise was cordially received. Doubtless this was made possible since he bore a letter of introduction from the composer and theorist Antoine Reicha. He was then resident in Paris but had known Beethoven from their days together in Bonn. Perhaps the rapport between Beethoven and Trémont was also facilitated by the fact that Trémont was an informed and ardent music lover. When he eventually located the composer, he found him living in reduced circumstances:

> 'Picture to yourself the dirtiest, most disorderly place imaginable — blotches of moisture covered the ceiling; an oldish grand piano, on which the dust disputed the place with various pieces of engraved and manuscript music ... under the piano an unemptied *pot de nui* [chamber pot]!'

To Trémont's delight, he was privileged to hear Beethoven improvise:

> 'His tempestuous inspiration poured forth lovely melodies, and harmonies unsought because, mastered by musical emotion, he gave no thought

to the search for effects that might have occurred to him with pen in hand; they were produced spontaneously without divagation.'[63]

To add to our survey of contextual matters contingent upon the origins of the G major Concerto we make reference to the portrait made of Beethoven by the Berlin artist Isidor Neugass — a circumstance that may be taken as further indication of the composer's growing celebrity.

Neugass took the composer's likeness a few years before the meeting with Trémont and, judging by the portrait, Beethoven was then taking care with his appearance. Neugass chose to depict Beethoven in a half-length portrait that was fashionable at the time. The closely cropped hair, as depicted in the painting of the composer by Joseph Mähler of 1804, is transformed in Neugass's depiction into a stylish *bouffant!* Around his neck is suspended a double lorgnette to assist his reading — Beethoven being somewhat short sighted.

There are two version of the painting: one version originates from the Lichnowsky family and is said to have been made, according to the family tradition, by the order of Beethoven's patron Prince Karl von Lichnowsky; the second version was made for the aristocratic Brunswick family with whom Beethoven was on familiar and affectionate terms.[64]

Before we redirect our narrative to the creation origins of the G major Concerto, it will be helpful to add further remarks, to those previously stated, concerning the six-octave keyboard now available to Beethoven.

In his *A History of the Concerto*, the American musicologist Michael Thomas Roeder, writes:

'[The Concerto] No. 4 in G major, a key of high lyrical connotations for Beethoven, must, in many ways, have been inspired by the newly developed Viennese six-octave piano.'[65]

Leon Plantinga expresses similar thoughts:

'In his earlier sonatas and concertos, we hear Beethoven forever struggling against the restraint at the top of his instrument. Now [in the Fourth Piano Concerto] he positively luxuriates in the added upper reaches of piano tessitura (up to c'''').'[66]

We have previously noted that in the First Concerto (see related text) the high f sharp (f3) was not available to Beethoven and he had to be content with f natural. The Third Concerto was initially conceived for a piano with only two notes beyond the conventional five octaves; it was only later, when making revisions for Ferdinand Ries with an instrument of larger compass in mind, that he extended the upper writing to c4.

Not only did the new six-octave instrument have an additional octave at the top of the range but, as Roeder states, 'the entire character of its sound was radically altered'. In the case of instruments possessing the five-octave keyboard, the top two-and-a-half octaves only were triple-strung whereas, on the newer instruments, all the notes were triple strung. This imposed greater tension on the piano's frame that in turn required heavier compensating construction. To quote Roeder once more:

'As a result the new instrument had a wider dynamic spectrum to which Beethoven responded by broadening his notated dynamic markings from *ff–pp* to *fff–ppp*.'[67]

In addition, the damper mechanism was now worked by a foot pedal — as with today's instruments — rather than by the cumbersome knee-lever characteristic of the older five-octave piano.

Today, the 'concert grand' reigns supreme in the concert hall, its great iron frame enabling it to hold its own against the orchestra. However, devotees of 'authentic performance' consider the delicate mechanism of the older-style instruments allow the performer to achieve subtleties of musical feeling not so readily achieved on a modern-day piano. To emphasise the point, we cite the views of the American pianist and fortepiano authority Robert Levin. Taking the *Andante con moto* of the G major Piano Concerto as his example, he remarks:

> 'The movement calls for a piano capable of true *una corda* — that is, with a lever that shifts the hammers from striking all three of the treble strings to two or one.'

He explains:

> 'The indication *una corda* — "one string" — is synonymous with the use of the soft pedal on today's pianos; its release is denoted by the indication *tre corde* — 'three strings'.

He adds: 'Modern-day instruments can shift only from three to two strings — thereby only an approximation to Beethoven's ideal can be realized.'[68]

In the Preface to his four-hand transcription of Beethoven's Op. 58, Hans-Werner Küthen observes: 'The source history of Beethoven's Fourth Piano Concerto is particularly interesting since the work's origins are as obscure as its unforeseen impact is obvious.' He describes the source materials as being 'sparse' and in the form of 'extremely rough sketches'.[69]

The available evidence suggests Beethoven resolved to write another piano concerto shortly after completing his Third Piano Concerto, Op. 37 in June or July 1804. Moreover, the G major Concerto is the only one of his five full-scale completed works in the genre for which there is no surviving autograph score. Küthen believes: '[Beethoven's] sole handwritten score went astray in 1807, while work was being prepared for publication by the Bureau des Arts et d'Industrie.' (see later) It is known that at that time Beethoven let the manuscript out of his hands to help the engraver enter his final changes. This action is consistent with a remark made by Ferdinand Ries to the effect that once a composition was engraved and in print, Beethoven was indifferent to the fate of his manuscripts. Ries once remarked how he found them scattered about the floor of Beethoven's apartment and that he could have carried away any number of them had he so requested.

Anton Schindler states:

> 'According to Ferdinand Ries, the Piano Concerto in G major ... was written in 1804 immediately after *Leonora-Fidelio*. It has not been possible to ascertain the exact date of its composition.'

In his footnote to Schindler's text, his editor Donald W. MacArdle, quoting the Kinsky-Halm Catalogue of Beethoven's works, assigns the G major Concerto to 1805–06, making it contemporaneous with the composer's work on the first two versions of *Fidelio*.[70] In addition, the indefatigable Thayer, drawing on the evidence available to him at the period of his researches, states: 'There is a sketch for the opening of the first movement near the end of the *Eroica* sketchbook, thus early 1804.'[71]

Modern-day Beethoven scholars confirm the foregoing remarks. For example, Braunstein comments:

> 'The first ideas for the G major Concerto were jotted down in a voluminous sketchbook that Beethoven filled with sketches for the Opera *Leonore*, later named *Fidelio*.'

Beethoven worked on the Opera during 1804 and 1805. After its completion he concerned himself with the Fourth Symphony, the series of three String Quartets, Op. 59, the Piano Concerto in G major, and the Violin Concerto. The Concertos were completed in 1806 and the Violin Concerto reached the public in the same year.[72]

In his discussion of Beethoven's work on his Opera, Barry Cooper states:

> 'Among the first sketches for *Leonora* are very early ones for three major works that were not completed for several years and had to wait until 1808 for their public premiere ...'.

He cites the Fifth and Sixth Symphonies and the Fourth Piano Concerto. Also found are preliminary sketch ideas for the Piano Sonata in F, Op. 54 and the Triple Concerto, Op. 56 — illustrative of Beethoven's capacity for working on several compositions at once. Cooper proposes Beethoven may have turned his attention to these compositions while waiting to receive the later sections of the Opera's libretto. Regarding the G major Piano Concerto he comments:

'Beethoven's initial sketch ['concept sketch'] for the Concerto in early 1804 is already very close to the final version of these five [opening] bars and it is remarkable how many ideas in the rest of the Concerto are generated by this opening phrase.'[73]

In his study of Beethoven at work during the period 1806—08, Cooper further remarks on the composer's creation of what he describes as 'a cluster of masterpieces'. The works for 1806, alone, include: String Quartets, Op. 59 (1805—06); G major Piano Concerto, Op. 58 (1805—06); *Leonora* (*Fidelio*), Version No. 2, Op. 72; Violin Concerto, Op. 61; Symphony No. 4, in B-flat major, Op. 60; and Thirty-two Variations for Piano WoO 16. To these may be added the Symphony No. 3 in E-flat major, Op. 55, dedicated to Prince Franz Joseph von Lobkowitz that was published by the Kunst- und Industrie-Comptoir. Truly, 'a wonderment of masterpieces' states Alexander Wheelock Thayer.

In his reflection on this period, and its related compositions, Maynard Solomon suggests Beethoven 'finds a sense of inner repose'. He explains:

'In a deepening trend, which began in 1806 with the Fourth Symphony, the Fourth Piano Concerto, and the Violin Concerto, [Beethoven] now seemed to imbue many of his works with a sense of inner repose that no longer required turbulent responses to grand challenges. A new lyrical strain enters his music, along with a pre-Romantic freedom of harmonic motion and structural design ... This practice results in a sense of calm, spaciousness, and measured nobility of rhetoric ...'.[74]

Barry Cooper believes the G major Piano Concerto was not sketched in detail until work on his Opera took its more-or-less final form. Beethoven resumed work on the Concerto only to set it aside once more to complete the 1806 revisions of the Opera. Cooper further suggests 'a score of some sort', was ready by 5 July 1806. As we shall see, Beethoven wrote to Breitkopf and Härtell on that day intimating that his brother Caspar Carl was about to travel to Leipzig taking with him, amongst other things, the score of 'a new piano concerto'. Cooper concludes 'the essential elements of the Concerto were evidently fixed by that time, for later sketches are associated with relatively minor details'.[75] Later, however, he adds:

> 'Over a year after preparing the work for publication, [Beethoven] saw many places for minor adjustment and this revised version [a reference to the score he used at the 22 December 1808 concert – see later] is much more virtuosic, sophisticated, sparkling, and original than the standard one.'[76]

In our discussion of the Piano Concerto No. 3 In C minor, Op. 37, we have seen how the cadenza assumed growing importance in Beethoven's writing for the genre of the piano concerto. This is no less evident in the G major Concerto on which Beethoven expended considerable time and effort. The Swiss musicologist and Beethoven scholar Willy Hess – who attained the great age of a hundred-and-one – has created audio re-creations of Beethoven's sketches for cadenzas to the Fourth Piano Concerto. A first movement cadenza, 'Hess 81', is derived from part of the H. C. Bodmer collection of sketches – Beethoven House Archives Mh 16, 17 and 18 – together with cadenzas for the final movement, 'Hess 82 and 83' and a brief cadenza for the *Rondo*.[77]

Tovey reminds us that the cadenza should be in accord with the spirit of the original music: 'The ideal classical cadenza would be an actual extemporization by a player capable of using the composer's language and above the temptation to display anything so banal as a review of the progress of music since the composer's date.' In support, he recalls Beethoven's remark: 'No artist deserved the title of *virtuoso* unless his extemporizations could pass for written compositions.' Tovey adds:

> 'The immense labour shown in Beethoven's innumerable sketches for all manner of works, from the greatest to the slightest, is mainly devoted to giving the written work the rhetorical perfection of extemporization.'

Notwithstanding his recognition of the care Beethoven took in the writing out of his cadenza passages, Tovey was — uncharacteristically — unimpressed by those he wrote for the Op. 58 Concerto:

> 'Of Beethoven's cadenzas for the G major Concerto, one set is tolerable and, when played by Schnabel, almost convincing. The other, inscribed by Beethoven with the pun *Cadenza per non cadre* [see later], is far sillier than the pun.'[78]

In an earlier essay, Tovey's estimation was even more bleak:

> 'Beethoven himself subsequently scribbled some astoundingly bad cadenzas to this work. Clara Schumann's cadenzas [see later] are better, but

feverishly Schumannesque; and a good musician is justified in doing his own best.'[79]

According to some authorities, Beethoven's first thoughts for the cadenzas to the first and third movements of the G major Concerto had their origins in the manuscript score that he was preparing for a chamber-music version of the composition for a private performance in 1807 (see later). 'These versions represent a first stage *en route* to his definitive copy of the cadenzas.'[80]

In the summer of 1809, Beethoven wrote cadenzas for the first and third movements of Mozart's Piano Concerto in D minor, K. 466 that may have been intended for his pupil Ferdinand Ries. At the same time, he turned once more to his own earlier piano concertos: Op. 15, three cadenzas for the first movement; Op. 19, one for the first movement; and Op. 37, one for the first movement. Of the cadenzas completed for the G major Concerto, Op. 58, he supplied two for the first movement and one for the third movement – other cadenzas are fragmentary.[81]

An incentive to write these cadenzas may have been to provide challenging keyboard material for his composition pupil, and patron, the Archduke Rudolph, as remarked the youngest son of Emperor Leopold II. Rudolph was an accomplished pianist and started to receive instruction from Beethoven at this time. For this undertaking, Beethoven assembled study materials

'drawing on the works of his own counterpoint teachers Albrechtsberger and Haydn and additionally those from the treatises of Fux and Kirnberger'.[82]

Musicologist Hans-Werner Küthen comments:

'Whether Beethoven intended these surviving cadenzas for the exclusive use of his pupil the Archduke Rudolph is a question requiring further study — they did not, after all, appear in any contemporary print and had to wait until 1864 for their partial publication in Breitkopf and Härtel's *Gesamtausgabe* [complete edition].'

He adds,

'Given their elemental significance within the framework of Beethoven's other late cadenzas for the Concertos Nos. 1 and 3, it is hardly likely that [the cadenzas for the G major Concerto] were intended exclusively for a single performer.'[83]

We reserve our discussion of the G major Concerto's musicology to the closing section of our text, but it will be useful here to make a few remarks about the character of Beethoven's cadenza writing.

Of the cadenzas Beethoven wrote for the first movement, pianists show a preference for the first. To quote Roeder once more:

'The longer and more brilliant cadenza for the G major Concerto is the most popular of the [first movement's] two. It is based on three of the movement's four themes and oscillates between 6/8 and common time. Once again, as in the Third Concerto, the soloist continues through the coda with lavish ornamentation in a great crescendo to the final cadence.'[84]

Michael Steinberg, mindful of the merits of the second cadenza Beethoven wrote, states:

> '[The] composer, aware of its musical and pianistic land-mines and never one to deny himself a pun, headed the piece *Cadenza ma senza cadere* ('Cadenza, but without falling down'). It also exemplifies to perfection Alfred Brendel's characterisation of Beethoven, the cadenza-composer, as "the architect [turned] into a genius running amok".'

Of the piece's spirited nature, Steinberg comments:

> 'Calculated to scare an audience into a state of extreme wakefulness, it begins with a violent version of what Beethoven does so poetically at the Concerto's beginning — an excursion into the "wrong" key. The game continues to give him pleasure, and in what appears to be a peace-making gesture he returns to the piano's first statement, *dolce*.'[85]

The American musician-musicologist Martin Meyer, in conversation with Alfred Brendel, raised the question with him is 'shock' and perhaps even 'humour' were to be found in Beethoven's cadenza-writing? In response, Brendel cited the second, less often played, cadenza for the first movement of the G major Concerto:

> '[In] its audacity [it] hits the listener like a slap in the face and shows absolutely no consideration for the character of the movement. It really does leave the virtuoso a free rein — or free path on

which to run amok and abandons all classical principles. There is still just about a certain amount of harmonic thread that runs through it and holds it all together.'

Brendel told Meyer how he had played, what he describes as 'the alternative cadenza', since the beginning of his career explaining: 'I found that it adds something to our knowledge of Beethoven.' He elaborated:

'The usual cadenza remains true to the dramatic lyricism of the first movement; the second cadenza, however, breaks all possible rules, and I think that the listener should not be spared.'[86]

We direct our narrative next to Beethoven's negotiations with his publishers. In so doing, it will be useful to recall the assistance he received for a period from his brother Carl. He had a reputation for driving hard bargains, was known as a 'skinflint' and did not always act circumspectly in his relationships with Beethoven's publishers. However, such was Beethoven's trust in Carl's negotiations, that he wrote to Breitkopf and Härtel on 22 April 1802: 'You can rely entirely on my *brother* – who, in general, attends to all my affairs.'[87] On 25 May 1806, Carl married Joanna Ries, a woman of whom Beethoven strongly disapproved; her amorous proclivities disposed him to refer to her as 'The Queen of the Night' – a thinly veiled reference to the vengeful character in Mozart's Opera *The Magic Flute*. From 1812, Beethoven's reliance on his brother ceased when Karl contracted tuberculosis – he died the following year.[88]

The music publishers Breitkopf and Härtel were based in Leipzig with Gottfried Christoph Härtel as head of the firm – his partner Breitkopf had died in 1800. Beethoven wrote a long letter of introduction to Härtel on 26 August 1804 in which he expressed the wish to establish a working relationship with the prestigious firm with the ultimate prospect of them publishing his works. This letter is illustrative of Beethoven's conviction of his worth and the value he set by his compositions. He offered Härtel: Symphony No. 3, Op. 55; Triple Concerto, Op. 56; Oratorio *Christ on the Mount of Olives*, Op. 85; and the three Piano Sonatas Op. 53, Op. 54, and Op. 57. He requested a fee of 2000 gulden (c.f. florins). He considered this to be a reasonable sum on the grounds 'people [publishers] give me up to 60 ducats for a single sonata for pianoforte solo'.[89]

Härtell responded to Beethoven on 30 August. His letter reveals the challenges confronting publishers at this time. He opens: 'We highly esteem and value your kind application to us concerning the four works that you have produced.' Härtell is referring here to the piano sonatas to which Beethoven makes reference and had assumed that the three sonatas mentioned were in fact a single opus — as then typical in eighteenth-century terms.

Härtell proudly described his music engraving and publishing house as being well organized and capable of producing large works in considerable numbers. He regretted, though, that his business was not in a position at present to fulfil the composer's requirements. He explained: 'The reason for this is that sales in Germany have been greatly diminished by pirate printings.' He gave the following illustration:

> 'We have had this experience with Mozart's *Requiem* and *Don Giovanni*, Handel's *Messiah*, Haydn's *Masses* and similar works which caused us too great a loss ...'.[90]

Beethoven, with the assistance of his brother Carl, continued to negotiate with Breitkopf and Härtell through the autumn of 1804 but with no definite outcome. Beethoven did, however, eventually establish a productive relationship with Breitkopf and Härtell — as the firm continued to be named despite the death of Breitkopf. Between 1809 and 1812 they published, for example: the Fifth and Sixth Symphonies, the Cello Sonata, Op. 69, the Piano Trios, Op. 70, and the Fifth Piano Concerto, Op. 73.

In 1805, the Austrian-born French composer, music publisher and piano manufacturer Ignaz (Ignace) Pleyel travelled to Vienna with his son Camille with the intention of establishing a branch of his firm there. During his stay he heard Beethoven improvise at a musical gathering at the salon of Prince Lobkowitz, the composer taking as his theme a melody from one of Pleyel's recently composed string quartets. According to Carl Czerny, who was present, Pleyel was so moved he kissed Beethoven's hands in admiration.[91] On 26 April 1807, Beethoven wrote in affectionate terms to Camille and offered him 'new works' for publication in Paris that he was simultaneously offering for publication in Vienna and London. The new works were: the Fourth Symphony, the Overture to *Coriolan*, the Violin Concerto — and its arrangement as a Piano Concerto, the three *Razumovsky* String Quartets, and the Fourth Piano Concerto. Pleyel's reply has not survived but it is known he did not take up Beethoven's offer; perhaps, once more, the price was too high — Beethoven had requested payment of 1,200 florins in Augsburg currency.[92]

In approaching Pleyel in Paris, Beethoven was endeavouring to have his works published simultaneously in France, England and Germany. Thereby, he hoped to sell more copies and increase his income. Muzio Clementi had already acquired some of his compositions for England and the publisher Kunst- und Industrie-Comptoir had similarly acquired them for the German market. Beethoven has sometimes been censured for allegedly negotiating nefariously, in this way, with several publishers at once. However, on this occasion, he took care to stipulate in his correspondence the dates of publication for the three different publishers — so as to circumvent the likelihood of financial loss to either party.[93]

On 27 March 1806, Carl wrote to another publisher, Franz Anton Hoffmeister, on his brother's behalf. Hoffmeister was himself a prolific composer and in 1800 established the Bureau de musique at Leipzig with his partner, the organist Ambrosius Kühnel — the partnership, thereby, being known as Hoffmeister and Kühnel. It was largely Kühnel who managed the firm's business from Leipzig. In his letter, Carl offered Hoffmeister and Kühnel the Fourth Piano Concerto together with the Oratorio *Christus am Ölberge* for 600 florins.[94] On 12 April, Kühnel replied to Beethoven requesting further information regarding the offer to publish his 'new Piano Concerto' and 'its fairest price'. He also requested more details about the composer's Opera *Leonora* that had been premiered, unsuccessfully, on 20 November 1805. Kühnel observed: 'When determining the fee, I always keep in mind that I spend more for elegance and correctness than other publishers do.'[95]

On 5 July, Beethoven himself wrote to Breitkopf and Härtel intimating that Carl would be travelling to Leipzig and would be taking with him 'the Overture to my Opera [*Fidelio*, Leonora No. 3] in pianoforte arrangement, my Oratorio [*Christus am Ölberge*], and a *new Pianoforte Concerto*' [Beethoven's emphasis] — which may be taken as a reference to the G major Concerto, Op. 58.[96] There is no evidence, however, that Carl did in fact undertake the intended journey to Leipzig.

Notwithstanding his independence of mind, Beethoven was not immune to criticism, as we can infer from a swipe he took at Härtell whose firm was responsible for the publication of the *Allgemeine musikalische Zeitung*. The *AmZ* had brought out an unfavourable review of the *Eroica* Symphony, prompting Beethoven to add in his letter of 5 July:

'If you fancy that you can injure *me* by publishing articles of that kind, you are very much mistaken. On the contrary, by so doing you merely bring your Journal into disrepute ...'.[97]

By the autumn, Beethoven appears to have made his peace with Härtel. On 3 September he wrote to reassure his publishing firm that it was his intention they should have exclusive rights to publish his work in Germany – save in a few cases. The reason for this was that Breitkopf and Härtell were aware the composer was also receiving offers from others to publish his works. Beethoven revealed that he even contemplated a time when he might leave Germany and be free then to publish his music in Paris or London. He closed his letter to Härtel stating:

'I can ... send you immediately *three Violin Quartets* [Op. 59], a *new Pianoforte Concerto* [Op. 58], a new Symphony [Op. 60], the score of my opera [*Leonora*], and my oratorio [*Christus am Ölberge*]'.[98]

On 18 November, Beethoven sought to further reassure Härtell that any works he sold his publishing house would belong to it exclusively '*and would be quite different from those for France or England or Scotland*'. Beethoven always used italics (in the form of underlining) to give emphasis to his meaning. To secure publication of the three String Quartets, Op. 59, he requested payment of 600 gulden and for the G major Piano Concerto a further 300 gulden.[99]

Our consideration of negotiations with publishers takes us into the following year.

We recall that in 1804 Muzio Clementi had expressed an interest in publishing a number of Beethoven's compositions (see above). Clementi first became personally acquainted with Beethoven when on a business trip to Vienna in 1807. On 22 April 1807 he wrote to his business partner William Frederick Collard in London: 'By a little management and without committing myself, I have at last made a complete conquest of that *haughty beauty* [Clementi's italics] Beethoven.' Clementi explained how he had persuaded the composer to have his works published in England (London) and how his publishing house would take care of him. Beethoven obligingly gave an undertaking to prepare a list of his available publications. Clementi told Collard he had agreed with Beethoven to take the Concerto for Pianoforte No. 4. Op. 58; the three String Quartets Op. 59; the Symphony No. 4, Op. 60; and the Overture *Coriolan*, Op. 62. He also requested the Violin Concerto, Op. 61 that Clementi described as being 'very beautiful' and which, at his request, Beethoven had offered to adapt for the pianoforte — what would in effect become Piano Concerto, Op. 61a. For all these works Beethoven was to receive two hundred pounds sterling — a considerable sum.[100]

On the same day, Clementi wrote to Breitkopf and Härtell informing the publisher of the personal friendship he had established with Beethoven and of the Contract he had agreed with the composer. He explained, it ceded to him the proprietary rights to publish in England the Piano Concerto No. 4, Op. 58, the three *Razumovsky* String

Quartets, Op. 59, the Symphony No. 4, Op. 60, the Violin Concerto, and the Overture *Coriolan*, Op. 62.[101] The Quartets were later published by Clementi in London (1809–10) together with the Violin Concerto – also, as adapted by Beethoven, as a Piano Concerto.

The Contract between Clementi and Beethoven, written in French, was signed by the signatories to both parties and dated 20 April 1807.[102] The Symphony, Overture and Piano Concerto were duly despatched to England by courier but it seems they never reached Clementi and were never published by him, despite the handsome price he had paid for this set of compositions. The military conflict in Europe may have disrupted the already tenuous postal services.[103] If Clementi did in fact receive the works in question, a disastrous fire that consumed Clementi and Co.'s London premises may offer an alternative explanation for his failure to fulfil all his publication intentions. This may also explain why Beethoven had to wait until the spring of 1810 to receive his payment.

Setting aside these tribulations, Beethoven was clearly pleased with his business dealings with Clementi as is evident from a letter he wrote on 11 May to Count Franz von Brunswick. He was an excellent cellist and his wife an accomplished pianist. Beethoven dedicated his celebrated *Appassionata* Piano Sonata, Op. 57 to Franz. By way of interest, Franz was the brother of Josephine and Therese to whom Beethoven jointly dedicated his Piano Duet Variations on *Ich denke dein*, WoO 74 when they were his piano pupils in the years 1799–1804. Moreover, he was in love at various times with both sisters and the two of them have, as a consequence, been considered as candidates for the composer's *Immortal Beloved* – Josephine in particular.

Schindler describes Franz von Brunswick as: 'One of the most enlightened connoisseurs of Beethoven's music who could truly call himself Beethoven's pupil.'[104] In his letter, Beethoven enthused to the Count:

> 'This is just to tell you that I have come to a very good arrangement with Clementi — I am to get two hundred pounds sterling and, what is more, I shall be able to sell the same works in Germany and France — and, in addition, he has given me further orders — so that by this means I may hope, even in my early years, to achieve the dignity of a true artist.'[105]

On 26 April, Beethoven, in the role of musician-business-man, corresponded with Nikolaus Simrock, resident in the composer's native township Bonn — we have encountered Simrock already (see above). He explained his intention to sell six of his new works — those just mentioned — to publishers in France (Ignaz Pleyel in Paris), in England (Muzio Clementi) and in Vienna (Bureau des Arts et d'Industrie). He offered the same six works to Simrock for 1200 gulden 'in Augsburg currency' — a stable currency of high-value denomination; although Beethoven was not very good at arithmetic he was shrewd in his financial dealings with publishers.[106] By offering these works to more than one publisher, with the prospect of them being published more-or-less simultaneously in France, England, and Austria, this would not only, as remarked, increase his sales but would also protect himself from piracy — then prevalent at the time.

Simrock replied to Beethoven on 31 May expressing his interest in publishing the works the composer had offered for sale. However, his letter is interesting in that it sheds light on the challenges to the music publishing business at this time in Austria — in addition to the problems of piracy.

Simrock complains of the effect the French occupation was having: '[At] no time ... has the music business been as very slow as it is now, and keeps getting slower daily'. He could not meet Beethoven's demands explaining, with reference to the French currency that was then in circulation: 'All that I can do in my lean situation is to scrape together 1,600 livres.'[107]

The Bureau des Arts et d'Industrie was to be Beethoven's principal publisher between the years 1802–08 and was also known as the Kunst- und Industrie-Comptoir. One of the partner's in the firm was Joseph Sonnleithner, a Director of the Theater an der Wien and remembered today for supplying Beethoven with the libretto to his Opera *Fidelio*. 1808 would be a particularly significant one in Beethoven's association with the firm. It saw the publication of the first editions of the Fourth Symphony, the Fourth Piano Concerto, the Violin Concerto, and Beethoven's arrangement of it as a piano concerto, the three *Razumovsky* String Quartets, and the *Coriolan* Overture.[108]

The sketch sources for the G major Piano Concerto, Op. 58 have their tentative origins in the so-called Autograph 19 E. This consists of a miscellaneous collection of autograph scores, sketches, and letters that was purchased by the former Royal Library, Berlin in 1874. It now forms part of the Beethoven archive in the Staatsbibliothek Preussischer Kulturbesitz, West Berlin.

'The Autograph consists of several parts of which 19E has 20 leaves (40 pages). Sketches for Op. 58 are found between folios 32–35 alongside sketches for the Fifth Symphony, Op. 67 and passages for *Christ on the Mount of Olives*, Op. 85.'[109]

Between June 1803 to about April 1804, Beethoven made use of the Landsberg 6 source — the so-called *Eroica* sketchbook. It was formerly owned by the collector of manuscripts Ludwig Landsberg and was later purchased by the Royal Library, Berlin. Its 91 leaves contain 'concept sketches' for the start of the G major Piano Concerto together with sketches for the Fifth and Sixth Symphonies. Sketches for the first movement of the Concerto are found at p. 148 and are considered to date from the early months of 1804.[110] Formerly in the Staatsbibliothek Preussischer Kulturbesitz, it was removed in wartime to the Biblioteka Jagiellońska in Krakow.[111]

Describing Beethoven's early sketches, Braunstein comments:

> 'The first ideas for the G major Concerto were jotted down in a voluminous sketchbook that Beethoven filled with sketches for the Opera *Leonore*, later named *Fidelio*. Beethoven worked on the Opera during 1804 and 1805. After its completion he concerned himself with the Fourth Symphony, the series of three String Quartets, Op. 59, the Piano Concerto in G major, and the Violin Concerto.'[112]

Authorities are in agreement that few sketches survive for the period when it is believed Beethoven worked most intensively on the G major Concerto. Douglas Porter Johnson observes, 'Op. 58 was substantially written in 1805–06' and further remarks, 'there is no extant evidence for Beethoven's detailed working-out of the Fourth Piano Concerto'. This, he suggests, indicates a sketchbook for this period has been lost.[113] Similarly, Barry Cooper states:

'[From] 1806–07 ... there are very few sketches for such major works as the Fourth Piano Concerto, the Fourth Symphony, the Violin Concerto, and the Overture *Coriolan*.'

He concludes:

'It is impossible to believe that no other sketches were made for such complex works; and it is more likely that a single book has been lost in each case than a lot of loose leaves are missing.'

He attributes the compositional process of the Fourth Piano Concerto to 'late 1805 to early 1807'.[114]

Alan Tyson's researches reveal fair copies of passages of piano-writing for Op. 58 are found in the Staatsbibliothek Preussischer Kulturbesitz collections and the Landsberg 10, sketchbook at pp. 1–4 and pp. 13–16. He suggests: 'These probably date from around the time of the Concerto's first performance (March 1807).'[115]

A corrected manuscript score for the G major Concerto is preserved in the archives of the Gesellschaft der Musikfreunde, Vienna. The copyist is thought to be 'Copyist D' who has been identified as Joseph Klumper. The score was sold at the auction of Beethoven's estate on 5 November 1827, being purchased by Ferdinand Pringer — a friend of the composer.[116] From Leon Plantinga's study of this score, we learn:

'The first and third movements of this manuscript appear to have served as the engraver's copy (*Stichvorlage*) for the first edition; it bears engraver's markings and the plate number of the edition as well as a number of corrections in Beethoven's *röthel*, the red crayon he characteristically used in proofreading ... The second movement in this manuscript is a much later copy ....'.[117]

The majority of Beethoven's autograph entries are confined to the piano part of the first movement. Plantinga remarks: 'In an often fleeting "private" notation they record a startling elaboration of the solo part as we know it, an elaboration that clearly represents a stage of Beethoven's ideas *subsequent* [emphasis added] to that of the first performance, from which all later ones were derived.' He describes Beethoven's adaptations as being 'sketchy in the extreme' and how they 'consist only of a stream of noteheads'. As they stand

> 'these notations look very much as if they were for [Beethoven's] own use — much like the sketches he typically made for cadenzas shortly before his performances'.

The score reveals evidence of Beethoven responding to the newly available six-octave keyboard: '[The] revisions in the Vienna manuscript ... explore the uppermost reaches of the expanded keyboard, all the way up to f´´´´, in the interests of new brilliance in the solo part ...'.[118]

Sketches for the cadenzas to the Fourth Piano Concerto are preserved in the Beethoven House Archives in Bonn. Of the three cadenzas he wrote for the first movement, one is incomplete. Of the three cadenzas for the finale one is fragmentary and another 'although incomplete, resembles the one which appeared in the first edition'.[119] The Bonn sketches originally belonged to the Swiss autograph collector Hans Conrad Bodmer, from whose name they derive their catalogue numbers. From these sources we derive the following.

First movement: H.C.B. Mh 14 is an eight-page manuscript facsimile of a cadenza for the first movement that was originally intended for Beethoven's pupil the Archduke Rudolph. It still bears the reference number 101 indicating it once belonged to the Archduke's own Library. H.C.B. Mh 15 is a six-page manuscript facsimile of a cadenza also intended for the first movement. It is marked *Cadenza ma senza cadre* which may be taken to mean 'but without falling'. The wording is illustrative of Beethoven's typical puns, in this case implying the pianist should not 'fall' – that is 'stumble' – in encountering the challenges posed by Beethoven's dextrous keyboard writing. The cadenza was intended to be inserted at page 18 in the Concerto score.[120] H.C.B. Mh 16 is a further two-page manuscript facsimile, also intended for the first movement. It is written out in bold, clearer handwriting than the foregoing with no corrections or amendments. The accompanying text informs:

> '[The] manuscript was clearly inserted into an original [performing] edition of the Concerto, which was in the Archduke Rudolph's collection, bearing the call number [catalogue number] 101 [as written on the top left of the manuscript].'[121]

Rondo finale: H.C.B. Mh 17 illustrates Beethoven's thoughts for a cadenza to the *Rondo* of the final movement. The accompanying text states:

> 'As with all of Beethoven's cadenzas for the Fourth Piano Concerto, this one was also inserted into the original edition of the Concerto in the music collection of Archduke Rudolph.'

The writer qualifies this remark stating, it is not a cadenza in the strictest sense 'but rather a transition, which has been fully written out, within the last movement'. He explains:

> 'This movement is constructed like a circle because the refrain keeps returning. The circular form is interrupted by different interludes. Before the theme returns each time in the orchestra, the solo piano has a transitional part, which is written out.'

Beethoven marks the text: '*Rondo* first entry to the theme remains; second entry into the theme.' The Beethoven House editor comments: '[Beethoven] therefore considered the first transition to be fitting but intended the second to be replaced by this manuscript.'[122]

HCB Mh18 is a short cadenza designated *Cadenza nel Rondo* that the Beethoven House editor suggests, with a touch of humour, may have been intended 'for tired pianists' and that Beethoven thereby 'contented himself here with a further transition, sparing himself the virtuoso exhibition of an expansive cadenza'. The supporting text states:

> '[As] with most of the other cadenzas there is a note under the [catalogue] number showing the place in the solo part at which the manuscript was to be inserted.' In this case it is 'p. 34'.[123]

HCB Mh19 consists of four pages of sketches for the second cadenza of the *Rondo* finale. The supporting text informs: 'Beethoven actually composed his cadenzas in pairs. A cadenza for the first movement was paired with a cadenza for the last one — like cadenza "full version" for the whole cadenza ... HCB Mh 19 is the second cadenza of one of these pairs, its other half being HCB Mh 14. The latter was also logically given the heading *Zweite kadenz* by the composer.'[124]

In the summer of 1808, Beethoven wrote to Baron Ignaz von Gleichenstein who, as we have seen, was both a friend of the composer and one who rendered him various services particularly with his correspondence. He was also a witness to the composer's Contract with Clementi. At this time, Beethoven was spending the summer in Heiligenstadt and wrote of his delight in seeing Gleichenstein and told him he was planning

> 'something which presumably will greatly surprise you ... because another work is appearing in which you will be given what is due to you – or to our friendship'.[125]

Beethoven is referring here to the Fourth Piano Concerto that he intended to dedicate to Gleichenstein. However, he later had a change of mind and dedicated the work to his composition pupil the Archduke Rudolph. By way of compensation, Gleichenstein, as we have seen, received the dedication to the Cello Sonata, No. 3, Op. 69 – the cello being Gleichenstein's chosen instrument.

The G major Piano Concerto was eventually published by the Bureau des Arts et d'Industrie with a dedication to Rudolph. The Title Page of the original edition announces, in translation:

> 'Fourth Piano Concerto with first and second Violins, Violas, Flute, two Oboes, two Clarinets, two Horns, two Bassoons, Trumpets, Drums, Cellos and Bass. Most respectfully dedicated to His Royal Highness the Archduke Rudolph von Oesterreich, by L. van Beethoven, Op. 58.

Vienna and Pesth Society of Arts and
Industries.'[126]

We have remarked Rudolph was an accomplished pianist.
In fact some authorities consider had he not followed his
clerical vocation, and not withstanding his princely status,
he might have had a career as a performing artist. Over time,
Beethoven honoured his distinguished pupil with an impressive list of dedications including, in addition to the G major
Concerto: the Piano Concerto in E-flat major; the Piano
Sonatas E-flat major, Op. 81a and B-flat major, Op. 106;
the Violin Sonata in G major, Op. 96; the Trio in B-flat
major, Op. 97; the vocal score to *Fidelio*; the *Missa Solemnis*; and the piano transcription of the *Great Fugue*, Op.
133. Perhaps Rudolph's most personal enduring legacy to
music, however, are his own forty variations on a theme set
him by Beethoven (WoO 200). These were published in
1818 with a dedication to his teacher.

The first full score of the G major Piano Concerto, with
piano and orchestral parts combined, did not appear in
Beethoven's lifetime. It was published first by C. F. Peters
in Leipzig, but not until 1861. In 1863, Breitkopf and Härtell
brought out the score in their complete edition of
Beethoven's works.

Given that the G major Piano Concerto is a cornerstone
of today's concert repertory, and forms a part of most
classical-pianists' repertoire, it seems almost unbelievable
that it should have been performed twice only, in public, in
the composer's lifetime and languished thereafter until it
was rescued from neglect, largely as a consequence of the
endeavours of the youthful Felix Mendelsohn. (see later)

Musicological tradition maintains the G major Concerto was first heard in a private chamber performance in
March 1807 that took place in the great salon of

Beethoven's patron Prince Franz Joseph Lobkowitz. By this time, he had supplanted Prince Lichnowsky as the composer's principal benefactor. In due course, Beethoven honoured Lobkowitz with dedications to the Third, Fifth, and Sixth Symphonies, and the String Quartets, Op. 18 and Op. 74.

Quoting from the April 1807 issue of the pioneering *Journal des Luxus und der Moden,* Thayer states:

> 'Beethoven gave two concerts in the house [Vienna residential Palace] of Prince L. at which nothing but his own compositions were performed; namely his first four Symphonies, an Overture to the tragedy *Coriolan,* a Pianoforte Concerto, and some airs from the Opera *Fidelio.*'

Thayer conjectures the reference to 'Prince L.' may be taken to signify Prince Lobkowitz and not his former benefactor Prince Lichnowsky, with whom Beethoven had quarrelled the previous autumn. Some authorities consider the reference to 'a Pianoforte Concerto' signifies the G major Concerto, but others remain undecided. (see below) There is no doubt, however, that the concert at which the Concerto in question was performed took place sometime in March. The contributor to the *Journal des Luxus und der Moden* enthused:

> 'Richness of ideas, bold originality and fullness of power, which are the particular merits of Beethoven's muse, were very much in evidence to everyone at these concerts; yet many found fault with a lack of noble simplicity and all too fruitful accumulation of ideas which, on account of their number, were not always adequately

worked out and blended, thereby, creating the
effect more often of [a] rough diamond.'[127]

In support of the belief that it was indeed a chamber
adaptation of the G major Concerto that was performed in
March 1807, Hans-Werner Küthen makes the following
observations:

'The Bohemian nobleman [Lobkowitz] was so
impressed with the new Concerto that he himself
probably instigated the plan to arrange a chamber-
music version for string quintet (the Prince's
preferred ensemble).'

Küthen considers proof that Beethoven sanctioned, and
even helped to produce this arrangement, is provided 'by
the changes he jotted down in the solo part of the outside
movements in more than eighty passages'. On the basis of
his researches, Küthen suggests:

'Beethoven assigned the task of reducing the
orchestral part to Franz Alexander Pössinger,
whose acquaintance he had made in 1803 when
Pössinger had appraised the String Quintet, Op.
29.'

Küthen concludes:

'The resultant version for piano and five-part string
ensemble saw the light of day in the early weeks of
summer 1807, a full year before the original
edition of the orchestral version was offered for
sale by the Bureau des Arts et d'Industrie.'[128]

Leon Plantinga makes the case for a later date than March 1807 for the unveiling of the G major Concerto:

> '[It] is tempting to think this was the composition performed at Lobkowitz's concerts in March of that year. But the evidence is weak. There seemed to be no hesitation at these concerts about presenting earlier works ... As the reports make no mention of Beethoven as soloist, the piano part for the Concerto may well have been taken by another pianist, and there were several such in Vienna who had earlier concertos of his in their fingers.'

He adds:

> '[One] might well wonder why, Reichardt, listening to the December 1808 concert from Lobkowitz's box, should speak of the Concerto as "new" if it had been performed some twenty-one months earlier at the home of the man sitting next to him.' Plantinga suggests the performance of December 1808 (see shortly) should be regarded as the occasion of the true premiere of the G major Concerto.'[129]

The following year, a moving incident occurred arising as a consequence of Beethoven's deafness. Friedrich Reichardt describes attending what he refers to as 'an amateur concert' that took place on 10 December 1808. The venue was 'three small rooms' into which a large crowd was assembled such that Reichardt 'could hardly breath'. Moreover, he found 'the blare of the trumpets, kettledrums and all manner of wind instruments was quite deafening'. The programme included Beethoven's Overture to Collin's *Coriolan* that, in the confined space, Reichardt found 'gigantic and over-whelming' all the more so since 'everyone tried with all his might to increase the noise'. The reason for this excess was that Beethoven was present and the instrumentalists were doing their utmost to ensure he could hear their rendering of his music. Reichardt set aside his misgivings reflecting: 'It gave me great pleasure to see dear Beethoven being much fêted.'[130]

A few days later, Beethoven was centre-stage in a concert of his works — his Musical *Akademie* — that has passed into legend. On 17 December a notice was displayed in the *Wiener Zeitung* announcing:

'On Thursday 22 December, Ludwig van Beethoven will have the pleasure of giving a concert in the Imperial and Royal Court Theater an der Wien. All the items are works of his own composition, are absolutely new, and have not yet been heard in public:

First half: 1, A Symphony entitled *Memories of Country Life*, in F major, No. 5 [in fact this was the composer's *Sixth* Symphony known as the *Pastoral*, Op. 68]; 2, Aria [*Ah! perfido*, Op. 65]; 3, Hymn with Latin text with chorus and solos [the *Gloria* from the C major Mass, Op. 86]; 4, Piano Concerto with Beethoven as soloist [G major Concerto, Op. 58].

Second half: 1, Grand Symphony in C minor, No. 6 [the celebrated *Fifth* Symphony]; 2, Sacred item with Latin text with chorus and solos [the *Sanctus* from the C major Mass, Op. 86]; 3, *Fantasia* for pianoforte solo [Op. 77]; Pianoforte *Fantasia* with the participation of the whole orchestra and with the introduction of choruses [Op. 80].'

In Thayer's words: 'Such a programme ... was certainly an ample provision for an evening's entertainment of the most insatiably musical enthusiast ...'.[131]

On the night in question, the very newness and number of the works performed, misunderstandings between Beethoven and the performers and their subsequent exhaustion, hectic last-minute preparations, and, not least, a freezing cold concert hall – the heating system had failed – all conspired to deprive the occasion – and Beethoven – of the adulation so richly deserved.

To accommodate all the works on the programme, the concert commenced at 6.30 p.m. Reichardt had been invited to attend the concert as the guest of Beethoven's patron Prince Lobkowitz and to join his party in the Prince's box. He relates:

'There we held out in the bitterest cold from half-past six until half-past ten, and experienced the fact that one can easily have too much of a good – and even more of a strong – thing.'[132]

A detailed account of the concert is outside the scope of our study and we confine ourselves to a few of the ensuing circumstances.

Ignaz von Seyfried, the Director of the Theater an der Wien, states the Choral *Fantasia* received only a single rehearsal 'with wet voice-parts as usual' – Beethoven was still writing out some of the parts at 6 30 a.m. on the morning of the concert. According to Seyfried's account, the orchestra broke down prompting Beethoven 'to shout from the piano for a new beginning'. Ferdinand Ries also states the clarinet player lost his way in the Choral *Fantasia* prompting Beethoven to call the orchestra to a halt — and abusing the players 'in the coarsest of terms'. He relates that although at the repeat 'the success was great', the players, aggrieved at their treatment, 'resolved not to play again if Beethoven was to conduct'. In his *Autobiography*, Louis Spohr describes Beethoven's overly demonstrative attempts to conduct from the piano. He describes how his gestures swept the candles from the piano, illuminating his music, and of the efforts of a choirboy attempting to hold a replacement candle. Standing too close to the animated conductor-pianist, he received a blow on the face — prompting 'Bacchanalian jubilation' amongst some members of the audience.

The premier of *Ah Perfido* should have gone well since it was intended to be performed by Anna Milder-Hauptmann who had sung the title role of *Leonora* just three years previously — when only twenty years old. Beethoven appears to have quarrelled with her at the last moment and, as a consequence, a less-experienced singer took her place — only to be overcome with stage fright and 'made wretched work of the aria'.

Reichardt, somewhat dismissively, considered the Fifth Symphony to be too long but enjoyed the *Pastoral* Symphony, finding it to be 'full of gorgeous painting and brilliant images'. He also thought Beethoven played the Piano Concerto in G 'marvellously well in the quickest time', despite what he believed to be its 'monstrous difficulty'.[133]

Reichardt's description of the technical challenges posed by the G major Concerto is of particular interest. Carl Czerny, who was present at the December concert, relates that Beethoven played the Concerto *muthwilligkeit* ('roguishly') and 'added more notes than were written in the score' — suggesting Beethoven introduced a measure of 'improvisation' in his performance. Perhaps it was this additional *bravura* that had seized Reichardt's attention, disposing him to remark as he did.

The available evidence supports the view that Beethoven had indeed elaborated the piano part of the Concerto:

> 'The manuscript score that Beethoven evidently used for directing the performance still survives (the middle movement is missing), and over a hundred bars there are minute, sketchy annotations of variants in Beethoven's handwriting. These were probably made in preparation for the performance, and they demonstrate how he was never fully satisfied with even his greatest works.'[134]

Leon Plantinga remarks:

> 'The Vienna manuscript copy that served as the *Stichvorlage* ('copy template') for the first edition evidently documents something of this *muth-willigkeit.*'

He cites its 'startlingly agile ornament that appreciably escalates the degree of virtuosity in the solo part and sometimes palpably alters its effect'. He summarizes:

> '[What] the audience at the Theater an der Wien heard that long December evening in 1808 was probably not quite the Fourth Concerto as we know it, but a richly elaborated version of it, the piano's expansive music planned, partly improvised. In its creator's hands, the Fourth Piano Concerto continued to be less the presentation of a "work" than a live activity, a unique event

subject to whim, its nature flowing partly from the mood of the moment.'

Plantinga suggests the work seemed to exist for Beethoven on two levels: One for publication — the work as we know it containing 'a certain intimate and subdued quality' — and the other in which the solo part is 'more dazzling and astonishing'. He concludes, this version 'must remain largely in our imagination'.[135]

We recall the *Wiener Zeitung* announced a further concert that was programmed to take place the following evening on 23 December. This was, in part, intended as an act of homage to the venerable Haydn — then age 76 — and some of his vocal works were respectfully performed. Beethoven, former pupil of Haydn, wanted to take advantage of this occasion and requested Ferdinand Ries to play the G major Piano Concerto.

Ries explains:

'One day Beethoven visited me carrying his Fourth Piano Concerto in G major, Op. 58 tucked under his arm. "Next Saturday you have to play this in the Kärnthnertor Theater".'

*

This gave only five days for Ries to learn and practice the work. Accomplished pianist as he was, Ries was no Franz Liszt — who had once learned to play the C minor Concerto in a single day — and so he declined. As he relates: 'Unluckily I remarked to him that the time was too short to learn to play it well; would he not permit me to perform the C minor Concerto?' Beethoven, in a characteristic rage, approached another pianist — Carl Friedrich Stein — who was the brother of Nanette Streicher — wife-member of the celebrated Viennese firm of piano manufacturers.

Stein initially agreed to play the new Concerto but, eventually, realizing the challenge of the undertaking, he too later declined and, like Ries, asked permission to play the C minor Concerto. With time so short, Beethoven had little option but to give his consent. Ries reports the Concerto 'made no effect' and that 'Beethoven was very angry'. Could it be that Ries had foresight of the 'decorative passages and many more notes' to which we have made reference and was, thereby, intimidated from attempting to master the music in the short time available? Beethoven later made his peace with Ries. He realized there had been a misunderstanding on the composer's part, as he later explained to his former pupil: 'I though you just did not particularly want to play the G major Concerto.'[136]

The following year, the *Allgemeine musikalische Zeitung* reported a performance of what the music correspondent described as 'the newest of Beethoven's pianoforte concertos, in G major [published by] the Vienna, Industrie-Comptoir'; this had taken place on 11 May 1809. At the concert in question, a flute concerto by the contemporary German composer August Müller was also performed – coincidentally in the same key of G major. The music critic praised this for being 'most superior, effective and also most gratifying to the solo player'. Of the G major Concerto, Op. 58 he remarked:

> 'The one by Beethoven is the most wonderful, unusual, artistic, and difficult of all those that [Beethoven] has written, yet less gratifying to the solo player than, for example, that in C [Op. 15, No. 1].'

He found aspects of the work challenging: 'The first movement, in particular, will be heard many times before we are able to follow it completely and therefore truly enjoy it.'

The second and third movements, though, earned the critic's unqualified praise:

> 'This is, however, less the case with the second movement, uncommonly expressive in its beautiful simplicity, and with the third, which rises up exuberantly with powerful joy.'

He concluded: 'Properly performed, they will find full approval everywhere on first hearing.'[137]

We now consider the fortunes of the G major Concerto in the ensuing years and into the nineteenth century.

From Anton Schindler we learn that towards the end of his life Beethoven complained of the public neglect of many of his works. This appears to have been the fate, in particular, of the concertos. Schindler laments:

> '[The] virtuosi of the time approached the Beethoven concertos with unconcealed reluctance, while the public showed no liking or very little of them.'

He adds:

> 'The C minor Concerto and The *Choral Fantasy* were each performed perhaps twice in fifteen years, and the Violin Concerto was performed ... by Franz Clement in 1806 with no success at all ... The Piano Concerto in G major suffered a similar fate. It lay untouched for twenty years after its first performance, while the Triple Concerto was neglected for an even longer time.'

He reflects:

> 'The principal cause of this neglect was a change
> in the style of piano playing introduced by
> Hummel, Moscheles, Czerny, and others. This
> new style was totally foreign to Beethoven's music,
> both in form and in material. Its salient character-
> istics — elegance, polish, and technical display —
> were inappropriate to Beethoven's piano compo-
> sitions and failed to convey to audiences the
> profound spiritual nature of the concertos.'[138]

Schindler may have somewhat exaggerated the extent of the
neglect of the Fourth Piano Concerto since on 8 April 1818,
the *Allgemeine musikalische Zeitung* reported on a performance of the G major Concerto performed by the German
composer-conductor-organist-pianist Friedrich Schneider.
The occasion prompted the *AmZ's* critic to comment:

> 'This *little-known composition* [emphasis added],
> which is nevertheless one of the most original
> and, particularly in the first two movements, was
> performed by the soloist and orchestra master-
> fully throughout and with the most beautiful
> effect.'

The editors to the text we have just quoted add:

> '[The] relative neglect of the G major Concerto
> in Beethoven's lifetime may have been attributa-
> ble, in part, due to the difficulty of the piano part
> and, more plausibly, to the fact that pianists
> typically performed their own concertos in public

performance — a thing no longer possible for the deaf composer.'[139]

In 1824 the Berlin music critic Adolph Bernhard Marx wrote an essay titled — in translation — 'Some words about concert life, especially in large cities.' In this he expressed the desire 'to hear the *Pastoral* Symphony and the Fourth Piano Concerto played more often'. He deplored the all-too frequent performance of 'worthless compositions' and the 'ill-mannered craving for the new'. He asked: 'When so many operas in many cities obtain fifty, a hundred performances, should not a Beethoven concerto deserve ten performances?' Of Beethoven's Op. 58, Marx enthused: 'What can be more simple than the immortal *Adagio* in Beethoven's G major Concerto?' He further enthused how the work had delighted him the first time he read it in score and, after hearing it three times, he still did not dare to presume 'he had grasped its entire profundity'.[140]

We learn of the first performance of the G major Concerto in England from an account of the early years of the (Royal) Philharmonic Society of London and of Cipriani Potter's contribution to its affairs. The Notes to the 1825 Concert Season record:

'This year is a memorable one in the history of the Society, for at the third concert, on 21 March [1825], was performed, for the first time in England, Beethoven's *Choral* Symphony, the immortal No. 9.'

It was described in the Programme as a 'New Grand Characteristic *Sinfonia* with vocal finale'. Of related interest is that at a Directors' Meeting on 10 November 1822, it had

310

been resolved to offer Beethoven fifty pounds sterling for the composition of the Symphony.

The 1825 Concert Season of the Philharmonic Society was also memorable for realizing the first performance in England of the G major Concerto. This took place at the second concert in the season, held on the evening of 7 March. The soloist was Cipriani Potter, described as 'having the distinction of introducing several great pianoforte works to English audiences'.[141]

In March 1818, the English-born musician Cipriani Potter was on tour in Europe and when in Vienna made a point of meeting the capital's distinguished composer. Potter appears to have made a favourable impression on Beethoven: he was well qualified to do so being variously a composer, pianist, conductor, teacher and, later, Principal of the Royal Academy of Music, London. He wrote an account of his recollections of Beethoven that was subsequently published in *The Musical Times*, 1861. Potter recalled Beethoven's objection to unwelcome visitors, particularly those who were merely 'ambitious of contemplating the greatest genius in [Vienna] and of hearing him perform'. He regarded such visits as 'an intrusion and an impertinence' and exhibited his displeasure 'to those who were so unlucky as to expose themselves to rebuke'.[142]

According to the records of the Philharmonic Society, the G major Concerto had to wait until the 1867 Concert Season before it was performed once more. However, the occasion was memorable for the work was played by Clara Schumann. Evidently her performance and the composition were received with enthusiasm since she gave a further rendering of the music on 25 April 1870. Of passing interest is that since this was the year of Beethoven's Birth Centenary, subscribers to the Philharmonic Society purchased a bust of the composer by the Viennese sculptor J. Schaller.

It was commissioned originally by Karl Holz, a personal friend of the composer and a member of Ignaz Schuppanzigh's celebrated string quartet.

A memorable performance of the G major Concerto is recorded in the account of the Concert Season for 1874. The artist for the concert on 13 July was Camille Saint-Saens, then resident organist at La Madeleine, Paris. This was his first appearance at a concert of the Philharmonic Society. His original intention was to play a concerto of his own, however, on learning that this suggestion had 'alarmed the Society', he undertook to play the Beethoven Op. 58 instead. His remarks about pianos of the period are of interest. He is on record as saying: 'I esteem [the English] Broadwood, but I prefer [the French] Érard.'[143]

The honour for being the most noteworthy early champion of the G major Concerto should be awarded to Felix Mendelssohn. To substantiate this remark, we return to the period 1831–32. Ferdinand Hiller was in Paris for the winter of 1831–32 at which time Mendelssohn was completing his travels in Europe, making a brief sojourn in Paris – he was twenty-two at the time. Hiller was a close friend of Mendelssohn and was himself an individual of high musical-standing; at the age of ten he had performed a Mozart piano concerto in public. On 18 March 1832, Mendelssohn gave the first performance of the G major Concerto in Paris. Of his interpretation Hiller recalls that the contributor to the *Revue Musicale* wrote: '[Mendelssohn] displayed a refinement, technical finish, and sensibility that deserved the greatest praise.'

Referring to the *Adagio* he remarked:

'I have heard it said to pianists that there is no piano music there: God be praised! I hope these

312

gentlemen always obtain success as flattering, as genuine with all their notes, as that which M. Mendelssohn obtained with these passages, so simple and so well delivered.'[144]

In her Diary entry of 11–16 January 1841, Clara Schumann wrote of being too unwell to attend a concert at the Gewandhaus Concert Hall, Leipzig. She relates:

'Because of my indisposition I had to miss the Gewandhaus concert which created a not insignificant conflict for me because Mendelssohn was playing the G major Concerto by Beethoven which, by Robert's account, he performed masterfully (that after all was predictable). I missed a great treat for which I had long yearned.'[145]

Clara Schumann evidently did have occasion to hear Mendelssohn play the G major Concerto as the celebrated English pianist Fanny Davies confirms. Writing in 1927, on the occasion of Beethoven's Birth Centenary, she relates:

'Madame Clara Schumann told me that Mendelssohn played the most difficult of all beginnings — the opening bars of the G major — as no one else. That his tone in the opening chord, so round and yet so *piano* and full of melody, with a never-dry staccato but just detached notes, the rounding off of the two D chords joined by the little pearl melodic run, and the exquisite shape of the whole scheme, was something that she could not forget.'

On a more personal note, Davies adds: 'And here let me

say that I can never forget Anton Rubinstein's playing of the G [major].'[146]

On 11 December 1842, Mendelssohn wrote from Berlin to his mother in Leipzig of the success he was having with his compositions. The King had promised to honour him, prompting the composer to express his embarrassment at the prospect of possessing 'a greater number of decorations than he had composed good compositions'. Whilst in Berlin he gave a subscription concert, concerning which he writes:

> 'I think I never played the Beethoven G major Concerto so well — my old *cheval de bataille*; the first cadence especially, and a new return to the solo, pleased me exceedingly, and apparently the audience still more.'[147]

In the mid-nineteenth century in England, the enthusiasm for Mendelssohn and his music was universal amongst the musically-minded public; for example, he could count amongst his personal friends no less than Prince Albert and Queen Victoria. In his *A Portrait of Mendelssohn* Clive Brown writes:

> 'The idea was prevalent amongst the musically informed that Mendelssohn was as uniquely gifted as a performer as he was a composer. Such was his absorption in the music he played, that many considered his interpretation had unparalleled authority.'

This is evident in a review of a concert Mendelssohn gave on 24 June 1844 when, once more, he played the G major Concerto — at a further concert of the London Philharmonic Society. The reviewer enthused:

'Of the playing of this extraordinary master we can never have enough: he is simply the greatest pianist of the day ... whatever he does is not only worth hearing, but worth remembering.'

The reviewer drew attention to Mendelssohn's 'fine extemporaneous power', his 'extraordinary memory', his 'deep reading', and his 'poetic fire and vivacity'. Of his interpretation of the G major Concerto he reported:

'The Concerto of Beethoven was played by him from memory [innovative for the period], that comprised not only his part but the entire instrumentation. His delivery of the work was characterised by truth and simplicity.'

Mendelssohn supplied his own cadenzas. This disposed the reviewer to enthuse how in the first movement 'these combined Bach with Beethoven ... in a profusion of grand sequences and imposing harmonies'. In the final movement, he states Mendelssohn captivated the audience 'with extraordinary ingenuity and science'.[148]

In his *Autobiography*, the English composer-pianist and teacher Walter MacFarren recalls Mendelssohn's tenth, and last, visit to England in 1847 – the year of his untimely death. MacFarren studied piano at the Royal Academy of Music under Cipriani Potter, to whom reference has been made. It was from these apprentice years that MacFarren's recollections of Mendelssohn derive. He describes the occasion when Mendelssohn performed the G major Concerto at a concert once more given by the Philharmonic Society. Of related interest is that the conductor on that occasion was the pioneering Michael Costa. He is remembered in musicology for introducing baton-conducting in its modern form, for encouraging higher standards in rehearsal, and adopting a new orchestral layout for the players.[149]

MacFarren writes:

'I well remember Mendelssohn's wonderful cadences [cadenzas] in the first and last movements, and how, on Costa raising his baton in the expectation that the soloist had nearly finished, the latter gently put up his hand again and again and smilingly shook his head.'

At the close of the concert, when Mendelssohn was congratulated on his performance, he responded: 'I am glad that I did well as there were two ladies present I particularly wished to please.' They were Queen Victoria and the singer Jenny Lind — 'The Swedish Nightingale'.

MacFarrenn had heard Mendelssohn play the G major Concerto previously, in 1844, on which occasion he conducted the orchestra from the piano. He relates how Mendelssohn intimated his wishes to the orchestra 'by the motion of his head' and that his 'impromptu cadences [cadenzas] were equally astonishing'.[150]

In 1895, the musicologist Aloys Unterreiter amended the score of the Piano-Quintet version of the G major Concerto that, as we have mentioned, is believed to have been performed originally at the town palace of Prince Lobkowitz. His emendations were ostensibly 'to fill some gaps'. This was at the request of the Austrian musicologist and collector of Beethoven manuscripts Aloys Fuchs. A chamber performance of the Concerto was given on 1 December in 1895 at the Gesellschaft der Musikfreunde; the soloist was Joseph Fischhof. At the close of the concert Fischhof was given the score as a present — it being known he was an avid collector of Beethoven manuscripts and related memorabilia.[151]

An anecdote from the recollections of the American pianist Amy Fay (1844–1928) connects us with the European musical scene of the 1870s. Fay was an accomplished performer who had travelled to Europe to study with Franz Liszt; she also had lessons with two other lions of the keyboard, namely, Theodor Kullak and Carl Tausig. Her letters sent home from Germany include descriptions of her training and the concerts she attended; these were published in 1880 as Music Study in Germany. Notwithstanding her considerable pianistic gifts, on 25 June 1871 she felt disposed to write:

'I have been learning Beethoven's G major Concerto lately, and it is the most horribly difficult thing I've ever attempted. I have practised the first movement a whole month, and I can't play it any more than I can fly ... Kullak gave me a regular rating over it at my last lesson and told me I must stick to it till I could play it. It requires the greatest rapidity and facility of execution, and I got perfectly desperate over it. Kullak took advantage of the occasion to expand upon all the things what an artist must be able to do, until my heart died within me.'

As if to emphasize the point, Kullak asked Fay what she knew about 'double thirds'. To her response 'nothing' he rushed to the piano and 'like lightning [played] from top to bottom in a scale in double thirds, just as if it were a common scale.'[152]

During a visit to England in 1874, Camille Saint-Saëns played Beethoven's Fourth Piano Concerto once more in

London at another concert of the Philharmonic Society — held in St. James Hall. Invited to remark on his choice of the G major Concerto he responded, 'I love [it] passionately'. In 1886 Saint-Saëns was once again in London for the first hearing there of his recently composed Third Symphony, presented at a concert attended by the Prince and Princess of Wales. Before conducting his new Symphony he gave a further rendering of the G major Concerto.[153]

We have occasion to refer to Fanny Davies once more. She was particularly admired for her interpretations of the piano music of Beethoven, Schumann, and Brahms but she was also an early London performer of the works of Debussy and Scriabin. She studied under Clara Schuman, at Frankfurt, and took part in the Beethoven Festival at Bonn in 1893. She was not only the first person to give a piano recital in Westminster Abbey but made her first English appearance in the celebrated concert series held at the Chrystal Palace. On 17 October 1875, she performed the G major Piano Concerto when she was just fourteen years old.[154] Davies also performed the Concerto on 28 February 1894 at a concert in the London season of the Philharmonic Society. For this rendering, she played the cadenzas composed by Clara Schumann — to the acclaim of non-other than the music critic George Bernhard Shaw.[155]

We remain with Shaw, in his capacity as music critic, for the London music season of 1877. On 17 February of that year he attended a concert at the Crystal Palace. The German-born pianist Marie Krebs was the soloist in the G major Concerto. Shaw's account sheds light on music-making of the period. Writing in *The Scottish Musical Monthly*, he remarks:

'Marie Krebs played Beethoven's Fourth Piano
Concerto in her characteristic style, crisply and

steadily. Throughout the concert the orchestra acquitted themselves most satisfactorily.'

He elaborates:

'The performances to which we are accustomed, in London, seem to move in a narrow circle from weak incompetence or coarse violence to the perfection of lifeless finish, according to the incapacity, the misdirected energy, or the cold autocracy which distinguishes the conductors.'

Shaw was prepared, however, to make an exception of the German-born British conductor Sir August Friedrich Manns — Director of music at the Crystal Palace. Of Manns, Shaw writes:

'At Sydenham, thanks to Manns, we can hear an orchestra capable of interpreting with refinement and expression the greatest instrumental compositions, more especially those of Beethoven.'[156]

In December 1891, Shaw attended a concert at St. James's Hall, London given by students of the Royal Academy of Music. The centrepiece of the occasion was the playing of the nineteen-year old Ethel Barns. Shaw writes:

'The only performance which rose above student level, into the region of beautiful execution and sympathetic interpretation, was that of Beethoven's Fourth Piano Concerto by Miss Ethel Barns, who very far surpassed Stavenhager's recent performance of the same work at the Crystal Palace.'

Shaw is referring here to the German pianist and composer Bernhard Stevenhagen. Concerning Miss Barn's, she was clearly an accomplished musician since, five years later, she made her professional debut as a *violinist* at the Chrystal Palace and later in her career was elected to a professorship at the Royal Academy of Music.[157]

Our final reference to the music criticism of George Bernhard Shaw draws us to the close of the nineteenth century. In June 1892, Shaw attended another concert at St. James Hall where he heard the Scottish pianist-composer Frederic Lamond perform the G major Concerto. For many years, Lamond enjoyed the reputation in England for being the foremost authority on Beethoven's piano sonatas, before being supplanted in that capacity by Artur Schnabel – when Breitkopf and Härtell published his edition of these works in 1893. Lamond also had the distinction of being the second-last pupil of Franz Liszt. Contemporaries praised Lamond for his phrasing and singing tone, but on the occasion when Shaw heard him play perhaps too much of the characteristic vigour of the style of playing of his teacher Liszt was evident.

Shaw opens his account by subscribing to the, by then established, view that the Fourth Concerto is 'as great in a feminine way as the Fifth is in a masculine way'. Regarding Lamond's interpretation, he laments (no pun intended):

> 'I never dreamt that he, or any musician, could miss the grace and tenderness of the opening phrase, even if Beethoven's *dolce* were erased from the pianoforte copy.'

He accused Lamond of treating the opening as 'a mere battery of chords' that he likened, in characteristic Shavian manner, to 'a slater finishing a roof'.[158]

In the same year that Shaw was writing his music criticism, on 29 July the Italian Ferruccio Busoni — composer, conductor, editor, writer, teacher, and, above all, titan of the keyboard — wrote from Boston to his concert agent Theodore Thomas. He informed Thomas of the pleasure he had in Boston of playing Beethoven's G major Concerto for which he had performed his own cadenzas. He composed these in 1890 and entered them for the Anton Rubinstein Prize — Rubinstein being himself a celebrated performer of Beethoven's piano works. We do not know of the eventual outcome of Busoni's competition entry but if he did not win it would be no loss since he had previously won the Rubinstein Prize for his one-movement piano sonata.[159]

We draw our survey of responses to the G major Concerto, Op. 58 to a close in the form of a selection of recollections derived from the accounts of artists performing in the twentieth century.

The relationship between orchestral conductor and soloist can sometimes be fraught. In his Autobiography *My Young Years*, Arthur Rubinstein recalls an early encounter with the characteristically strong mindedness typical of some orchestral conductors. At the close of 1909, when he was twenty-two, he was invited to play concertos at concerts in Berlin's Philharmonic Hall — the city's largest. His preference was to play Chopin or Saint Saëns. The maestro for the occasion was the Polish conductor-composer Gregor Fitelberg. Rubinstein relates how his forebodings were confirmed when Fitelberg dismissed his suggestions and insisted Beethoven's G Major Concerto and Brahms's B flat Concerto should be played. Rubinstein reflects:

'I guessed right away why he was so adamant. Both the Beethoven and Brahms are predominantly symphonic, orchestral works giving the pianist little chance to shine as a virtuoso and provoke enthusiastic demonstrations, a thing all conductors dread.'[160]

In the concert season 1936–37, Rubinstein was commissioned to perform the G major Concerto at the Concertgebouw, Amsterdam. Instead of Willem Mengelberg, its regular conductor, the orchestra was directed by George Szell. The encounter was not a happy one for Rubinstein. He relates at the rehearsal Szell stopped him at the close of the piano's first solo entrance and exclaimed in a loud voice, 'Artur Schnabel took it slower'. Worse was to follow. At the intermission, in the artists' room, Szell took up the score and lectured Rubinstein how Artur Schnabel had played the Concerto 'to his full satisfaction'. Rubinstein responded very angrily: 'Tell your Artur that this Artur feels in a different way ... and I did not speak to him anymore.'[161]

In the 1940s, Rubinstein played the G major Concerto at Los Angeles's famous Hollywood Bowl, this time under the direction of Sir Thomas Beecham. The rehearsal was challenging for all concerned. Beecham grew impatient with the orchestra 'addressing this or that player with sharp criticisms' and making Rubinstein sit waiting 'with the hot sun beating down on him'. Rubinstein describes the rehearsal as closing in 'undisguised hostility'. Chance, however, favoured him seeking his revenge. Beecham requested a lift back to his hotel. Rubinstein agreed and, as the journey progressed, made out — notwithstanding being a competent driver — that he had only just passed his driving test. He describes driving deliberately erratically, pretending not to see red warning lights and so on. To his satisfaction, they arrived at their destination with Beecham 'tottering out of the car unsteadily' and giving Rubinstein a 'murderous look'![162]

The Italian conductor Arturo Toscanini is renowned for the intensity and fervour that he brought to his interpretation of music and the attention — devotion — he demanded of the artists who worked under him. Notwithstanding, musicologist Mortimer Frank writes — following his study of Toscanini's many recordings:

'Two overlooked qualities of Toscanini, as an accompanist, emerge here; flexibility and rapidity in assimilating a soloist's conception. Moreover, when he found that conception to be musical, he would go along with it, even where he found it differed from his own.'

By way of illustration, he cites the recording Toscanini made of Beethoven's Fourth Piano Concerto in 1936 when directing the New York Philharmonic Orchestra with Rudolph Serkin as soloist — this was Toscanini's debut with an American orchestra. Frank characterises the performance as possessing 'delicacy and repose'.[163]

The music historian Richard Holt wrote a tribute to the Russian composer-pianist Nikolai Medtner. He describes the hardships he experienced in post-revolutionary Moscow, attempting to keep warm by burning books and pieces of furniture. Despite these many deprivations, Medtner, and his fellow musicians, summoned the energy to make music. In the winter of 1920, Medtner performed the G major Concerto to an audience consisting of soldiers, workmen, and officials of the Kommissarits — the great majority of whom had never attended a concert in their lives. Alfred Jarosy, a contemporary recalling the performance, relates such was the influence of Beethoven's music on the audience that any doubts were immediately set aside regarding how it would be received. He states:

'Hardly had [Medtner] finished the first bars, when an atmosphere of religious devotion spread through the hall ['House of the People']. Pianist and piano were forgotten ... they listed to Beethoven alone.'[164]

From an entry in the Diary of the nineteen-year old Benjamin Britten, for 9 November 1932, we learn he heard Myra Hess perform the G major Concerto at the Queen's Hall, London. The BBC Symphony Orchestra for the occasion was conducted by Henry Wood. Britten's cryptic entry goes: 'Myra Hess plays the Beethoven G major ... She plays it technically very well – but ridiculous cadenzas.' It is unclear here whether Britten is referring to Beethoven's cadenzas or, more probably, those supplied by Hess herself. He continues: 'She and Wood have no idea of the second movement – It's *Andante* not *Adagios-sississimo*.' Perhaps Britten had been influenced by hearing the Concerto played the previous year by the German pianist Wilhelm Backhaus. His Diary entry for 11 February 1931 commends him for having performed the work 'beautifully'.[165]

Michael Tippett composed his Concerto for piano and orchestra between 1953 and 1955, written to a commission from the City of Birmingham Symphony Orchestra. According to the composer, its overall character was influenced by his hearing the German pianist Walter Gieseking rehearse Beethoven's G major Concerto, sometime in 1950. Writing of the influence of Beethoven on Tippett, the musicologist and academic Ian Kemp comments:

'[The] final section [of Tippett's Concerto] is strongly reminiscent of the "taming of the orches-

tra" in the slow movement of Beethoven's Piano
Concerto No.4. No doubt, the allusion is delib-
erate ... and as such it can be read as his tribute
to Beethoven.'

Kemp continues: 'But it can also be read as another example
of how he reinterprets his forebears in order to say something.' In his comparison of the Tippet and Beethoven
Concertos, Kemp observes:

'In Beethoven the "taming" comes at the beginning of the [slow] movement. But in Tippett it is
at the end, and the piano is tamed not the
orchestra: the individual is reconciled with the
collective.'[166]

The Canadian pianist Glenn Gould describes the occasion
when his teacher suggested he should make his debut with
an orchestra; Gould was then still a mere thirteen-year old
student at the Toronto (Royal) Conservatory of Music. It is
a tribute to Gould's remarkable pianism that his teacher
considered that such a challenging work as the G major
Concerto was within his capabilities. Gould narrates how he
enthusiastically accepted the challenge — for the reason that
he was familiar with Artur Schnabel's recoding of the music.
Gould relates:

'Almost every day during the two years I owned
... all eight 78-rpm sides [they] served as accompaniment for practice sessions in which I faith-
fully traced every inflective nuance of the
Schnabelian rhetoric, surged dramatically ahead
whenever he thought it wise ... and glided to a
graceful cadential halt every four minutes and

twenty-five seconds or so while the automatic changer went to work on the turntable.'

The present writer can interpose a personal observation here. He has in his possession the very same set of Schnabel's 78-rpm recordings of the Beethoven G major Concerto to which Gould makes reference — recused at the very moment they were about to be tossed into a skip!

According to Gould's account, his Schnabel impersonation acquired 'awesome authenticity'. Gould was pleased with his resulting performance. However, the following day the discerning music critic of the Toronto *Globe and Mail* wrote: 'Beethoven's elusive Fourth Piano Concerto was left in the hands of a child last night. Who does he think he is, Schnabel?'[167]

Dennis Matthews recalls the celebrations, held in March 1960, when five-hundred people assembled in the Connaught Rooms, London to pay homage to the pianist-arranger-composer-teacher Harold Craxton. The occasion in question was Craxton's seventy-fifth birthday and Matthews, a former student of Craxton, was asked to speak on behalf of his fellow students. He paid tribute to the manner in which Craxton had never sought to impose ready-made interpretations on his students or of telling them "how". Matthews closed his address:

'We thank Harold because he always told us "Why" and encouraged us to respond to the music in our own way. For, as Beethoven showed us in the *Andante* of the G major Concerto, persuasion can move mountains, when it is backed up by love and affection.'[168]

Writing in 1961 of John Ogden, his wife — and fellow pianist

— Brenda Lucas makes passing reference to his personal concerto enthusiasms:

> 'Of the many Beethoven works that John plays, he particularly loves the Fourth Piano Concerto, while he believes the Third to be a superbly balanced composition not allowed its worth even today.'[169]

In Helena Matheopoulos's study of the relationship between orchestral conductors and soloists, she reveals that finding a balance of views between the two can sometimes be a challenge. For example, she recalls the occasion in 1967 when maestro Carlos Kleiber conducted a performance of the G major Concerto in Munich with Alfred Brendel as soloist. She quotes Brendel as remarking:

> 'I had known Carlos for years, he is an old friend and a conductor of extraordinary character. But it was very difficult to arrive at our result, because he has very rigid views, very precise views about every semiquaver of the piece, and one has to struggle and reach some kind of compromise. But I think that the performance was very good!'[170]

We draw our discussion of Beethoven's Piano Concerto No.4 in G major, Op. 58 to a close in the form of a documentary-style collection of texts. These are derived from the writings of musicologists and performing artists bearing on the musicology of the Op. 58 Concerto.

Worthy of remark, first of all, is that in choosing a key for a new work, Beethoven took several factors into consideration. Schindler states:

'One of the most important was the key of previous works in the same genre. He tended to think of each genre as a separate category ... Thus, any composition would normally be not only in a different key from the one immediately preceding but also in a different key from the previous work in the same genre.'

Schindler also relates that Beethoven was interested in the writings of the contemporary mystical poet and musician Christian Schubart. He characterised the musical keys with feelings and ascribed to them a certain 'psyche.'[171] Combing Schubart's key-attributes with those that Beethoven chose for his five piano concertos gives us the following — the text in quotation marks is that of Schubart:

C MAJOR (OP. 15, NO. 1): 'Completely pure. Its character is innocence and simplicity.'

B-FLAT MAJOR (OP. 19, NO. 2): 'Cheerful love, clear conscience, hope and aspiration for a better world.'

C MINOR (OP. 37, NO. 3): 'Declaration of love and at the same time the lament of unhappy love. All languishing, longing, sighing of the love-sick soul lies in this key.'

G MAJOR (OP. 58, NO. 4): 'Everything rustic, idyllic and lyrical, every calm and satisfied passion, every tender gratitude for true friendship and faithful love — in a word every gentle and peaceful emotion of the heart is correctly expressed by this key.'

E-FLAT MAJOR (OP. 73, NO. 5): The key of love, of devotion, of intimate conversation with God.

The philosopher and musicologist Theodore Adorno offers what he refers to as 'a theory of Beethoven's *types* and of his *characters*'. Within this intellectual construct he distinguishes between *intensive* and *extensive* types. (Adorno's emphasis) With regard to the latter, he remarks:

'The greatest and most successful example is perhaps the first movement of the G major Concerto — The absence of smoothness is very characteristic of the extensive type.'[172]

The texts that follow are presented in the chronological order of their publication.

FIRST MOVEMENT
ALLEGRO MODERATO

'With this solo the Concerto begins, and the *tutti* follows in the sixth bar. The character of the first movement — which is as beautiful as it is original — is calm, simple and agreeable, almost in the pastoral style; but the performance of the same is considerably difficult, as the pianoforte part is very closely interwoven with the orchestra and the player must have regard to this nearly in every passage. A strict preservation of the time is therefore essentially requisite, and the expression chiefly depends on the light, clear and accurate performance of the various difficulties in which it abounds.'

Carl Czerny, as quoted in: Paul Badura-Skoda, *Carl Czerny: On the Proper Performance of all Beethoven's Works for the Piano*, 1970, p. 99.

> 'As if sensing high attainment, the recapitulation begins with the opening phrase of the Concerto *fortissimo* in the solo; but this intensity is only momentary. Gentleness is resumed and the whole substance of the exposition, as the solo presented it, is repeated with the usual alterations of key. After the cadenza (Beethoven wrote two, of which the second is nowadays usually the choice of discriminating artists) there is a brief but very pertinent Coda.'

Donald Nivison Ferguson, *Masterworks of the Orchestral Repertoire: A Guide for Listeners*, 1954, pp. 106–07.

The opening theme of the G major Concerto, Op. 58 displays similarities with the first theme of the Fifth Symphony, and originally the figure of the accompaniment in the *Rondo* of the same Concerto was still more closely related to that in the *prisoners'* chorus in the Opera *Leonore*. This likeness was so marked that it invoked the musicologist Paul Mies to recall the conjectures of the pioneering Beethoven musicologist Gustav Nottebohm who reflected: 'Would Beethoven have written the first movement of the G major Concerto if he had not written the C major Symphony?' And, again: 'Would Beethoven have written the *prisoners'* chorus as he did if he had not also written the G major Concerto?'

Paul Mies, *Beethoven's Sketches: An Analysis of his Style based on a Study of his Sketchbooks*, reprint, 1969, p. 126.

'Although [the piano] contributes only five bars, its absence throughout the rest of the *tutti* is a positive factor in the total musical experience. At its re-entry, it asserts its importance with a caden-za-like passage before allowing the thematic argument to proceed.'

Basil Deane, *The Concertos*, in: Denis Arnold and Nigel Fortune editors, *The Beethoven Companion*, 1973, p. 326.

In the course of his Ernst Bloch Lectures for 1972, the American musicologist Edward T. Cone stated:

'During the opening of the ritornello of Beethoven's Third Concerto, not only is the piano waiting for its moment to enter, but the orchestra is determining that moment. At the beginning of his Fourth, the orchestra listens to the piano and then comments on what it has heard, and the piano is conscious of being so attended. That is what distinguishes the one from a symphony, the other from a piano sonata, even at the outset.'

Edward T. Cone, *The Composer's Voice*, 1974, pp. 124–25.

'At the beginning, the piano emerges gently from dreams; this is truly Beethoven improvising. Two romantic themes, renunciation and hope, are gradually developed. When, after an orchestral interlude, the piano is heard again solo, it is as if a butterfly rose ecstatically from its cocoon. There are no *fortissimos* here, and when the call to new

adventures sounds, the butterfly sinks back,
dreaming. The whole thing is wrapped in dark-
red velvet; at times, it is as if one were caressing
it with one's hands.'

Ludwig Emil, *Beethoven, Life of a Composer*, 1943,
translated by George Stewart McManus, as quoted in:
Jacques Barzun, *Pleasures of Music: An Anthology of
Writing about Music and Musicians*, 1977, p. 354.

Arthur Rubinstein performed the G major Concerto in
Cincinnati in the 1920s under the direction of the Belgian
violinist and conductor *Eugène Ysaÿe*. In recalling the
occasion, Rubinstein reveals the Beethoven Concerto had
been a favourite of his since hearing the work performed by
Eugène *d'Albert*. Discussing the opening of the work he
states: 'I used to take the [opening] theme at a slower tempo
in order to give it all the weight and lay a solid foundation
for the whole movement.'

Arthur Rubinstein, *My Many Years*, 1980, pp. 55–56.

'It would be wearisome to catalogue all the events
in this remarkable movement, but one moment of
sheer delight must be mentioned. Having for once
asserted authority in a display of uncharacteristic
virtuosity, the soloist seems to say, "I didn't really
mean to bully you" and offers a new theme of
child-like innocence based on the five descending
notes of the scale of **C** sharp minor. The effect is
so beguiling that we sometimes fail to notice how
the cellos and bases relate this to the initial repeat-
ed-note theme.'

Antony Hopkins, *The Concertgoer's Companion*, 1984, p. 93.

'To allow the soloist the first word in a Classical concerto would have been a rarity [for the period], though Mozart approached it in his early E flat Concerto, K. 271; but the masterstroke in the G major is the gentle manner of the opening, with its half-close that surprises the orchestra into its still quieter reply in the distant key of B major.'

Denis Matthews, *Beethoven, Master Musicians*, 1985, p. 177.

'As regards rhythm, Beethoven was particularly fond of the [four-note] motif ... Some form of it is used conspicuously not only in the Fifth Symphony but also in several other works, among them the Piano Sonata in C minor, Op. 10, No.1 (third movement), the *Appassionata* Sonata, Op. 57 (first movement), the *Egmont* Overture, and the Fourth Piano Concerto, Op. 58 (first movement) [piano entry].

Barry Cooper, *Beethoven and the Creative Process*, 1990, p. 63.

Cooper returned once more to the G major Concerto:

'The piano opens the movement alone. This is not, of course, the first time the soloist has appeared at the start of a concerto, but in Mozart's Piano Concerto in E flat, K. 272 the concept is different. There, the piano was treated as an extra dimension of the orchestra and was then reintroduced in its "proper" place. Here, the solo part is more self-contained, and the piano then remains silent during the rest of the orchestral exposition.'

Barry Cooper, *The Beethoven Compendium: A Guide to Beethoven's Life and Music*, 1991, p. 218.

Hopkins returned once more to the G major Concerto:

'If this work (like the Haydn symphonies) were to be given a nickname it might well be the *Unexpected.* Over and over again, throughout this first movement, Beethoven exploits the element of surprise. Surprise number one was the opening with the piano; number two was the soft orchestral entry in the "wrong" key of B major. Now, we have an orchestral exposition which ends on an extreme dissonance ... Cascading arpeggios, covering nearly five octaves at a time and a huge chromatic run, lead, via some trills, to an unexpected new development. Marked very soft and sweetly (*pp dolce*), the pianist introduces a brand-new theme based, one might almost think, on a child's five-finger exercise. Charming though it is, we should not disregard the mutterings of the cellos and bases, who keep reminding us of the rhythm of the original theme.'

Antony Hopkins, *The Seven Concertos of Beethoven*, 1996, p. 47 and p. 50.

'Like several other works from this period, this Concerto displays a quality of spacious lyrical serenity. In the opening *Allegro moderato*,

Beethoven gives special prominence to the dialogue between solo and *tutti* by beginning with a short piano passage, whose initial G major sonority is reinterpreted with wonderful sensitivity by the strings on a B major harmony, marked *pianissimo*.'

William Kinderman, *Beethoven*, 1997, p. 110.

'[The] Fourth Piano Concerto opens with a sonorous statement of the theme in the solo instrument followed by the *tutti*, whereas in the Violin Concerto the entry of the soloist is deferred as long as possible ... In the one, the *tutti* rises from the solo, in the other the solo emerges from the orchestral fabric ...'.

Maynard Solomon, *Beethoven*, 1997, pp. 202–03.

'Experienced listeners in the audience at the Lobkowitz *Palais*, or at the marathon [concert] in the freezing Theater an der Wien, would have expected to wait for the soloist to make his first entrance after a substantial *tutti*, lasting a couple of minutes and introduce several themes. That is how concertos began. They were in for a shock ... With the piano fallen silent, after setting the music into motion, the orchestra generously expands the first paragraph, carries it briefly to *fortissimo*, then introduces a new theme, gentle but full of melancholy passion.'

Michael Steinberg, *The Concerto: A Listener's Guide*, 1998, p. 64 and p. 67.

'[This] movement joins many others among Beethoven's instrumental works that conjure up the idea of voices and song and dramatic situation, works such as the *Tempest* Sonata, Op. 31, No. 2, the Sonata Op. 110, the middle movement of the *Waldstein* (more remotely), the introduction to the finale of the String Quartet, Op. 132, and (of course most especially) the finale of the Ninth Symphony ... [The] piano [is] leader, showing occasional fine bursts of virtuosity, but remaining all the while devoted to the cause of tranquil and nuanced reflection, a curb on the orchestra's propensity for energetic motion, for direct action.

[The] voice of the piano achieves mastery of a very particular kind, and it does so only as the end result of a process of working out, a dialectic, we might say, whose conclusion is a greatly enriched encapsulation of its parts ... The Concerto begins with the solo instrument; this simple fact has been much noted — together with the ritual naming of its nearest known precedent in Mozart's Concerto in E flat, K. 271. And such a reversal of roles is to be sure startling; it calls attention at the outset to issues about the individual and the group that will be raised to a higher power in the second movement, and it suggests, from the first, a particular musical persona for the soloist.'

Leon Plantinga, *Beethoven's Concertos: History, Style, Performance,* 1999, p. 186, p. 195 and p. 204.

'Never before had a composer begun a concerto with a piano solo, and a barely audible one at that. The orchestra's entry in an audibly alien key is no less surprising. Within a few bars, then, Beethoven destroyed all his audience's preconceptions about concerto form. The first movement's ceaselessly modulating exposition similarly keeps its listeners guessing. The piano's recently extended keyboard is gloriously exploited in music filled with ethereal sweetness, though the material is also energised by much use of sparkling triplet figures.'

Conrad Wilson, *Notes on Beethoven: 20 crucial works*, 2003, p. 46.

'The most famous thing about this Concerto is its opening: an exquisitely gentle, questioning theme for the soloist, richly scored in the keyboard's resonant middle register. No previous classical concerto had announced itself with the soloist alone; and none had begun so poetically and speculatively. The orchestra then responds, as if entranced, in a distant, luminous B major, before softly re-establishing the home key.'

Richard Wigmore, *Notes to the BBC Radio Three Beethoven Experience*, Friday 10 June 2005, www.bbc.co.uk/radio3/Beethoven

SECOND MOVEMENT
ANDANTE CON MOTO
'In this movement, (which, like the entire Concerto, belongs to the finest and most poetical of

Beethoven's creations), one cannot help thinking of an antique tragic scene, and the player must feel with what intense, pathetic expression his solo is performed, in order to contrast with the powerful and austere orchestral passages, which are, as it were, gradually withdrawn ... It must not be played too slow; though the pianist may restrain the time rather more than the orchestra. It produces a good effect when, after a brief pause, the Finale immediately follows.'

Carl Czerny, *On the Proper Performance of all Beethoven's Works for the Piano*, in: Paul Badura-Skoda, 1970, p. 100.

'Perhaps nothing more touchingly beautiful has ever been written than that tragic lyric — the second movement of the G major. And how wonderfully Beethoven has enshrined it between the other two movements. After that middle movement of the G, with its deepest depths of sadness, nothing could follow but a finale of intense and pure joy. And what a world of joy he takes us in order to balance artistically, those depths of sadness. Schumann is said to have likened that middle movement to Orpheus in the Underworld — with which one may or may not agree, but at any rate that thought suggests the ruggedness of the orchestral parts at the outset.'

Fanny Davies, *The Pianoforte Concertos in: The Musical Times. Special Issue*, editor John A. Fuller-Maitland, Vol. VIII, No. 2, 1927, p. 21.

'The slow movement reveals at once — if the first

has not already done so — how far Beethoven has been emancipated from the conventions of the eighteenth century ... Toward the end, the orchestra's rage subsides. Its *forte* phrases become *piano*, and with a few docile notes it accompanies the few final bars of the solo, whose strains are sung, not on triumph or self-vindication, but only as if there could never have been any doubt as to the outcome of the strife. There is a moment of high excitement in the brief cadenza, but this is soon subdued, and a lingering phrase suggests and prepares for the final *Rondo*.'

Donald Nivison Ferguson, *Masterworks of the Orchestral Repertoire: A Guide for Listeners*, 1954, p. 107.

'The slow movements [of the G major Concerto and the Violin Concerto] are both conceived as dialogues, but that in the Piano Concerto is a recitative dialogue of disputants, whereas in the Violin Concerto we have a lyrical discussion between agreeable conversationalists.'

Maynard Solomon, *Beethoven*, 1977, pp. 202–03.

'The middle movement of the Concerto, an *Andante* in E major, is unique in the concerto literature. Formally, it is a dialogue between the piano and the strings, which play in unison except for a few measures. The classification of *tutti* and solo, however, seem meaningless in view of the integration of the piano sound into the orchestral sonority. There is a tradition that sees in the orchestra the pitiless forces of Hades and in the piano the lamenting, and imploring voice of Orpheus. Putting aside poetic hermeneutics, we feel, as listeners, utterances of spiritual forces that carry us into sublime spheres.'

Joseph Braunstein, *Musica Aeterna, Program Notes for 1971–1976*, 1978, p. 23.

'The slow movement presents us with a unique musical drama, the perfect symbol of the soft answer turning away wrath. The orchestra is reduced to strings only, but they begin with a savage intensity; their stark unisons have something of the character of the introduction to a Handel aria. The ensuing passage for piano is not so much a response as a total disregard for the orchestra's aggression. It is like a chorale, enabling the soloist to withdraw into a world of inner contemplation.'

Antony Hopkins, *The Concertgoer's Companion*, 1984, p. 94.

'The *Andante* of the G major is a unique drama carried out with the simplest of means. Only the orchestral strings are used, playing in octaves until the closing bars. They begin in an aggressive *forte*, to which the piano responds in quiet but fully harmonised phrases ... The Romantics understandably read extra-musical meanings into the *Andante*, whether Orpheus taming the forces of nature, or more simply, "A soft answer [that] turneth away wrath" [Proverbs 15:1].'

Denis Matthews, *Beethoven, Master Musicians*, 1985, p. 177.

> 'According to tradition, stemming from Liszt and others, the *Andante con moto* is associated with Orpheus and the Furies. In this movement, the classical *topos* juxtaposing stark, unharmonized unisons and plaintive, harmonized lyricism is imposed on the relationship between *tutti* and soloist, investing the music with a mythic aura ...The music assumes a human face; the stern forbidding posture of the orchestral phrases is injected with inner life ... the orchestral level softens to pianissimo ... yet another concession in the struggle with the soloist ... From this point on the dominance of the pianist is absolute, and a new stage in the narrative design of the movement has been reached ... The *Andante con moto* of the G major Concerto ... provides a paradigm of musical transformation, whereby the detached, objective idiom of the *tutti* is gradually infused with human subjectivity, won over by the power of the [composer's] artistic imagination ... The *Andante con moto* is an intrinsically musical narrative, which urgently invites interpretation without allowing itself to be displaced thereby.'

William Kinderman, *Beethoven*, 1997, p. 110, pp. 113–14 and p. 116.

> 'The sort of musical rhetoric Beethoven gives us seems intimately bound up with situation, character, speech. And there can be no doubt about elements of implied human drama here: a pro-

tagonist and antagonist, a relationship between the two that changes over time from implacable opposition — even their [soloist's and orchestra's] very worlds of discourse seem at first opposed — to some agreement, reconciliation, maybe sympathy.'

Leon Plantinga, *Beethoven's Concertos: History, Style, Performance*, 1999, p. 186 and p. 189.

The British cellist Alexander Kok recalls hearing Artur Schnabel play the G major Concerto. His rendering of the music so affected him that he describes being 'in a state of shock at the wonderful way in which he had performed'. A later meeting with Schnabel offered him the opportunity to posit 'whether one first has to *experience* a deeper awareness before being able to share it with others'. Kok was thinking, in particular, of the bridge-passage in the slow movement after what he describes as 'the angry orchestral statement'. He relates, Schnabel suggested how, in Beethoven's music, 'it was possible to think of sound as if it were a language' and sometimes, as in speech, 'there had to be silence' and this was the moment 'when the intangible becomes a living experience'.

Alexander Kok, *A Voice in the Dark: The Philharmonia Years*, 2002, pp. 150–52.

THIRD MOVEMENT
RONDO (VIVACE)

'The solos of this finale are so often interrupted by the orchestra, that the greatest care and accuracy are required on all sides, in order, by a well-studied combined effect, to produce a whole that may be intelligible to the hearer. The pianist has here therefore, in particular, to observe a strict keeping of the time and great accuracy in coming in. Moreover, this movement must be performed in a very lively, humorous and decided manner, and the pedal is often required in order to complete the effects.'

Carl Czerny, *On the Proper Performance of all Beethoven's Works for the Piano*, in: Paul Badura-Skoda, 1970, p. 101.

'The finale breaks in, *pianissimo*, with an intensely lively theme in that prosaic daylight by which Beethoven loves to test the reality of his sublimest visions. The daylight is more grey from the strong emphasis the theme gives to the subdominant chord, almost producing the impression of C instead of G major ... [At the close] the irrepressible woodwind and pianoforte have little more to say before ending this audacious masterpiece of gigantic and inexhaustibly varied proportions with that punctuality which gives solemnity to Beethoven's utmost exuberance of high spirits.'

Donald Francis Tovey, *Essays in Musical Analysis*, 1935–41, Vol. 3, p. 81 and p. 84.

'This [Rondo] is incredibly light in character — joyous without blatancy; imbued with every spiritual vigour, yet avoiding all vulgar display of energy; leading its inner exuberance of feeling to a second subject that is the very pinnacle of ecstasy ... An improvisatory cadenza (which Beethoven warned the performer, if he preferred to substitute his own, to make it short) was also supplied, with the expected appropriateness, by the composer.'

Donald Nivison Ferguson, *Masterworks of the Orchestral Repertoire: A Guide for Listeners*, 1954, pp. 107–08.

'Characteristic for the subtlety of the whole is the opening of the final *Rondo*: it emerges very quietly after the last chord of the slow movement ... reserving a straightforward statement for the first orchestral *tutti* ... The way in which Beethoven achieves his second theme, a solemnity of utterance, the expression, as it were, of some universal truth, without losing the momentum of what is basically a gay and light-hearted movement, is composition of the highest order. No wonder that this Concerto, even more perhaps than the *Emperor*, has been the favourite among musicians for a very long time.'

R. Kinloch Anderson, Liner notes to: *Beethoven, Piano Concerto, No. 4*, EMI *Classics for Pleasure*, 1977.

'The ebullient rondo-finales [to the G major Concerto and the Violin Concerto] are equally differentiated. Beethoven finds a pastoral solution in the Violin Concerto, but gives a more urgent "military" character to the Piano Concerto, with its snare-drum rhythms and "bayonet motif" opening theme.'

Maynard Solomon, *Beethoven*, 1977, pp. 202–03.

'With little respect for our emotions, Beethoven breaks the spell [of the slow movement] with a crisp march that seems to come from a great distance. The soloist takes up the tune, all sadness fled. It is as though Puck has flitted into the Capulet's Tomb, and takes a moment or two to adjust to this lightning change of mood. In this final Rondo the dialogue between piano and orchestra is totally good humoured, sometimes boisterous, sometimes witty, occasionally smilingly content.'

Antony Hopkins, *The Concertgoer's Companion*, 1984, p. 94.

Hopkins returned once more to the G major Concerto:

'As if from a great distance we hear the strains of a crisp little march, though more for Oberon's fairy retinue than the brigade of guards. The soloist instantly embroiders the first phrase in a somewhat frivolous mood, as the little bubbling trills indicate. The change of mood from deep despair to sheer delight could scarcely be more extreme ... The cadenza which follows must be short according to Beethoven's instructions (*la cadenza sia corta*) and ends in a flurry of trills. The music calms with beautiful and nostalgic versions of the march theme to which the piano adds delicately spicy decorations which gradually have a soporific effect. Just as the music threatens to come to a complete halt Beethoven appears to say "This won't do", and launches into a final *presto*.'

Antony Hopkins, *The Seven Concertos of Beethoven*, 1996, p. 53 and p. 55.

> 'The air is crystalline and sparkling with joy — so much so that the second subject, especially when we hear it in D major in the orchestra following bar 92, strongly anticipates the great tune in the finale of the Ninth Symphony. The chief glory of the splendid Rondo is its magnificently expansive, vigorous yet leisurely Coda, for which a shortened recapitulation makes room.'

Robert Simpson, *Beethoven and the Concerto* in: Robert Layton editor, *A Guide to the Concerto*, 1996, p. 120.

> 'The vivacious rondo-finale shows a special richness of thematic material. The main theme has a dance-like character and begins not in G major but in C major ... The transition to the coda is marked by that speciality of Beethoven's piano playing showcased in each movement of this great work — the triple trill — and the final *Presto* section resolves the main theme to the tonic G major with irresistible energy and compelling finality.'

William Kinderman, *Beethoven*, 1997, pp. 110–11.

> 'The second movement has ended with a chord of E minor with E on top. Still *pianissimo*, the strings play a series of chords that also have E on top, but now they are chords of C major, and they dance. That is how Beethoven makes his way into this beguiling finale. He pulls a lot of amusing

surprises in the manner of when and how solo and orchestra take over from each other. The finale also has moments that remind us of the first movement's *dream interludes* [emphasis added] and, with its two sections of violas, it is also given to outrageously lush sounds — one more unexpected element in this most subtle, suggestive, and multifaceted of Beethoven's concertos.'

Michael Steinberg, *The Concerto: A Listener's Guide*, 1998, p. 71.

'For all its swagger and playfulness, this movement shares with the opening *Allegro moderato* both its elaborate symphonic development and its core of rich, tranquil lyricism ...'.

Richard Wigmore, *Notes to the BBC Radio Three Beethoven Experience*, Friday 10 June 2005, www.bbc.co.uk/radio3/Beethoven

[1] Maynard Solomon, 1977, p. 143.
[2] Anton Neumayr, 1994–1997, p. 253.
[3] Anton Felix Schindler, *Beethoven as I Knew Him*, edited by Donald W. MacArdle and translated by Constance S. Jolly from the German edition of 1860, 1966, p. 134. See also: Elliot Forbes editor, *Thayer's Life of Beethoven*, 1967 p. 391.
[4] As quoted (with adaptations) in: H. C. Robbins Landon, 1992, p. 109.
[5] Joseph Braunstein, 1978, p. 22.\
[6] R. Kinloch Anderson, *Liner notes to Beethoven, Fourth Piano Concerto*, EMI, Classics for Pleasure, 1977.
[7] Robert Levin, *Liner notes to Piano Concerto, No. 4*, Deutsche Grammophon, 1998 — quoting musicologist Hans-Werner Küthen, *Ludwig van Beethoven, Piano Concertos*, Nos. 4 and 5.
[8] Michael Steinberg, 1998, p. 65.
[9] Dennis Matthews, 1968, p. 52.
[10] Derived from Wayne M. Senner, Robin Wallace and William Meredith, editors, 1999, Vol. 1, pp. 32–33. Authorities consider the three concepts of music to which the *AmZ* contributor alluded, owe a debt to Friedrich

Schiller's *Über naive und sentimentalische Dichtung* – 'On Naïve and Sentimental Poetry' of 1795, regarded as a landmark text of classical literary theory.

11 *Ibid*, Vol. 1, p. 37.
12 Michael Thomas Roeder, 1994, p. 186.
13 Barry Cooper, 2000, pp. 156–57.
14 With acknowledgment, and with adaptations, to: Michael Steinberg, 1998, p. 65.
15 Owen Jander, *Nineteenth-Century Music*, 8:3 (Spring 1985): 195–212.
16 Michael Thomas Roeder, 1994, p. 187.
17 Michael P. Steinberg, 2004, p. 62.
18 Anton Felix Schindler, *Beethoven as I Knew Him*, edited by Donald W. MacArdle and translated by Constance S. Jolly from the German edition of 1860, 1966, p. 368. See also: Michael Thomas Roeder, 1994, p. 187.
19 Donald Francis Tovey, *Essays in Musical Analysis*, 1935–41, Vol. 3, pp. 80–81.
20 Paul Badura-Skoda, Carl Czerny: *On the Proper Performance of all Beethoven's Works for the Piano*, 1970, p. 100.
21 Michael P. Steinberg, 2004, p. 62. See also Owen Jander (above).
22 Leon Plantinga, 1999, pp. 186–95.
23 Barry Cooper, 2000, p. 157.
24 Antony Hopkins, 1996, pp. 52–53.
25 Theodore Albrecht editor and translator, 1996, Vol. 1, Document, 78, pp. 133–34. Dorothea's portrait is reproduced in the Beethoven House Digital Archives, Library Document B 486/b.
26 Reichardt's reminiscences were recalled by Alexander Wheelock Thayer as published in Thayer-Forbes, 1967, p. 412.
27 Emily Anderson editor and translator, 1961, Vol. 1, Letter No. 107, p. 125. For a facsimile reproduction of Mähler's portrait see: Beethoven House Digital Archives, Beethoven Gallery and Library Document B 2388. Although this portrait situates Beethoven in a somewhat idealised pastoral setting, the artist is not considered to have sacrificed his appearance in striving for Romantic effect.
28 Theodore Albrecht, translator and editor, 1996, Vol. 1, Letter No. 80, pp. 133–8.
29 Emily Anderson editor and translator, 1961, Vol. 1, Letter No. 108, p. 129.
30 *Ibid*, Vol. 1, Letter No. 110, pp. 130–32.
31 Theodore Albrecht editor and translator, 1996, Vol. 1, Letter No. 114, pp. 177–78.
32 *Ibid*, Vol. 1, Letter No. 117, p. 184.
33 *Ibid*, Vol. 1, Letter No. 116, pp. 179–83.
34 Elliot Forbes editor, *Thayer's Life of Beethoven*, 1967 p. 404.
35 Emily Anderson editor and translator, 1961, Vol. 1, Letter No. 136, pp. 154–56. See also: Elliot Forbes editor, *Thayer's Life of Beethoven*, 1967 pp. 405–06. The original letter is now preserved in the British Museum (Library).
36 Theodore Albrecht editor and translator, 1996, Vol. 1, Letter No. 122, pp. 192–3.
37 Peter Clive, 20001, pp. 318–19.

38 As recounted in, *Vienna and its Musical Life*, in, *Haydn: The Years of the Creation*, H. C. Robbins Landon, 1977, p. 25.

39 As recalled in: Hans Conrad Fischer and Erich Kock, 1972, pp. 29–30.

40 The annuity was set at 4000 florins, the equivalent of an upper-middle class income. However, personal misfortunes to Kinsky and Lobkowitz, combined with inflation, soon undermined its purchasing power. Of Lobkowitz's support, Schindler remarks: 'The great love this princely family felt for Beethoven was constant and unwavering.' He adds: 'In fact, for ten to twelve years, nearly all Beethoven's works were first tried out in the music circle of Count Lobkowitz.' See: Anton Felix Schindler, *Beethoven as I Knew Him*, edited by Donald W. MacArdle and translated by Constance S. Jolly from the German edition of 1860, 1966, p. 50.

41 As recalled by Carl Czerny in: Paul Badura-Skoda, 1970, p. 14. See also: Elliot Forbes, 1967, p. 391.

42 Theodore Albrecht, editor and translator, 1996, Vol. 1, Letter No. 116, pp. 179–183.

43 As recounted in: Elliot Forbes, 1967, p. 402.

44 H. C. Robbins Landon, 1970, p. 118.

45 See, for example, the account by Martha Frohlich, 1991, pp. 127–8.

46 From the recollections of Josef August Röckel as recounted in: Oscar George Theodore Sonneck, *Beethoven: Impressions of Contemporaries*, 1927, p. 60.

47 Emily Anderson editor and translator, 1961, Vol. 3, Appendix I, Document I, pp. 1444–46.

48 *Ibid*, Vol. 1, Letter No. 143, pp. 168–69.

49 Elliot Forbes editor, *Thayer's Life of Beethoven*, 1967 pp. 421–22.

50 *Ibid*.

51 *Ibid*, p. 439.

52 *Ibid*, Vol. 1, Letter No. 169, pp. 191–93.

53 *Ibid*, Vol. 1, Letter No. 170, pp. 193–94.

54 Elliot Forbes, editor, *Thayer's Life of Beethoven*, 1967, p. 442 and Peter Clive, 2001, pp. 39–40.

55 Denis Matthews, *Beethoven, Master Musicians*, 1985.

56 Emily Anderson, editor and translator. 1961, Vol. 1, Letter No. 179, p. 200.

57 As quoted in: Hans Conrad Fischer and Erich Kock, 1972, p. 32.

58 Elliot Forbes, editor, *Thayer's Life of Beethoven*, 1967, pp. 453–9.

59 Theodore Albrecht editor and translator, 1996, Vol. 1, Letter No. 129, March 1808.

60 Karl Geiringer, 1982, pp. 186–7.

61 H. C. Robbins Landon, 1977, pp. 124–25 and Ludwig Nohl, 1880, pp. 58–9.

62 As recorded in: H. C. Robbins Landon, 1970, pp. 125–26.

63 Oscar George Theodore Sonneck, 1927, pp. 69–75. For an extended account of Trémont's meeting with Beethoven, see: H. C. Robbins Landon, 1992, pp. 147– 48.

64 A facsimile reproduction of the portrait, with accompanying historical information, can be seen at the Beethoven House, Digital Archives, Library Document B 1093 and Library Document B 1925.

[65] Michael Thomas Roeder, pp. 184–85.
[66] Leon Plantinga, 1999, p. 202.
[67] Michael Thomas Roeder, pp. 184–85.
[68] Robert Levin, *Liner notes to Piano Concerto, No. 4*, Deutsche Grammophon, 1998. Levin has recorded the G major Concerto on a Paul McNulty instrument (Prague 1997) based on an original Walter & Sohn fortepiano of 1805 now in the collection of instruments of the University of Harvard. The instruments in question are illustrated in the Deutsche Grammophon *Liner notes.*
[69] Hans-Werner Küthen, Preface to: *Beethoven: Konzert für klavier und orchester, Nr. 4, Op. 58* – transcription for four hands, undated.
[70] Anton Felix Schindler, edited by Donald W. MacArdle and translated by Constance S. Jolly from the German edition of 1860, 1966, p. 135.
[71] Elliot Forbes editor, *Thayer's Life of Beethoven*, 1967 p. 407. Note: the text is Forbes's footnote 17 to Thayer's text.
[72] Joseph Braunstein, *Musica Aeterna, Program Notes for 1971–1976*, 1978, p. 22.
[73] Barry Cooper, 2000, pp. 138–39.
[74] Maynard Solomon, 1977, pp. 208–09.
[75] Barry Cooper, 2000, p. 155. See also: Thayer Forbes, 1967, p. 407.
[76] *Ibid*, pp. 179–80. Barry Cooper has created a 'transcription' of the G major Concerto that includes these elaborations. See: footnote 29 to the text cited.
[77] Website: *The Unheard Beethoven, Fourth Piano Concerto.*
[78] Donald Francis Tovey, 1949, p. 315.
[79] Donald Francis Tovey, *Essays in Musical Analysis*, 1935–41, Vol. 3, p. 80.
[80] Hans-Werner Küthen, Preface to: *Beethoven: Konzert für klavier und Orchester, Nr. 4, Op. 58*, transcription for four hands, undated. According to Küthen the manuscript in question is preserved today in the archives of the Gesellschaft der Musikfreunde, Vienna – Catalogue A82b.
[81] Elliot Forbes editor, *Thayer's Life of Beethoven*, 1967, p. 478 and footnote 25.
[82] Barry Cooper, 1990, p. 173
[83] Hans-Werner Küthen, Preface to: *Beethoven: Konzert für klavier und Orchester, Nr. 4, Op. 58*, transcription for four hands, undated.
[84] Michael Thomas Roeder, 1994, p. 187.
[85] Michael Steinberg, 1998, p. 68.
[86] Alfred Brendel, *The Veil of Order: Alfred Brendel in Conversation with Martin Meyer*, 2002, p. 116.
[87] Emily Anderson, editor and translator, 1961, Vol. 1, Letter No. 58, p. 74.
[88] For a detailed account of Caspar Karl and his dealings with Beethoven's publishers see Peter Clive, 2001, pp. 20–1.
[89] Emily Anderson editor and translator, 1961, Vol. 1, Letter No. 96, pp. 115–17.
[90] Theodore Albrecht editor and translator, 1996, Vol. 1, Letter No. 83, pp. 140–41.
[91] Peter Clive, 2000, pp. 268–69.
[92] Emily Anderson editor and translator, 1961, Vol. 1, Letter No. 140, p. 165.
[93] See text to: Beethoven House, Digital Archives, Library Document, Bonn. NE 161.

[94] Elliot Forbes editor, *Thayer's Life of Beethoven*, 1967 p. 407.

[95] Theodore Albrecht editor and translator, 1996, Vol. 1, Letter No. 113, pp. 176–77.

[96] Elliot Forbes editor, *Thayer' Life of Beethoven*, 1967 p. 407. See also: Beethoven House, Digital Archives, Library Document, H. C. Bodmer, HCB Br 67 – an 'audio letter' with German text.

[97] Emily Anderson editor and translator, 1961, Vol. 1, Letter No. 132, pp. 150–51.

[98] *Ibid*, Vol. 1, Letter No. 134, pp. 152–53. See also: Beethoven House, Digital Archives, Library Document, H. C. Bodmer, HCB Br 6B – an 'audio letter' with German text.

[99] *Ibid*, Vol. 1, Letter No. 137, pp. 156–58.

[100] Theodore Albrecht editor and translator, 1996, Vol. 1, Letter No. 119, pp. 186–88. For an audio version of this letter, together with the German text, see: Beethoven House, Digital Archives, Document Sammlung H. C. Bodmer, HCB BBr 84.

[101] Theodore Albrecht editor and translator, 1996, Vol. 1, Letter No. 118, p. 185.

[102] Emily Anderson editor and translator, 1961, Vol. 3, Document 3, pp. 1419–20.

[103] Alan Tyson, 1963, pp. 51–52.

[104] Anton Felix Schindler, *Beethoven as I Knew Him,* edited by Donald W. MacArdle and translated by Constance S. Jolly from the German edition of 1860, 1966, p. 305.

[105] Emily Anderson editor and translator, 1961, Vol. 1, Letter No. 143, pp. 168–69.

[106] *Ibid*, Vol. 1, Letter No. 141, pp. 166–67. See also: Beethoven House, Digital Archives, Library Document, H. C. Bodmer, HCB Br 222.

[107] Theodore Albrecht editor and translator, 1996, Vol. 1, Letter No. 121, pp. 189–90. As suggested by Alan Tyson, 1963, pp. 51–52.

[108] For discussion of Beethoven's relationship with the Bureau des Arts et d'Industrie see: Peter Clive, 2000, pp. 200–01.

[109] Douglas Porter Johnson editor, *The Beethoven Sketchbooks: History, Reconstruction, Inventory*, 1985, p. 89.

[110] Alan Tyson, editor, *Beethoven studies 3*, 1982, p. 108, footnote 2.

[111] Douglas Porter Johnson editor, *The Beethoven Sketchbooks: History, Reconstruction, Inventory*, 1985, p. 141.

[112] Joseph Braunstein, 1978, p. 22.

[113] *Ibid*, p. 141 and p. 161.

[114] Barry Cooper, 1990, p. 80 and p. 89.

[115] Alan Tyson, editor, *Beethoven Studies 3*, 1982, p. 108, footnote 2.

[116] Hans-Werner Küthen, Preface to: *Beethoven: Konzert für klavier und Orchester, Nr. 4, Op. 58,* transcription for four hands, undated. See also: Barry Cooper, 1991, p. 191.

[117] Leon Plantinga, *Beethoven's Concertos: History, Style, Performance*, 1999, pp. 213–14.

[118] *Ibid*.

[119] Barry Cooper, 1991, p. 221 and p. 285.

[120] *Ibid*, H. C. Bodmer, HCB Mh 15.

[121] *Ibid*, H. C. Bodmer, HCB Mh 16.

[122] *Ibid*, H. C. Bodmer, HCB Mh 17.

123 *Ibid*, H. C. Bodmer, HCB Mh 18.

124 *Ibid*, H. C. Bodmer, HCB Mh 19.

125 Emily Anderson editor and translator, 1961, Vol. 1, Letter No. 172, p. 195.

126 For a facsimile reproduction of the Title Page see: Beethoven House, Digital Archives, Library Document, Bonn, C 58 / 20.

127 Elliot Forbes editor, *Thayer's Life of Beethoven*, 1967 p. 416.

128 The chamber version is attributed to being a 'discovery' of Hans-Werner Küthen's. See: Hans-Werner Küthen, Preface to *Beethoven: Konzert für klavier und Orchester*, Nr. 4, Op. 58, transcription for four hands, undated.

129 Leon Plantinga, 1999, pp. 211–12. On the occasion when all of Beethoven's compositions were performed by the BBC in a single week, Richard Wigmore, in his programme notes accompanying the performance of Op. 58, remarked: 'Tradition has it that Beethoven performed the G major Concerto at a private concert in Prince Lobkowitz's palace in Vienna in March 1807, though the evidence is far from watertight.'Richard Wigmore, *Notes to the BBC Radio Three Beethoven Experience*, Friday 10 June 2005, www.bbc.co.uk/radio3/Beethoven

130 H. C. Robbins Landon, 1992, p. 143.

131 Elliot Forbes editor, *Thayer's Life of Beethoven*, 1967 pp. 446–49. See also: Emily Anderson editor and translator, 1961, Vol. 3, Appendix H, No. 5, p. 1436.

132 H. C. Robbins Landon, 1992, pp. 149–50.

133 Accounts vary as to the precise mishaps that took place on the evening of 22 December 1808. See: Elliot Forbes editor, *Thayer's Life of Beethoven*, 1967 pp. 448–49, and H. C. Robbins Landon, 1992, p. 149. For a more recent study see: Leon Plantinga, 1999, p. 204.

134 Barry Cooper, 2000, pp. 179–80. They are described in detail and given musical notation in Barry Cooper's article, *Beethoven's revisions to his Fourth Piano Concerto*, in: *Performing Beethoven*, edited by Robin Stowell, Cambridge University Press, 1994.

135 Leon Plantinga, 1999, p. 216.

136 As recalled in: Franz Wegeler, *Remembering Beethoven: The Biographical Notes of Franz Wegeler and Ferdinand Ries*, 1988, p. 103. See also: Elliot Forbes editor, *Thayer's Life of Beethoven*, 1967 pp. 449–50.

137 Wayne M. Senner, Robin Wallace and William Meredith, editors, *The Critical Reception of Beethoven's Compositions by his German Contemporaries*, 1999, Vol. 1, pp. 50–51.

138 Anton Felix Schindler, *Beethoven as I Knew Him*, edited by Donald W. MacArdle and translated by Constance S. Jolly from the German edition of 1860, 1966, p. 368. See also: Michael Thomas Roeder, 1994, pp. 161–62.

139 *Ibid*, pp. 51–52 and footnote 1.

140 Marx's original text is titled 'Einige Worter über das Konzertwesen, besonders in grossen Städten'. It is available in translation in: Sanna Pederson, *A. B. Marx, Berlin Concert Life, and German Identity, 19th Century Music*, 18, 1994, pp. 97–98. As quoted in: Wayne M. Senner, Robin Wallace and William Meredith, editors, *The Critical Reception of*

Beethoven's Compositions by his German Contemporaries, 1999, Vol. 1, pp. 51–52.

[141] Myles Birket Foster, *History of the Philharmonic Society of London, 1813–1912: A record of a hundred years' work in the cause of music*, 1912, pp. 70–73 *et seq.*

[142] As recalled in: Oscar George Theodore Sonneck, 1927, p. 109.

[143] See reference cited at 140.

[144] Clive Brown, *A Portrait of Mendelssohn*, 2003, p. 208.

[145] Gerd Nauhaus editor, *The Marriage Diaries of Robert & Clara Schumann*, 1994, p. 52.

[146] Fanny Davies, *The Pianoforte Concertos* in: *The Musical Times*, Special Issue, editor John A. Fuller-Maitland, Vol. VIII, No. 2, 1927, p. 225.

[147] Paul Mendelssohn Bartholdy, *Letters of Felix Mendelssohn Bartholdy, from 1833 to 1847*, 1864, p. 316.

[148] Clive Brown, 2003, pp. 218–19.

[149] John Goulden, *Michael Costa: England's First Conductor, The Revolution in Musical Performance in England, 1830-1880,* 2016.

[150] Walter MacFarren, *Memories: An Autobiography*, 1905.

[151] As recounted by Hans-Werner Küthen, *Preface to Beethoven: Konzert für klavier und Orchester, Nr. 4, Op. 58,* transcription for four hands, undated.

[152] Amy Fay, *Music-study in Germany: From the Home Correspondence of Amy Fay*, Dover Publications (reprint), 1965, p. 123.

[153] Brian Rees, *Camille Saint-Saëns: a Life*, 1999, pp. 181–82.

[154] Michael Musgrave, *The Musical Life of the Crystal Palace*, 1995, p. 92.

[155] Myles Birket Foster, *History of the Philharmonic Society of London, 1813–1912: A record of a hundred years' work in the cause of music*, 1912, p. 439.

[156] Bernard Shaw, 1960, p. 14.

[157] *Ibid*, pp. 203–04.

[158] Originally published in: *The World*, 8 June 1892 and quoted by Dan H. Laurence editor, *Shaw's music: the complete musical criticism*, 1981, Vol. 2, p. 644.

[159] Antony Beaumont editor, *Ferruccio Busoni: Selected Letters*, 1987, p. 48.

[160] Arthur Rubinstein, 1973, p. 288.

[161] Arthur Rubinstein, 1980, p. 409.

[162] *Ibid*, p. 501.

[163] Mortimer H. Frank, *Arturo Toscanini: The NBC Years*, 2002.

[164] Richard Holt, *Nicolas Medtner (1879–1951): A Tribute to his Art and Personality, 1955,* pp. 159–60.

[165] Quoted in: Donald Mitchell editor, *Letters from a Life: The Selected Letters and Diaries of Benjamin Britten 1913–1976,* 1991, Vol. 1, p. 284.

[166] Ian Kemp, *Tippett: The Composer and his Music*, 1984, p. 310.

[167] Tim Page editor, *The Glenn Gould Reader*, 1987, pp. 438–40.

[168] Dennis Matthews, *In Pursuit of Music*, 1968, pp. 38–39.

[169] Brenda Lucas and Michßael Kerr, *Virtuoso: The Story of John Ogdon*, 1981, p. 104.

[170] Helena Matheopoulos, *Maestro: Encounters with Conductors of Today*, 1982, p. 461.

[171] Anton Felix Schindler, *Beethoven as I Knew Him, edited by Donald W. MacArdle and translated by Constance S. Jolly from the German edition of 1860*, 1966, pp. 366–67.

[172] Theodor W. Adorno, 1998, pp. 89–90.

PIANO CONCERTO NO. 5, E-FLAT MAJOR, OP. 73: *THE EMPEROR*

'In speaking of Beethoven's piano concertos, whose mind does not run at once to the G major and the E flat, those greatest of all pianoforte concertos? One does not try or wish to give the palm to either the one or the other – the G major of such wondrous lyrical beauty – the E flat in its glorious majesty. Both are supreme, both give us glimpses of another world, both are of the greatest Beethoven.'

Fanny Davies, *The Pianoforte Concertos* in: *The Musical Times. Special Issue*, editor John A. Fuller-Maitland, Vol. VIII, No. 2, 1927, p. 21.

'The magnificent Fifth Concerto in E-flat major,

Op. 73, was completed in 1809. As in the Fourth, Beethoven places the piano in the foreground from the outset, but here its imperial position is asserted by a couple of splendid preludings placed between ceremonial chords given out *fortissimo* by the orchestra before the first real *tutti* gets under way. The thematic material is so bold, ringing, triumphant, and its treatment so splendid that the origin of the nickname *The Emperor* Concerto is easily understood.'

Marion M. Scott, *Beethoven, Master Musicians*, 1940, p. 184.

'Nobody with a sense of style has the slightest doubt that Beethoven's three greatest concertos, the G major, Op. 58, and the E flat, Op. 73, for pianoforte, and the Violin Concerto, Op. 61, are among his grandest works. The orchestra is not only symphonic, but is enabled, by the very necessity of accompanying the solo lightly, to produce ethereal orchestral effects that are in a quite different category from anything in the symphonies. On the other hand, the solo part develops the technique of its instrument with a freedom and brilliance for which Beethoven has no leisure in sonatas and chamber music.'

Donald Francis Tovey, *Beethoven*, 1944, pp. 114–15.

'Beethoven's hero, in the *Eroica*, was a figure by which to measure the stature of pretenders; and the world would be a happier place if such an emperor, as is portrayed in this Concerto, had ever existed.'

Donald Nivison Ferguson, *Masterworks of the Orchestral Repertoire: A Guide for Listeners*, 1954, p. 111.

'The Concerto in E-flat major is Beethoven's last creation in the field ... He employed the standard classical symphonic scoring with pairs of flutes, oboes, clarinets bassoons, horns, trumpets, kettledrums and strings which he used in Symphonies Nos. 1, 2, 7, and 8. Keeping the time-honoured three-movement design, this Concerto shows, like the preceding one in G major and the Violin Concerto, several unusual features. The most important is the elimination of the virtuoso cadenza at the end of the symphonically-conceived first *Allegro* ...'.

Joseph Braunstein, *Musica Aeterna, Program Notes for 1961–1971*, 1972, p. 37.

'Beethoven's last Piano Concerto, No.5 in E-flat major, Op. 73, known in some countries as *The Emperor*, is also his largest in scale and represents a culmination of tendencies in his previous works ... The synthesis of concerto and sonata principles achieved in the two preceding concertos serves as a secure base for further evolution. He expands his form without loss of coherence; and he makes an unprecedentedly bold assertion of the virtuosic rights of the soloist, without impairing the essential balance between the protagonists.'

Basil Dean, *The Concertos* in: Denis Arnold and Nigel Fortune, editors, *The Beethoven Companion*, 1973, p. 327.

'The Concerto in E-flat major, Op. 73 was dedicated to the Archduke Rudolph of Austria; the date 1809 is to be found on the original manuscript copy at the Prussian State Library in Berlin, but the work was not completed until 1810 ... It is probable Beethoven never heard the popular title of *The Emperor* which has been applied to his Fifth Piano Concerto; as in the case of the *Jupiter* Symphony of Mozart, the expression probably originated with some overly enthusiastic admirer of the work. The first performance appears to have taken place at the Gewandhaus Concert on 28 November 1811 with Friedrich Schneider as soloist; it was later heard in Vienna with the famous pedagogue, Carl Czerny, at the piano.'

Albert E. Wier, *The Piano Concertos of Bach, Beethoven, Brahms*, foreword to *Miniature Score Series*, Belwin Mills, 1973.

'The magnificence of the music, its grand gestures and its superb panache are reasons enough for the title, but it is unnecessary. We do not need to think of emperors in order to appreciate the great sweep of this score. Much of it is extrovert music in which the composer seems to be glorying in his own strength and affirming his positive outlook on life. Technically, it represents Beethoven in a mood of supreme confidence. He had now been for years the absolute master of his craft and could mould his material as he wished.'

R. Kinloch Anderson, *Beethoven, Piano Concerto No. 5,* Liner notes to EMI *Classics for Pleasure*, 1977.

'The nickname *The Emperor* by which this work is commonly known would certainly not have gained Beethoven's approval, though it shows the special respect with which it is regarded in musical circles. Here at last it seems as though the piano has come to age and is able to stand up to the orchestra not merely as an equal but as master. Indeed, in the opening bars the orchestra is reduced to the level of a lackey opening doors, harmonic doors through which the pianist lets loose a flood of sound.'

Antony Hopkins, *The Concertgoer's Companion*, 1984, p. 95.

'The Fifth Concerto in E-flat major was the last Beethoven completed, a fact usually related to his gradual withdrawal from public performance, and Cramer's nickname has survived too long for us to quibble about its political implications. The title *The Emperor* at least befits the majesty of the work from its opening bars, which establish the pianist in the grandest manner before settling down to an equally grand orchestral exposition.'

Denis Matthews, *Beethoven, The Master Musicians*, 1985, p. 181.

'While it cannot be denied that the element of virtuosity is still present in Beethoven's later concertos, it may also be observed that as the technical demands on the soloist increase, so paradoxically the significance of the concerto as a vehicle for display seems to decrease. Beethoven's changing attitude to virtuosity is reflected in his handling of the cadenza and the solo episode. This may partly have resulted from his gradual withdrawal from the concert platform following the onset of his deafness, but the same apparent paradox may be observed in the later sonatas and quartets and is indicative of his unceasing search for the means whereby he might adequately express his unique musical thought.'

John B. Meyer *The Concerto* in: Philip Radcliffe, *Piano Music in the Age of Beethoven, The New Oxford History of Music*, Vol. VIII, Gerald Abraham, editor, 1988.

On 1 January 1897, Percy Grainger was in London preparing for a concert series and wrote to his friend Dr. Henry O'Hara — in his hometown of Melbourne:

'Concertos are lovely things to practice and Beethoven was such a master of them, for instance his glorious E-flat major is a real masterpiece.'

Malcolm Gillies, and David Pear, editors, *The All-round Man: Selected Letters of Percy Grainger, 1914–1961*, 1994, p. 280.

'Beethoven's Piano Concerto No. 5 in E-flat

major, Op. 73, is the composer's most ambitious and is the culmination of his work in this form. It was completed in 1809, the year of Napoleon's occupation of Vienna. The war may have delayed the work's first performance, but more likely Beethoven's deafness prevented him from performing, so he delayed its presentation until Czerny could present it in Vienna on 11 February 1812. There may have been a performance a few months earlier in Leipzig.'

Michael Thomas Roeder, *A History of the Concerto*, 1994, p. 188.

'Between the composition of his Fourth and Fifth Piano Concertos, Beethoven apparently came into possession of a new piano. [reference to the six-octave pianoforte introduced by Johann Andreas Streicher.] Despite his deafness, he at once realized the potentialities of the instrument, and in the so-called *Emperor*, we see the result of his reassessment of the relationship between piano and orchestra. Here, for the first time in musical history, the piano stands up to the orchestra as an equal, even indulging in open defiance at times.'

Antony Hopkins, *The Seven Concertos of Beethoven*, 1996, pp. 8–9.

'1809 might be thought of as Beethoven's E-flat year – it produced the so-called *Harp* Quartet, Op. 74, the Piano Sonata *Les Adieux*, Op. 81a, and the Fifth Piano Concerto whose pompous nickname *The Emperor* was certainly not the composer's. These were the major works of that year, which also saw the Piano Sonatas, Op. 78 and Op. 79 (the beautiful two-movement one in F sharp and the spirited little work in G), and the six songs of Op. 75. A rich year indeed ... Heroism is not ... the concern of this Concerto; it expresses the calm consciousness of achievement rather than heroic endeavour. That Beethoven's music has little to do with passing moods or sensations is well attested by the fact that while the unfortunate man was trying to save the remnants of his hearing, by burying his head in pillows during the bombardment of Vienna, he was also working on the serenely confident E flat Concerto ... Whatever the distractions, this Concerto must rank among his most unmistakably objective creations. It expresses with majestic joy a calm knowledge of its own vigour, a poetic appreciation of its own superb athletic form.'

Robert Simpson, *Beethoven and the Concerto*, in: Robert Layton, editor, *A Guide to the Concerto*, 1996, pp. 127–28.

'With the Fifth Piano Concerto (*The Emperor* in E-flat major, Op. 73), Beethoven reached a new zenith in his composing. The exalted nature of the work reflects Beethoven's reaction to events in 1809 when the French besieged and occupied Vienna.'

Anton Neumayr, *Music and Medicine,* 1994–1997, p. 253.

'One of the great joys of this Concerto is, of

course, its wealth of splendid keyboard sound. Beethoven makes palpable further advances in the surge of pianistic inventiveness that was so conspicuous in the Fourth Concerto (and so sorely wanting in the piano transcription of the Violin Concerto). Especially intriguing is the delicate interplay of thematic matter and figuration; the one may dissolve into the other while both somehow remain clearly present.'

Leon Plantinga, *Beethoven's Concertos: History, Style, Performance*, 1999, p. 262.

'The so-called *Emperor* Concerto from 1809 represents a pinnacle of Beethoven's pianistic virtuosity and a major monument in his "heroic" style cast in the same key as the *Eroica* Symphony, E-flat major. Its outer movements assume a majestic character, with rhythmic figures evocative of military style. This Fifth Concerto stems from that point in Beethoven's career when the composer curtailed his own performances on account of his incurable deafness; at the end of the first movement, Beethoven explicitly instructs performers not to play their own cadenzas, but inserts the cadenza-like passage to be played right into the score. The opening *Allegro* actually begins with an impressive cadenza-like passage, which is reaffirmed at the outset of the recapitulation.'

William Kinderman, *The Concertos* in: Glenn Stanley, editor. *The Cambridge Companion to Beethoven*, 2000, p. 111.

'Beethoven did not intend *The Emperor* to be his crowning piano concerto. Nor did he mean it to be one more tribute to Napoleon. The title was not his own, and he would have been surprised to know that was how posterity, particularly in Britain, would identify his Concerto in E-flat major. Yet, as nicknames go, it was relevant to the martial, nowadays somewhat disconcerting, side of the music, just as it would have been relevant to the unfinished Sixth Piano Concerto, if the surviving fragments of the first movement are anything to go by. But whether Beethoven's "heroic" style — as heard in the *Waldstein* and *Appassionata* Sonatas as well as in the *Eroica* Symphony and *Emperor* Concerto — was also a "Napoleonic" style remains debatable.'

Conrad Wilson, *Notes on Beethoven: 20 Crucial Works.* 2003, pp. 73–74.

'The Fifth Piano Concerto is known to English-speaking countries as *The Emperor* — an unauthentic title which has been attributed to Johann Baptist Cramer, a pianist and music publisher based in London, who was a long-time friend of Beethoven and champion of his music. The title seems apposite, though, given the work's majestic grandeur and breadth of conception. Interestingly, it is in the same key and on a similar scale to the *Eroica* Symphony of 1803, which had originally been dedicated to Napoleon — the Emperor who had, by the time of the Fifth Concerto, invaded Vienna, forcing many, including the Archduke Rudolph [Beethoven's pupil] to flee the city (it was for the absence of the Archduke that Beethoven composed the *Les Adieux* Sonata).'

David A. Thrasher, *Piano Concerto No. 5 in E-flat major*, BBC, Radio Three, *Beethoven Experience*, 5 June, 2005.

Beethoven's Fifth Piano Concerto in E-flat major, Op. 73 is popularly known to English speaking audiences as *The Emperor*. The origins of the work's nickname are uncertain but some authorities attribute it to the German-born, London-based pianist and publisher Johann Baptist Cramer. Beethoven and Cramer were on friendly terms — for the most part. Beethoven is reported to have remarked, 'Cramer had given him greater pleasure than any other pianist' and, for his part, Cramer considered Beethoven to be 'the supreme improviser'.[1] Notwithstanding their mutual regard, if Cramer did indeed crown Beethoven's Op. 73 Concerto *The Emperor* we can be sure it would not have received his sanction, since he seldom permitted anyone to take liberties with his music. We discuss the appropriateness of the Concerto's title in due course. Suffice it to say here, it has no connection with the Emperor Napoleon Bonaparte. We recall, when Beethoven received news the French Consul had assumed the title 'Emperor', he immediately — and in a rage — annulled the intended dedication to him of his Third Symphony, *The Eroica*. Donald Francis Tovey once remarked, dismissively:

'[The] wrathful republican ghost of Beethoven forbids me to call [Op. 73] by its popular English title of *The Emperor* Concerto, though Beethoven did, in fact, dedicate it to a Royal Archduke for whom he had a deep affection (see later).'[2]

Setting aside the reservations just expressed, the sobriquet *Emperor* is in many ways appropriate — albeit indirectly — insofar as it captures something of the turbulent atmosphere prevailing at the period of the music's composition. 1809, the period of gestation of Beethoven's Op. 73, was an inauspicious one for Austria's musical capital; Austria was at war with France. On 10 May, the French surrounded the city that the Archduke Maximilian had ordered to defend. On learning of his refusal to capitulate, the following day the French artillery opened their bombardment of the city's defensive walls. The windows of Haydn's apartment were shattered and a shell exploded in the grounds of the school then attended by the eleven-year old Franz Schubert — a schoolmaster was killed.

At this time Beethoven resided near the defensive city-wall (*Wasserkunst Bastei*) that became a specific target and blasts were discharged close to the windows of the composer's own apartment. Beethoven's biographer Alexander Wheelock Thayer comments: 'Every shot directed ... was liable to plunge into Beethoven's windows'.[3] He eventually sought refuge in the basement of the house of his younger brother Caspar Carl (Karl), protecting his remaining hearing with cushions that he placed over his ears.

The subsequent occupation of the city by Napoleon and his military entourage had immediate and severe consequences. On 26 July 1809, Beethoven wrote to his publisher Breitkopf & Härtel:

'[We] have been suffering misery in a most concentrated form ... The whole course of events has in my case affected both body and soul. I cannot yet give myself up to the enjoyment of country life which is so indispensable to me ... What a destructive, disorderly life and here around me, nothing but drums, cannons, and human misery in every form.[4]

In other letters Beethoven complains of the bad food, the cost of living and other material deprivations. Not least of his concerns was the soaring inflation that lessened the value of the money he received for his compositions and that of the annuity he had started to receive from his patrons the Princes Kinsky and Lobkowitz and the Archduke Rudolph.[5]

Beethoven's correspondence, concerning everyday matters, provides insights into the cost of living and its demands on his income. On 8 February 1810, he wrote to Peter von Leber to arrange his accommodation. Von Leber was part-owner of Baron Johann Pasqualati's large house that was situated on the Mölkerbastei, as remarked, close by Vienna's fortifications. Beethoven lived on the fourth floor at various times between 1804 and 1815. His annual rent was 500 gulden.[6] Later, in April, Beethoven had occasion to write to his then assistant Ignaz von Gleichenstein to help him secure various domestic items from the merchant Joseph von Henikstein — a competent cellist and a member of the Gesellschaft der Musikfreunde. Henikstein offered him 27.5 gulden in exchange for one pound sterling.[7] On 21 August, Beethoven wrote to his publisher Breitkopf & Härtel and gave expression to his feelings, complaining that a pair of boots cost 30 gulden and a new coat as much as 170 gulden. He remonstrates: 'The deuce take the economics of music.'[8] By way of interest, Breitkopf & Härtel charged between 60–80 ducats, in silver Viennese coinage, for the score of a major composition.[9]

Whilst he does not mention it in his correspondence, the

death of his teacher Haydn, on 31 May, must have increased Beethoven's sense of despondency — although, thereby, it elevated Beethoven to the position of Vienna's, and Europe's, pre-eminent living composer. He must also have felt the loss of his physician Johann Schmidt who died on 19 February. Although an ophthalmologist by training, Schmidt had treated Beethoven over a number of years for several of his ailments with the encouragement 'take hearty walks, work little, sleep — also eat well and drink spirits in moderation'.[10] As a token of appreciation, and as a gesture of friendship to his physician, Beethoven dedicated to him the Piano Trio, Op. 28 — an arrangement of his Septet, Op. 20.

As a consequence of his impaired hearing, Beethoven was progressively withdrawing from the public stage in the capacity of virtuoso pianist. The extent to which his hearing was impaired can be inferred from the recollections of his friend, the violinist, mandolinist and harp virtuoso, Wenzel Krumpholz. He gave Beethoven instruction in violin technique and sometimes played the composer's violin sonatas with him. Of this experience he writes:

'That was, however, truly dreadful music-making because in the throes of his enthusiasm he did not hear when he attacked a passage with the wrong fingering.'[11]

Thayer puts a gloss on the composer's adversity, remarking:

'Beethoven had surely assumed the right to retire and leave the virtuoso field to his pupils, of whom Baroness Ertmann and Carl Czerny were pre-eminent as performers of his music. In the more private concerts [in the salons of the nobility] he had long given place to the Baroness and now

Czerny began to take it before the public, even to the extent of introducing his last new composition for pianoforte and orchestra, Op. 73.'[12]

With the signing of an armistice, things gradually started to improve somewhat in Vienna, such that on 2 November Beethoven felt disposed to write to Breitkopf & Härtel:

'We are enjoying a little peace after violent destruction, after suffering every hardship that one could conceivably endure. I worked for a few weeks in succession, but it seemed to me more for *death* than for *immortality* ... I no longer expect to see any stability in this age ...'.[13]

Despite his sombre mood and enforced hardships, the evidence of Beethoven's sketchbooks (see later) reveals he not only turned his mind to the *Emperor* Concerto but also to other significant compositions. These include: String Quartet, Op. 74 (*The Harp*); Variations for Piano in D major, Op. 76; Fantasia for Piano, Op. 77; and Piano Sonatas, Op. 78, Op. 79 and Op. 81a *Das Lebe Wohl — Les Adieux.*

Reflecting on the compositions of this period, Barry Cooper contends: '[Beethoven's] C major/minor phase had now given way to an E-flat phase.' He elaborates:

'In choosing a key for a work, Beethoven apparently took several factors into consideration. One of the most important was the key of the previous works in the same genre ... He tended to think of each genre as a category.'[14]

In his discussion of the compositions under consideration,

Maynard Solomon suggests: '[In] his heroic symphonies Beethoven had generated the architecture of his compositions from the release of energy stored within condensed, explosive germinal motifs and rhythms ...'. Now, in 1809, Solomon maintains:

> '[A] sense of calm, spaciousness, and measured nobility of rhetoric ... is encountered in the Cello Sonata, Op. 69, the Violin Concerto, and the Fourth and Fifth Piano Concertos.'

Solomon describes Beethoven's Fifth Piano Concerto as belonging to 'the invasion year, 1809' but concedes, 'it may have been begun in the closing days of the previous year'. He proposes: 'Along with a March for Military Band, WoO 18 [composed 1808], [the Fifth Concerto] may well embody Beethoven's response to the tide of Napoleonic conquest.' However, he qualifies his suggestion: 'Of course, its grandeur and its unparalleled solutions of strictly musical problems far transcend such considerations.[15]'

The Mozart scholar Alfred Einstein called the *Emperor* Concerto, with its warlike rhythms, victory motifs, thrusting melodies, and affirmative character, 'the apotheosis of military concept' in Beethoven's music.'[16] Quoting Einstein, Solomon elaborates:

> 'According to Einstein, the "military style", which had its roots in the Viennese tradition, as well as in contemporary French music, was readily understood by Beethoven's audiences ... They expected a first movement in four-four time "of a military character" ... They reacted with unmixed pleasure when Beethoven not only fulfilled but surpassed their expectations.'[17]

As we shall see in due course, at its first performance in Leipzig, in 1810, the *Emperor* Concerto was greeted with bravos and ovations. In respect of the E-flat major Piano Concerto, Anton Schindler — Beethoven's biographer, writing in 1860 — considered it to be 'the summit of all concerto-music ever written for this instrument both regards its spiritual content and the technical difficulties it presents'.[18]

In this part of our study of Beethoven's five piano concertos, we consider the following: Beethoven's personal circumstances at the period of composition of the Piano Concerto, Op. 73; the work's composition chronology; Beethoven's negotiations with publishers; publication; records of contemporary performance; accounts of performance in the nineteenth and twentieth centuries; and references to a selection of performances in our own time. To close, we provide a documentary study of the musicology of the E-flat major Concerto as expressed in selected writings of musicologists and performing artists.

We direct our attention, first, to the period prior to Beethoven commencing work on his Op. 73.

In an attempt to improve his financial position, Beethoven was anxious to secure an official appointment within Vienna's musical establishment — as had Mozart twenty years previously. In this context, as H. C. Robbins Landon observes: 'Mozart's death, in dire poverty, was obviously a spectre that haunted Vienna for many years after.'[19] Doubtless with such considerations in mind, on 4 December 1807 Beethoven applied for the vacant post of Director at the Royal Imperial Court Theatre. Such a position would, he hoped, help to secure his financial prospects and provide an outlet for his ambitions to be a respected composer for the lyric theatre — a quest he was to pursue for many years as he considered one potential opera libretto after another.

Beethoven's application was no mere whim-of-the-moment impulse. He had previously been employed, from 1803 to 1804, by the Theater an der Wien as its musical director, but his back-stage residential accommodation was so miserable as to precipitate his early departure. In his application for the new post of Director, Beethoven describes how he had been obliged 'to struggle with difficulties of all kinds' and how he had not yet been able to establish himself in Vienna in a position that would enable him 'to fulfil his desire to live wholly for art, to develop his talents to a still higher degree of perfection ... and to make certain for the future the fortuitous advantages of the present'.

Beethoven gave an undertaking to compose an opera each year which, however, given the exacting artistic demands he made of librettists, he was most unlikely to have been able to fulfil. In addition, he promised to compose 'a divertimento or another work of similar proportions' for all of which he asked for a salary of 2,400 florins – about 240 pounds sterling. The theatre directors gave cursory consideration to Beethoven's application and promptly rejected it.[20]

In early November 1808, a further opportunity came Beethoven's way – arising, doubtless, as a consequence of a growing awareness of his fame beyond the confines of Vienna. Napoleon's younger brother Jérôme – recently installed as the King of Westphalia – invited Beethoven, through the diplomatic offices of his High Chamberlain, to consider an offer of appointment as his Senior Kapellmeister in Kassel.

Despite the somewhat archaic-sounding title, the post held distinct attractions for Beethoven. His duties would not be onerous; he would merely be required to play for

Jérôme's personal pleasure and to conduct occasional concerts. Moreover, he was offered a salary of 600 gold ducats (the equivalent of about 4000 gulden/florins or 200 pounds sterling) and an additional 150 ducats for travelling expenses.[21] Denis Matthews makes the interesting observation that although the title of kapellmeister was becoming somewhat antiquated, in the first decade of the nineteenth century, it may have had a particular resonance for Beethoven. His grandfather had held such an appointment, and this, combined with childhood memories, may, Matthews suggests, have exerted an influence on his subconscious mind.[22]

Beethoven was immediately attracted by the invitation and was disposed to accept it. In late November he wrote in enthusiastic terms to his new confident and general factotum Baron Ignaz von Gleichenstein:

> 'I have received the offer of a fine appointment as Kapellmeister to the *King of Westphalia*. I am to be paid handsomely — I have been asked to state how *many ducats* I should like to have — and so forth.'

He closed the letter by asking Gleichenstein for a meeting to seek his advice.[23]

In the New Year of 1809, Beethoven appears to have made up his mind regarding Jérôme Bonaparte's offer of employment. In a letter to his publisher Breitkopf & Härtel (7 January) he intimates how attractive the position appeared to him regarding the steady income he would receive and the post's other advantages. He complained of the standard of musicians in Vienna, some of whom he accused of hardly being able to read an orchestral score; Beethoven was still resentful of the poor standard of playing they had displayed at his mammoth concert on the previous 22 December. He also believed the composer Antonio Salieri intrigued against him — echoes of 'Mozart and Salieri' — disposing him to exclaim: 'At last, owing to intrigues and cabals and mean-nesses of all kinds, I am compelled to leave my German fatherland.'[24]

Comments by Carl Czerny shed light on Beethoven's feelings at this time and put them into perspective. He writes:

> 'It has often been said abroad that Beethoven was despised and repressed in Vienna. The truth is that even as a young man he received all possible support, attention and encouragement from our great aristocracy which could have been given to a young artist ... It is true that, as an artist, he had to deal with intrigues, but the public were not to blame for that. He was always admired as an unusual character, and his great-ness was assumed by everyone who didn't really know him.'[25]

In a postscript to his letter to Breitkopf & Härtel, Beethoven asked the publisher not to make anything public about his appointment until the final details were confirmed, although he did not object, somewhat conspiratorially, to 'a few hints' about his leaving Vienna being inserted into the *Allgemeine musikalische Zeitung* — the journal published by Breitkopf & Härtel.[26]

The 'few hints' of Beethoven's departure appear to have reached the ears of the Countess Anna Maria Erdödy. She was a competent pianist, an admirer of the composer's music and given to holding frequent musical soirées in her Vienna town house — her family also owned estates in the country. For a time, Beethoven occupied rooms in her apartments, held the Countess in high esteem, and dedicated to her the two Piano Trios Op. 70 and the two Cello Sonatas Op. 102.[27]

By virtue of her social standing, the Countess had the ear of Vienna's nobility, the outcome of which was she made known Beethoven's intended departure to a privileged inner-circle that included the Archduke Rudolph, Prince Ferdinand Kinsky and Count Franz Joseph Lobkowitz. In order to secure Beethoven's continuing presence in Vienna, they resolved to take immediate action and collectively agreed to settle upon him an annuity of 4000 gulden/florins – the equivalent offered to him by Jérôme Bonaparte. Beethoven's new secretary-assistant Baron Franz von Gleichenstein and Countess Erdödy assisted in drawing up an Annuity Contract that was duly ratified on 1 March.

Beethoven's patrons were doubly generous; not only did they offer to provide him with financial support, they did not try to control or monopolise him by placing restrictions on his place of domicile. The terms of their agreement allowed him to reside in Vienna 'or some other town situated in the hereditary lands of His Imperial Majesty'. The Contract also affirmed:

> '[The] undersigned have made the decision to place Herr Ludwig van Beethoven in a position where the most pressing circumstances shall not cause him embarrassment or impede his powerful genius.'

Despite this promised financial support, Beethoven did not secure the title he so much cherished, namely, that of *Imperial Kapellmeister*.[28]

Thayer remarks that the three signatories to Beethoven's Annuity Contract were doubtless motivated to assist the composer on the grounds: 'What an inexcusable, unpardonable disgrace to Vienna would be the departure of Beethoven under such circumstances!'[29]

Although Beethoven was to remain in Vienna for the rest of his life, the full extent of the reassurance his Annuity Contract offered proved to be relatively short-lived. In 1811, devaluation, resulting from the Napoleonic wars, reduced his 4000 gulden to about 1,600 gulden. Moreover, on 11 September 1811, Count Lobkowitz was obliged to stop his payments for four years because he was declared bankrupt, and on 3 November 1812 Prince Kinsky died suddenly as the result of an accident, compelling Beethoven to legally challenge his heirs to maintain Kinsky's share of the annual payment that he considered was due to him. It was not until around 1815 that his Annuity was restored to something like its original value — about 3,400 gulden.[30]

These experiences conferred in Beethoven a lasting mistrust of 'paper money' and he was eager ever after to transact his business affairs in terms of the coinage of the day, namely, gulden, florins, ducats and louis d'or. Reflecting on this formative episode in Beethoven's career, Solomon muses:

> 'With [the Annuity] Beethoven had attained the highest degree of independence and security possible within a semi-feudal mode of patronage. There was no longer a personal bond or commitment involving the slightest element of subservience.'[31]

We stay with the French occupation of Vienna a moment longer. Napoleon set up his headquarters in Schönbrunn Palace together with his Military Council, a member of which was Baron de Trémont (Louis-Philppe de Vienney), a senior French officer and an ardent music lover. He was eager to make Beethoven's acquaintance but was anxious as to how he would be received. On the day he resolved to call on the composer he was doubly anxious since, having attended a Council meeting, he was still wearing his official uniform — a circumstance he thought might ignite the composer's fiery temperament. To his surprise, and great pleasure, he was cordially received. Recalling the circumstances years later, Trèmont mused:

> 'I admired his genius and knew his works by heart ... he arranged several meetings with me during my stay in Vienna, and would improvise an hour or two alone for me ... I fancy that to these improvisations of Beethoven's I owe my most vivid musical impression. I maintain that unless one had heard him improvise well and quite at ease, one can but imperfectly appreciate the vast scope of his genius.'[32]

Trèmont was dismayed to find an artist of such manifest distinction living in modest circumstances; Beethoven by this time had left the refuge of his brother's rooms and had relocated to his own accommodation. Writing of this Trèmont records:

> 'Picture to yourself the dirtiest, most disorderly place imaginable — blotches of moisture covered the ceiling; an oldish grand piano, on which the dust disputed the place with various pieces of engraved and manuscript music ... under the piano an unemptied *pot de nui* [chamber pot]!'[33]

The composer's first biographer Johann Schlosser was disposed to remark: 'Beethoven's way of working did not fit the conventions of a regulated household'.[34] Perhaps Beethoven himself realized the need to take better control of his domestic circumstances since later in the year he set about seeking the services of a housekeeper to assist with his everyday affairs.[35]

Beethoven, together with other composers, undoubtedly felt a nationalistic impulse prompted by the French occupation of Vienna. This found expression in the writing of *Lieder Österreichischer Wehrmänner* — 'Lieder by Austrian Soldiers'. Beethoven's contribution was a collaboration with the dramatist and writer of patriotic verse Heinrich Joseph von Collin. Beethoven planned a work for chorus and orchestra titled *Österreich über alles* — 'Austria above all'. Sketches for this are found in the so-called Landsberg 5 sketchbook but, like so many other of the composer's musical thoughts, it was not carried through to completion.[36] Further evidence of Beethoven's patriotism is apparent in the autograph score to the Piano Concerto Op. 73. At the beginning of the second movement, Beethoven wrote: 'Austria shall retaliate against Napoleon'. This disposed Hans-Werner Küthen, the Concerto's editor, to deduce Beethoven composed much of the Concerto's music after the French occupation of Vienna.[37]

In the summer of 1809, Beethoven entered into a formal teaching arrangement with the youthful Archduke Rudolph that would have far reaching consequences. Rudolph was a patron of music and a capable pianist who, according to the testimony of Johann Reichardt, could perform Beethoven's compositions 'with great skill, accuracy and refinement'.[38] As the youngest son of the Emperor Leopold II, Rudolph's social standing was of the highest and Beethoven's many notes and letters to his pupil were always expressed with the utmost courtesy and respect, despite the fact that Rudolph's lessons often became a burdensome challenge to the composer.

Surviving notes from Beethoven to Rudolph frequently express the regret that he had to cancel a lesson. Rudolph was Beethoven's only composition pupil and, in preparation for the lessons he was to give, he diligently compiled a compendium of extracts from the relevant works of theory of the day from which he copied out interesting or important parts bearing on figured base and counterpoint. The texts Beethoven consulted included the *Gradus ad Parnassum* by Joseph Fux, regarded as the epitome of pedagogical counterpoint at the time. Beethoven had studied Fux's text closely and had a much-annotated copy of his own.[39] It is believed he may have copied out more than two-hundred pages of counterpoint studies — which suggests he had a personal agenda that went beyond the self-imposed obligations to his pupil.

Beethoven later give expression to this absorption in musicological pedagogy in such compositions as the slow movement of the String Quartet, Op. 95, the Piano Trio, Op. 97 — dedicated to the Archduke Rudolph and which bears his name — and the fugues found in more distant works such as the Cello Sonata, Op. 102, No. 2 and the *Hammerklavier* Piano Sonata, Op. 106.[40] Beethoven's most fruitful collaboration with his pupil was the set of forty variations composed by Rudolph — although heavily supervised by Beethoven — and published in the composer's subordinate catalogue of works as WoO 200. Beethoven dedicated more compositions to Rudolph than any other individual. These included the Fourth and Fifth Piano concertos and the Piano Sonata Op. 81a. His distinguished pupil was clearly familiar with his master's Piano Sonata Op. 78, since a rare letter from him to Beethoven has survived in which Rudolph requests a copy of the music.[41]

Testimony to Beethoven's international fame is evident in a letter he received on 9 August 1809 from the Royal

Institute of Sciences, Literature, and Fine Arts, Amsterdam. It informed him of his election as a Member in recognition of his 'contribution to music' and of his 'distinguished talents'.[42] At the close of a business letter to Breitkopf & Härtell on 19 September 1809, Beethoven could not refrain from telling of his honour, albeit with a touch of irony: 'So I now have a title – Ha, Ha, Ha, that makes me laugh.'[43] Nevertheless, on 20 December he respectfully replied to the Institute. He first apologised for the delay in acknowledging the Institute's letter, as a consequence of the disruptions caused by the war. He assured the Secretary (C. J. Roos) how flattered he was to receive the award and how he would continue to strive to be worthy of it. He took leave with – 'Your very humble and very obedient servant, Ludwig van Beethoven'.[44]

The esteem in which Amsterdam's Royal Institute held Beethoven's pioneering achievements at this period were not universally shared; they were proving hard to be accepted by even some of the composer's more gifted and enterprising composer-contemporaries. This is evident from remarks the Swiss publisher Hans Georg Nägeli made when he wrote to Carl Maria von Weber on 21 May 1810. Nägeli had stated that one of Weber's compositions (not identified) reminded him of Beethoven. Weber was neither flattered nor amused and his reply illustrates how far in advance of musical convention Beethoven's music appeared, even to so imaginative a musical mind as Weber's. Weber responded:

'[My] views differ far too much from those of Beethoven ever to come into contact with him. The fiery, almost incredible inventive faculty which inspires him is attended by so many complications in the arrangement of his ideas that it is only his earlier compositions that interest me; the later ones appear to me a confused chaos, unintelligible struggle after novelty from which occasionally heavenly flashes of genius dart forth, showing how great he might be if he chose to control his luxuriant fancy.'[45]

Years later, however, Weber tempered his views about Beethoven's music and, for example, came to admire Beethoven's Opera *Fidelio* that he introduced to Prague audiences in 1814 – its first performance outside of Vienna. Later, in 822, Weber presented *Fidelio* in Dresden to considerable acclaim. News of this subsequently reached Beethoven who, following an exchange of letters, invited Weber to meet him. The opportunity to do so arose when Weber premiered his own Opera *Euryanthe* at the Kärntnerthor Theater on 25 October 1823. Later in life, Weber left an account of his meeting with Beethoven together with his son Max. From this he relates:

'[Beethoven] had begun to forget the loss of real sound, as his own heavenly orchestra played more closely to his soul.'

Weber described Beethoven in the following florid terms:

'His thick grey hair was flung upwards and disclosed the sanctuary of his lofty forehead. His nose was square like that of a lion; his chin broad with those remarkable folds which all his portraits show; his jaws formed as if purposely to crack the hardest nuts; his mouth noble and soft. Over the broad face, seamed with scars from the smallpox, was spread a dark redness. From under the thick, closely compressed eyebrows gleamed a pair of small flashing eyes. The square broad form of Cyclops was wrapped in a shabby dressing gown, much torn about the sleeves.'[46]

In the winter of 1811, Schnyder von Wartensee, a young Swiss musician, was seeking to expand his education by living and studying in Vienna. Beethoven's reputation had preceded von Wartensee and he soon sought out the composer. On 17 December he wrote to his Swiss compatriot, the music publisher Hans Georg Nägeli about his resulting meeting: 'He is a highly exceptional man. In his mind hover great thoughts which he can express in no other way than through music; words are not at his command.'

It appears Beethoven was finding it irksome at this time to give composition lessons to the Archduke Rudolph since von Wartensee adds: 'He has only one [composition student] who gives him very much trouble and whom he would gladly be rid of, if he could.'[47] This latter remark may appear to be rather severe, particularly in light of the warmth of feeling Beethoven was bestowing upon his pupil at this time in the form of his E-flat major Piano Sonata, Op. 81a (*Les Adieux*) and would later reinforce in the many dedications to him in other of his works. It remains the case, though, that Beethoven would complain, on many an occasion, how a composition lesson of two-or-three hours with Rudolph would 'wear him out and render him useless for serious work of his own for the rest of the day'.

Two further encounters with Beethoven convey the impression he made on his contemporaries. Beethoven experienced abdominal pains throughout his adult life, frequently described as 'colic', and sought to remedy his condition at health spas such as that at Teplitz. On one such occasion, the German diplomat and soldier Karl August von Ense was also at Teplitz and made the composer's acquaintance. Writing of this to his friend, the poet and philologist Ludwig Uhland, confided:

> 'I soon was on intimate terms with him ... He lives only for his art ... On his walks he seeks out distant places along lonely paths ... finding peace in the contemplation of the great features of nature and thinking in musical tones.'

The second encounter to relate was that between Beethoven and none other than Germany's celebrated man of letters Johann Wolfgang von Goethe, who also met the composer at Teplitz. This was perhaps the only occasion in Goethe's life when he came face to face with an artist of his own stature. He wrote to his wife:

> 'I have never before seen a more comprehensive, energetic or intense artist. I understand very well how strange he must appear to the outside world.'

A few days later he wrote to his friend Carl Friedrich Zelter:

> 'His talent astounded me; but, unfortunately, he is a quite intractable person ... He does not make things enjoyable either for himself or for others.'[48]

Perhaps the most enduring visual image of the composer we have dates from this period. Beethoven was a close friend of the Viennese pianoforte manufacturers Nannette and Andreas Streicher; they adorned their music salon with busts of celebrated composers. In 1812 they commissioned the sculptor Franz Klein to take a likeness of Beethoven that required his face to be covered with gypsum plaster. Klein had earlier perfected this technique when preparing anatomical models — from corpses!

Beethoven had first to be persuaded to have his face lubricated with oil, to prevent his whiskers from adhering to the plaster, then to have his eyebrows covered with paper strips — for the same reason. Finally, before his face was covered with plaster, goose quills were inserted into his nostrils to enable him to breath. The ordeal proved too much for Beethoven and the taking of his likeness almost ended in disaster. Finding the process too uncomfortable, and fearing he would suffocate, he tore the cast from his face and dashed it to the floor.[49] Fortunately for posterity, Klein was able to reassemble the broken pieces that were later used to create the well-known bust that is considered to be a particularly authentic likeness of the composer — resolute expression, pock marks and all.[50] Klein later created a bust of the composer that remained in possession of the Streicher family for many years. In 1890 a mould was made from this in order to obtain a copy for presentation in the Beethoven House in Bonn.[51] (see the text to our frontispiece)

The events attendant upon The Congress of Vienna of 1814-15 prompted the creation of a further likeness of Beethoven. The Conference was convened with the intention of securing Europe's future, following the downfall of the French Emperor.

The French portraitist Louis Letronne, then resident in the capital, was called upon to create portraits of the various monarchs and statesmen who had come to the imperial city to participate in this event — what today would be called 'a summit'. During this time, Letronne also took a likeness of Beethoven. His portrait was intended to be the draft for a copperplate engraving to be undertaken by Blasius Höfel — a member of Vienna's Academy of Fine Arts.

In the event, Höfel was dissatisfied with Letronne's sketch and requested the composer to sit for second time – no small undertaking given Beethoven's irascible nature. The publishing house Artaria & Co. subsequently published Höfel's portrait in connection with some of the composer's works – further evidence of Beethoven's public popularity and fame. This new popularity derived mainly from the success of the two compositions he composed and performed on the occasion of the Vienna Congress, namely: the Cantata *Der glorreiche Augenblick (The Glorious Moment)*, Op. 136, and the Symphony *Wellingtons Sieg* (*Wellington's Victory*) or the *Schlacht bei Vittoria* (*Battle near Vittoria*), Op. 91, to which may be added the acclaim accorded to the composer's Seventh Symphony – the only one of the three compositions to remain in today's concert repertoire. Höfel's study was used for the frontispiece of the Leipzig periodical *Allgemeine musikalische Zeitung* and became widely known thereby. [52]

In our wider portrait of Beethoven, at the period of composition of the E-flat major Concerto, reference should be made to his increasing deafness and its influence upon him. A measure of the depression he was experiencing can be judged from a letter he wrote on 2 May 1810 to the German physician Franz Gerhard Wegeler; the two had been friends from their school days together in Bonn. In his letter Beethoven laments how beautiful life would be for him had it not been 'poisoned forever'. He remarks how for the last two years he had sought respite by trying to lead a quiet life away from society and concludes, with a combination of despair and fortitude:

> 'If I had not read somewhere that a man should not voluntarily quit this life so long as he can still perform a good deed, I should have quit this earth long ago.' [53]

*

From about 1812, Beethoven's deafness was compelling him to withdraw ever more from society. With the hope of professional success and public recognition fading, and disappointed at his failure in marriage, he came to realize all he had to fall back upon was his self-reliance and belief in his art. This is evident in a cryptic diary entry for the start of 1812. It reads: 'Submission, the deepest submission to your fate.' Beethoven's self-injunction may have been influenced by his reading of Zacharias Werner's Tragedy, *The Templars of Cyprus*. In the copy in his possession, he annotated passages where the hero of the work has to accept his fate — as expressed in such passages as: 'He can be defeated but not destroyed'.[54]

We learn of Beethoven's isolation from society from the recollections of the composer-violinist Louis Spohr; he was in Vienna in 1812 when he was scheduled to conduct some of his oratorios. In his *Autobiography* he writes how he wished to meet the composer at one of Vienna's many musical parties but learned Beethoven had withdrawn from such reunions, 'for his deafness had so much increased that he could not hear music readily or clearly, and he had become exceedingly shy of society'.

Spohr eventually met Beethoven by chance in a restaurant, recalling: 'One had to shout loud enough to be heard three rooms off.' He describes Beethoven as being a little abrupt 'but a pair of sparkling eyes gleamed under his shaggy eyebrows'. Spohr expressed his opinion of Beethoven's music that he states was current at the time, and with which he concurred for many years afterwards:

> 'His ear could no longer guide him in his constant strivings after originality and new forms. Was it, then, [not surprising] that his works should

386

become more and more strange, incoherent and incomprehensible? ... I ... freely confess that I have never been able to acquire a taste for Beethoven's later works.'[55]

Amidst this somewhat sombre account of Beethoven, it should be remarked his sense of humour – albeit frequently somewhat ribald – does not appear to have deserted him. A glimpse into his correspondence with Nikolaus von Zmeskall, at the period under consideration, confirms this. Zmeskall was a civil servant employed at the Hungarian Court Chancellery. Musically inclined, he was an excellent cellist and a founder member of the Gesellschaft der Musikfreunde; he probably first met Beethoven at one of the morning concerts of the composer's patron Prince Lichnowsky. Beethoven maintained an extensive correspondence with Zmeskall, usually regarding domestic matters, mostly expressed in brief note-form and styled, as remarked, in a humorous manner.

In the autumn of 1809, Beethoven wanted Zmeskall's help in arranging a performance of his String Quartet, Op. 74 that was to be rehearsed at Prince Lobkowitz's. He opened with a typical salutation, 'CURSED TIPSEY DOMANOVETZ – not Count of music, but Count of gluttony, Count of Supper and the like' – this may in part be explained by the fact that the two friends frequently dined together.[56]

At about the same time, Beethoven sent a typical note to Zmeskall requesting 'a few quills' – a reminder this was the era of the quill pen and of the composer's reliance on such close friends as Zmeskall to assist him with his everyday needs. With a characteristic touch of humour, he promised Zmeskall he would receive 'the grand award of the Order of the Cello'[57] – his friend being, as stated, a competent cellist. Beethoven acknowledged this, more properly, by conferring on Zmeskall the dedication of his String Quartet, Op. 95 – paradoxically, one of his most serious. On another occasion, he asked Zmeskall to let him have the recipe for boot polish, remarking: 'A well-polished head needs also a well-polished boot.'[58] It is a measure of the regard Beethoven's friends and associates felt for him that such unedifying notes – couched in harmless badinage – were carefully retained as keepsakes.

Beethoven's increasing success with the public doubtless contributed to maintaining his spirits. For example in Vienna, in 1808, he achieved thirty-two public performances of his works compared with only two of Mozart and five of Haydn. As Tia de Nora comments in her study *Beethoven and the Construction of Genius*:

> 'Beethoven's popularity can in part be explained by the all-Beethoven concerts programmed that year, some of which took place in the Theater an der Wien and the Burgtheater where princes and counts subscribed to boxes and barons to the partier.'[59]

Worthy of reiteration is that Beethoven's major compositions of 1809 were: Piano Concerto, Op. 73; String Quartet, Op. 74; Variations for Piano, Op. 76; Fantasia for Piano, Op. 77; Sonatina for Piano, Op. 79; and Piano Sonata, Op. 81a *Das Lebe Wohl*.

On 25 September 1809, the Scottish music publisher George Thomson wrote to Beethoven requesting he should set 'forty-three short airs' and provide suitable 'ritornellos and possible accompaniments for the piano or pedal harp'. In so doing, Thomson established a fruitful working-relationship with the composer that was to last for several years.

Thomson was generous to Beethoven, offering him one-hundred Viennese ducats (about fifty pounds sterling) adding 'if you do not find the one-hunded ducats sufficient consideration, I intend to add a few ducats more'. He did stipulate, though, that the composition of the accompaniments for the piano should be 'easy to play, because our young ladies, when singing our national airs, do not like, and hardly know how to play, a difficult accompaniment'.[60]

Beethoven initially responded with fifty-three song settings and over the next decade contributed some 156 simple melodies that would eventually be published in Thomson's five-volume series *A Select Collection of Original Scottish Airs for Voice*. It has been suggested, 'the seeds planted in 1809, and later, in these song-settings exerted an influence on Beethoven's later sense of musical lyricism'.[61]

On 5 August 1812, Thomson confirmed he had received the fifty-three song settings from Beethoven. He enthused: 'They are all worthy of the greatest applause.' He identified those he considered would find the most favour

'because they are the simplest and easiest to play
on the piano ... and that at the same time, there
is not one that does not bear the stamp of genius,
knowledge and taste.'

Thomson singled out for praise the 'delightful *conversations* [his emphasis] between the violin and violincello.' He closed by recalling how some years previously another composer (unnamed) had set nine airs for him but he considered

'It would grieve me to mix his with yours ...
Indeed, I know of no other living composer
whose name merits the honour of being found in
the same book with that of Beethoven'.[62]

We recall the impression Beethoven's powers of improvisation had made on Baron de Trémont. A further illustration of his pianistic accomplishments derives from an account of his performing left by the horn player and composer Friedrich Starke. He had heard Mozart play, held the post of horn player in the Court Opera, and assisted Beethoven's nephew Karl with his piano studies. One morning, Starke was invited to breakfast – that included coffee – ground by Beethoven, as was his custom. Later, Starke relates hearing Beethoven improvise 'in three different styles', describing these as

> 'first, restrained, second, fugal – where a heavenly theme in sixteenth notes was developed in the most wonderful way – and third, in chamber style in which Beethoven knew how to combine the greatest intricacies in projecting his special mood'.

Anticipating they would play together, Starke had his horn at the ready and suggested they should play the composer's Horn Sonata in F, Op. 17 – to which he records, 'Beethoven agreed with pleasure'. Of particular interest is that when it was discovered the piano was a semitone low, Beethoven played the piano part raised to F-sharp major and 'played it in a wondrously beautiful way; the passages rolled along so clear and fine that one couldn't believe at all that he was transposing.'[63]

Devotees of the school of piano playing advocated by Tobias Matthay, in his influential compendium *The Act of Touch*, will find what Starke next has to say, of Beethoven's hand position, of particular interest.

> '[Beethoven] held his fingers very curved, so

much so that they were completely hidden by the hand, what is called the old position, in brief, as contrasted to the present way in which the fingers are characteristically more extended.'[64]

Trémont and Starke were fortunate to hear Beethoven improvise. The recollections of the Austrian writer and dramatist Franz Grillparzer reveal how sensitive Beethoven could be on occasions, particularly if he thought anyone was eavesdropping when he was at work at the piano. In the summer of 1808, Grillparzer and his mother shared lodgings in the same house as Beethoven situated at Heiligenstadt, in the Döbling district of Vienna. In 1861 he recalled these days of his youth – he was seventeen at the time – to Beethoven's biographer Alexander Wheelock Thayer. The Grillparzer's shared a common staircase and when Beethoven played, or worked at, the piano it could be heard throughout the house. This encouraged Grillparzer's mother to open their door to hear more clearly. One day, temptation got the better of her and she went out into the vestibule – only to be caught by Beethoven eavesdropping on his playing. According to Grillparzer, 'he never played again all summer despite his mother's entreaties never to disturb him at his work'.[65]

We discuss the musicology of the E-flat major Concerto later. For the moment, it will help to take our narrative forward by calling to mind some thoughts of the multi-talented musician Anthony Hopkins – composer, pianist, conductor, writer, and radio broadcaster. Remarking on the manner in which the Concerto opens with sonorous chords, he states: 'This was an entirely new development for which the instrument-makers must take some of the credit.' As he observes, this was a time of technical improvement for wind, brass and keyboard instruments. Beethoven, with his deafness by then becoming debilitating, realised a new style of piano was available to him and which was, in Hopkins' words, 'for the first time capable of dominating the orchestra.' Hopkins suggests: 'It was for this reason that the opening of the [E-flat major] Concerto is so radically different from that of its predecessors.' He adds:

'[One] feels that the [Concerto's] three mini-cadenzas or flourishes are a sort of celebration. At last, they seem to say, "We pianists no longer have to court the orchestra; we are the masters now and [the orchestra] must bend to our will".'[66]

In his reference to 'a new piano', Hopkins may have had in mind the splendid state-of-the-art instrument Beethoven received in 1803 from the French manufacturer Sébastien Érard.[67] This, the reader may recall, from our study of the B-flat major Concerto, Op. 19, incorporated several innovations such as foot pedals that replaced the cumbersome knee-action lever-arrangement typical of earlier instruments of the time. Érard's pianos were sturdily constructed and offered greater sonority than most other fortepianos of the day — characteristics particularly valued by Beethoven in his quest for an evermore resonant keyboard-sound. The gift was in recognition of Érard's esteem of Beethoven and of his growing reputation abroad as a pianist. Other distinguished musicians of the day, who owned an Érard piano, included Beethoven's teacher Haydn and fellow pianist Ignaz Moscheles.

Such were the rapid advances in the development of the fortepiano, though, that by 1809–10 even Érard's instrument was being superseded — technologically speaking — by that of Vienna's own piano maunfacturers. This is evident from a letter Beethoven wrote on 18 September 1810 to the piano-maker Johann Andreas Streicher. Pianos continued to be one of Beethoven's preoccupations and he wrote to Streicher requesting one of his newest instruments. He complains: 'My French piano is no longer of much use; in fact, it is quite useless.' He is clearly referring to the Érard piano of 1803. Despite it once having been considered to be a state-of-the-art instrument, Beethoven had taxed it to its limits. He even asked Streicher to help him 'find a home for it'.[68]

In mid-November, Beethoven wrote once more to Streicher. He first proclaims: 'My motto is either play on a good instrument or not at all.' He reflected he had considered disposing of his Érard, but was apparently having second thoughts: 'As for my French piano, which is certainly quite useless now, I still have misgivings about selling it, for it is really a souvenir such as no one here has so far honoured me.'[69] Attempts to sell the Érard proved unsuccessful and Beethoven kept it until about 1824 when he gave it to his brother Johann. By then he may have wanted to make room for a new piano he was given by the English maker John Broadwood. By way of interest, in 1845 Johann presented the Érard piano to the Oberösterreichisches Landesmuseum in Linz, where he lived for a period; it was subsequently loaned, fully restored, to its present location in the Kunsthistorisches Museum, Vienna.[70]

That Streicher was endeavouring to improve his pianos is evident from the recollections of Carl Czerny who wrote:

'In 1807 I met Andreas Streicher, a famous piano teacher, who had begun to manufacture pianofortes; by devoting thought to it, and by imitating English instruments, he was able to give his own a fuller tone and a firmer action than older pianofortes had had.'[71]

On his tour of Vienna, in 1809, the German composer and music critic Johann Reichardt became acquainted with Beethoven's piano music and recalled:

> 'Streicher has been persuaded away from the compliant ... musical characteristics of other Viennese instruments. On Beethoven's insistence he has given his instruments more resistance and elasticity. A forceful performer thus has a greater basic and continuous control over the instrument ... He has given his instrument a greater and more diverse character.'[72]

Some idea of the cost of a good Viennese piano from this period can be ascertained from Beethoven's correspondence with his then assistant Ignaz von Gleichenstein. Frau von Malfatti, the mother of Therese and Anna – with whom Beethoven was on affectionate terms – had requested Beethoven's advice on the purchase of a piano – and its cost. Beethoven informed von Gleichenstein, who was acting as intermediary, to inform Frau von Malfatti that a good one could be purchased for 500 gulden. However, because of his standing in Vienna he informed Gleichenstein: 'I can obtain an *expensive instrument* for a *very* low figure.' [Beethoven's emphasis] On this occasion, Beethoven recommended Johann Schanz – one of Vienna's leading pianoforte manufacturers.[73]

It was probably as a consequence of searching for a suitable instrument for the elder Therese, that prompted Beethoven once more to reflect on the state of the pianoforte of the time. On 6 May 1810, he wrote to Streicher about the state of his own piano (one of Streicher's). He complains how it is 'very worn out' and adds 'I frequently hear the same expressed by other people'. He asked Streicher not to be offended and took leave of him saying: 'You know that my sole object is to promote the production of good instruments.'[74]

Improvements continued to be made with regard to the design and construction of the piano as Carl Czerny remarked — writing in the 1840s:

> 'With the present perfection of the pianoforte, which, in power and fullness of tone vies with the instruments of the orchestra, the performer of a concerto is more easy and grateful, than at a time when Beethoven himself played his First Concerto at the Kärntnerthor Theatre in Vienna (in 1801).'

Czerny enthused:

> 'We can now produce effects of which he had then no idea; and, in reference to the expression, we can now also reckon on a much more accurate accompaniment on the part of the orchestra than was the case at that period.'[75]

With Czerny's observations, we close our remarks regarding the pianos of Beethoven's time and direct our narrative to a discussion of the sketch origins of the Piano Concerto, Op. 73.

In the composition of *The Emperor* Concerto, Beethoven followed his established procedure of noting down his thoughts in sketch form, initially making use of such music paper that came to hand and later by organising his thoughts in the form of bound sketchbooks. From December 1808 to early 1809, he made use of the so-called

Grasnick 3 Sketchbook. It derives its name from the collector of autograph scores Friedrich August Grasnick who acquired it from the art and music dealer Tobias Haslinger – a close friend of Beethoven. In 1879, it came into the possession of the Royal Library – the *Deutsche Staatsbibliothek*. Today, 43 leaves of music paper (sketch leaves) survive from an original compilation of some 48 leaves (96 pages); leaves appear to have been removed from three locations. About three-quarters of Grasnick 3 is devoted to sketches for the Fantasy for piano, chorus and orchestra, Op. 80. Early sketches for the Fifth Piano Concerto are found at the close of Grasnick 3 – at leaves 38 (verso) through to 43 (verso). One of the 'missing' leaves from Grasnick 3 is preserved today in the Pierpont Morgan Library, New York. The recto side contains early ideas for the second and third movements of Op. 73 and on the verso are well-developed sketches for the first movement.[76]

From February through to October 1809, Beethoven made use of the Meinert Sketchbook; it derives its name from the collector of manuscripts Carl Meinert of Dessau. In 1879, the *Musikalische Wochenblatt* ('Weekly Musical Journal') published an article describing a number of sketch leaves belonging to Carl Meinert. The Paris-based collector Charles Malherbe acquired these in 1903 and are the origin of the eight bifolia (double-format pages) that are now preserved in the collections of the Bibliothèque Nationale. This source reveals Beethoven at work extensively on the first movement of the E-flat major Concerto together with preliminary sketches for the Concerto's second and third movements.[77]

Between March and October 1809, Beethoven resorted to the Landsberg 5 desk sketchbook. It was acquired, following Beethoven's death, by the resourceful manuscript collector Ludwig Landsberg from whom it eventually passed into the possession of the Berlin Royal Library. Today, the sketchbook consists of 56 leaves; in its original form it was probably made up of 61 leaves. Beethoven used Landsberg 5 for the development of the following compositions: Opp. 73, 74 75, 76, 79, 81a, and 115. The sequence of the sketches for these works is illustrative of how Beethoven's mind turned from one composition to another. Their order in Landsberg 5 is: Op. 73 (III); Op. 81a (I); Op. 115; Op. 74 (I, II, III); Op. 81a (II, III); Op. 74 (IV); Op. 79 (I); Op. 76; and Op. 75 (Nos. 6 and 5).[78]

A sketch leaf for the first movement of Op. 73 is preserved in the Archive of the Beethoven House, Bonn. It is thought to be a remnant of the larger gathering of related sketches preserved, as remarked, at the Bibliothèque Nationale, Paris.[79]

Seventy-four leaves of sketches are held in the Archives of the Beethoven House in Bonn, known as the Petter Collection. They are named after the Viennese collector Gustav Petter and are considered to represent Beethoven at work over the period September 1811—December 1812. Thayer writes:

'Scattered along ... part of the sketchbook are diverse subjects for pianoforte works; as if Beethoven had in mind a companion piece to the E flat Concerto for the further display of his powers.'[80]

By way of illustration of the 'further display of Beethoven's powers', the principal contents of the Petter sketchbook include ideas for: *Ruins of Athens — Die Ruinen von Athen*, Op. 113; Seventh Symphony, Op. 92; Eighth Symphony, Op. 93; Opera *Macbeth* — sketches for but not completed; and the Violin Sonata, Op. 96.[81]

The autograph score of the *Emperor* Concerto has survived and is preserved today in the Deutsche *Staatsbibliothek*, Berlin where it is catalogued as 'Klavier Conzert 1809, von L. v. Bthwn'.

The Fifth Piano Concerto reveals a changing attitude to concerto writing that had become evident in the preceding Fourth Piano Concerto. It will be recalled, from our earlier study, Op. 58 was published before its premier. In the words of Leon Plantiga: 'The autograph score was no longer a vehicle for demonstrating [Beethoven's] fabled prowess as a pianist.' The autograph of Op. 73 reflects these changes as Plantinga further elucidates:

> 'In this manuscript, in stark contrast to his scores for all earlier piano concertos, Beethoven wrote out the solo part meticulously, including articulation marks, pedaling, verbal performance directions, and even alternative passages (marked *osia*) for shorter keyboards. And he wrote a good bit of music into the piano part in the orchestral tuttis, with the intriguing addition of systematic figured bass notation.'

These features, Plantinga maintains, are characteristic of other printed piano concertos of the period and support the contention that the function of the score of Op. 73 was to facilitate publication and not performance — and certainly not by Beethoven.[82]

For the piano concertos prior to the *Emperor*, Beethoven had typically sketched the soloist's cadenza passages in anticipation of his personal performance at the keyboard and, for adornment, placing reliance on his powers of extemporization. This changed with his writing for the Op. 73 Concerto and, with it, he established a precedent that would influence other composers throughout the nineteenth century — not always for the better. An extended cadenza runs the risk of introducing a sense of 'foreignness' and 'distortion' of the original text. Commenting on Beethoven's cadenza-writing for Mozart's Piano Concerto K. 466, the American musicologist Richard Cramer states — in a manner that may be controversial to some:

> 'Beethoven's additions have been characterised as a violation of the ground-rules of the Mozartian cadenza, as a repudiation of the Classical ideal of cadential elaboration', and 'a "revealing indiscretion", an act of "impropriety", situating a moment in history "in which the past is vilified and a precarious future glimpsed".' [83]

We consider for a moment the origins of the cadenza and Beethoven's response to it.

In 1752 the German composer Joachim Quantz defined the cadenza quite simply as 'an extempore embellishment'. As a mark of virtuoso display, the instrumental cadenza owed much to the art of the vocal cadenza of the Baroque era. It was a period when virtuosi were eager to manifest their skills and thereby secure public esteem. In 1796, a *Yearbook of Musical Art* appeared (*Jahrbuch der Tonkunst von Wien und Prag*) that contained remarks devoted directly to the performance-custom of embellishments of melodies. The author's words of caution have relevance with respect to the temptation of over-elaborating cadenza-writing in the genre of the piano concerto:

> 'From singers, it is expected and demanded that they have a *method.* By this, one generally understands certain ornaments and graces which

are inserted by the singer. To place these graces capably and suitably requires exceptional taste and feeling. Thus, it happens that many singers insert too many runs and chromatic notes; their singing line often becomes too overloaded and obscured, so that the subjects and melodies become lost.'[84]

The (conservatively minded) Tovey reminds us that the cadenza should be 'in accord with the spirit of the original music'. He stipulates:

'The ideal classical cadenza would be an actual extemporization by a player capable of using the composer's language and above the temptation to display anything so banal as a review of the progress of music since the composer's date.'

In support of his contention, he recalls Beethoven's remark

'No artist deserved the title of *virtuoso* unless his extemporizations could pass for written compositions.'[85]

On another occasion, Tovey defined the cadenza as being 'a medium that enables the soloist to display his skill as a performer ... by doing things which the rest of the orchestra cannot do'. He could not, however, resist from becoming censorious:

'But the idea that it is a vulgar occasion for vulgar display is due to the obvious fact ... that vulgar people did see in it an opportunity for vulgar display, and used it accordingly.'[86]

In our discussion of the Piano Concerto in C minor, Op. 37, we have seen how the cadenza assumed growing importance for Beethoven in the genre of the piano concerto. We have also seen that in the summer of 1809, not only did Beethoven write cadenzas for the first and third movements of Mozart's Piano Concerto in D minor, K. 466 — that may have been intended for his pupil Ferdinand Ries — but he also turned once more to his own earlier piano concertos. For Op. 15, he wrote three cadenzas; for Op. 19, one for the first movement; and for Op. 37, one for the first movement.

Of the cadenzas completed for the G-major Concerto, Op. 58, he supplied two for the first movement and one for the third movement — other cadenzas being fragmentary.[87] Writing of Beethoven's concern to achieve 'formal integration' in the *Emperor* Concerto, the American composer-musicologist Glenn Watkins believes elaborate cadenza-writing would have militated against Beethoven's desired intentions. For this reason, he wrote in the score of the first movement: 'Non si fa cadenza, ma s'attacca subito il seguente' — 'Do not play a cadenza, but attack the following at once.'[88] Tovey comments: 'The written cadenza to the E-flat Concerto is, of course, an integral part of the composition. It is not, as often described, "accompanied by the orchestra"; for the actual cadenza is only eleven bars of purely cadential flourish ...'.[89] In the same spirit, Cooper remarks on 'the grand, three chordal-flourishes' with which the Concerto opens and the manner in which these later return with different piano decorations. He adds:

'With so much bravura figuration in those prominent places, Beethoven considered a full-scale cadenza unnecessary, and instead wrote out just a short one, more motivic than decorative that is fully integrated into the movement.'[90]

On 4 February 1810, Beethoven resumed his correspondence with Gottfried Härtel, the surviving partner of the Breitkopf and Härtel partnership. He offered him several publications for sale remarking, modestly, 'Here are some works'. Testimony to his creativity and industry, together with the *Emperor* Concerto, these included: String Quartet, Op. 74; Six Variations — on an original theme, Op. 76; Piano Fantasia, Op. 77; Three Piano Sonatas Op. 78, Op. 79, Op. 81a; and Choral Fantasia, Op. 80. For these compositions he requested payment of 1,450 florins. He justified himself to Härtel: *'I don't think I am making excessive demands if I ask for a fee of 1450 gulden.'* [Beethoven's italics] He further explained how he also intended to have these compositions published in England (London). That raised the question of copyright. Beethoven, therefor, asked Härtel to hold back his publication until September in order for him to facilitate negotiations with his London publisher. He then complained, one of the reasons for the slow recovery of his health was 'due to the bad provisions' occasioned by the military conflict. He added: 'We have bad food and have to pay exorbitant sums for it.'[91]

On 20 June, Härtel responded to Beethoven's concerns regarding the copyright of his works and aired anxieties of his own concerning the problem of the nefarious actions of unscrupulous publishers. Härtell was particularly anxious about the consequences that might follow from Beethoven's intended publication overseas, remarking:

'[Very] soon thereafter, following the London edition, they will also appear from all the [pirate]

German publishers, who will take care not to offer you an adequate fee, because they are really accustomed to paying none at all.'

Härtel cites his recent experience: 'Thus, as a legal publisher of Haydn's last Quartet [Op. 103 in D minor, published in 1806] (as I can prove at the moment), I have sold, up to this time, no more than about 250 copies; while perhaps two or three times as many of the cheap pirate reprints were sold.'

Setting aside his doubts, Härtel offered Beethoven 250 ducats in gold for the works he had received; Härtel was mindful Beethoven was now wary of transacting business in paper money because of the effects of inflation. Härtel stipulated the works in question should not appear in London before they did in Leipzig – the location of Breitkopf and Härtel's business address. Having been rebuked by Beethoven for errors that had appeared in previous works of his that his firm had published, Härtell took the precaution of concluding his letter: 'I would like to receive your original manuscripts for greater accuracy in the engraving.'[92]

Beethoven responded to Härtel on 2 July, opening his letter in a typically forthright manner:

'I will let you have the works I have mentioned for a fee of 250 gold ducats. But I will not reduce this figure, particularly as with the help of my brother I could obtain more in Vienna. Would to Heaven that in order to get some money out of you I have always to wrestle with you first.'

He proposed to send his compositions in three lots, assigning to each a delivery and publication date. He requested the first lot to be published by 1 September. This consisted of the String Quartet, Op. 74 — that actually appeared in November; Op. 77 (Fantasia); Op.78 and Op. 79 (Piano Sonatas) — all of which also appeared in November; Op. 75 (Lieder) and Op. 76 (Piano Variations) — that appeared in October. The second lot was to be published by 1 November and contained the Fifth Piano Concerto, Op. 73; the Choral *Fantasia*, Op. 80; and three Lieder Op. 83. The third and last lot was to be published by 1 February the following year and comprised the Piano Sonata Op. 81a; the four Ariettas and a Duet, Op. 82; and the score of the Incidental Music to *Egmont*, Op. 84.[93]

Despite the reassurances Beethoven had given Härtel that his publishing house, in Leipzig, would have precedence with regard to the appearance of his works in London, Härtel had lingering concerns. This is evident from a letter he wrote on 20 July to Christian Hasse, a musician and dealer in music with connections in London. Härtel was still worried about the possibility of pirate editions undermining his business transactions with Beethoven. Moreover, Härtel was aware that Beethoven's publisher in London, Clementi and Co., had received much the same offer, as his firm, to publish the compositions to which we have made reference — including the E-flat major Piano Concerto. Härtel informed Hasse:

'Several new and interesting works by Beethoven will appear from us shortly, of which we notify you ... You do not lack for musical acquaintances in London. You would, therefore, greatly oblige me if you would be so kind as to commission an acquaintance in London to be on the watch, and to send us anything about these items as soon as it comes out.' With a conspiratorial touch, he asks for Hasse's discretion in this matter.[94]

On 21 August, Beethoven wrote a further letter to Breitkopf and Härtel of some twelve quarto-pages — testimony to his diligence in business matters. First, he alluded once more to his financial insecurity, complaining of the effect inflation was having on his Annuity: 'Last year, before the arrival of the French, my 4000 gulden were worth something. This year they are not even worth 1000 gulden [an exaggeration].' He adds: '[My] purpose in life is not to become a profiteer in musical art ... God forbid! ... But I like to live independently; and that I cannot do without a small income.' He sought to reassure Härtel that the fee to of 250 gold ducats he was asking was 'a very low fee'. Regarding the E-flat major Concerto he informed Härtel:

'The Concerto is dedicated to the Archduke R[udolph] and the title is just "Grand Concerto dedicated to His Imperial Highness the Archduke Rudolph of, and so forth".'

In closing, Beethoven raised a subject he held dear to the end of his life, namely, the publication of a complete edition of his works. He enthused:

'[I] intend to produce an authentic edition of my collected works to be prepared by myself and, if we can come to an agreement, to be published by your firm.'

He offered to supervise the work himself so as to ensure 'the production of an accurate, correct and permanent work'. He hoped the project would benefit them both financially and looked forward to receiving Härtel's reply.[95]

Härtel responded to Beethoven's suggestion on 24 September; his reply must have been disappointing to Beethoven. He comments:

> 'As you know, I have ... published the greatest number of, and the most significant, piano compositions of Haydn, Mozart, Clementi, Dussek, Cramer, and Steibelt.'

He adds, reflecting his integrity, how he would have suggested himself a new and complete edition of Beethoven's works if he had not been constrained by 'the proprietary rights [copyright] of several other publishers'; he cites the Kunst- und Industrie-Comptoir in Vienna, Kühnel in Leipzig and Simrock in Bonn, all of which had published one or other of Beethoven's works. In any case, Härtel adds, editions of Beethoven's works were already in circulation and it would only be

> 'a few well-to-do zealous worshippers of your art, who would purchase a new complete edition that, by its nature, would be expensive to produce with the likelihood of only limited sales'.

Härtell also referred to the parlous state into which music-publishing had declined, as a result of the Napoleonic wars: '[You] may have difficulty imaging the paralysis in which northern Germany (to which I am limited as long as the northern shipping remains blocked) finds itself, and the repercussions that this dismal condition has on music.' Härtel complained once more about the problems of pirate editions. To give added testimony to his concerns, he cited the unauthorised publication of Beethoven's own works:

'They have not only been published and pirated individually [but also] in France, England, Offenbach, Bonn, Mainz, Augsburg, Berlin, Amsterdam, Hamburg, Munich, and even Leipzig.'

Härtell concluded his letter by expressing the hope that he can make a mercantile success of selling the works of Beethoven he was being offered. He was doubly anxious, though, in part for the reasons just explained but he was also mindful that Beethoven's compositions had a reputation for being 'difficult' and, as he put it: '[I] cannot accurately judge of their success.'[96]

On 15 October, Beethoven wrote again to Härtel this time asking for the return of some of his manuscripts. He states: 'I hardly possess any manuscripts [for the reason] 'some good friend here and there asks for them.' He explains: 'For instance, the Archduke has the score of the Concerto [Op. 73] and refuses to let me have it back.' Perhaps Rudolph was learning the work and needed the score since it was not yet in print?[97]

From our previous remarks (Piano Concerto, Op. 58), we recall the London-based Muzio Clementi had established a working relationship with Beethoven and had negotiated with him the English publication rights for his Fourth Piano Concerto, Op. 58, together with the three String Quartets Op. 59, the Symphony No. 4, Op. 60, the Violin Concerto, Op. 61 – also transcribed as Piano Concerto, Op. 61a – and the Overture *Coriolan*, Op. 62. For all these works, Beethoven was to receive two hundred pounds sterling – a considerable sum.

During his stay in Vienna, in 1808–10, Clementi renewed his association with Beethoven that produced further commissions for the English (London) market. Relevant to our narrative is that these included the *Emperor*

Concerto. Clementi's relationship with Beethoven would, over time, prove to be particularly fruitful. In collaboration with his partner Frederick William Collard, Clementi's editions included the following English editions: Opp. 31/3, 59, 61 and 61a, 73–80, 81a, 110–11, 119, 136– and 139.[98]

It so happens that Muzio Clementi in London was quicker off the mark, regarding the publication of the *Emperor* Concerto, than Gottfried Härtel in Leipzig. Under the copyright procedures then in force in England, at the period under consideration, Beethoven's Op. 73 was received at Stationers Hall, London on 1 November 1810. The Law of Copyright then required eleven copies of newly printed works to be deposited at Stationers' Hall, the London home of the Worshipful Company of Stationers and Newspaper Makers, a Livery Company that regulated the affairs of the printing and publishing industry. On receipt of new works, the Company then passed these to the eleven libraries that were privileged to exercise their right of demand to receive new works – the equivalent of today's system of Legal Deposit. As Pamela Willets explains in her study *Beethoven and England*:

'This is the principal source of the collections of the English Beethoven [first] editions preserved in the British Museum, the Bodleian Library at Oxford, [and] the University Library at Cambridge.'[99]

Thereby, the *Emperor* Concerto came to be published in England (London) before its appearance in Germany (Leipzig). This also proved to be the case with other works assigned to Clementi including and the String Quartet, Op. 74, and the Piano Sonatas, Opp. 78, 79, and 81a.

The London edition of Op. 73 duly appeared in

November 1810 with its Title Page, styled in Clementi's nomenclature, as Op. 64:

'Grand Concerto / for the / PIANO FORTE, / As newly constructed / BY CLEMENTI & Co. / with additional Keys up to F, and also arranged for the Piano Forte up to C, / with Accompaniments for a / Full Orchestra, / COMPOSED BY / Lewis [sic] van Beethoven. / Op. 64. London printed by Clementi, & comp[any], 26 Cheapside ...'.

The Title Page also made it known that other of the composer's works were available from Clementi including the Piano Sonatas and Fantasia for piano. Of particular interest is Clementi's stated adaptation of the E-flat major Concerto to enable the work to be played on a pianoforte of shorter compass, in recognition that the newer, more extended keyboard, was not universally available. Alan Tyson reports few major discrepancies exist between the editions of Clementi and Breitkopf and Härtell but he does identify more than forty minor textual differences between the two editions.[100] With these variants in mind, he suggests, in some instances, Clementi's London editions may be considered 'too early' insofar as they may have escaped Beethoven's last-minute improvements such as 'adding extra dynamics and marks of expression'. Notwithstanding, he further observes that for the compositions Opp.73–82 there is close correspondence between Clement's texts and those of Breitkopf and Härtel.[101]

Turning to the New Year 1811, Thayer writes:

'There were now, or soon to be, in the hands of Breitkopf and Härtel's engravers, the Pianoforte

Concerto, Op. 73, the *Fantasia*, Op. 80, the Piano
Sonata *Les Adieux*, Op. 81a ... and the *Christus
am Ölberg*, Op. 85 ... The revision of these works
for the press, with his duties to the Archduke, are
all the professional labours in these months ...'.[102]

The first edition of the Fifth Piano Concerto was duly
published by Breitkopf and Härtel in February 1811 with
the Title Page:

'Grand / CONCERTO / Pour le Pianoforte /
avec Accompagnement / de l' Orchestre /
composé et dédié / à / Son Altesse Impériale /
ROUDOLPHE / par ' L. v. Beethoven / Pro-
priété des Editeurs / à Leipsic / Chez Breitkopf
& Härtel.'[103]

It shows the piano part in reduced form in the orchestral
tuttis, consisting of bass and melody plus continuo figuration. Beethoven – uncharacteristically – made some
concessions for the less able performer: 'The shimmering
decent in double notes at the end of the first movement
(mm 562ff) has a right-hand replacement (marked *'o sia
più facile*) – ['in single notes'].' Leon Plantinga, whose
words we have just quoted, points out a conundrum faced
by music publishers: 'Glittering virtuosity in concert
performance was counted on by publishers to spur sales
that had most excited audiences in the first place [but] was
the element least reproducible at the living-room piano.'
Concerning Beethoven's changing attitude – away from
performance to publication – he adds: 'There was no plan,
so far as we know, for early performance of the Concerto,
and certainly no talk of holding it back until it had been
heard; this Concerto simply joined that majestic flow of

major works to be recorded in print and preserved for posterity.'[104]

The Bonn Archives contain a final version of the first movement of the piano part to Op. 73 that is thought was created in parallel with the engraver's model for Breitkopf and Härtel. It was formally in the library of the work's dedicatee the Archduke Rudolph.[105] As was customary for the period, publication comprised the solo and orchestral parts only. The full score was not printed by Breitkopf and Härtel until 1857. C. F. Peters, in Leipzig, also brought out a full score in 1864.

On 2 May 1811, Beethoven learned that Härtel had sent the score of the Concerto to the Industriekomptoir – Bureau des Arts and d'Industrie – without his consent; he was anxious because it contained errors that he had not yet corrected. He had in fact sent Härtel the corrected proofs the previous day.[106] Beethoven was clearly very cross. Four days later he wrote once more to the hapless Härtel over his concerns regarding the errors remaining in the Concerto score. He railed 'Mistakes – mistakes – you yourself are a unique mistake.' He threatened to send his own copyist to Leipzig to have the work done to his satisfaction. In more conciliatory mood he took leave of Härtel jesting in typical fashion:

> 'Make as many mistakes as you like ... All the same, I do esteem you very highly. As you know it is the custom with human beings to esteem one another for not having made even greater mistakes.'[107]

We can infer Beethoven and his publisher were soon reconciled from a further letter Beethoven sent to Härtel on 9 October. Härtel had invited Beethoven to join him in

Leipzig to enjoy the countryside. Beethoven had to decline, though, for reasons of being too busy. Of interest is his reference to the changing status of his pupil the Archduke. He informs the publisher that Rudolph is about to be made Primate of Hungary with 'an income of three million' [florins?]. He concludes, with a touch of humour, that Rudolph should confer on him 'one million a year' that he would then devote 'for the good votaries of music'.[108]

Public performance of the *Emperor* Concerto may have been obstructed as a consequence of the political situation and upheavals caused by the military conflict. Cooper conjectures the *Emperor* Concerto may have received 'a trial run at some private venue'.[109] It has even been suggested the Archduke Rudolph himself may have performed the work on 13 January 1811 at the palace of Prince Lobkowitz.[110]

The first authenticated public performance took place on 28 November 1811 at the Leipzig Gewandhaus.[111] The soloist was the German composer-pianist Friedrich Schneider. The triumphalist character, evident in much of the music, appears to have been seized upon by the audience. One critic reported: 'The audience was roused to a degree of enthusiasm such as could not be manifested by the ordinary evidences of appreciation and pleasure.'[112]

The first public performance of the *Emperor* Concerto in Vienna took place on 12 February 1812 at the Opera House. The poster for the occasion announced the dedication of the work: 'To his Imperial Majesty, Archduke Rudolph.' Anton Schindler comments:

'Such a public statement of dedication was not customary, and it may be taken as an indication of Beethoven's desire to proclaim to all his deep gratitude to the most illustrious of his patrons.'

The depth of Beethoven's feeling towards Rudolph may be judged by our reaffirming how many, and significant, works, he dedicated to him: Piano Concerto No. 4 in G major, Op. 58 (1808); Piano Concerto No. 5 in E-flat major, Op. 73 (1811); Piano Sonata in E-flat major (Les Adieux), Op. 81a (1811); Fidelio, Op. 72 (vocal score) (1814); Violin Sonata in G major, Op. 96 (1816); Trio in B flat, Op. 97 (1816); Piano Sonata in B-flat major, Op. 106 (1819); Missa Solemnis, Op. 123 (autograph dated 1823); Grosse Fuge, Op. (autograph dated 1823); and Grosse Fuge (piano transcription for four hands), Op. 134 (autograph dated 1826).[113]

The Vienna concert was a social occasion for the benefit of The Society of Noble Ladies of Charity. For this reason, the music was heard with an accompanying tableau of pictures by Raphael, Poussin, and Troyes. These were described as having offered 'a glorious treat' but may have detracted from the effect of Beethoven's new Concerto. As Joseph Braunstein observes: 'Beethoven's extraordinary creation surely was out of place there.'[114]

The audience's response to the Concerto was reported in the Journal *Thalia* that had recently (1810) been established by Franz Castelli. It took its name from an earlier enterprise of the same name that had been founded by Friedrich Schiller in 1784 in which his *An die Freude* – set to music by Beethoven as the finale to the Ninth Symphony – first appeared in 1786. Franz Castelli was himself a dramatist, librettist, poet, and a friend of Beethoven; he endeavoured to collaborate in an opera project but to no effect. He wrote of Beethoven with the greatest admiration, describing calling him as 'a giant' and 'one of the greatest practitioners of his art, the Shakespeare of music'.[115]

With regard to the reception of the *Emperor* Concerto, the music correspondent to Castelli's Journal could only respond in muted terms:

'If this composition ... failed to receive the applause which it deserved, the reason is to be sought partly in the subjective character of the work, partly in the objective nature of the listeners.'

The critic continued:

'Beethoven, full of proud confidence in himself, never writes for the multitude; he demands understanding and feeling, and because of the intentional difficulties, he can receive these only on the hands of the knowing minority of whom is not to be found on such occasions.'[116]

The *Emperor* Concerto was the most expansive composition yet written for piano and orchestra. This disposed the critic of the *Allgemeine musikalische Zeitung* to carp: 'The immense length of the composition robs it of the impact that this product of a gigantic intellect would otherwise practise upon its hearers.' This induced Schindler to respond: 'Who would today find this Concerto excessively long?' He adds:

'This critical remark shows us once more that it was then, as later, the external form of Beethoven's works that gave most offence. For even today there are learned persons who busy themselves by counting measures in a movement, comparing Beethoven's works with Mozart's on the basis of mere volume.'

Beethoven, having withdrawn from public life, as a pianist,

414

entrusted the Vienna performance to his former pupil. Of this, Schindler writes: 'The pianist was Carl Czerny who, as a result of Beethoven's coaching, brought out the very best in the music.'[117] The *AmZ* reported favourably on Czerny's playing: 'Czerny played with much accuracy and fluency and showed that he has the power to conquer the greatest difficulties.'

On 16 June 1812, the *Journal de la Roer* reported on a concert that had taken place at Aachen. A concerto was performed which may have been the *Emperor*. The pianist was Rahel Varnhagen, the wife of the diplomat Karl von Varnhagen; both were known to Beethoven who once played personally for Rahel's pleasure.[118] The *Journal's* correspondent relates: 'This young lady plays with much taste; she overcomes the greatest difficulties and was greatly applauded.' The report of the concert is of particular interest for the observations made concerning the pianoforte used for the occasion:

'It is simply too bad that such a beautiful talent was fruitlessly squandered on such an unsatisfactory instrument in such large premises. Its dry and monotonous tones competed to its great disadvantage with an entire orchestra, the combination of so many different instruments.'[119]

Later in the summer, Beethoven received the distressing news that on 26 July a fire had engulfed much of Baden, the spa town to which he was in the habit of making frequent visits for hydrotherapy and relaxation in the countryside. His response was to enlist the aid of Giovanni Polledro to collaborate with him in a benefit concert that took place on 6 August. Polledro was an accomplished violinist who had studied with Paganini and became acquainted with

Beethoven when the two were residing in Carlsbad. Beethoven set aside his reluctance to play in public and contributed an improvisation.[120]

It is a measure of the neglect of the *Emperor* Concerto – certainly in Vienna – that we have to look to 1824 for further reference to it. On 20 May, Beethoven wrote to Czerny to ask if he would perform two movements of the work.[121] The Beethovenian will be aware this was a time of considerable musical significance. On 23 May 1824, the Ninth Symphony received its second performance. A month later this disposed Czerny to write to his composer-pianist friend Johann Pixis, then living in Paris:

> 'There is surely no more significant musical news that I can write about from your dear old Vienna than that Beethoven finally gave repeated performances of his long-awaited concert, and in the most striking manner.'

The Ninth Symphony had received its premier on 7 May and the work was to receive its second performance together with other works that included, the Overture *Consecration of the House*, Op. 124 as well as the *Kyrie, Credo,* and *Agnus Dei* from the *Missa Solemnis*, Op. 123 – styled as 'Three Grand Hymns' in the Concert Programme.

From Beethoven's Conversation Book for the period, we learn the composer's nephew Karl suggested 'Czerny ought to play the Concerto'. From what followed, this can be taken to be a reference to the E-flat major, Op. 73. Beethoven concurred, and instructed his secretary-assistant Anton Schindler to 'write a few lines to Czerny' adding, 'He has already played the E flat often [?], so it would cause him little trouble'. On reflection, Beethoven suggested Czerny should play the first movement only since a performance of the whole work would make the concert too long. Schindler's response is of interest. He enthused: 'Czerny's presence on the programme would attract his large following among the nobility.' Although Czerny was of a retiring nature, and shunned the limelight as a virtuoso pianist, Schindler's remarks suggest he was widely acknowledged in the musical salon as an outstanding performer.

Something of Czerny's caution can be detected from his response to Beethoven's request to perform at the 23 May concert. He explained how he had been devoting the last fifteen years to teaching and giving lessons and, as a consequence, he had not cultivated his playing 'to the degree now expected of his abilities'. He explained: 'In order to appear as a virtuoso, I need at least three months to get my technique fully back into practice.' He added: '[The] greatest pianists of our time devote their health and their entire existence to this purpose.' He closed by regretting that with, only two days remaining to practice the Concerto, he had 'necessarily to forgo this honour'.

Beethoven was not angered by Czerny's refusal. On the contrary, he responded to his 'dear and beloved Czerny' that he had no idea of his present situation and offered to help him improve it if he could. To fill the gap left in the concert by the Concerto's first movement omission, a movement from Rossini's *Tancredi* was substituted in its place. This was a gesture to popular taste, suggested by the theatrical manager of the Grosse Redoutensaal where the concert eventually took place. In the event, it was poorly attended and, to Beethoven's dismay, was not a financial success.[122]

In the nineteenth century, the *Emperor* Concerto became established in the concert repertoire. It is to this aspect of the composition's reception-history that we now direct our narrative.

A concert performed on the evening of 1 November 1829, at the Paris Conservatoire, was auspicious for two reasons. It was the first time the *Emperor* Concerto was performed in France and was the first time that Hector Berlioz had appeared in public as a composer. The soloist in the Concerto was Ferdinand Hiller — then just 18 years old. Hiller later achieved celebrity in the diverse roles as composer, conductor, writer, and music director. The conductor was François Habeneck who had begun to perform Beethoven's symphonies the year before at the Conservatoire — to considerable acclaim. This, however, proved to be to Berlioz's disadvantage. The musical correspondent of the *Allgemeine musikalische Zeitung* considered his music to be 'crazy, bizarre, [and] extravagant' and that it 'lacked education'. He concluded: 'If he had this, perhaps he would become a Beethoven.'[123]

Ferdinand Hiller had played through the Concerto for Berlioz at a private performance a month before the Conservatoire concert. The impact upon him was immediate. Berlioz described the work as 'sublime' and 'immense' and subsequently in his writings he made reference to the composition more than any other of Beethoven's concertos. A further measure of his enthusiasm is that he conducted the *Emperor* Concerto several times during his career, including performances at the Paris Conservatoire, with Liszt as soloist (25 April 1841), in London (13 June 1855), and at his last concert in St. Petersburg (25 January 1868). In his *Treatise on Orchestration* (1843–44), in the chapter on piano, he cites a passage from the second movement to illustrate the use of the solo piano to accompany the orchestra.[124]

The honour of performing the *Emperor* Concerto in England for the first time goes to Felix Mendelssohn. He visited London in 1829 when just twenty years old — he was then quite unknown to English audiences. He played for the first time on 30 May in the Argyll Rooms, then a fashionable venue for concerts and recitals. He created something of a stir for 'playing without notes' — that is from memory — something unknown at the time. Ignaz Moscheles, already established in London, introduced the young pianist-composer to influential circles. In addition, his letters of introduction opened such doors to him as Devonshire House and Lansdowne House where he was fêted for his pianism and endearing personality. He performed the E-flat major Concerto on 24 June 1829 and had the pleasure of hearing a performance of his miraculously youthful Overture *Midsummer Night's Dream.* Of musical-sociological interest is that several women played in the orchestra — including double-bass, bassoon, horns, and tympani. One wit was disposed to pun 'there were more *belles* than *bows* in the orchestra'.[125]

In his *Felix Mendelssohn, Letters and Recollections,* Ferdinand Hiller recalls the 1831—32 music-season in Paris. Hiller first payed tribute to Mendelssohn's powers of recall: 'Felix's wonderful musical memory was a great source of enjoyment to us all as well as to himself.' Hiller was a considerable pianist and relates being asked to play the E-flat major Concerto at an informal gathering of musicians. All the music was available save for the wind parts. When this became known, Hiller relates: 'I will do the wind', said Mendelssohn, and sitting down to a small piano, which, stood near the grand one, he filled in the wind parts from memory so completely that I don't believe even a note of the second horn was wanting, and all was as simply done as if it were nothing.'[126]

The honour of being the first woman to perform the *Emperor* Concerto in England goes to Lucy Philpot (Mrs. Anderson). She is considered to be the most eminent of

English pianists of the early Victorian era and shared the renown of such eminent contemporaries as (Sir) William Sterndale Bennett. Anderson, as she was professionally known, was the first woman pianist to play at the (Royal) Philharmonic Society concerts. Between 1822 and 1862 she appeared no fewer than 19 times — eventually earning her honorary membership of the Society. She was an early champion of Beethoven's piano concertos and performed the *Emperor* Concerto on 3 March during the Philharmonic Society's 1834 concert season. She also appeared under the baton of Ignaz Moscheles in Beethoven's Choral *Fantasia*.[127]

In 1841, Edinburgh commenced a series of concerts known as the Ried Concerts. These were established under a bequest by General John Reid, a major benefactor to the University of Edinburgh. He bequeathed funds for the establishment of the Chair of the Theory of Music at The University of Edinburgh with a condition attached to the bequest that a concert be held each year in his memory. The Ried Concerts were subsequently held under the auspices of the professors of Music at the University of Edinburgh — that eventually included in their number the celebrated Beethovenian Sir Donald Francis Tovey.

Worthy of remark is that Edinburgh could lay claim to having a direct association with Beethoven dating from 1810. It was then when he established a long and fruitful relationship with the Edinburgh-based music publisher George Thomson.

Over time, the Ried Concerts attracted the support of Clara Schumann and Sir Charles Hallé. Beethoven's symphonies and piano concertos feature in the early programmes of the Ried Concerts.[128] At one early concert Beethoven's Piano Concerto, Op. 73 was performed, but it did not find favour with the music critic of the time. Writing in an Edinburgh Journal he complained:

'[In] Beethoven's *Emperor* Concerto in E-flat major, the treatment shows throughout a poverty of thought, the opening movement especially is arid and diffuse and full of meaningless arpeggios and scale passages, and the work can in no way be placed among the composer's "masterpieces".'

On reading these words, Sir Charles Hallé pronounced them to be 'horrible nonsense'.[129]

In the 1840s, Hallé was becoming established in Paris as a virtuoso pianist. He was celebrated in both recitals and concerts but his ambition to perform at the *Concerts du Conservatoire* had at that stage in his career eluded him — Hallé, though, was still in his early twenties. In 1843, a chance encounter with the conductor François-Antoine Habeneck provided Hallé with his sought-after opportunity. 'Why don't you play at our concerts?' asked Habeneck. 'Call tomorrow and we will arrange it'. Thereby, the following year, Hallé achieved his ambition of playing the E-flat major Concerto at the *Conservatoire*. His playing pleased all but one, namely, the discerning principal viola player. He chastised Hallé 'for changing Beethoven' — by which he meant for not keeping strictly to the score. It appears Hallé played certain passages in double octaves, instead of single notes, to achieve, as he believed, greater effect. Hallé had apparently followed the example of his teacher Franz Liszt. On reflection, he conceded the rebuke 'was well-merited'.[130]

Later, in 1845, Hallé had a further opportunity to hear Liszt perform the Op. 73 Concerto. The occasion in question was the Festival in Bonn at which Beethoven's statue was unveiled. Hallé dutifully observed, 'Liszt kept scrupulously to the text', resolving himself henceforth to do likewise.[131]

A competition for the design of a sculptural monument to Beethoven had been organised by the *Bonner Verein für Beethovens Monument* ('Bonn Association for Beethoven's Monument'). After the study of sketches and plaster models, the jury expressed preference for the design by Ernst Julius Hähnel. The resulting bronze cast statue was unveiled on 12 August 1845 in the Münsterplatz, Bonn —

> 'in the presence of the king and queen of Prussia, Queen Victoria and Prince Albert, and numerous other distinguished personages and prominent musicians from Germany and elsewhere'.[132]

The ceremony was the centrepiece of a Beethoven festival (10–13 August) in which Liszt not only played a prominent role as organiser, conductor, and pianist but also contributed the considerable sum of 10,000 francs. Ignaz Moscheles gave a fund-raising concert at the Drury Lane Theatre, London as did Frédéric Chopin at the Salle Playel and the Conservatoire de Paris — his last public appearance.

Anton Schindler was present and recalls Liszt's playing. '[Liszt] had indeed mastered Beethoven's music, and some of these pieces that conformed to his style made up a considerable portion of his repertoire.' Schindler considered Liszt's more demonstrative manner occasionally 'did more harm than good' but he acknowledged

> 'Liszt's feeling for [Beethoven's] works was not devoid of a poetic sense, and there were moments when his playing, though far from Beethoven's, was still in the master's spirit. His performances were never ordinary!'

He continues: '[Liszt] even had occasional times of

tranquillity, and even reverence, when he might have completely satisfied the great composer himself — for instance, his performance of the Concerto in E-flat major at the ceremony in Bonn, in 1845, for the unveiling of the Beethoven monument.'[133]

From February to March 1826, Beethoven used a set of sketch leaves that later came into the possession of the collector H. C. Bodmer. Schindler gave a selection of sixteen of these leaves to Ignaz Moscheles as a keepsake in recognition of his close association with Beethoven. Moscheles did not keep his bundle intact. When the Beethoven memorial was being erected, in 1845, he removed a leaf and gave it to Ernst Julius Hähnel. Moscheles inscribed a dedication:

'Beethoven's manuscript. To Herr Professor Ernst Julius Hähnel in memory of the unveiling of the monument in Bonn, with the greatest admiration in me for the perfect manner in which it has captured the immortal master. August 1845. I. Moscheles.'

This leaf is now in possession of the Beethoven House, Bonn.[134] In 1856, Schindler sold the rest of the sketchbook to the Berlin Royal Library, today the Staatsbibliothek Preussischer Kulturbesitz.

In 1848 Hallé was obliged to leave Paris, where he was then living, as a consequence of the revolutionary disturbances in France. In London, where he relocated, he soon established himself as a virtuoso pianist; a measure of Hallé's musical standing is that in Paris he had been a close associate of Frédéric Chopin and Franz List. In his Autobiography, Hallé records, 'instead of having to solicit engagements, the opportunity of playing in public [in London] was offered to me spontaneously'. Amongst his engagements were invitations to play at the Covent Garden series of 'grand orchestral concerts'. He writes: 'I soon received an invitation to play Beethoven's E-flat major Concerto at one of them' — a work that at the time would be unknown to many in the audience. Of related interest is that Hallé was the first pianist in England to play the complete series of Beethoven's Piano Sonatas; it was due in great measure to his pioneering of these works that they became an established part of the recital repertoire in English musical society.

Despite being in demand later in life as a conductor, Hallé continued to appear before the public as a concert pianist. For example, on 2 April 1881 he wrote to his daughter:

> 'I have at last played in Vienna, and I may say that I have every reason to be pleased. I played Beethoven's Concerto in E-flat major and three pieces by Chopin, and after each performance I was recalled five times to the platform.'

At a subsequent concert in Prague, Hallé was recalled seven times prompting him to remark '[I] had a great mind to take a chair and sit down on the platform for greater convenience.'[135]

On 2 June 1849, the nineteen-year old Hans von Bülow wrote to his mother about his meeting with Franz Liszt. Although remembered today by musicologists as one of the foremost conductors of his day, Bülow is also recognised for being one of the most celebrated pianists of the nineteenth century. He received lessons from Liszt alongside Alexander Winterberger — a gifted organist and editor of an edition of Beethoven's piano sonatas, to which he contributed interpretive annotations. Liszt once listened to Winterberger play through the E-flat Concerto prompting Bülow to relate to his mother of Liszt's 'splendid hints with regard to the conception of it, even in apparently trifling matters'. Bülow described Winterberger as 'a very talented fellow' and how Liszt's remarks were of 'very great use' to him.[136]

Clara Schumann (née Wieck) is recognised for being one of the most distinguished pianists of the Romantic era and whose compositions — solo piano pieces, a piano concerto (Op. 7), chamber music, choral pieces, and songs — are also recognised for their individuality and merit. We commence our remarks — albeit somewhat inauspiciously — concerning Clara's style of performance with the views of Anton Schindler. He attended one of Clara's concerts in Frankfurt, sometime in November 1854. He was not impressed by her interpretation of the music she played — perhaps her style was too virtuosic for his more conservative taste. Her programme included the *Waldstein* Piano Sonata, the *Emperor* Piano Concerto and Weber's Piano Sonata in C major. Schindler acknowledged the public's high esteem of Clara's playing:

> 'Frau Schuman's extraordinary reputation has led us to expect that she understood the art of playing classical music in the classical style, by grasping its very fundamentals and presenting the whole in their light.'

He then cautions:

> 'But we were all wrong; we had to admit reluctantly that she was in this respect just another virtuoso, capable of literally wearing out classical music, but not truly presenting it.'

Schindler conceded:

> 'Subjectivity, in the conception and performance
> of substantial works, is permissible up to certain
> limits [but] within which the character of the
> composition must always be recognisable.'

He was of the opinion that contemporary art criticism had 'raised great talents to heights of acclaim despite glaring defects'. In the interest of objectivity, Schindler sought the views of two respected music authorities concerning Clara's style of interpretation.

The first of these was the pianist and Munich court composer, Aloys Schmitt. He affirmed, 'Frau Schuman's great talent as a pianist' but considered she played the C-major Piano Sonata too fast 'and thereby the character was lost'. In particular, he considered 'she made improper use of the pedal by using it in the wrong place, so that notes often become blurred'. Schindler next consulted the Swiss composer Schnyder von Wartensee. In his opinion, Clara 'did not overstep the bounds [of tempo] in the Beethoven Concerto but did so in the *Allegro* and *Rondo* of the Piano Sonata'.[137]

Clara's correspondence some years later conveys a more elevated estimation of her playing. On 6 April 1862, she wrote to her friend and confident Johannes Brahms of the public reception of her recent concert at the Paris Conservatoire:

> 'The Beethoven E-flat major Concerto went very
> well, and was received with a storm of applause.
> It was well accompanied, and all the players were
> delightful to me ... Except in Vienna I have never
> had such a reception anywhere. You can easily
> see how this has stimulated me.'[138]

*

From Clara's Diary for April-May 1865 we learn of her concert engagements in London. She describes a visit to see the Chrystal Palace where she was escorted by 'Mr Grove', the not-yet knighted Sir Charles Grove, in his capacity as Secretary to the Chrystal Palace Committee; he had responsibility for arranging concerts and recitals. On 3 May she played the *Emperor* Concerto at the *Musical Society*, disposing her to remark: 'I succeeded in playing it wonderfully well, and the applause was enormous.' This was Clara's first success in London and from this time on she endeared herself on several further occasions with English audiences.[139]

Two years later Clara returned to London as she outlined in a letter of 26 February 1867 to her friend Elsie Junge. She performed the *Emperor* Concerto once more, this time at the Chrystal Palace, and wrote enthusiastically to Elsie:

> 'The Beethoven Concerto was magnificently accompanied ... I had to take an encore, as I usually do when I play a solo in England. You cannot think how warmly the public is disposed to me, and what a reception they always give me.'[140]

We learn of Charles Hallé once more on the occasion of the Beethoven Centenary Festival held (a year late) in Bonn in August 1871. Hallé appeared as soloist in the Choral *Fantasia* and the *Emperor* Concerto. Of particular interest is that he used a concert grand that had been specially sent over by Broadwood from London.[141] We recall Thomas Broadwood had arranged for one of his firm's finest instruments to be sent as a gift to Beethoven in 1817.

On 19 March 1873 (Dr.) Hans von Bülow performed the *Emperor* Concerto at a concert of the Philharmonic

Society. This was his first such appearance in England and music critics of the day (such as Otto Goldschmidt) wrote of his 'great powers' and 'marvellous memorising' — he played without the music that was still something of an innovation at this period. In recognition of his contribution to music — and in particular that of Beethoven — Bülow received the Philharmonic Society's Gold Medal.[142]

Amy Fay was an accomplished American pianist who travelled to Europe to study with Franz Liszt; she also had lessons with two other lions of the keyboard, namely, Theodor Kullak and Carl Tausig. Her letters sent home from Germany include descriptions of her training and the concerts she attended; these were published in 1880 as *Music Study* in Germany. From Fay's Diary entry of 25 December 1873, we learn of her acquaintance with the pianist and fellow student Anna Steiniger. She describes her playing as being remarkable, not so much for sentiment or poetry but for 'her *mastery* of the instrument'. In particular, Fay admired 'the clarity and limpidity of her trills' and her runs 'which surprised and delighted'. Fay, as fellow pianist, also admired Steiniger's hand position beneath which 'all difficulties seemed to melt away like snow'. Notwithstanding being the possessor of these attributes, Fay records that when she (Steiniger) prepared the *Emperor* Concerto for the pianist-conductor Ludwig Deppe, his response was bleak. 'We poor conductors!' he exclaimed. 'Will artists *always* keep bringing us Beethoven's E-flat major Concerto?' He lamented: 'Why not, for once, the B-flat major [Op. 19] or a Mozart concerto?' Fay further relates Deppe complaining 'everybody wants to play on a grand scale nowadays ... The mighty rushing torrent is the fashion!' Nevertheless, Fay tells how Deppe 'listened patiently for the thousandth time to the E-flat Concerto as Steiniger played it' and finally agreed to accept her as his pupil.[143]

In 1875 Wagner was occupied in raising funds for the completion of his Bayreuth Festspielhaus that was planned to open the following year. It so happened Franz Liszt proved crucial to the enterprise; it is possible Liszt may have been disposed to assist Wagner in his undertaking since Cosima Wagner was his daughter and, thereby, Wagner was his son-in-law. A benefit concert was planned to take place on 10 March for which initially there was some opposition and tickets failed to sell. When Liszt was informed of this he volunteered to play the *Emperor* Concerto. News of this soon circulated throughout the musically-minded community. According to Count Apponyi, the organiser of the concert:

'On the day when this decision of the Master became known, all tickets were sold out and artistic success which no other town could rival was assured.'[144]

Count Apponyi, a Hungarian and compatriot of Liszt, recorded the impression made on him by Liszt's playing:

'I think I am safe in asserting that Liszt's playing of the E-flat major Concerto ... marked [the] highest achievement of which artistic interpretation is capable. As if bewitched, Hans Richter and the orchestra followed the indications of the great Master whom they were privileged to accompany, and in no way did their playing disturb the perfection of the impression, or rather the impression of perfection, which one received from Liszt ... One could feel how, at every important turn in that marvellous work ... pianist and listener were in spiritual communion with

each other, happy in their common understanding of the dead genius.'

Three thousand attended the concert and included the
Estonian physician Dr. Georg von Schultz and his gifted
daughter Ella. She studied with Liszt from the age of twelve
and three years later made her début at Saint Petersburg
playing none other than the E-flat major Concerto — a
remarkable feat. Schultz cryptically declared the Wagner
concert to be 'a treat for the ears!' and described how Liszt
appeared:

'Liszt now wears the dress of an *abbé*, similar to
what our pastors once wore. His long, thick hair
has turned grey, but he still plays as beautifully as
in his prime.'

The music critic of the *Neues Pester Journal* declared the
concert to be 'the most important event of the music
season' and described how it had kept the capital's musical
circle 'in a state of suspense'. He declared the concert to
be 'a full and complete triumph for Franz Liszt', who he
regarded as 'the unparalleled pianistic interpreter of
Beethoven'.[145]
Cosima Wagner attended the rehearsal and recorded
her impressions of the occasion in her Diary:

'Dress rehearsal; an ugly hall, bad acoustics ... my
father absolutely overwhelms us the way he plays
the Beethoven Concerto — a tremendous impression! Magic without parallel — this is not playing,
it is pure sound.'

Richter also left an account of the rehearsal in his Diary and concurred, albeit somewhat cryptically: 'Liszt played the E-flat major Concerto by Beethoven with heavenly beauty.'[146]

1877 marked the fiftieth anniversary of Beethoven's death. Several European cities observed the occasion, none more so than Vienna that had been the composer's musical home for more than thirty years. Liszt was invited to participate in the ensuing ceremonies, fittingly since he had devoted so many years of his own life to the interpretation and advancement of the composer's music. Ironically Vienna, unlike Bonn, did not yet have a public Beethoven statue. Proceeds from Liszt's concert were intended to contribute to such a purpose. In his acceptance to play, Liszt responded how he intended to 'work with a full heart and with both hands' to help the Monument Committee with its task.

He did so fulsomely on 16 March when he played the *Emperor* Concerto in Vienna's Musikvereinssaal that was specially illuminated for the occasion, with the piano festooned with flowers. Liszt was sixty-five years old and he no longer practised. Yet, according to the music critic Eduard Hanslick who attended the concert, his playing 'delighted the audience' and was characterised by 'nobility and refinement'. Unknown to the audience, on the morning of the concert Liszt had injured a finger that required him to redistribute the notes to his other fingers, thereby depriving his playing of some of its typical bravura. He had cut his finger whilst shaving — this being the era of the cutthroat razor — that obliged him to play without making use of the fourth finger on his right hand. Hanslick perceived some lack of strength in his playing, disposing him to remark 'old age was knocking at the artist's door' but he added: 'The younger generation [of pianists] should not rejoice too loudly, since they will not catch up with the old man.' The following day, 17 March, Liszt received a gold medal from the mayor of Vienna 'in recognition of his services'.[147]

Attending Liszt's concert was the Austrian dramatist Eduard von Bauernfeld – one of the last surviving members of the circle of Franz Schubert. Of Liszt's playing he states:

> 'His touch is superb as ever, the quiet passages enchanting ... In the trill and powerful passages, no longer his old strength. On the other hand, he was calmer, played the fool less than he used to.'

The latter remark is a reference to the days of Liszt's youth when he was given to adding double octaves and similar embellishments to the score.

Such was the stir caused by the prospect of Liszt appearing once more in Vienna, that those unable to obtain a ticket for the concert itself were permitted, on payment of admission, to attend the rehearsal. One such was the Austrian composer Wilhelm Kienzel. In his recollections of Liszt he writes:

> 'The impression I received from his performance of the E-flat major Concerto of Beethoven remains ineffaceable. It was an absolutely personal interpretation, yet without any violation, wholly in the spirit of Beethoven. Liszt played the work in such a free, improvisatory manner, that it was as though he were composing it under the very eyes of his listeners.'[148]

On 7 February 1871, the Gesellschaft der Musikfreunde established a Beethoven Monument Committee. The jury decided in favour of the design by Caspar von Zumbusch who had already created a bust of Richard Wagner and who later created a monumental statue of the Empress Maria

Theresa. Beethoven's nephew Karl attended the unveiling ceremony held in Vienna's Beethovenplatz.[149]

On 27 May 1882, a number of Franz Liszt's former pupils were united at a social occasion that included the eighteen-year old Eugen d'Albert. Liszt had heard him play the previous month disposing him to exclaim: 'In my younger days I should have enjoyed competing with you – nowadays I can no longer do so!' Later in life, d'Albert maintained that Liszt's performance of the *Emperor* Concerto reminded him of Beethoven's remark: 'Music is a higher revelation than all wisdom and philosophy.' In somewhat similar fashion, the musicologist Wilhelm von Lenz was disposed to remark:

> 'Let all pianists come together and attack the E-flat major Piano Concerto of Beethoven ... and the moment Liszt touches the keys his hearers will know that it is he and no other! Where Liszt appears, all other pianists disappear in his shadow as though in a magic cloak.'[150]

On 11 January 1885, Hugo Wolf, in his capacity as music critic, attended a concert performed under the auspices of Vienna's Gesellschaft der Musikfreunde. Eugène d'Albert performed the E-flat major Concerto, disposing Wolf to respond:

> 'Herr Eugène d'Albert played Beethoven's Concerto in E-flat major with great refinement. His technique is complete, his touch round and soft, his conception, however, governed more by the score markings than any imaginative grasp of the spiritual substance of this wonderful work.'

Despite these reservations, Wolf acknowledged d'Albert's playing aroused the audience to such demonstrations of approval that an encore was required. D'Albert elected to play Chopin's Waltz in A flat but which incurred Wolf's wrath. Although he considered the Chopin to be 'charming in its own right' he considered it to be 'the last thing in the world that one would want to wish to hear after the magnificent E-flat major Concerto'. He concluded his review with a characteristically excoriating blast: 'Any halfway sensitive person ... could have consigned the pianist and the Chopin Waltz to the devil the minute the Concerto was over.'[151]

In our study of the G-major Concerto, we have remarked that George Bernhard Shaw was respected in his day as a discerning observer of the London musical scene, notably in his six-year capacity as music critic of *The Star* and *The World* and later for other journals, notably in the 1880s and 1890s. On 7 June 1889, *The Star* included Shaw's review of a performance of the *Emperor* Concerto by the Norwegian pianist Agathe Backer Grondahl – a pupil of Franz Liszt and Hans von Bülow. Following a London performance of Grieg's Piano Concerto, Shaw proclaimed Grondahl to be 'one of the very greatest pianists in Europe'. He praised her interpretation of the *Emperor* Concerto for

> 'now urging the pianoforte almost violently to do what a piano cannot do, and anon caressing it to exquisite ripples of sound and streams of plaintive melody'.[152]

The following year Shaw had a further opportunity to hear Agathe Backer Grondahl perform at a concert given at the Chrystal Palace. This offered Shaw to air one of his (many) prejudices. He opens his review of her concert remarking, 'Last year she played Beethoven's E-flat major Concerto amid storm and thunder' — a great storm had almost brought her playing to a close. He continues: 'On Saturday [3 March] she came to the Chrystal Palace in clouds of boreal snow. I should not have minded her bringing the snow if she had left Grieg's Concerto at home ... Madame Grondahl's powers of interpretation are wasted upon scrappy work like Grieg's.'[153]

Shaw's prejudices are further evident in his review of a concert he contributed to the 10 June 1891 issue of *The World*. In this he reported on a performance of the E-flat major Concerto performed by the Polish pianist and statesmen Ignacy Paderewski. Audiences typically responded to his brilliant style of playing with almost extravagant displays of admiration; this was perhaps in part induced by his striking appearance, made instantly recognisable by his mass of red hair. Shaw was not so moved as is evident in his opening remarks: 'I do not admire Paderewski's style.' Shaw complained it revealed too much of the influence of his teacher Theodor Leschetitzky who, he considered, 'had done more to dehumanize pianoforte-playing than any other leading teacher in Europe'. Shaw dismissed Paderewski's interpretation of the *Emperor* Concerto with the sweeping diatribe:

> 'When I hear pianists with fingers turned to steel hammers, deliberately murdering Beethoven by putting all sorts of *accelerandos* and *crescendos* into the noblest and most steadfast passages, I promptly put them down without further inquiry as pupils of Leschetitzky.'[154]

The Irish pianist Bettina Walker studied piano first with Sterndale Bennett in England and then in Europe with Carl Tausig (Berlin), Franz Liszt (Weimar), and Giovanni Sgambati

(Rome) — himself a pupil of Liszt. Bettina's *Memoirs — My Musical Experiences* (1890) — detail her encounters with these and many other musicians. Writing of Sgambati she states:

'Sgambati's playing of Beethoven's E-flat major Concerto was (I should rather say *is*) one of the finest I have ever heard; such beautiful tone, such perfect taste, such broad simple phrasing, such reserve of force; never have I heard any artist sink so poetically from *forte* to *piano* in the two octave pages of the first movement. I had, moreover, the advantage of hearing him play it several times, both in the *Sala Dante* with orchestra, and in his own house with the accompaniment of a second pianoforte.'[155]

In September 1899, Sir George Grove was completing work on his much-acclaimed *Dictionary of Music and Musicians*. In a letter from this time to his friend Mrs Wodehouse, he makes reference to Adela Verne. Although her name is remembered today only by musicologists, she was in her day regarded as the equal of any male pianist — not least for the strength and physicality of her playing. Some idea of this can be inferred from the fact that when age thirteen she performed Tchaikovsky's taxing Piano Concerto No.1 in B-flat minor at the Chrystal Palace. One day Grove, having listened to Adele practising the Beethoven E-flat major Concerto, shared his thoughts about the work, and the composer, with Mrs Wodehouse: 'I agree with you about the "tenderness" and "everlasting freshness" of that Concerto (e*wig jung und ewig neu*)'. Grove further confided to his lady friend:

'There is no one like Beethoven for taking one off and out of misery, and making one forget all the ills of this life. And I do not believe one can ever exhaust the merits and virtues of his works until the very end.'[156]

We draw this part of our remarks, bearing on the reception history of the *Emperor* Concerto, to a close with a selection of recollections and observations expressed by pianists and musicians in the twentieth century and nearer to our own time.

On 20 August 1901, the composer Gustav Mahler attended a recital at which a selection of Beethoven's piano sonatas was performed. This prompted his friend to ask Mahler's opinion of performing these compositions. Mahler responded saying the performance of piano sonatas demanded a freer, more improvisational style of perform-ance than was suitable for orchestral works. Mahler main-tained, in the case of the latter, the composition was 'already held together by the interaction of the various instruments'. Mahler then recalled the occasions in Leipzig and Hamburg when he had heard Anton Rubinstein play Beethoven. He acknowledged his 'elemental force' and 'boundless power of execution' but on hearing Rubinstein play the *Emperor* Concerto he confessed he was disappointed. For Mahler, Rubinstein's playing, in the final movement, was 'too delicate' and 'merely graceful' instead of being, as he believed, 'stormy and vigorous'.[157]

In his *Autobiography, Theme and Variations*, the German-born conductor Bruno Walter reflected upon his early years when he was intending to be a concert pianist; at the age of thirteen he had performed a piano concerto with the Berlin Philharmonic Orchestra. It was his subsequent encounter with, and encouragement from, Gustav Mahler that later disposed him to the vocation of orchestral conductor. Walter's early enthusiasm for the piano is evident in the part of his *Autobiography* in which he describes his encounters with various lions of the keyboard of his youth. From these we learn:

> 'I remember well the radiant fame achieved by young Eugen d'Albert in his rapid rise. I shall never forget the Titanic force in his rendering of Beethoven's Concerto in E-flat major. I am almost tempted to say he didn't play it, that he personified it. In his intimate contact with his instrument he appeared to me like a new centaur, half piano and half man.'

Walter regretted he had not heard Franz Liszt or Anton Rubinstein play but, had he been privileged to do so, he believed that they too, on the strength of their reputations, might have played in like manner.[158]

In his *Autobiography, My Own Trumpet*, the English conductor Sir Adrian Boult recalls his early musical experiences. During his study of music at Oxford University (1908–12) – where he failed to secure honours and was awarded a basic 'pass' degree – he relates how he had the good fortune to meet the Italian composer-pianist Ferrucio Busoni. Boult recalls:

> 'I heard him play a number of times. He often gave memorable sonata recitals with [Eugène-Auguste] Ysaÿe [Belgian violinist], and I once heard him give a Chopin recital in the Bechstein (Wigmore) Hall. His last performance of the *Emperor* in Queen's Hall was at times startlingly unexpected; his reading began where others left

off and some of his audience did not follow him all the way. But no one could deny the great power of his playing and the deep thought behind it.'[159]

In his *Autobiography, With Strings Attached*, the Hungarian violinist Joseph Szigeti recalls the occasion when Busoni was preparing to perform the *Emperor* Concerto under the direction of Gustav Mahler. This was during Mahler's tenure in 1908 at the New York Philharmonic. According to Szigeti, the two resolved to 'cleanse the masterpiece of all the interpretative accretions of past decades' and to give a model performance 'based entirely on the score and not on "tradition".' Szigeti remarks that the German conductor Hans von Bülow was disposed to disdain "tradition" as *Tradition ist Schlamperei!* — 'Tradition is slovenliness!' In that spirit, Busoni and Mahler set about exorcising the score of the Concerto of interpretive pencil-markings they considered dimed the lustre of the work 'just as surely as successive carelessly applied coats of varnish dim the glow of a masterpiece of painting'. Notwithstanding the pairs' well-intended endeavours, at the rehearsal of the Concerto a prominent member of the Philharmonic Committee — enamoured of tradition — rose ostentatiously and left declaring in loud voice: 'No, this will not do!'[160]

In the London 1909 music season, the German composer-pianist Emil von Sauer played the E-flat major Concerto on the 3 March at a concert of the (Royal) Philharmonic Society. He was a pupil of both Anton Rubinstein and Franz Liszt and was regarded as one of the most distinguished pianists of his generation. Josef Hofmann called him 'a truly great virtuoso' and the Philharmonic Society recognised his gifts by awarding him its Gold Medal. By way of passing interest, , (Dame) Ethel Smyth conducted two compositions of her own – the first occasion a woman had conducted at a Philharmonic Society Concert.[161]

In February 1921, Ferruccio Busoni played Mozart's Piano Concerto No. 22, K. 482 in Manchester; this was his first appearance with the Hallé Orchestra. At this period, the chief music critic of the *Manchester Guardian* was Samuel Langford. Himself an accomplished pianist; he was regarded as one of the most influential English music critics of the early twentieth century. Two years previously, Langford heard Busoni perform the Emperor Concerto that to him was 'a revelation'. He described the effect of the slow movement as being 'like the passing of an august spirit'.[162] Busoni himself once remarked:

> 'Music is so constituted that every context is a new context and should be treated as an "exception".'

He maintained:

> 'The solution of a problem, once found, cannot be reapplied to a different context. Our art is a theatre of surprise and invention, and of the seemingly unprepared. The spirit of music arises from the depths of our humanity and is returned to the high regions whence it has descended on mankind.'[162]

The British-born pianist Fanny Davies was an ardent admirer of Beethoven and was acknowledged as an accomplished interpreter of his work. For example, she performed in the Berlin Philharmonic Concerts (1886), at the Leipzig Gewandhaus (1888), at the Bonn Beethoven Festival (1888), and with the Vienna Philharmonic (1895). Being an artist of such standing, Davies was invited to contribute to the

Beethoven Death-Centenary Issue of the *The Musical Times*. She opens her account:

> 'In speaking of Beethoven's piano concertos, whose mind does not run at once to the G major or the E-flat major, those greatest of all pianoforte concertos? One does not try or wish to give the palm to either the one or the other — the G major of such wondrous lyrical beauty — the E-flat major in its glorious majesty.'

Davies recalled the encouragement — exhortation — of her former teacher Clara Schumann

'Jede Note muss mit Liebe gespielt werden' — 'Each note must be played with love'.

She closed with the generalization:

> 'Practically all passages in Beethoven should be treated as melody — one sees them in melodic shape — and the tempo, whether quick or slow must be that which can adequately express the musical intention.'[163]

Dennis Matthews recalls the first time he played the *Emperor* Concerto in public; he was twenty-four at the time and embarking on his career as a concert pianist. He was scheduled to play with the Liverpool Philharmonic Orchestra under the baton of Malcolm Sargent. It was wartime (1943) and rehearsal time was strictly limited, consequently Sargent allowed Matthews a few minutes only to try out the agreed tempi. Matthews recalls he had wanted to rehearse the challenging chromatic run at the opening of the first movement but time did not allow for this. Notwithstanding, according to Matthews's account, the evening performance went well prompting Sargent to complement his youthful novitiate: 'With musicians like *us*, what's the point of rehearsing?' At a following concert, Sargent took this sanguine outlook to extremes and required Matthews to perform Beethoven's C minor Concerto with him without *any* prior rehearsal, confining his negotiations to hastily exchanged opinions in the car on the way to the concert!

Matthews tells an amusing story — somewhat to the discredit of the then music critic of the *Manchester Guardian*. Following his performance of the *Emperor* Concerto with the Northern Sinfonia Orchestra, the critic in question complained, 'the performance lacked the support of a proper wind section, *especially trombones'*. Mathews relates how Sir John Barbirolli came to the rescue by writing a letter to the editor of the paper drawing his attention to the fact that the *Emperor* Concerto does not include parts for the trombone![164]

The pianist-composer James Butt recalls an occasion when he was receiving composition lessons from Benjamin Britten. He confided in him how he had been learning the five Beethoven piano concertos. Although Britten is considered to have had some antipathy towards Beethoven — not entirely justified — on this occasion he responded enthusiastically exclaiming: 'Ah yes', and, turning to the piano, remarked: 'I think this has always been rather a lovely sound'. Butt then relates '[Britten] sat down to play the last 22 bars of the last movement of the *Emperor*, most gracefully and without effort'.[165]

In 1975, the musicologist Robin Daniels was in conversation with the English writer and music critic Neville Cardus. In the course of their conversation Cardus expressed his opinion of the performing styles of various pianists of his acquaintance. He remarked: 'I would not expect a great performance by Rubinstein of the *Emperor*

Concerto.' He elaborated: 'I'd expect a good technical performance, a very good musical performance, but not the Beethoven "thing in itself".' He justified himself saying:

'Artur Rubinstein would be the first to tell you that — like [Moritz] Rosenthal — he belongs to a different school from [Artur] Schnabel. Rubinstein is the artist, first; the musician, second; and third, the thinker.'

In a later part of his reflections, Cardus acknowledged that for him Artur Schnabel was the pre-eminent interpreter of Beethoven. He relates:

'In the Thirties, Schnabel was a great revelation to me. He used to come to Manchester and he played Beethoven and Brahms in a way I'd never heard before and have never heard since.'

The conversation then turned to the question of interpretation and adherence to the composer's directions. Cardus responded:

'The composer may label a movement *andante cantabile*, but no two musicians will interpret that marking in the same way. They will have different ideas of the tempo, rhythmic emphasis, *rubato*.'

He recalled the occasion when the Hungarian-American conductor George Szell was rehearsing a Beethoven piano concerto (not identified) with Artur Schnabel but the two could not agree upon the required tempi. It prompted a heated exchange. Szell asserted:

'Artur, I have seen the manuscript in Vienna, in
the museum, I have seen it in the *Handschrift* of
Beethoven. I have seen the metronome mark
written by the pen of Beethoven.'

To which Schnabel replied: 'Yes, and I have seen his
metronome. It could not have been very accurate.'[166]

In his writing for *The New Criterion*, Alexander
Coleman reflected on what he considered to be the idiosyn-
cratic views of some pianists of his acquaintance. In this
context he made reference to the celebrated Russian pianist
Svyatoslav Richter. Richter studied at the Moscow Conservatory with the renowned teacher Heinrich Neuhaus who
became not merely his mentor but a spiritual father. On
hearing Neuhaus perform the *Emperor* Concerto, Richter
considered his performance could not be surpassed and
resolved never to play the work himself. He not only held
to his resolve but declined to play Beethoven's C minor and
G major Concertos nor the *Moonlight* Sonata.[167]

We draw our discussion of Beethoven's Piano Concerto
No.5 in E-flat major, Op. 73 to a close in the form of a
documentary-style collection of texts. These are derived
from the writings of musicologists and performing artists
bearing on the musicology the *Emperor* Concerto. The texts
that follow are presented in the chronological order of their
publication.

FIRST MOVEMENT
ALLEGRO

'In this grand concerto, the pianoforte begins with
three very powerful and brilliant cadences, which
must be played in a noble style, and each of which
is preceded by a single chord given by the orchestra. In the third cadence, the more tranquil passage

must be played very *legato* and *ritardando* with great expression ... The solo begins *piano*, but very clearly and in a steady degree of movement.'

Carl Czerny as related in: Paul Badura-Skoda, *On the Proper Performance of all Beethoven's Works for the Piano*, 1970, p. 102.

'The Fifth Concerto has a majestic introduction, in which the key of E-flat major is asserted in the orchestra and pianoforte in a rhapsodic outburst. This introduction reappears once at the beginning of the recapitulation, and plays no further part in the narrative. As in the first movements of all classical concertos, including Brahms's, the main threads of the story are set forth broadly, but with explicit avoidance of anything like development or combination, in the opening tutti, which is best called by its primitive title of ritornello.'

Donald Francis Tovey, *Essays in Musical Analysis*, 1935–41, Vol. 3, p. 84.

Tovey returned once more to the E-flat major Concerto:

'In the G major Concerto, Beethoven allows the pianoforte to play the first two bars, and in the E flat Concerto there is a cadenza-like introduction, in which key-chords from the full orchestra are answered by with arpeggios and declamation *senz tempo* by the pianoforte.

Donald Francis Tovey, *Beethoven*, 1944, pp. 116. Elsewhere Tovey writes:

'His Fifth and last Pianoforte concerto in E-flat major begins with a rhapsodical introduction for the solo player, followed by a long tutti confined to the tonic major and minor with a strictness explained by the gorgeous modulations with which the solo subsequently treats the second subject.'

Donald Francis Tovey, *The Forms of Music: Musical articles from The Encyclopaedia Britannica*, 1944, p. 16.

'Like the G major Concerto, this one offers the soloist the opportunity at the outset. The orchestra strikes a resounding tonic chord, and this evokes an impressive solo flourish on that general harmony ... The theme is set forth by the orchestra at considerable length, its few pregnant motives being fertile in suggestion; but the grip the theme has upon us is never relaxed ... The main theme ... will not be silenced. It asserts itself at once, whether in fragments or as a whole, and dominates the thought ...'.

Donald Nivison Ferguson, *Masterworks of the Orchestral Repertoire: A Guide for Listeners*, 1954, p. 109.

'Note the varying ways in which the second theme is presented: first in the mysterious atmosphere in E-flat minor, then as a romantic horn melody in a deft episode in C-flat major, and finally, as a powerful march sounded by the entire orchestra.'

Joseph Braunstein, *Musica Aeterna, Program Notes for*

1961–1971, 1972, p. 37.

'The great opening prelude of the soloist, while
not a complete innovation, is on a scale
unthought-of earlier, and it is repeated in varied
forms at the recapitulation. The orchestral ritornello is massive but not one note too long.'

R. Kinloch Anderson, Beethoven, *Piano Concerto No. 5,*
Liner notes to EMI *Classics for Pleasure*, 1977.

'One might write in technical terms of the first
movement's long-term key-scheme, of Neapoli-
tan relations and enharmonic modulations, and
of the orchestra's peremptory returns to the
dominant or tonic; but the great popularity of the
Emperor testifies to the drama, colour, and
emotion that these moves convey.'

Denis Matthews, *Beethoven, The Master Musicians*, 1985,
pp. 181–82.

'Between each of the majestic [opening] chords
the piano is given a cadenza of considerable
virtuosity, establishing a new relationship quite
different from anything Beethoven had employed
so far. The dominance established beyond doubt,
the soloist is able to relax for a while and allow
the orchestra a full-scale exposition, unusually
rich in thematic materials ... Two grand flourishes
from the piano and heavily scored martial chords
from the orchestra lead us to expect a substantial
cadenza. Beethoven expressly forbids the performer to improvise one of his own; instead he

provides one of exemplary but unusual brevity which even dispenses with the formality of a concluding trill. The Coda begins with a beautiful shimmering effect high on the keyboard that gradually descends to less ethereal regions. Some final flourishes in E flat bring this immense movement (582 bars) to an end.'

Antony Hopkins, *The Concertgoer's Companion*, 1984, p. 95 and p. 97.

'The opening of this work, with the soloist's entry in fantasia style, is one of the most noteworthy features in the concerto literature, and even with repeated hearings, it remains arresting. It consists of three chords ... richly figured by the soloist in preludial style, after which the orchestral ritornello begins. Tempting as it is to call these measures "introduction", that would be misleading, since a similar passage occurs at the beginning of the recapitulation (mm. 359–368). What is at issue here is the style and what it says about the soloist's function. The opening puts the relationship between the soloist and the orchestra into a certain context, one which forces the soloist to fantasize.'

Philip G. Downs, *Classical Music: The Era of Haydn*, 1992, p. 602.

'Many of the musical devices with which Beethoven experimented in the Fourth Concerto are found in the Fifth, but in a more developed form. The soloist steps broadly to the front at the very beginning; the age of the virtuoso concerto is upon us ... The enormous first movement (582 measures of 4/4 time, *Allegro*) begins with a decisive tonic chord in the full orchestra followed by a rhapsodic improvisatory, cadenza-like passage for the soloist.' [The opening movement of the *Emperor* Piano Concerto is the longest concerto-movement Beethoven wrote; in an expansive interpretation it has a performing time approaching twenty-five minutes.]

Michael Thomas Roeder, *A History of the Concerto*, 1994, p. 189.

Hopkins returned once more to the E-flat major Concerto:

'The key of E flat is established beyond all possible doubt at the start of the Concerto. Like footmen at some grand occasion proclaiming the arriving guests' names, the orchestra gives out in a stentorian voice in the order tonic, sub-dominant, dominant ... Each of these three "announce-ments" is followed by a virtuoso flourish by the soloist, flourishes which increase in length and complexity each time as if to demonstrate the importance and supremacy of the piano ... Expansive arpeggios re-establish the predomi-nance of the soloist, leading to a passage that everyone who knows the Concerto awaits with some eagerness. It is an extension of the first theme ... with a stirring accompaniment in chro-matically descending triplets. The music is irre-sistibly march-like here, and one can almost see banners waving in the breeze, and plumed helmets tossing. After a while the soloist is so carried away that the right hand is thrown completely off beat as the left-hand part bubbles upwards like champagne from a bottle.'

Antony Hopkins, *The Seven Concertos of Beethoven*, 1996, p. 59 and p. 63.

'The first movement is the broadest and most massive [Beethoven] achieved in the concerto field. Like its predecessor in No. 4, it deploys the piano from the outset, but where the G major Concerto uses the device with delicate poetry, here the opening has an architectural effect not unlike that to come later, and on a still larger scale, in the introduction of the Seventh Symphony.'

Robert Simpson, *Beethoven and the Concerto*, in: Robert Layton, editor, *A Guide to the Concerto*, 1996, p. 128.

'An expression of *pride*, in that one is allowed to be present at such an event, to be its witness; [is found] for example, in the first movement of the E-flat major Concerto and the *Eroica*.'

Theodor W. Adorno, *Beethoven: The Philosophy of Music; Fragments and Texts,* 1998, p. 76.

'Beethoven had begun his Fourth Piano Concerto in an unprecedented way, with an unaccompanied lyric phrase for the soloist, and only after that bringing in the "normal" exposition of material by the orchestra. Starting to sketch the Fifth

Concerto, he again turned his mind to the question of how one might begin a concerto in an original and striking manner. Here, too, he introduces the piano sooner than an audience 185 years ago expected to hear it – not, however, with a lyric or indeed any sort of thematic statement, but in a series of cadenza-like flourishes.'

Michael Steinberg, *The Concerto: A Listener's Guide*, 1998, p. 73.

'[The Concerto's] grand, majestic first movement, which gave rise to the work's [English] nickname, shows several innovations, especially in the role of the piano. In the previous piano concerto Beethoven had broken with tradition by allowing the soloist to initiate the opening orchestral ritornello before falling silent. This idea was extended in the *Emperor*, where the opening consists of three grand orchestral chords each followed by elaborate decorations from the soloist; only with this curtain-raiser is the main theme heard, with the soloist once again falling silent for the rest of the ritornello.'

Barry Cooper, *Beethoven: The Master Musicians*, 2000, pp. 182–83.

'There is imperial splendour about the orchestra's series of opening chords, each of them unleashing a torrential piano solo. From its very first note, the music continues the innovations in concerto form previously made in the Fourth Piano Concerto, itself more imperial than it is traditionally made out to be. By now, Beethoven was one step further away from the Mozart concerto — as Mozart knew it. In Mozart's concertos, aggression is never allowed to disrupt the surface good-manners of the music, no matter what was simmering beneath. In Beethoven's last completed concerto, aggression does break through, and the future of the concerto, as a purveyor of conflict and revolution, was thereby established.'

Conrad Wilson, *Notes on Beethoven: 20 Crucial Works*, 2003, p. 74.

'The scale and virtuosity of the *Emperor* Concerto are stated categorically at the outset: a long piano cadenza punctuated by three orchestral chords, rather than the more usual orchestral exposition — a startling opening even by the standards of this most individual and innovative of early 19th century composers. The Fourth Concerto had brought the piano in at the outset of the work, but for a different effect, treating the piano as a self-contained element, thereafter remaining silent for the rest of the exposition. Mozart had had a similar idea in 1777, in his *Jeunehomme* Concerto, K. 271, in which the piano becomes part of the orchestral texture at the opening of the work, later to be reintroduced in the expected place. But the *Emperor* Concerto's explosion of virtuosity was something new in 1809.'

David A. Thrasher, *BBC, Radio Three, Beethoven Experience, Piano Concerto No. 5 in E-flat major*, 5 June, 2005.
SECOND MOVEMENT

ADAGIO UN POCO MOSSO

'When Beethoven wrote this *Adagio*, the religious songs of devout pilgrims were present in his mind, and the performance of this movement must therefore perfectly express the holy calm and devotion which such an image naturally excites. The *Adagio* (*alla breve*) must not be dragging, but it must be played nearly always with the pedal, where an harmonious effect has to be attained.' [Worthy of recall is that Czerny was writing with the pianoforte of the early and mid-nineteenth century in mind.]

Carl Czerny as related in: Paul Badura-Skoda, *On the Proper Performance of all Beethoven's Works for the Piano*, 1970, p. 103.

'The *Adagio* has but one theme — a heartfelt strain, as simple and as lofty as a hymn ... The solo has, for continuation, passages of quiet improvisatory comment that seem to recall the theme although they never really utter it ... The noble melody is played quietly in the solo against a simple pizzicato accompaniment to which a few notes in the winds make unbelievably rich addition. Thereafter, flute, clarinet, and bassoon sing the theme against light notes in the strings and a quietly persistent figuration in the solo.'

Donald Nivison Ferguson, *Masterworks of the Orchestral Repertoire: A Guide for Listeners*, 1954, p. 111.

'The slow movement is in B major, a key rather remote but already emphasised in an episode of the first movement; it opens with a melody almost hymn-like in its spirit of quiet devotion and continues with passages of exquisite writing for the piano which showed the way for many other future composers.'

R. Kinloch Anderson, *Beethoven, Piano Concerto No. 5, Liner notes to EMI Classics for Pleasure*, 1977.

'The last few bars of the opening tune seem almost to disintegrate, creating a sense of expectancy as we wait for the "arrival" of the soloist. He brings not only a new theme but a new texture, wide-spread after the warm dark harmonies of the strings. Two descending passages drift downwards in an almost Chopinesque fashion leading to an openly expressive melody whose sequences might sound trite were it not for the sheer beauty of each curved phrase.'

Antony Hopkins, *The Concertgoer's Companion*, 1984, p. 98.

The soloist's quiet reflections on an orchestral subject of great beauty and serenity set a pattern for many concertos of the Romantic period, whether the nationalist Grieg or the classically-minded Brahms and the celeste-like treatment of the piano towards the close was praised by Berlioz.'

Denis Matthews, *Beethoven, The Master Musicians*, 1985, p. 182.

'The *Adagio* is delicately scored, beginning with muted strings and avoiding strong contrasts of orchestral sound. The writing for the piano has a strongly improvisatory quality as the piano plays material based on the opening theme, often without clearly stating it. The movement has the overall effect of a set of variations ... A magical and compelling moment occurs at the end of the slow movement. Here Beethoven has composed one of his most dramatic links to a succeeding movement. All instruments reach B natural, the tonic note of the movement, which then sinks a semitone to B flat, the dominant of the final movement's tonic. Over this B flat pedal in the horns, the piano in *adagio* tempo hints at the finale's rondo theme, before it bursts out in the *allegro* tempo of the finale.'

Michael Thomas Roeder, *A History of the Concerto*, 1994, p. 190.

Hopkins returned once more to the E-flat major Concerto:

'For fifteen bars the strings, only occasionally reinforced by the wind, present us with a chorale-like tune of great solemnity that would surely by now have been appropriated by the editors of hymn books, were it not for the fact that the vocal range is perhaps a little much for the average congregation.'

Antony Hopkins, *The Seven Concertos of Beethoven*, 1996, p. 68.

'The beautiful and mysterious *Adagio* follows ...
The form is variations broken by improvisatory
matter, a mutation from the slow movement of
the Violin Concerto and the main body of the
Choral *Fantasia*, and the mood is of felicitous
contemplation. Here it is possible to give the
soloist extemporary air purposely denied him
after the opening of the first movement.'

Robert Simpson, *Beethoven and the Concerto*, in: Robert
Layton, editor, *A Guide to the Concerto*, 1996, p. 129.

'Playing the *Adagio un poco mosso* of the Fifth
Concerto as solemnly as possible has become an
impressive habit. [Czerny] and [Theodor] Kullak
are the only ones to give the correct metre, *alla
breve*; Czerny does so quite specifically with the
words "the *Adagio* (a*lla breve*) should not drag"
('darf nicht schleppend gehn'). It was Czerny,
after all, who gave the first Vienna performance
in 1812 under Beethoven's eyes.'

Alfred Brendel, *Alfred Brendel on Music: Collected Essays*,
2001, p. 129.

'After the ringing climax of the first movement,
nothing could be more peaceful than the gentle,
hymn-like beauty of the *Adagio* in B major, though
the idyllic simplicity of the main theme evidently
cost Beethoven much trouble before he got it right.
Apart from the dreamily descending triplets with
which the soloist enters, the movement is devoted
to the opening melody, which on each repetition
is bathed in different, ever more delicate light.'

Conrad Wilson, *Notes on Beethoven: 20 Crucial Works*, 2003, p. 75.

> 'The slow movement is in the sumptuous key of B major, and presents cumulative elaborations on the static hymn-like theme that rests like an oasis between the titanic outer movements. The coda hints subtly at the subsequent rondo's theme — but without giving away too many clues — before leaping into the exuberant finale.'

David A. Thrasher, BBC, Radio Three, Beethoven Experience, *Piano Concerto No. 5 in E-flat major,* 5 June, 2005.

THIRD MOVEMENT
RONDO — ALLEGRO

> 'At the end, the passage in which the pianoforte is concerted with the drums, *ritardando,* must be well practised. By means of the pedal, which is here required, the lower E flat sounds as the ground bass. At the conclusion of the powerful run the orchestra must come in *exactly* with the highest E flat. The whole finale very lively, fiery and brilliant.'

Carl Czerny as related in: Paul Badura-Skoda, *On the Proper Performance of all Beethoven's Works for the Piano*, 1970, p. 104.

> 'In this Concerto Beethoven ... organises the only undigested convention of the form, namely, the cadenza, a custom elaborated from the operatic

aria, in which the singer was allowed to extempo-
rize a flourish on a pause near the end.'

Donald Francis Tovey, *The Forms of Music: Musical
Articles from The Encyclopaedia Britannica*, 1944, p. 16.

'The continuation is a thumping phrase from a
German dance-song, the *Grossvatertanz* −
another stroke of genius, since that tune would
enliven the muscles even of a social paralytic.
The orchestra takes over the theme and adds
vitality to it ...'. [*Grossvatertanz* 'Grandfather
Dance') is a German dance tune from the 17th
century, generally considered to be a traditional
folk tune.]

Donald Nivison Ferguson, *Masterworks of the Orchestral
Repertoire: A Guide for Listeners*, 1954, p. 111.

'The delicate lyricism of the *Adagio* in which the
strings are muted and the trumpets and kettledrums are silenced, is contrasted with the joyous
Rondo finale, which displays significant parallels
to the *Rondo* in the Violin Concerto ... [The] finale
of both works is cast in 6/8 meter which was
associated with *la chasse* (the hunt), in the classical
period ... Note how the strings break into a long
trill of the solo instrument (this also occurs in the
Violin Concerto). Finally, note that the rhythmic
element, and the dactylic rhythm in particular, is
of great significance in both concertos, and in the
Piano Concerto in E-flat major it is especially
important in the duet of the piano and the kettledrums which precede the conclusion.'

Joseph Braunstein, *Musica Aeterna, Program Notes for 1961–1971, 1972*, p. 38.

> 'The movement is on a bigger scale than any concerto rondo which had been attempted before. Its combination of massive power, bounding energy and withdrawn thoughtfulness make it unique (as is every great work of art). The E-flat-major Concerto made the finest of the later 19th-century concertos possible. Without it, some of the best-loved works in this repertoire could not have existed.'

R. Kinloch Anderson, *Beethoven, Piano Concerto No. 5*, Liner notes to EMI *Classics for Pleasure*, 1977.

> 'Scarlatti-like leaps emphasise the mischievous mood of the soloist, who ultimately has to be called to order by a peremptory use of the repeated-note rhythm originally established by the brass. This time it is on violas, then clarinets and bassoons, violas again (more angrily) and, lastly, surprisingly quiet horns. In just such a spacious mood the soloist reintroduces the theme *pianissimo* in A-flat Major before indulging in a dizzy flight of chromatic scales.'

Antony Hopkins, *The Concertgoer's Companion*, 1984, p. 99.

Hopkins returned to the E-flat major Concerto once more:

> 'In a remarkable coda, the timpani player con-

stantly reminds us of the motto rhythm as the piano part starts a slow descent through a series of beautifully spaced chords. Finally the music appears to have come to a halt, as though Beethoven's inspiration has truly failed him. Just when it seems that total exhaustion has set in, the pianist, in a sudden burst of renewed energy, embarks on a virtuoso scale-passage that, ultimately aided by the full orchestra, brings this masterpiece to a glorious close.'

Antony Hopkins, *The Seven Concertos of Beethoven*, 1996, p. 72.

'When the finale comes, it is the most spacious of all Beethoven concerto rondos. Its main theme is dimly adumbrated in the mysterious link from the *Adagio*, with its softly arresting drop of a semitone; then it leaps out with a sweeping enthusiasm that causes it to catch its breath before the orchestra fierily bears the music up again.'

Robert Layton, editor, *A Guide to the Concerto*, 1996, p. 129.

'The choice of tympani for [the] final playing of the primal rhythms of the movement, and their sudden emergence into a solo role for such a purpose, seem rife with symbolism. Until now these instruments have only added their supporting sounds to the big climaxes of the movement ... But now the tympani instantly transform that amiable, galloping rhythm into something quite different: it has become tense, portentous, martial. It recalls the military music of the first movement. Perhaps Beethoven was even stirred by a memory of the tympani strokes that had haunted the Violin Concerto, whose martial intent he had made clear in the cadenza to its piano transcription, composed at about the same time as the Fifth Concerto. His last concerto ends with a closing reference to that archetypal emblem of the genre, a vision of leader and followers engaged in common struggle and coop-eration. The imagery is military, the meaning ultimately humane.'

Leon Plantinga, *Beethoven's Concertos: History, Style, Performance*, 1999, p. 272.

We close our study of Beethoven's Piano Concerto No. 5 in E-flat major, Op. 73 with the contemplative words of the British musicologist and composer Robert Simpson:

'Here he stopped, and to try to imagine what kind of concertos Beethoven would have written in the period of the late quartets can be no more than frustrating. Perhaps he was no longer interested in works with elements of display – yet who knows? If someone had commissioned a con-certo, how might he have responded? There can be no doubt that he would have explored new and profound aspects of the relationship between the individual and the mass, and that no one since has moved into the regions he alone knew.'

Robert Simpson, *Beethoven and the Concertos*, in: Robert Layton, editor, *A Guide to the Concerto*, 1996, p. 129.

1. Peter Clive, 2001, p. 78. Beethoven's opinion concerning Cramer is derived from the recollections of his piano pupil Ferdinand Ries as recalled in his *Biographische Notizen.*

2. Donald Francis Tovey, 1944, p. 48.

3. Elliot Forbes, editor, *Thayer's Life of Beethoven*, 1967, pp. 465–6.

4. Emily Anderson, editor and translator, 1961, Vol. 1, Letter No. 220, pp. 233–6.

5. In order to secure Beethoven's presence in Vienna, Kinsky, Lobkowitz and Rudolph conferred an annuity on Beethoven of 4,000 florins.

6. Emily Anderson, editor and translator, 1961, Vol. 1, Letter No. 246, pp. 264–65.

7. *Ibid*, Vol. 1, Letter No. 252, p. 267.

8. *Ibid*, Vol. 1, Letter No. 272, pp. 283–8. For a facsimile copy of this long letter – some twelve quarto pages – see: Beethoven House, Digital Archives, Library Document, H. C. Bodmer, HCB Br 88. This includes the full text transcribed in German.

9. Theodore Albrecht, editor and translator, 1996, Vol. 1, Letter No. 148, pp. 223–6.

10. *Ibid*, Vol. 1, Letter No. 122, pp. 192–3.

11. As related in: Franz Wegeler, *Remembering Beethoven: The Biographical Notes of Franz Wegeler and Ferdinand Ries*, 1988, p. 106. See also: Peter Clive, 2001, p. 197.

12. Elliot Forbes editor, *Thayer's Life of Beethoven*, 1967 p. 526.

13. Emily Anderson, editor and translator, 1961, Vol. 1, Letter No. 228, pp. 245–47.

14. Barry Cooper, 2000, p. 182.

15. Maynard Solomon, 1977, p. 207 and p. 209.

16. Alfred Einstein, *Essays on Music*, 1958, p. 247.

17. Maynard Solomon, 1977, p. 207.

18. Anton Felix Schindler, edited by Donald W. MacArdle and translated by Constance S. Jolly from the German edition of 1860, 1966, p. 160.

19. H. C. Robbins Landon, 1992, p. 153.

20. For a full translation of Beethoven's application, see: Elliot Forbes, editor, *Thayer's Life of Beethoven*, 1967, pp. 426–7. Beethoven clearly spent considerable time composing his application that runs to several manuscript pages. A Facsimile copy of a portion of the application can be seen at the Beethoven House, Digital Archives, Library Document H. C. Bodmer Collection, HCB BBr 111.

21. Elliot Forbes, editor, *Thayer's Life of Beethoven*, 1967, p. 442 and Peter Clive, 2001, pp. 39–40.

22. Denis Matthews, 1985.

23. Emily Anderson, editor and translator, 1961, Vol. 1, Letter No. 184, p. 200. See also letter No. 179. Beethoven frequently addressed his letters to Gleichenstein with the salutation 'Dissolute Baron' – a characteristic example of the word play he inflicted on his close friends and associates.

24. Emily Anderson, editor and translator, 1961, Vol. 1, Letter No. 192, pp. 211–12.

25. As quoted in: Hans Conrad Fischer and Erich Kock, 1972, p. 32.

26. Emily Anderson, editor and translator, 1961, Vol. 1, Letter No. 192, pp. 211–2.

27 For a fuller account of Countess Anna Maria Erdödy, see: Peter Clive, 2001, pp. 101–2.

28 The wording of the Contract is reproduced in full in: Theodore Albrecht, editor and translator, 1996, Vol. 1, Document No. 134, pp. 205–6. The following is an extract: 'The daily proofs that Herr Ludwig van Beethoven gives of his extraordinary talents and genius as a musician and composer awaken the desire that he surpass the greatest expectations that are justified by his past achievements. Since it has been demonstrated, however, that only a person who is as free from care as possible can devote himself to one profession alone and create great works that are exalted and that enable art, the undersigned have made the decision to place Herr Ludwig van Beethoven in a position where the most pressing circumstances shall not cause him embarrassment or impede his powerful genius.'

29 Elliot Forbes, editor, *Thayer's Life of Beethoven*, 1967, pp. 453–9.

30 Hans Conrad Fischer and Erich Kock, 1972, pp. 27–9.

31 Maynard Solomon, 1977, p. 149

32 Paul. Nettle, 1975, pp. 278–80 and Thayer-Forbes, 1967, p. 466.

33 Oscar George Theodore Sonneck, 1927, pp. 69–75.

34 Johann Schlosser, *Beethoven: The First Biography, 1827*, Barry Cooper, editor, 1996, p. 77.

35 Elliot Forbes, editor, *Thayer's life of Beethoven*, 1967, p. 469.

36 Beethoven House, Digital Archives, Library Document, HCB Mh 79.

37 Beethoven House, Digital Archives, Library Document, Konzert für Klavier und Orchester Nr. 5, Op. 73.

38 Emily Anderson, editor and translator, 1961, Vol. 1, Letter No. 273, pp. 289–1.

39 Historical information is provided in the text to the four-part fugue Beethoven copied out for his pupil that is reproduced in the Beethoven House, Digital Archives, Library Document, H. C. Bodmer Mh 45.

40 With acknowledgment to Stephen C. Rumph, 2004, p. 99.

41 See: Beethoven House, Digital Archives, Library Document, NE 2.

42 Theodore Albrecht editor and translator, 1996, Vol. 1, Letter No. 144, pp. 217–18.

43 Emily Anderson, editor and translator, 1961, Vol. 1, Letter No. 226, pp. 243–4.

44 *Ibid*, Vol.1, Letter No. 231, pp. 249–50. This letter was written in French by another hand and signed by Beethoven, as was his practice in his dealings with much of his international correspondence. For the text of the letter from the Royal Institute of Science and Fine Arts see: Theodore Albrecht, editor and translator, 1996, Vol. 1, Letter No.143, pp. 216–7. For a facsimile reproduction of Beethoven's letter of response to the *Gesellschaft Schöner Künst und Wissenschaften* see: Beethoven House, Digital Archives, Library Document, H. C. Bodmer, HCB Br 81.

45 Quoted in: John L. Holmes, *Composers on Music*, 1990, p.101. See also: John Palgrave Simpson, *Carl Maria von Weber: The Life of an Artist, from the German of his son Baron, Max Maria von Weber*, 1865.

46 John Palgrave Simpson, *Carl Maria von Weber: The Life of an Artist, from the German of his son Baron, Max Maria von Weber*, 1865, pp. 323–24.

47 Theodor Albrecht, editor and translator, Vol. 1, Letter No. 157, p. 248.

48 H. C. Robbins Landon, 1970, pp. 143–4.

49 For a vivid description of the ordeal Beethoven had to undergo in order to have his facial likeness reproduced, see: John Ella, 1869, Vol. 1, pp. 6–10.

50 For additional information see: Beethoven House, Digital Archives, Library Documents Ley, Band VIII, Nr. 1311; B 257; p 2; B 447; B 448; B 1153; and B 450. See also: Peter Clive, 2001, pp. 186–7.

51 See: Beethoven House, Digital Archives, Library Document Bonn P 2.

52 For a reproduction of Höfel's portrait see: Beethoven House, Digital Archives, Library Document, Sammlung Wegeler, W 25; Bonn 2315; and Bonn B 9/a. Höfel's study of the composer also exists in the form of a colour lithography that was considered by his contemporaries to be a faithful likeness.

53 Emily Anderson editor and translator, 1961, Vol. 1, Letter No. 257, pp. 270–71. Franz Wegeler is remembered today for his 1838 biography of Beethoven Biographische Notizen über Ludwig van Beethoven, published in collaboration with the composer's former pupil Ferdinand Ries.

54 See: Beethoven House, Digital Archives, Library Document, BH 57.

55 As recounted in Ludwig Nohl, *Beethoven Depicted by his Contemporaries*, 1880, p. 94–100.

56 Emily Anderson editor and translator, 1961, Vol. 1, Letter No. 234, p. 251.

57 *Ibid*, Vol. 1, Letter No. 336, p. 347.

58 *Ibid*, Vol. 1, Letter No. 282, p. 299.

59 Tia De Nora, 1997, pp. 31–32.

60 Theodore Albrecht editor and translator, 1996, Vol. 1, Letter No. 145, pp. 218–20.

61 Rumph Stephen C. 2004, pp. 100–1.

62 Theodore Albrecht editor and translator, 1996, Vol. 1, Letter No. 163, pp. 255–60.

63 Elliot Forbes editor, *Thayer's Life of Beethoven*, 1967 pp. 525–26.

64 As recalled in: Gerhard von Breuning, *Memories of Beethoven: From the House of the Black-Robed Spaniards*, (1874), 1992, p. 78.

65 *Ibid*, p. 48.

66 Antony Hopkins, 1996, p. 59. Additional quotation marks have been added to the last sentence.

67 This is the date Érard despatched the piano to Beethoven; he may not have received it, however, until sometime later.

68 Emily Anderson, editor and translator, 1961, Vol. 1, Letter No. 275, p. 292. For a facsimile reproduction of this letter see: Beethoven House, Digital Archives, Library Document, H. C. Bodmer, HCB Br 252.

69 Emily Anderson, editor and translator, 1961, Vol. 1, Letter No. 283, p. 300.

70 Edwin Marshall Good, 1982, p. 71.

71 Paul Badura-Skoda, Carl Czerny: *On the Proper Performance of all Beethoven's Works for the Piano*, 1970, p. 6.

72 Cited in: Hans Conrad Fischer and Erich Kock, 1972, p. 13. See also: Edwin Marshall Good, 1982, p. 71 and Tia de Nora, 1970, p. 179.

73 Emily Anderson, editor and translator, 1961, Vol. 1, Letter No. 255, p. 269.

74 *Ibid*, Vol. 1, Letter No. 257, p. 271. For a facsimile reproduction of this letter

see: Beethoven House, Digital Archives, Library Document, H. C. Bodmer, HCB Br 248.

[75] Paul Badura-Skoda, Carl Czerny: *On the Proper Performance of all Beethoven's Works for the Piano*, 1970, p. 93.

[76] Douglas Porter Johnson, editor, 1985, pp. 174–79 and Barry Cooper, 1990, p. 89.

[77] Elliot Forbes editor, *Thayer's Life of Beethoven*, 1967 p. 476 and Douglas Porter Johnson, editor, 1985, pp. 527–29.

[78] Barry Cooper, 1990, p. 90 and p. 182 and Douglas Porter Johnson, editor, 1985, p. 72 and p. 185.

[79] Beethoven House, Digital Archives, Library Documents, Bonn NE 39 and HCB Mh 77.

[80] Elliot Forbes editor, *Thayer's Life of Beethoven*, 1967 pp. 518–19.

[81] Douglas Porter Johnson, editor, 1985, p. 215.

[82] Leon Plantinga, 1999, p. 39 and pp. 251–78.

[83] Richard Kramer. 1992, pp. 125–26.

[84] Quoted in: Eva Badura-Skoda, *Performance Conventions in Beethoven's Early Works*, in: Robert Winter, editor, *Beethoven*, Performers, and Critics: the International Beethoven Congress, Detroit, 1977, 1980, 37.

[85] Donald Francis Tovey, 1949, p. 315.

[86] Michael Tilmouth, editor, *Donald Francis Tovey: The Classics of Music: Talks, Essays, and other Writings Previously Uncollected*, 2001, pp. 599–600.

[87] Elliot Forbes editor, *Thayer's Life of Beethoven*, 1967, p. 478 and footnote 25. See also the texts to the Piano Concertos 1–4.

[88] Glenn Watkins, 1994, pp. 425–27.

[89] Donald Francis Tovey, 1949, p. 317.

[90] Barry Cooper, 2000, p. 183.

[91] Emily Anderson, editor and translator, 1961, Vol. 1, Letter No. 245, pp. 260–61. For a facsimile reproduction of Beethoven's letter to Breitkopf and Härtell together with its German text, see: Beethoven House, Digital Archives, Library Document, Sammlung H. C. Bodmer, HCB Br 85.

[92] Theodore Albrecht, editor and translator, 1996 Vol. 1, Letter No. 148, pp. 223–6.

[93] Emily Anderson, editor and translator, 1961, Vol. 1, Letter No. 262, pp. 276–7. For a facsimile reproduction of Beethoven's letter to Breitkopf and Härtell together with its German text, see: Beethoven House, Digital Archives, Document Sammlung H. C. Bodmer, HCB Br 322.

[94] Theodore Albrecht, editor and translator, 1996 Vol. 1, Letter No. 151, pp. 231–3.

[95] Emily Anderson, editor and translator, 1961, Vol. 1, Letter No. 272, pp. 283–88. For a facsimile reproduction of Beethoven's letter to Breitkopf and Härtell together with its German text and audio recording, see: Beethoven House, Digital Archives, Document Sammlung H. C. Bodmer, HCB Br 88.

[96] Theodore Albrecht, editor and translator, 1996 Vol. 1, Letter No. 152, pp. 233– 8.

[97] Emily Anderson, editor and translator, 1961, Vol. 1, Letter No. 281, pp. 295–99.

[98] For Clementi's publication of Beethoven's works see: Barry Cooper, 1991, p. 194.

[99] Pamela J. Willetts, 1970, pp. 27–31.

[100] Alan Tyson, 1963, pp. 79–81.

[101] *Ibid*, 1963, p. 19, p. 26, pp. 31–32, p. 39, p. 52, and p. 141.

[102] Elliot Forbes editor, *Thayer's Life of Beethoven*, 1967 p. 507.

[103] For facsimile reproductions of the Title page to the Piano Concerto Op. 73, see: Beethoven House, Digital Archives, Library Documents, HCB C Op. 73 and Bonn C 73 / 9.

[104] Leon Plantinga, 1999, pp. 273–73.

[105] Beethoven House, Digital Archives, Library Document, Bonn NE 157.

[106] Emily Anderson, editor and translator, 1961, Vol. 1, Letter No. 305, pp. 319–20. For a facsimile reproduction of this letter, together with the German text, see: Beethoven House, Digital Archives, Library Document, Bonn BH 8. Note: this version of the letter is dated 3 May 1810.

[107] *Ibid*, Vol. 1, Letter No. 306, pp. 320–21. For a facsimile reproduction of this letter, together with the German text, see: Beethoven House, Digital Archives, Library Document, HCB BBr 9, HCB Br 94.

[108] Emily Anderson, editor and translator, 1961, Vol. 1, Letter No. 325, pp. 336–40.

[109] Barry Cooper, 2000, p. 184.

[110] Beethoven website. This claim appears to be based on text relating to a sketchleaf auctioned at Sothebys – *www.sotherbys.com*

[111] Anton Felix Schindler, edited by Donald W. MacArdle and translated by Constance S. Jolly from the German edition of 1860, 1966, p. 196, editor's footnote 117.

[112] Cited in: Donald Nivison Ferguson, 1954, p. 109.

[113] Anton Felix Schindler, edited by Donald W. MacArdle and translated by Constance S. Jolly from the German edition of 1860, 1966, pp. 160–61.

[114] Joseph Braunstein, 1972, p. 37.

[115] Peter Clive, 2000, pp. 68–69.

[116] Elliot Forbes editor, *Thayer's Life of Beethoven*, 1967, p. 526.

[117] Anton Felix Schindler, edited by Donald W. MacArdle and translated by Constance S. Jolly from the German edition of 1860, 1966, pp. 160–61.

[118] Peter Clive, 2001, pp. 377–71.

[119] Wayne M. Senner, Robin Wallace, and William Meredith, editors, 1999, Vol. 1, pp. 39–40.

[120] Theodore Albrecht editor and translator, editor and translator, 1996, Vol. 1, Document No. 164, pp. 260–61.

[121] For a facsimile reproduction of the letter in question, together with the German text, see: Beethoven House, Digital Archives, Library Document, HCB BBr 12.

[122] Theodore Albrecht editor and translator, 1996, Vol. 1, Letter No. 366, pp. 36–39.

[123] Wayne M. Senner, Robin Wallace, and William Meredith, editors, 1999, Vol. 1, p. 132.

[124] Quoted, with adaptations, from: Website text: *Berlioz, Beethoven.*

[125] Stephen Samuel Stratton, 1901, pp. 56–57.

[126] 2 Ferdinand Hiller, *Felix Mendelssohn, Letters and Recollections*, 1874, pp.

28–29, reprinted: 1972. For related accounts of Mendelssohn see: Michael Tilmouth, editor: Donald Francis Tovey; *The Classics of Music: Talks, Essays, and other Writings Previously Uncollected*, 2001, pp. 374–75.

[127] Cyril Ehrlich, *First Philharmonic: A history of the Royal Philharmonic Society*, 1995, p. 129.

[128] For the history of the Ried School of Music and its associated concerts, see: Fiona McCallum Donaldson, *Reid Concerts at The University of Edinburgh: the first 100 years, 1841-1941*, PhD Thesis, 2017.

[129] Edward Murray Oakeley, 1904, pp. 123–24.

[130] Michael Kennedy, editor, *The Autobiography of Charles Hallé; With Correspondence and Diaries*, 1972, p. 10. See also: Michael Kennedy, *The Hallé Tradition: A Century of Music*, 1960.

[131] Charles Rigby, 1952, pp. 59–60.

[132] Peter Clive, 2001, pp. 143– 45.

[133] Anton Felix Schindler, edited by Donald W. MacArdle and translated by Constance S. Jolly from the German edition of 1860, 1966, p. 433.

[134] Beethoven House, Digital Archives, Library Documents BSK22 and MH 96.

[135] C. E. Hallé, *Life and Letters of Sir Charles Hallé: Being an Autobiography (1819–1860) with Correspondence and Diaries, 1896,* pp. 102–03 and p. 306.

[136] Adrian Williams, 1990, p. 254.

[137] Anton Felix Schindler, edited by Donald W. MacArdle and translated by Constance S. Jolly from the German edition of 1860, 1966, pp. 435–36.

[138] Berthold Litzmann, editor, *Clara Schumann: An Artist's Life, based on material found in diaries and letters, 1913*, Vol. 2, p. 205.

[139] *Ibid*, p. 237.

[140] *Ibid*, pp. 250–51.

[141] Peter Clive, 2001, p. 59.

[142] Cyril Ehrlich, *First Philharmonic: A History of the Royal Philharmonic Society*, 1995, p. 339.

[143] Amy Fay, 1965 (reprint) , pp. 294–96.

[144] Alan Walker, *Franz Liszt*, Volume 3: *The Final Years, 1861–1886*, 1997, p. 279.

[145] Adrian Williams, 1990, pp. 515–16.

[146] Christopher Fifield, 1993, pp. 80–81.

[147] Alan Walker, *Franz Liszt*, Volume 3: *The Final Years, 1861–1886*, 1997, p. 366.

[148] Adrian Williams, 1990, pp. 533–34.

[149] Peter Clive. 2001, pp. 406–07.

[150] Adrian Williams, 1990, pp. 600–01.

[151] Henry Pleasants, editor and translator, *The Music Criticism of Hugo Wolf*, 1978, pp. 103–04.

[152] Dan H. Laurence, editor, *Shaw's Music: The Complete Musical Criticism in Three Volumes*, 1981, Vol. 1, pp. 654–55. See also: Bernard Shaw, *London Music in 1888–89 as heard by Corno di Bassetto (later known as Bernard Shaw): With some further Autobiographical Particulars*, 1937, pp. 161–62. Tragically, like Beethoven, Agathe Backer Grondahl progressively lost her hearing.

[153] Bernard Shaw, 1960, p. 176.
[154] Dan H. Laurence, editor, *Shaw's Music: The Complete Musical Criticism in Three Volumes*, 1981, Vol. 2, pp. 366–65.
[155] Bettina Walker, 1890, pp. 70–71.
[156] Charles L. Graves, *The Life & Letters of Sir George Grove, Hon. D.C.L. (Durham), Hon. LL.D. (Glasgow), formerly Director of the Royal College of Music*, 1903, pp. 454–55.
[157] Natalie Bauer-Lechner, 1980, p. 174.
[158] Bruno Walter, 1948, p. 53.
[159] Adrian Boult, 1973, p. 17.
[160] Joseph Szigeti, 1949, pp. 228–29.
[161] Cyril Ehrlich, 1995, p. 505.
[162] As quoted by Alfred Brendel, 1976, p. 211.
[163] Fanny Davies, *The Pianoforte Concertos* in: *The Musical Times, Special Issue* edited by John A. Fuller-Maitland, Vol. VIII, No. 2, 1927, pp. 224–26.
[164] Dennis Matthews, 1968, pp. 107–08 and p. 171.
[165] Donald Mitchell, editor, *Letters from a Life: The Selected Letters and Diaries of Benjamin Britten 1913–1976*, 1991. Vol. 2, p. 1229.
[166] Robin Daniels, 1976, pp. 118–19 and pp. 168–69.
[167] Alexander Coleman, editor, *Diversions & Animadversions: Essays from The New Criterion*, 2005, pp. 170–71.

VIOLIN CONCERTO
D MAJOR, OP. 61
PIANO TRANSCRIPTION
OP. 61A

'Here then is a work which, as far as we can see,
will endure for all time. If it has survived the most
critical century in the history of music, there is no
reason why it should not live another hundred
years and retain its supremacy unchallenged.'

Ferrucio Bonavia, writing about Beethoven's Violin Concerto on the occasion of the composer's Birth Centenary,
The Musical Times, Vol. VIII, No. 2, April, 1927.

'Beethoven's Violin Concerto is gigantic, one of
the most spacious concertos ever written, but so
quiet that when it was a novelty most people
complained quite as much of its insignificance as

of its length. All its most famous strokes of genius
are not only mysteriously quiet, but mysterious
in radiantly happy surroundings. The whole
gigantic scheme is serene.'

Donald Francis Tovey, *Essays in Musical Analysis*, Vol. 3,
1935–41, p. 88.

'My enduring affection for the Beethoven [Violin
Concerto] is rather like what I might feel towards
a keepsake. It grows more precious with the
passing of the years; it accumulates importance
through a subtle kind of companionship and
mutual trust.'

Yehudi Menuhin in: Robin Daniels, *Conversations with
Menuhin*, 1979, p. 46.

'It is gratifying to learn that the problematical
conversion [Op. 61a], which it is assumed was
done by somebody else under the composer's
supervision, was not the result of artistic considerations but part of a business deal.'

Joseph Braunstein, *Musica Aeterna, Program Notes for
Musica Aeterna*, 1972, p. 41.

'Pianists have almost always completely neglected
Op. 61a, largely because it is "highly unsatisfactory" [Norman Del Mar, *Conducting Beethoven*,
1993, p. 107] and because Beethoven's five other
piano concertos are in their various different ways
so much more fulfilling. One wonders, however,
whether it would be quite so maligned if listeners

were not so familiar with the *original* version for violin.'

Robin Stowell, *Beethoven: Violin Concerto*, 1998, pp. 48–49.

'It is possible, perhaps even likely, that Beethoven merely authorised this transcription rather than undertaking it himself, but if that is so, he would probably have contributed some suggestions of his own anyway. No question, though — Beethoven (or whoever) did a perfunctory, ineffectual job with what may have been an impossible task to begin with; the one thing of value in this version is the cadenza — with timpani! — for the first movement.'

Michael Steinberg, *The Concerto: A Listener's Guide*, 1998, p. 81.

In this text we first consider the creation origins of Beethoven's Violin Concerto, Op. 61 and the role of its protagonist the violinist Franz Clement (Klement). We then direct our narrative to the origins, and later reception, of the Piano Transcription, Op. 61a and the role of its protagonist, the polymath of music, Muzio Clementi — pianist, pedagogue, conductor, music publisher, editor, and piano manufacturer.

Although Beethoven's instrument was the piano, in his youthful days in Bonn he had acquired an understanding of the character and potential of string instruments. As assistant organist at the Elector's Court he had initially earned a reputation for being able to play the most difficult passages from sight. Moreover, and central to our introductory remarks bearing on the Violin Concerto, we learn the following from Beethoven's biographer Alexander Whee-lock Thayer:

> 'As organist the name of Beethoven appears still in the Court Calendar [1788], but as viola player ... Thus, for a period of full four years, he had the opportunity of studying, practically, composi-tions in the best of all schools — the orchestra itself.'[1]

From 1786, when Beethoven was sixteen years old, we have a silhouette of him by the illustrator Joseph Neesen depicting the composer in his pig-tailed perruque and lace-trimmed neckerchief. He, like Mozart before him, was obliged to dress on formal occasions in a frockcoat complete with silken waistcoat and hose.[2]

Beethoven doubtless benefited from the company of the cousins Andreas and Bernhard Romberg who were respec-tively Court Violinist and Court Violoncellist. It has been suggested he would, in due course, have become familiar with the violin schools and style of playing of such virtuosi as Giovanni Battista Viotti, Pierre Rode, Rodolphe Kreutzer and Pierre Baillot.[3] It is not surprising, therefore, that an extensive 259-bar fragment exists, from sometime between 1790 and 1792, for a Violin Concerto, in C major, desig-nated WoO5. This is recognised for being Beethoven's first attempt at such a composition; it was left incomplete and was not discovered until 1870.[4]

Musicologist Michael Steinberg suggests Beethoven's Violin Sonata Op. 47 (1802–03) — the so-called *Kreutzer* — can almost be considered as 'an honorary concerto'.[5] Beethoven himself inscribed words to this effect on the work's draft title page: '*scritta in uno stilo molto concertante quasi come d'un Concerto*' – 'written in a very concerto-like style, almost like that of an actual concerto'. It was, however, with the two Romances for Violin and Orchestra that Beethoven more fully embraced the compositional genre of the violin concerto; the term Romance was an expression in use at the period in question to describe the slow movement of a violin concerto. The Romances Op. 40 in G major and Op. 50 in F major were published in 1803 and 1805 respectively and their *cantabile* manner is considered to anticipate that of the Violin Concerto, Op. 61.

An anecdote from June 1879 connects Richard Strauss with the F major Romance. He had just heard a performance of it by the twelve-year old violin prodigy Maurice Dengrement. He enthused to his childhood friend, Ludwig Thuille, how Dengrement's playing was 'really something to marvel at' and 'completely suited to the Romance'. Dengrement later performed the Mendelsohn Violin Concerto, prompting Strauss to further remark: 'Next to Mozart's [unspecified] and Beethoven's it must be reckoned among the most beautiful violin concertos that Germany has produced.'[6]

It is to the origins of Beethoven's Violin Concerto that we now direct our remarks.

We have referred to Franz Clement as being a protagonist in the creation origins of the Violin Concerto. By this we mean he was a formative influence in bringing the work into being. Before we substantiate this assertion, Clement requires a few words of introduction.

Franz Joseph Clement was born in Vienna in 1780 and was soon recognised for his remarkable aptitude for violin playing. He was also blessed with a remarkable memory; it is on record that he could recall whole passages of music after but a single hearing – a circumstance that will assume significance later in our narrative. To showcase his talent, he went on tour with his father, much as Mozart had done years before. At the age of ten he toured Germany, Belgium, and England and when in London he performed a concerto of his own composition at the Hanover Square Rooms. This was so well received that he gave a second performance of the work in Oxford on the occasion (July 1791) when Haydn was honoured with the degree of Doctor of Music.

In 1804, Clement was appointed leader of the orchestra at the Theater an der Wien and in 1805 became its *Musikdirektor.*[7] Beethoven met Clement in 1794 and, like others, was captivated by his style of playing. A contemporary described this in the following terms:

> 'His is not the marked, bold, strong playing, the moving, forceful *adagio*, the powerful bow and tone which characterize the Rode-Viotti School; rather, his playing is indescribably delicate, neat and elegant; it has an extremely delightful tenderness and cleanness that undoubtedly secures him a place among the most perfect violinists. At the same time, he has a wholly individual lightness, which makes it seem as if he merely toys with the most incredible difficulties, and a sureness that never deserts him for a moment, even in the most daring passages.'[8]

Another contemporary proclaimed Clement to be 'the most artistic violinist in Vienna'. Consistent with the foregoing, he describes Clement's playing to have been graceful and lyrical rather than vigorous, with a comparatively small yet expressive tone, and an assured left-hand technique especially in the high registers of the instrument.'[9] Beethoven was clearly enamoured of Clement's playing and had occasion to write to him: 'Nature and art vie for each other in making you a great artist.'[10]

Clement is also said to have been a fine pianist and an accomplished orchestral conductor. Not surprising, then, that he was at the centre of Vienna's musical activity at the beginning of the nineteenth century. From 1803, Thayer reports an article describing the 'Amusements of the Viennese after Carnival'; this provides insights into salon music-making of the period. Franz Clement is identified as being amongst the 'most notable artists' for his violin playing in his role as Director of the orchestra of the Theater an der Wien.[11] On 7 April 1805, Clement gave a benefit concert at the Theater an der Wien that is memorable for being the occasion when Beethoven publicly conducted his *Eroica* Symphony. Clement also premiered his Violin Concerto in D major — one of his six known concertos. In his capacity as conductor, Clement later programmed the *Eroica* Symphony and Beethoven's first two symphonies.

Clement was present on 20 November 1805 when Beethoven's only Opera was premiered in its three-act version as *Leonora*. It became apparent to a close circle of the composer's friends that the work required revising and shortening. In the events that followed, Clement's participation proved invaluable. The tenor Joseph August Röckel, who was entrusted with the role of *Florestan* in the second version of *Leonore* (*Fidelio*) — performed on 10 April 1806, has left an account of the ensuing proceedings.

Röckel recalls how amidst Beethoven's protests — he did not want to excise a single bar of his music — a group sympathetic to the composer's interests assembled in the apartments of his patron Prince Lobkowitz. These included: Clement, leader of the orchestra; Beethoven's brother Caspar Carl van Beethoven; Beethoven's close friend Stephan von Breuning; the poet Heinrich von Collin; the librettist Georg Friedrich Treitschke; the conductor Ignaz von Seyfried; and Princess Lichnowsky, wife of Beethoven's patron Prince Lichnowsky. Röckel recalls Princess Lichnowsky played through the score whilst Clement, 'sitting in a corner of the room, accompanied with his violin the whole opera by heart, playing all the solos of the different instruments'. Röckel, who had not witnessed Clement's prodigious feats of memory before adds: 'The extraordinary memory of Clement, having been universally known, nobody was astonished by it except myself.'[12] The collective efforts of the assembled gathering were not in vain. With their encouragement the over-long *Leonora* was transformed into its final form, the universally admired *Fidelio*.

A few days later, Röckel had to visit Beethoven to learn more about the changes to his part in the Opera. He describes Beethoven's apartment:

> 'I entered a place consecrate to supreme genius.
> It was almost frugally simple and a sense of order
> appeared never to have visited it; [in] one corner
> was an open piano, loaded with music in wildest
> confusion. Here, on a chair, a fragment of the
> *Eroica*. The individual parts of the Opera, with
> which he was busy lay, some on chairs others on
> and under a table ... amid chamber music com-
> positions, piano trios and symphonic sketches.'[13]

Together with this description of the composer's apartments, the painter Joseph Mähler has left a contemporary impression of Beethoven dating from 1804–05; that his likeness was sought is a measure of the composer's growing fame. Mähler portrayed Beethoven in an Arcadian setting, striking a lyre and in the background is a temple of Apollo. Beethoven evidently liked the painting and it remained in his possession until his death.[14]

To round out our descriptive picture of Beethoven at

the period in question, we draw on an account of him from the recollections of Ignaz von Seyfried who, as we have seen, took part in the dramatic events in the apartments of Prince Lobkowitz. Von Seyfried remarks that he spent time in Beethoven's company between 1803 and 1805, when the composer was at work on the Violin Concerto and other contemporaneous works including his Oratorio *Christus am Ölberg* – *Christ on the Mount of Olives* – and his early symphonies. He remarks how Beethoven used to play passages from his newly composed works, asking von Seyfried his candid opinion of them. Moreover, it was von Seyfried who conducted the première of the original version of *Fidelio*. Writing of Beethoven's prowess as a virtuoso pianist, he recalls, albeit in a somewhat florid style:

> 'When once he began to revel in the infinite world of tones, he was transported also above all earthly things ... Now his playing tore along like a wildly foaming cataract, and the conjurer constrained his instrument to an utterance so forceful that the stoutest structure was scarcely able to withstand it ... Again, the spirit would soar aloft, triumphing over transitory terrestrial sufferings.'[15]

Returning to Clement and his association with Beethoven, he was doubtless touched by the violinist's enthusiasm for, and support of, his music. It is not surprising, therefore, that when Clement asked him to write a violin concerto, expressly for him, Beethoven readily acquiesced. The work was to be premiered at another of Clement's benefit concerts that was scheduled for 23 December 1806 – leaving Beethoven very little time to work on the composition. Since the Violin Concerto, Op. 61 and the Piano Transcription Op. 61a share close affinities, rather in the manner in which the obverse and inverse sides of a precious coin share the same attributes, it will assist our narrative to briefly outline the origins of the Violin Concerto together with associated remarks concerning its subsequent reception.

Sketches for the Violin Concerto appear amongst those for the Fifth Symphony, Op. 67 and the Cello Sonata. Op. 69. Early accounts relate that the work was completed only just in time to meet the performance deadline and that Clement had to virtually play the solo part *a vista*.[16] This traditional view of the circumstances of the first performance is, however, now considered to be something of an overstatement. Robin Stowell, an authority on the Beethoven Violin Concerto, suggests that Clement may have contributed suggestions to Beethoven regarding the writing of the violin part— and would, thereby, have gained some insight into the challenges the soloist has to confront.

Stowell proposes Clement's participation in the compositional process may explain the many alterations to the manuscript that he describes as presenting 'a disorderly appearance' with many emendations being made only at the last minute before the first performance. He concludes:

> 'It would be wrong to underestimate the interaction between the composer's initial thoughts, the special requirements of the instrument, and Clement's artistic and technical values.'[17]

Joseph Braunstein writes:

> 'It is perhaps Beethoven's most interesting manuscript because of the numerous additional entries. These can be divided into two categories: alterations to the solo part, perhaps suggested by

Clement, and the adjustments connected with the conversion of the work into a piano concerto.'[18]

Beethoven authority Barry Cooper comments:

> 'The autograph score is not the definitive version. The first Viennese edition was based on a copy annotated by Beethoven, and the first English edition, by Clementi [see later], was based on a set of parts copied from the autograph, thereby, producing slight differences. Both editions reveal that Beethoven considerably revised the solo part, but no source exists.'[19]

After Beethoven's, death the autograph of the Concerto was acquired by Beethoven's pupil Carl Czerny who subsequently bequeathed it to the Court Library (Austrian National Library).

From the foregoing it follows that at its premier, Clement would have had prior acquaintance with the challenges the work held in store. That said, there was inadequate time for the Concerto to be properly rehearsed.

In recognition of his debt to Franz Clement, Beethoven added a typically punning superscript to the autograph acknowledging his *clemency*: '*Concerto par Clemanza pour primo violino e direttore al theatro di Vienna. Dal. v. Bthvn. 1806.*'[20]

Beethoven, however, subsequently dedicated the Concerto not to Clement but to Stephan von Breuning. This was, perhaps, not merely an act of regard for his old friend but an acknowledgement of their days together as violin pupils of Franz Anton Ries.[21]

At the premiere of the Concerto on 23 December 1806, tradition maintains Clement declared that the concerto's opening movement would be played prior to the intermission, and that its conclusion would follow after the intermission. In between, it is alleged that, by way of demonstrating his technical prowess, Clement improvised on a theme of his own whilst holding his violin upside down. Some authorities, however, disavow this lack of respect for Beethoven's majestic work. Whilst acknowledging that Clement yielded to the temptation of seeking to captivate the audience with his showmanship, they maintain he reserved his antics for the end of the concert. Michael Steinberg writes:

> 'The legend persists that Clementi performed a set of variations of his own with the violin held upside down between the first two movements of Beethoven's Concerto; he did indeed play such a piece, but it came at the end of the programme, which included works by Méhul, Mozart, Cherubini, and Handel.'[22]

The premier of the Concerto took place in the Schauspielhaus an der Wien. Thayer relates how the occasion offered Beethoven the opportunity for him

> 'to give the general public as fine a taste of his quality as a composer for the violin as he had just given to the frequenters of Razumovsky's quartet parties in the Op. 59'.[23]

Notwithstanding, the composition received a mixed reception. In the 7 January 1807 issue of the *Allgemeine musikalische Zeitung*, the critic contributed a somewhat anodyne account of the concert:

480

'The admirers of Beethoven's muse will be interested to hear that this composer has written a violin concerto — as far as I know, his first — which the locally beloved violin player Klement performed with his customary elegance and grace at the academy given for his benefit.'[24]

The music critic of the *Wiener Theater-Zeitung* was more fulsome:

'The superb player Klement played amongst other exquisite pieces, a violin concerto by Beethhofen [sic], which was received with exceptional applause due to its originality and abundance of beautiful passages.'

Clement's playing was praised: 'In particular, Klement's proven artistry and grace, his power and confidence on the violin, which is his slave, were received with loud bravos.' He also observed how Clement's cadenzas were 'exceptionally well received'. But Clement was censured for his showmanship — doubtless a reference to performing the fiddle upside down:

'The educated world was struck by the way that Klement could debase himself with so much nonsense and so many tricks in order to delight the crowd.'

The reviewer in question was probably Johann Nepomuk Möser, a critic of considerable social standing in Vienna.[25]

The Concerto received a mention on 24 January 1808 in a celebratory announcement citing various compositions of Beethoven that appeared in the *Journal des Luxus und der Moden*. The article was titled 'Beethoven's most recent works in Vienna' and its author enthused:

> 'With great pleasure I offer you the news that our Beethoven has just completed an extraordinarily beautiful Mass, which is quite worthy of him [Op. 86] ... His Fourth Symphony [Op. 60] is being engraved, also a very beautiful Overture to *Coriolan* [Op. 62], and a big Violin Concerto [Op. 61] ... in addition three Quartets are being engraved [Op. 59]. From that you see how ceaselessly active the brilliant artist is!'.[26]

Whilst several of these works duly found favour, the Violin Concerto was relatively neglected. However, Anton Schindler reports that Clement kept Beethoven's Concerto in his repertoire, performing it in Dresden and once more in Vienna. Luigi Tomasini, the violinist-son of Haydn's concertmaster at Eisenstadt, also performed the work in 1812 in Berlin.

Following Beethoven's death in 1827, a memorial concert was arranged by, amongst others, the violinist Joseph Böhm. He was active in the musical scene at the *Gesellschaft der Musikfreunde* and had earned Beethoven's gratitude for assisting in first performances of his last string quartets. It is a measure of Böhm's admiration for Beethoven that he was a torchbearer at his funeral. At the Beethoven memorial concert, Böhm gave a rendering of the composer's Op. 61. The following year Pierre Baillot — remembered for his *L'Art du Violon* — played the Concerto in Berlin where it had otherwise been neglected; it had not been performed there since 1812. In 1834, the Belgian composer and violinist Henri Vieuxtemps resurrected the Concerto and gave it an airing in

Vienna. He was just fourteen-years old at the time; Robert Schumann, no less, compared Vieuxtemp's art to that of Niccolò Paganini.

In Paris, Hector Berlioz was an early champion of Beethoven's orchestral music. Alongside him, in the genre of chamber music, was Pierre-Marie Baillot. In 1828 he played Beethoven's Concerto twice at the Paris Conservatoire but with little success. It was not until 1847, in France, when Jean-Delphin Alard, who succeeded Baillot at the Conservatoire, established the work more fully in the repertoire. At about the same time, the Estonian Jerome Louis Gulomy played the Concerto in an all-Beethoven programme conducted by Felix Mendelsohn; Beethoven's late string quartets had exerted an influence on him. On 27 May, 1844 Mendelsohn included the Beethoven Concerto in a programme of the London Philharmonic Orchestra. The thirteen-year old Joseph Joachim, a student of Böhm, was the soloist. The concert has been described as: '[A] triumph for Beethoven and Joachim, who has come to be regarded as *the* interpreter of Beethoven's Violin Concerto in the nineteenth century.'

Clara Schumann recalled in her Diary the Karlsruhe Music Festival of 1853 at which Joachim performed the Beethoven Concerto. She reflected:

> '[Among] many striking and stimulating impressions, the greatest of all, and one which those present could never forget, was Joachim's plying of the Beethoven Violin Concerto. Joachim was the crown of the evening ... Joachim won a victory over us all with the Beethoven Concerto – he played it with a finish, a depth of poetic feeling, his whole soul in every note, that I never heard violin-playing like it ... And how that grand work

was accompanied! How perfectly! It was as if the whole orchestra felt a holy awe!'[27]

Before we consider the circumstances that brought about the transcription of the Violin Concerto into piano-concerto form, we briefly reflect on the character of the composition.

We recall Beethoven composed the Violin Concerto in close proximity to the Fourth Piano Concerto, Op. 58, that he completed in the summer of 1806. The Fourth Symphony Op. 60 was completed in the autumn of the same year with the Thirty-two Variations in C minor WoO 80 being written at that time. Reflecting on these compositions, Maynard Solomon remarks:

> 'Compared with such works of his *grand manner* as the Piano Sonatas Opp. 53 and 57 and the *Razumovsky* String Quartets, Op. 59, his latest orchestral works reveal "a temporary retreat from exalted rhetoric into a more lyrical, reflective, and more serene style".'

He suggests his works have taken on 'certain qualities of magnified chamber music ... characterised by quiet, reflective gravity'.[28]

Concerning the Violin Concerto, in Antony Hopkins' words:

> 'It shares with the Fourth Piano Concerto an absence of mere technical display, and just as that work begins with an unprecedented gesture, the piano playing alone, so does [the Concerto], the four, quiet drum-taps instantly arresting our attention without recourse to drama.'[29]

Beethoven eschews violin theatricality by eliminating conventional eighteenth-century bravura display; Op. 61 is closer to the symphonic genre.

> 'Its symphonic character is never impaired by purely virtuoso passages, for the solo violin speaks movingly as the soul and eloquent voice of the orchestral commonwealth ... The solo instrument does not dominate the orchestra, but rather is a prominent member with a special task.'[30]

With his characteristic insight and turn of phrase Theodore Adorno remarks: 'Pieces like the G major Piano Concerto and the Violin Concerto ... belong together ... The idea of *expressing tranquillity through motion.*' [italics added][31]

In its original form, Beethoven did not leave a cadenza for the Violin Concerto — consistent with the level of theatrical restraint in the writing of the violin part. In the nineteenth century, Joseph Joachim contributed cadenzas that for some years became inseparable from the work. The doyen of Beethovenians Donald Tovey went so far as to enthuse: 'Joachim's cadenzas have the right to be treated as integral parts of the composition ...'. He recalled:

> 'I heard them from him only in an abbreviated form: but he included the full version in one of his last publications, the volume of concertos in his violin school; and it is interesting to note that in this form the cadenza to the first movement still contains a certain famous chromatic scale in octaves which made a tremendous impression when he played the concerto in London as a boy of twelve ...'.[32]

Having established the origins of the Violin Concerto, we now direct our attention to the circumstances that brought about the piano-concerto version. Central to this part of our narrative is the second of our so-called protagonists, Muzio Clementi.

Beethoven respected the Italian-born English composer and pianist. We learn from Beethoven's close associate and biographer, Anton Schindler, that the composer's relatively modest musical library contained almost all of Clementi's sonatas for which; 'He had the greatest admiration ... considering them the most beautiful, the most pianistic of works.' Also in Beethoven's possession was Clementi's *Introduction to the Art of Playing on the Piano Forte* of 1801.[33] In 1798, Clementi founded a firm of music publishers and instrument manufacturers in London with his partner Frederick William Collard — known as Clementi & Co. In his business capacity, Clementi travelled widely on the continent to seek out clients for his company's pianos and also to secure financial arrangements, with composers, for the English publication of their most recent publications. It is this latter context that unites Beethoven, Clementi and the piano version of the Violin Concerto.

Beethoven's burgeoning creativity, in the early 1800s, was not lost upon Clementi the composer, pianist, publisher, and piano-maker. He was aware of Beethoven's standing when he visited Vienna in 1802 and 1804 but remained somewhat aloof from the composer, notwithstanding the mutual respect each had for the other. Beethoven's brother Caspar Carl played a part in this; he considered Beethoven should wait until Clementi approached him with his business proposals rather than that Beethoven should be seen soliciting for them himself.

Doubtless Clementi, himself a pianist of great accomplishments, was drawn to Beethoven's new keyboard style and his willingness to explore daring and remote key-relationships. As Cooper remarks:

> '[His] textures are richer and more complex; modulations are more frequent and daring; motivic development is more intensive; contrasts are sharper and more dramatic; and emotions, whether of exuberance, tenderness or anguish, are much more strongly characterized.'[34]

Caspar Carl's machinations could not hold off Clementi forever. Relationships between himself and Beethoven improved during Clementi's further visit to Vienna between November 1806 and April 1807. The two established what would become a close and lasting friendship and on 20 April 1807 they signed a contract – drafted in French. This conceded to Clementi the English publication-rights for the Fourth Piano Concerto, the Fourth Symphony, the *Razumovsky* String Quartets, the Overture *Coriolan*, and the Violin Concerto. Two days later, Clementi wrote enthusiastically to his partner William Collard in London: 'By a little management ... I have at last made a complete conquest of that haughty beauty, Beethoven.'[35] He explained to Collard the terms of the contract. For these compositions, Beethoven was to receive payment of two hundred pounds sterling (about 2000 Viennese florins). In addition, the contract granted Beethoven two printed-copies of each of his published works – although he often inveigled publishers to supply him with half a dozen. To put this remark into context, the publishers Breitkopf & Härtel typically charged between 60–80 ducats, in silver coinage, for the score of a major composition.[36]

Of greater significance to our narrative, than the foregoing, is that Clementi commissioned Beethoven to rewrite the Violin Concerto as a Piano Concerto. He intimated to Collard that Beethoven was to accommodate the higher register of the solo part 'with additional keys'. This was to enable the new composition to be performed on the six-octave keyboard that was coming into vogue. With the possibility of selling his compositions in France in mind, on 26 April Beethoven wrote to Camille Pleyel offering him the Piano Transcription Op. 61a, and the other compositions to which we have just made reference. He requested payment of 1,200 florins.[37] In the event, however, Pleyel did not take up Beethoven's offer.

On the same day that he wrote to Pleyel Beethoven sent an almost identical letter to Nikolaus Simrock in Bonn with a view to securing the sale of his compositions in Germany. He once more explained the piano transcription would be *avec des notes additionelles'*.[38] [39]

By offering these works to more than one publisher, Beethoven hoped to have his works published more-or-less simultaneously in France, England, and Austria. This would not only increase his sales but would also protect himself from piracy — then prevalent at the time.

Simrock replied to Beethoven on 31 May, expressing his interest in publishing the works the composer had offered for sale. His letter is interesting in that it sheds light on the music-publishing business at this time in Austria. Simrock complains of the effect the French occupation was having: '[At] no time ... has the music business been as very slow as it is now, and keeps getting slower daily'. He could not, therefore, meet Beethoven's demands explaining, with reference to the French currency that was then in circulation: 'All that I can do in my lean situation is to scrape together 1,600 livres.'[40] In Germany the works in question were subsequently published by the Kunst- und Industrie-Comptoir — also known as the Bureau des Arts et d'Industrie.

In Beethoven's lifetime it was commonplace for compositions of all kinds to be arranged for the keyboard, thereby making then more accessible to the wider music public. Stowell writes:

> 'Piano transcriptions of violin concertos were fairly common at that time, several of [Giovanni] Vioti's violin concertos, for example, were arranged by eminent pianists such as Steibelt and Dussek. Similarly, a large number of Beethoven's works were arranged for other media in order to make them more widely available to an eager public.'[41]

Moreover, by the late eighteenth century the piano was beginning to hold sway over the violin. In this context the ever-increasing sonority and expansion of the keyboard, at the period in question, is worthy of remark — Beethoven had an interest in the development of the piano all his adult life.

During the early 1800s, piano makers such as Nanette and Johann Andreas Streicher — with whom Beethoven was on close terms — developed ever more powerful instruments capable of producing a correspondingly large volume of sound. This development would continue well into the nineteenth century and the era of the 'ivory crushers' and 'lions of the keyboard' such as Franz Liszt and Anton Rubinstein. A consequence of this was that, whereas orchestral accompaniments for the solo violin were heard to better effect over a restrained orchestral sound, the more powerful piano was better equipped to hold its own against the full orchestra. To quote Stowell once more:

> 'To compensate for the difficulty of making the

solo violin stand out from the orchestra, composers tend to place the solo violin part in its high
registers, clearly separated in range from the
orchestral violins ... Composers of piano concertos do not have this problem, and thus the piano
can easily occupy the same tonal-range as the
orchestra.'[42]

Beethoven was prepared to sanction transcriptions of his
own music when the work was to be undertaken by musicians whom he could trust, such as his piano pupils Carl
Czerny and Ferdinand Ries. When pressed, he was prepared to do the work himself. For example, he made a
partial transcription for piano of the Seventh Symphony and
a four-hand arrangement of the Great Fugue from his String
Quartet in B-flat major, Op. 130 — but only after rejecting
an attempt by the pianist-composer Anton Halm. Mention
may also be made of the composer's arrangement for string
quartet of his Piano Sonata Op. 14, No. 1 — his one-and-only
such undertaking.

Beethoven expressed his disaffection for transcriptions
on 13 July 1802 in a letter to his publisher Breitkopf and
Härtel:

'The *unnatural mania* [Beethoven's italics], now
so prevalent, for transferring even *pianoforte
compositions* to stringed instruments, instruments which in all respects are so utterly different
from one another, should really be checked.'

He added: 'I firmly maintain that only *Mozart* could arrange
for other instruments the works he composed for the
pianoforte; and Haydn could do this too.'[43]

What vexed Beethoven most were unauthorised

490

arrangements of his works. This is evident in protests he made public by writing once more on 20 October, this time to the *Wiener Zeitung*. He protested that a quintet arrangement of his Septet, Op. 20, and another derived from his First Symphony Op. 21, were not sanctioned by him. He states:

> 'The making of transcriptions is on the whole a thing against which nowadays (in our prolific age of transcriptions) a composer would merely struggle in vain; but at least he is entitled to demand that the publishers shall mention the fact on the title page, so that his honour, as a composer, may not be infringed nor the public deceived.'

On 22 January the following year he had further cause to write a letter of complaint to the *Wiener Zeitung*. A plagiarised edition of his Quintet, Op. 29 had appeared that Beethoven publicly declared to be 'extremely faulty, inaccurate and quite useless for the performer.'

Notwithstanding his aloofness from the making of arrangements and transcriptions, as we have seen Beethoven consented to Clementi's request for his Violin Concerto to be reworked in such a fashion. Critics of the outcome exonerate him on the grounds that he was doubtless motivated be a desire to further the popularity of his original creation and, ever relevant to his personal circumstances, the pressing need to earn additional money from his labours. Leon Plantinga expresses doubts about the transcription's authenticity, asking: 'Could Beethoven have written all this music?' He suggests another hand may have contributed to the final version of the transcription that he, thereby, considers absolves Beethoven from what he describes as its 'most glaring inadequacies'. He considers

Beethoven probably regarded the transcription as being essentially a commercial project undertaken for Clementi and not really a part of his 'typical artistic undertaking'.[44]

The Austrian pianist, and sometime musicologist, Paul Badura-Skoda expressed similar views but also acknowledged the transcription's occasional merits:

> 'Beethoven's arrangement of the Violin Concerto is by and large so faithful to the original (adding only some uninteresting figures in the left hand) that a public performance can scarcely be justified today. Still, some fine differences in the passage-work deserve attention, for the piano-version contains several runs in Beethoven's original version that he subsequently altered for the violin on grounds of playability.'

Badura-Skoda adds: 'The quite extended and very pianistic cadenza in the first movement, which includes a wild duet with the timpani, is also worthy of notice.'[45]

Beethoven may have been obliged to accept assistance in the writing out of the solo part of the piano transcription as a consequence of the pressure of work he was experiencing at the time; his correspondence, from the summer of 1807, coveys this impression. On 11 May he wrote to Countess Josephine Deym — for whom he had a lasting affection — explaining how he had 'so many things' that were keeping him busy.[46] Amongst his obligations, was the pressing need to complete his Mass in C, Op. 86 that had been commissioned by Prince Nikolaus Esterházy. On 26 July he reassured the Prince he would receive the Mass by 20 August at the latest.

One of the reasons for the delay was illness, as he explained:

'I was afflicted somewhat ... by an illness which affected my head. This prevented me at first from working at all and later, and even now, has allowed me to do very little work.'

To convince the Prince, he sent him some of the letters from his physician at the time — the ophthalmologist Dr. Johann Schmidt; amongst his many ailments Beethoven was prone to debilitating headaches. In passing, he could not refrain from mentioning to Esterházy the business he was transacting with Clementi. He refers to his dealings as being 'extraordinarily advantageous'.[47]

Beethoven clearly regarded his negotiations with Clementi as being of some significance to his advancement as a composer. This is evident from a further letter he sent on 11 May to his close friend Count Franz Brunsvik; amongst his other accomplishments he was an excellent cellist. Beethoven enthused:

'This is just to tell you that I have come to a very good arrangement with *Clementi* — I am to get 200 pounds sterling and, what is more, I shall be able to sell the same works in Germany and France — and, in addition, he has given me further orders — so that by this means I may hope even in my early years to achieve the dignity of a true artist'.[48]

Commenting on Beethoven's preparedness to rewrite his Violin Concerto in piano transcription form, Cooper suggests there may have been a precedent in his earlier compositions. He cites a piano cadenza in G that he describes as being 'thematically related' to the existing fragment of the early Violin Concerto in C, WoO 5 to which we have made reference. Cooper concludes: 'This could signify that in 1790—92, Beethoven had considered adapting for piano a work conceived for the violin.'[49] He also suggests that reworking the Concerto for piano may have disposed him to reconsider the configuration of the violin part.[50]

Stowell doubts if the transcription can be considered as truly-authentic Beethoven. He considers

> 'many of the accompanying figures for the left hand ... are surprisingly banal and unimaginative, comprising largely of chords and single notes ... and octave doublings'.

He has praise, though, for Beethoven's setting of the main rondo theme and 'the highly original cadenza for the first movement' that he considers 'a *tour de force* of pianism'. Assuming that another hand did assist Beethoven in amplifying his sketched ideas for the piano version, Stowell assumes Beethoven at least must have checked and corrected the transcription. On that basis he concludes it must have met with his approval 'and should be recognised as his work'.[51]

In the piano transcription, Beethoven retained the original orchestral accompaniment whilst adapting the solo part to the idiomatic requirements of the keyboard — notably in the lower register of the instrument.'[52] As Plantinga shows in his study of the score, the right hand of the piano part is not merely a rendition of the violin line that Clement played at the premier, 'it derives from the many transformations to which Beethoven presented it for publication'.[53]

The autograph score of the Violin Concerto, now a prized possession of the National-bibliothek, Vienna, is dated 1806. This represents Beethoven's first thoughts bearing evidence of the creative process in the form of alterations, revisions and re-scorings. Interestingly, the solo line is assigned four staves in order to leave room for alternative versions and alterations that may have been at Clement's suggestion. In many places all four staves have been filled in, an indication of Beethoven's pursuit for perfection.[54] The piano transcription is only indicated in the form of lightly pencilled sketches at the bottom of the score.[55] The orchestral score of the Violin Concerto was not published until 1861. The piano arrangement appears to have been overlooked and the subsequent publication of the composer's collected works included only the piano part and the cadenzas.[56]

The autograph score of the piano arrangement has not survived, but sketch leaves in possession of the Beethoven House Archive shed light on the composer's creative process. Twelve such leaves trace the workings-out of the original cadenzas with insertions for timpani that feature so strikingly in the piano version. The commentary to these sketches reads: 'It is unique amongst piano works, as a timpani part (of all parts) has been added to the solo piano.' The author reminds us of the originality of the composition's opening: 'Even at the beginning of the Concerto the timpani has an extremely important role — the work opens with four solo beats.' He concludes: 'Perhaps Beethoven wanted to underline this role in the cadenza?'[57]

In two related sketch leaves, Beethoven wrote out ideas for the cadenzas for the piano arrangement. The transition from the second to the third movement is indicated with the textual indication 'Eingang von dem andante into the rondo' — 'Lead-in from the andante into the rondo'. In addition, the recapitulation to the rondo theme within the third movement is headed 'Zwieiter Eingang in's Thema vom Rondo' — 'Second lead-in to the theme of the rondo'.[58]

Commenting on these commentaries, Plantinga remarks:

> 'The modesty of these ornamental additions contrasts vividly with the cadenza for the first movement, a gigantic, powerful thing. More than four minutes in duration featuring all the virtuoso piano playing.'

In effect the timpani play a protracted duet with the piano. 'One is reminded', writes Plantinga, 'of the piano-timpani duet just after the corresponding cadenza in the Third Piano Concerto.' Beethoven designates the second section of the cadenza *Marcia* in which the timpani-figure persists. To Plantinga this is reminiscent of the March of the Guards that opens the second act of *Fidelio*.[59]

By way of further interest, and relevant to our discussion in general of Beethoven's piano concertos, sometime around 1809 he wrote out a cadenza for the first and third movements of Mozart's Piano Concerto in D minor, K. 466 for his pupil Ferdinand Ries. At this time, he also wrote cadenzas for his first four pianoforte concertos: Op. 15, three cadenzas for the first movement; Op. 19, one for the first movement; Op. 37, one for the first movement; and Op. 58, two for the first movement and one for the third movement.[60]

The Viennese editions of the Violin Concerto and the pianoforte adaptation were published by the Bureau des Arts et d'Industrie in August in 1808. The London editions were published later that autumn by Clementi. The Title Page of his edition of the Piano Transcription reads:

'THEMA / WITH / VARIATIONS / for the / Piano Forte, / Composed by / Lewis van Beethoven. / LONDON, / Printed by Clementi,

Banger, Collard, Davis & Collard, / 26 Cheapside, / Ent[ered] at S[tationers] Hall Price 2
s[hillings].'[61]

The London copy was entered at Stationers Hall on 18
August 1808. In England at this time the Law of Copyright
required eleven copies of newly printed works to be deposited at Stationers' Hall, the London home of the Worshipful
Company of Stationers and Newspaper Makers, a Livery
Company that regulated the affairs of the printing and
publishing industry. On receipt of new works, the Company
then passed these to the eleven libraries that were privileged
to exercise their right of demand to receive new works — the
equivalent of today's system of Legal Deposit. As Pamela
Willets explains in her study of *Beethoven and England*:

> 'This is the principal source of the collections of
> the English Beethoven [first] editions preserved
> in the British Museum, the Bodleian Library at
> Oxford, [and] the University Library at
> Cambridge.'[62] [63]

Beethoven dedicated the transcription to Julie von Vering,
the daughter of his physician the surgeon Gerhard von
Vering. She was an accomplished pianist with whom
Beethoven is said to have enjoyed playing duets. Julie had
recently married Beethoven's childhood friend Stephan von
Breuning; his first wife having died at the tragically early age
of nineteen.

To further the sale of his publications in England, in
1816 Beethoven entered into negotiations with Charles
Neate. Neate was an accomplished pianist and proficient
composer who lived to the considerable age of 93 — he died
in 1877. He visited Vienna in 1815 with the hope of

receiving piano lessons from Beethoven but who declined; he did agree, however, to appraise some of Neate's piano compositions. Beethoven established a warm relationship with Neate and on his departure from Vienna, in February 1816, he made him a gift of a copy of the manuscript score of the Violin Concerto that included both solo parts (violin and piano) written in by a copyist and corrected by Beethoven.[64] It subsequently came into the possession of the British Museum (Library) in 1953.

Neate himself claimed to have performed the piano arrangement.[65] Some of the correspondence between Beethoven and Neate is preserved today in the Beethoven House Archives.[66] It reveals the trust Beethoven placed in Neate to act as his London agent in selling and promoting a considerable number of his compositions. Interestingly, these included piano arrangements of his *Wellingtons Sieg — Wellington's Victory* and the Seventh Symphony. As his agent, Neate, though, proved to be somewhat tardy — for which he had to apologise to Beethoven. He explained he had fallen in love and, thereby, had neglected his business obligations![67]

Little is known of the fortunes of the Piano Concerto, Op. 61a in the nineteenth century but it was included in the 1863 complete edition of Beethoven's compositions (*Gesamtausgabe*) of Breitkopf and Härtell.

We give our closing summative words to Leon Plantinga:

'What we value in the two instruments is much too different: we delight in the richness and flexibility of tone colour in a single line played in almost any register of the violin, while the same line, played alone on the piano, will seem by comparison poverty stricken. What counts in transcribing music from the one instrument to the other is the invention of textures that sound convincing on the piano, an art in which Beethoven's solo piano works of course excel! This virtue is conspicuously missing in the transcription of the Violin Concerto. In a great many passages, the violin line is simply doubled down an octave: the merest expedient, it seems, adopted to give the left hand something to do.'

Plantinga concludes, perhaps too dismissively for some:

'We are left with the impression that the piano transcription of Beethoven's Violin Concerto ranges in quality from satisfactory to incompetent — and that it is more heavily weighted to toward the latter end of the scale.'[68]

[1] Elliot Forbes editor, *Thayer's Life of Beethoven*, 1967 pp. 95–96.

[2] For a depiction of the silhouette see: Beethoven House, Digital Archives, Library Document Wegeler, W 171.

[3] Michael Thomas Roeder, 1994, p. 192.

[4] Elliot Forbes editor, *Thayer's Life of Beethoven*, 1967, p. 123. See also: Beethoven House, Digital Archives, *Konzert für Violine und Orchester, D-Dur, Op. 61.*

[5] Michael Steinberg, 1998, p. 82.

[6] As recoded by Bryan Gilliam editor, *Richard Strauss and his World*, 1992, pp. 223–24.

[7] Peter Clive, 2001, pp. 72–73.

[8] Recollected in Clive Brown, *The Violin Concertos of Franz Clement and Ludwig van Beethoven*, 2008.

[9] As recounted by Robin Stowell, 1998, p. 20.

[10] *Ibid*, pp. 20–22.

[11] Elliot Forbes editor, *Thayer's Life of Beethoven*, 1967, pp. 324–25.

[12] *Ibid*, pp. 388–89.

[13] Oscar George Theodore Sonneck, *Beethoven: Impressions of Contemporaries*, 1927, pp. 60–68.

[14] See: Beethoven House Digital Archives, *Beethoven Gallery* and Library Document B 2388. After Beethoven's death the portrait passed to the widow of Carl van Beethoven.

[15] Elliot Forbes editor, *Thayer's Life of Beethoven*, 1967, pp. 206–07.

[16] *Ibid*, p. 410.

[17] Robin Stowell, 1998, pp. 20–22.

[18] Joseph Braunstein, *Musica Aeterna, program notes for 1961–1971, Musica Aeterna*, 1972, p. 27.

[19] Barry Cooper, 1991, p. 221.

[20] Robin Stowell, 1998, p.50.

[21] For a portrait of von Breuning with his family, see: Beethoven House, Digital Archives, Library Document, Bonn, Ley, Band VI. Nr. 1161.

[22] Michael Steinberg, 1998, p. 81.

[23] Elliot Forbes editor, *Thayer' Life of Beethoven*, 1967, p. 410.

[24] Wayne M. Senner, Robin Wallace and William Meredith editors, *The Critical Reception of Beethoven's Compositions by his German Contemporaries.* Lincoln: University of Nebraska Press, in association with the American Beethoven Society and the Ira F. Brilliant Center for Beethoven Studies, San José State University, 1999, Vol., 1, pp. 68–69.

[25] H. C. Robbins Landon, 1992, p. 141.

[26] See note 24, Vol., 1, p. 144.

[27] Berthold Litzmann editor, *Clara Schumann: An Artist's Life, Based on Material found in Diaries and Letters*, 1913, pp. 40–41. Also with acknowledgement to: Anton Felix Schindler, *Beethoven as I Knew him*, edited by Donald W. MacArdle and translated by Constance S. Jolly from the German edition of 1860, 1966; Johann Schlosser, *Beethoven: the first Biography, 1827*, edited by Barry Cooper, 1996, pp. 120–23; Joseph Braunstein, *Musica Aeterna, Program Notes for 1961–1971, Musica Aeterna*, 1972, pp. 26–27; and Robin Stowell, 1998, pp. 32–33.

[28] Maynard Solomon, 1997, pp. 202–03.

[29] Antony Hopkins, 1984, p. 9.

[30] Joseph Braunstein, See endnote 27, p. 27.

[31] Theodore Adorno, 1998, p. 88.

[32] Donald Francis Tovey, *Essays in Musical Analysis*, Vol. 3, 1935–41, pp. 87–88.

[33] Anton Schindler, 1860, English edition: Donald MacArdle, editor, 1966, p. 379.

[34] Barry Cooper, 2000, p.58.

[35] Theodore Albrecht editor and translator, 1996, Vol. 1, Letter No. 119, pp. 186–88.

[36] *Ibid*, Letter No. 148, pp. 223–6.

[37] See Beethoven House, Digital Archives, Library Document, NE 161.

[38] Emily Anderson editor and translator, 1961, Vol. 1, Letter No. 141, pp. 166–67.

[39] For a facsimile reproduction of this letter see: Beethoven House, Digital Archives, Library Document, H. C. Bodmer, HCB Br 222. The letter appears to have been written by Beethoven's brother Caspar Carl who was by then assisting his brother with his affairs.

[40] Theodore Albrecht, editor and translator, 1996, Vol. 1, Letter No. 121, pp. 189–90.

[41] Robin Stowell, *Beethoven: Violin Concerto*, 1998, p. 48.

[42] See, for example, Michael Thomas Roeder, 1994, p. 191.

[43] Emily Anderson editor and translator, 1961, Vol. 1, Letter No. 59, pp. 74–75.

[44] Leon Plantinga, 1999, pp. 243–50.

[45] Paul Badura-Skoda in his commentary to: Carl Czerny, *On the Proper Performance of all Beethoven's Works for the Piano*, Universal edition: A. G. Wien, 1970, p. 104 and p. 114. Badura-Skoda also refers the reader to: Alan Tyson, *The Text of Beethoven's Op. 61*, *Music and Letters*, April, 1962.

[46] Emily Anderson editor and translator, 1961, Vol. 1, Letter No. 142, p. 167.

[47] *Ibid*, Letter No. 150, p. 174.

[48] *Ibid*, Letter No. 143, pp. 168–69.

[49] Barry Cooper, 1991, p. 272.

[50] Barry Cooper, 2000, p. 167.

[51] Robin Stowell, 1998, pp. 48–49.

[52] See: Michael Thomas Roeder,1994, p.195.

[53] Leon Plantinga, 1999, p. 243.

[54] Donald Francis Tovey, *Essays in Musical Analysis*, Vol. 3, 1935–41, p. 88.

[55] Alan Tyson, 1963, pp. 56.

[56] Joseph Braunstein, See endnote 27, p. 27.

[57] Beethoven House, Digital Archives, Library Document, H. C. Bodmer, HCB Mh 20.

[58] *Ibid*, H. C. Bodmer, HCB Mh 21. See also Barrie Cooper, 1991, p. 272 and Elliot Forbes editor, *Thayer's Life of Beethoven*, 1967, p. 478.

[59] Leon Plantinga, 1999, p. 243–50.

[60] Elliot Forbes editor, *Thayer's Life of Beethoven*, 1967, p. 478.

[61] Alan Tyson, 1963, p. 56. Tyson remarks the work was probably sold for 3 shillings since the printed copy was inked over to this effect.

[62] Pamela J. Willetts, 1970, pp. 27–31.

[63] Facsimile reproductions of the score of the first, and early editions, of the Violin Concerto can be viewed on the Beethoven House Digital Archives, Library Documents: HCB C Op. 61; Bureaux des Arts et d'Industrie, 583; and Haslinger 4022 and 4032.

[64] Peter Clive, 2001, pp. 243–44.

[65] Emily Anderson editor and translator, 1961, Vol. 2, Letter No. 606a, p. 557.

[66] See, for example, Beethoven House, Digital Archives, Library Documents Bonn NE 28 and H. C. Bodmer, HCB Br 175.

[67] Emily Anderson, editor and translator, 1961, Vol. 1 Vol. 1, Letter No. 664, pp. 604–7.

[68] Leon Plantinga, 1999, p. 243.

BIBLIOGRAPHY

The author has individually consulted all the publications listed in this bibliography and can confirm that each makes reference, in some way or other, to Beethoven and his works. It will be evident from their titles which of these are publications devoted exclusively to the composer. Others that make only passing reference to Beethoven and his compositions, nevertheless unfailingly bear testimony to his genius and humanity. The diversity of the titles listed testifies to the centrality of Beethoven to western culture and beyond; the mere survey of these should be of itself a rewarding experience for a lover of so-called classical music. The entries are confined to book publications, reflecting the scope of the author's researches. The cut-off date for this was 2007; no works after this date are listed, notwithstanding the author is mindful that Beethoven musicology, and related publication, continue to be a major field of endeavour.

Abraham, Gerald. *Beethoven's second-period quartets*. London: Oxford University Press: Humphrey Milford, 1944.

Abraham, Gerald. *Essays on Russian and East European music*. Oxford: Clarendon Press: New York: Oxford University Press, 1985.

Abraham, Gerald, Editor. *The age of Beethoven, 1790-1830*. London: Oxford University Press, 1982.

Abraham, Gerald. *The tradition of Western music*. London: Oxford University Press, 1974.

Abse, Dannie and Joan. *The Music lover's literary companion*. London: Robson Books, 1988.

Adorno, Theodor W., Translator. *Alban Berg: master of the smallest link*. Cambridge: Cambridge University Press, 1991.

Adorno, Theodor W. *Beethoven: the philosophy of music; fragments and texts*. Cambridge: Polity Press, 1998.

Albrecht, Daniel, Editor. *Modernism and music: an anthology of sources*. Chicago; London: University of Chicago Press, 2004.

Albrecht, Theodore, Translator and Editor. *Letters to Beethoven and other correspondence*. Lincoln, New England: University of Nebraska Press, 3 vols., 1996.

Allsobrook, David Ian. *Liszt: my travelling circus life*. London: Macmillan, 1991.

Anderson, Christopher, Editor and Translator. *Selected writings of Max Reger*. New York; London: Routledge, 2006.

Anderson, Emily, Editor and Translator. *The letters of Beethoven*. London: Macmillan, 3 vols.,1961.

Anderson, Martin, Editor. *Klemperer on music: shavings from a musician's workbench*. London: Toccata Press, 1986.

Antheil, George. *Bad boy of music*. London; New York: Hurst & Blackett Ltd., 1945.

Appleby, David P. *Heitor Villa-Lobos: a bio-bibliography*. New York: Greenwood Press, 1988.

Aprahamian, Felix, Editor. *Essays on music: an anthology from The Listener*. London, Cassell, 1967.

Armero, Gonzalo and Jorge de Persia. *Manuel de Falla : his life & works*. London: Omnibus Press, 1999.

Arnold, Ben, Editor. *The Liszt companion*. Westport, Connecticut; London: Greenwood Press, 2002.

Arnold, Denis and Nigel Fortune, Editors. *The Beethoven companion*. London: Faber and Faber, 1973.

Ashbrook, William. *Donizetti*. London: Cassell, 1965.

Auner, Joseph Henry. *A Schoenberg reader: documents of a life*. New Haven Connecticut; London: Yale University Press, 2003.

Avins, Styra, Editor. *Johannes Brahms: life and letters*. Oxford: Oxford University Press, 1997.

Azoury, Pierre H. *Chopin through his contemporaries: friends, lovers, and rivals*. Westport, Connecticut: Greenwood Press, 1999.

Badura-Skoda, Paul. *Carl Czerny: On the Proper Performance of all Beethoven's Works for the Piano*. Universal Edition: A. G. Wien, 1970.

Bailey, Cyril. *Hugh Percy Allen*. London: Oxford University Press, 1948.

Bailey, Kathryn. *The life of Webern.* Cambridge: Cambridge University Press, 1998.

Barenboim, Daniel. *A life in music.* London: Weidenfeld & Nicolson, 1991.

Barlow, Michael. *Whom the gods love: the life and music of George Butterworth.* London: Toccata Press, 1997.

Barrett-Ayres, Reginald. *Joseph Haydn and the string quartet.* New York: Schirmer Books, 1974.

Bartos, Frantisek. *Bedrich Smetana: Letters and reminiscences.* Prague: Artia, 1953.

Barzun, Jacques. *Pleasures of music: an anthology of writing about music and musicians.* London: Cassell, 1977.

Bauer-Lechner, Natalie. *Recollections of Gustav Mahler.* London: Faber Music, 1980.

Bazhanov, N. Nikolai. *Rakhmaninov.* Moscow: Raduga, 1983.

Beaumont, Antony, Editor. *Ferruccio Busoni: Selected letters.* London: Faber and Faber, 1987.

Beaumont, Antony, Editor. *Gustav Mahler, letters to his wife.* London: Faber and Faber, 2004.

Beecham, Thomas. *A mingled chime: an autobiography.* New York: Da Capo Press, 1976.

Bekker, Paul. *Beethoven.* London: J. M. Dent & Sons, 1925.

Bellasis, Edward. *Cherubini: memorials illustrative of his life.* London: Burns and Oates, 1874.

Bennett, James R. Sterndale. *The life of William Sterndale Bennett.* Cambridge: University Press, 1907.

Benser, Caroline Cepin. *Egon Wellesz (1885–1974): chronicle of twentieth-century musician.* New York: P. Lang, 1985.

Berlioz, Hector. *Evenings in the orchestra.* Harmondsworth: Penguin Books, 1963.

Berlioz, Hector. *The musical madhouse (Les grotesques de la musique).* Rochester, New York: University of Rochester Press, 2003.

Bernard, Jonathan W., Editor. *Elliott Carter: collected essays and lectures, 1937-1995.* Rochester, New York; Woodbridge: University of Rochester Press, 1998.

Bernstein, Leonard. *The joy of music.* New York: Simon and Schuster, 1959.

Bertensson, Sergei. *Sergei Rachmaninoff: a lifetime in music.* London: G. Allen & Unwin, 1965.

Biancolli, Louis. *The Flagstad manuscript.* New York: Putnam, 1952.

Bickley, Nora, Editor. *Letters from and to Joseph Joachim.* London: Macmillan, 1914.

Bie, Oskar. *A history of the pianoforte and pianoforte players.* New York: Da Capo Press, 1966.

Blaukopf, Herta. *Mahler's unknown letters.* London: Gollancz, 1986.

Blaukopf, Kurt and Herta. *Mahler: his life, work and world.* London: Thames and Hudson, 1991.

Bliss, Arthur. *As I remember.* London: Thames Publishing, 1989.

Block, Adrienne Fried. *Amy Beach, passionate Victorian: the life and work of an American composer, 1867–1944.* New York: Oxford University Press, 1998.

Bloch, Ernst. *Essays on the philosophy of music.* Cambridge: Cambridge University Press, 1985.

Blocker, Robert. *The Robert Shaw reader.* New Haven; London: Yale University Press, 2004.

Blom, Eric. *A musical postbag.* London: J. M. Dent, 1945.

Blom, Eric. *Beethoven's pianoforte sonatas discussed.* London: J. M. Dent, 1938.

Blom, Eric. *Classics major and minor: with some other musical ruminations.* London: J. M. Dent, 1958.

Blum, David. *The art of quartet playing: the Guarneri Quartet in conversation with David Blum.* London: Gollancz, 1986.

Blume, Friedrich. *Classic and Romantic music: a comprehensive survey.* London: Faber and Faber, 1972.

Boden, Anthony. *The Parrys of the Golden Vale: background to genius.* London: Thames Publishing, 1998.

Bonavia, Ferruccio. *Musicians on music.* London: Routledge & Kegan Paul, 1956.

Bonds, Mark Evan *After Beethoven: imperatives of originality in the symphony.* Cambridge, Massachusetts; London: Harvard University Press, 1996.

Bonis, Ferenc, Editor. *The selected writings of Zoltán Kodály.* London; New York: Boosey & Hawkes, 1974.

Bookspan, Martin. *André Previn: a biography.* London: Hamilton, 1981.

Boros, James and Richard Toop, Editors. *Brian Ferneyhough: Collected writings.* Amsterdam: Harwood Academic, 1995.

Boulez, Pierre. *Stocktakings from an apprenticeship.* Oxford: Clarendon Press, 1991.

Boult, Adrian. *Boult on music: words from a lifetime's communication.* London: Toccata Press, 1983.

Boult, Adrian. *My own trumpet.* London, Hamish Hamilton, 1973.

Boult, Adrian with Jerrold Northrop Moore. *Music and friends: seven decades of letters to Adrian Boult from Elgar, Vaughan Williams, Holst, Bruno Walter, Yehudi Menuhin and other friends.* London: Hamish Hamilton, 1979.

Bovet, Marie Anne de. *Charles Gounod: his life and his works.* London: S. Low, Marston, Searle & Rivington, Ltd., 1891.

Bowen, Catherine Drinker. *Beloved friend: the story of Tchaikowsky and Nadejda von Meck.* London: Hutchinson & Co., 1937.

Bowen, Meiron, Editor. *Gerhard on music: selected writings.* Brookfield, Vermont: Ashgate, 2000.

Bowen, Meirion. *Michael Tippett.* London: Robson Books, 1982.

Bowen, Meiron, Editor. *Music of the angels: essays and sketchbooks of Michael Tippett.* London: Eulenburg, 1980.

Bowen, Meiron, Editor. *Tippett on music.* Oxford: Clarendon Press, 1995.

Bowers, Faubion. *Scriabin: a biography.* Mineola: Dover; London: Constable, 1996.

Boyden, Matthew. *Richard Strauss.* London: Weidenfeld & Nicolson, 1999.

Bozarth, George S., Editor. *Brahms*

studies: analytical and historical perspectives; papers delivered at the International Brahms Conference, Washington, DC, 5-8 May 1983. Oxford: Clarendon Press, 1990.

Brand, Juliane, Christopher Hailey and Donald Harris, Editors. *The Berg-Schoenberg correspondence: selected letters.* Basingstoke: Macmillan, 1987.

Brandenbugh, Sieghard, Editor. *Haydn, Mozart, & Beethoven: studies in the music of the classical period: essays in honor of Alan Tyson.* Oxford: Clarendon Press, 1998.

Braunstein, Joseph. *Musica Æterna, program notes for 1961–1971.* New York: Musica Æterna, 1972.

Braunstein, Joseph. *Musica Æterna, program notes for 1971–1976.* New York: Musica Æterna, 1978.

Brendel, Alfred. *Alfred Brendel on music: collected essays.* Chicago, Iliinois: A Cappella Books, 2001.

Brendel, Alfred. *The veil of order: Alfred Brendel in conversation with Martin Meyer.* London: Faber and Faber, 2002.

Breuning, Gerhard von. *Memories of Beethoven: from the house of the black-robed Spaniards.* Cambridge: Cambridge University Press, 1992.

Briscoe, James R., Editor. (Brief Description): *Debussy in performance.* New Haven: Yale University Press, 1999.

Brott, Alexander Betty Nygaard King. *Alexander Brott: my lives in music.* Oakville, Ontario; Niagara Falls, New York: Mosaic Press, 2005.

Brown, Alfred Peter. *The symphonic repertoire. Vol. 2, The first golden age of the Viennese symphony: Haydn, Mozart, Beethoven, and Schubert.* Bloomington, Indiana: Indiana University Press, 2002.

Brown, Maurice John Edwin. *Schubert: a critical biography.* London: Macmillan; New York: St. Martin's Press, 1958.

Broyles, Michael. *Beethoven: the emergence and evolution of Beethoven's heroic style.* New York: Excelsior Music Publishing Co., 1987.

Brubaker, Bruce and Jane Gottlieb, Editors. *Pianist, scholar, connoisseur: essays in honor of Jacob Lateiner.* Stuyvesant, N.Y., Pendragon Press, 2000.

Buch, Esteban. *Beethoven's Ninth: a political history.* Chicago; London: University of Chicago Press, 2003.

Burk, John N., Editor. *Letters of Richard Wagner: the Burrell collection.* London: Gollancz, 1951.

Burnham, Scott G. *Beethoven hero.* Princeton, New Jersey: Princeton University Press, 1995.

Burnham, Scott G and Michael P. Steinberg, Editors. *Beethoven and his world.* Princeton, New Jersey; Oxford: Princeton University Press, 2000.

Burton, William Westbrook, Editor. *Conversations about Bernstein.* New York; Oxford: Oxford University Press, 1995.

Busch, Fritz. *Pages from a musician's life.* London: Hogarth Press, 1953.

Busch, Hans, Editor. *Verdi's Aida: the history of an opera in letters* and documents. Minneapolis: University of Minnesota Press, 1978.

Busch, Hans, Editor. *Verdi's Falstaff in letters and contemporary reviews.* Bloomington: Indiana University Press, 1997.

Busch, Marie, Translator. *Memoirs of Eugenie Schumann.* London: W. Heinemann, 1927.

Bush, Alan Dudley. *In my eighth decade and other essays.* London: Kahn & Averill, 1980.

Busoni, Ferruccio. *Letters to his wife.* Translated by Rosamond Ley. New York: Da Capo Press, 1975.

Byron, Reginald. *Music, culture, & experience: selected papers of John Blacking.* Chicago: University of Chicago Press, 1995.

Cairns, David. *Responses: musical essays and reviews.* New York: Da Capo Press, 1980.

Cardus, Neville. *Talking of music.* London: Collins, 1957.

Carley, Lionel. *Delius: a life in letters.* London: Scolar Press in association with the Delius Trust, 1988.

Carley, Lionel. *Grieg and Delius: a chronicle of their friendship in letters.* London: Marion Boyars, 1993.

Carner, Mosco. *Major and minor.* London: Duckworth, 1980

Carner, Mosco. *Puccini: a critical biography.* London: Duckworth, 1958.

Carroll, Brendan G. *The last prodigy: a biography of Erich Wolfgang Korngold.* Portland, Oregon: Amadeus Press, 1997.

Carse, Adam von Ahn. *The life of Jullien: adventurer, showman-conductor and establisher of the Promenade Concerts in England, together with a history of* those concerts up to 1895. Cambridge England: Heffer, 1951.

Carse, Adam von Ahn. *The orchestra from Beethoven to Berlioz: a history of the orchestra in the first half of the 19th century, and of the development of orchestral baton-conducting.* Cambridge: W. Heffer, 1948.

Casals, Pablo. *Joys and sorrows: reflections by Pablo Casals as told to Albert E. Kahn.* London: Macdonald, 1970.

Casals, Pablo. *The memoirs of Pablo Casals as told to Thomas Dozier.* London: Life en Español, 1959.

Chappell, Paul. *Dr. S. S. Wesley, 1810–1876: portrait of a Victorian musician.* Great Wakering: Mayhew-McCrimmon, 1977.

Chasins, Abram. *Leopold Stokowski, a profile.* New York: Hawthorn Books, 1979.

Charlton, Davi, Editor and Martyn Clarke Translator. *E.T.A. Hoffmann's musical writings: Kreisleriana, The Poet and the Composer.* Cambridge: Cambridge University Press, 1989.

Chávez, Carlos. *Musical thought.* Cambridge: Harvard University Press, 1961.

Chesterman, Robert, Editor. *Conversations with conductors: Bruno Walter, Sir Adrian Boult, Leonard Bernstein, Ernest Ansermet, Otto Klemperer, Leopold Stokowski.* Totowa, New Jersey: Rowman and Littlefield, 1976.

Chissell, Joan. *Clara Schumann: a dedicated spirit; a study of her life and work.* London: Hamilton, 1983.

Chua, Daniel K. L. *The "Galitzin" quartets of Beethoven: Opp.127, 132, 130*. Princeton: Princeton University Press, 1995.

Citron, Marcia, Editor. *The letters of Fanny Hensel to Felix Mendelssohn*. Stuyvesant, New York: Pendragon Press, 1987.

Clark, Walter Aaron. *Enrique Granados: poet of the piano*. Oxford, England; New York, N.Y.: Oxford University Press, 2006.

Clark, Walter Aaron. *Isaac Albéniz: portrait of a romantic*. Oxford; New York: Oxford University Press, 1999.

Clive, Peter. *Beethoven and his world*. Oxford University Press, 2001.

Closson, Ernest. *History of the piano*. Translated by Delano Ames and edited by Robin Golding. London: Paul Elek, 1947.

Cockshoot, John V. *The fugue in Beethoven's piano music*. London: Routledge & Kegan Paul, 1959.

Coe, Richard N, Translator. *Life of Rossini by Stendhal*. London: Calder & Boyars, 1970.

Coleman, Alexander, Editor. *Diversions & animadversions: essays from The new criterion*. New Brunswick, New Jersey; London: Transaction Publishers, 2005.

Colerick, George. *From the Italian girl to Cabaret: musical humour, parody and burlesque*. London: Juventus, 1998.

Coleridige, A. D. *Life of Moscheles, with selections from his diaries and correspondence by his wife*. London: Hurst & Blackett, 1873.

Colles, Henry Cope. *Essays and lectures*. London: Humphrey Milford, Oxford University Press, 1945.

Cone, Edward T., Editor. *Roger Sessions on music: collected essays*. Princeton, New Jersey: Princeton University Press, 1979.

Cone, Edward T. *The composer's voice*. Berkeley; London: University of California Press, 1974.

Cook, Susan and Judy S. Tsou, Editors. *Cecilia reclaimed: feminist perspectives on gender and music*. Urbana: University of Illinois Press, 1994.

Cooper, Barry. *Beethoven: The master musicians series*. Oxford: Oxford University Press, 2000.

Cooper, Barry. *Beethoven and the creative process*. Oxford: Clarendon Press, 1990.

Cooper, Barry. *Beethoven's folksong settings: chronology, sources, style*. Cambridge: Cambridge University Press, 1991.

Cooper, Barry. *The Beethoven compendium: a guide to Beethoven's life and music*. London: Thames and Hudson, 1991.

Cooper, Martin. *Beethoven: the last decade, 1817–1827*. London: Oxford University Press, 1970.

Cooper, Martin. *Judgements of value: selected writings on music*. Oxford; New York: Oxford University Press, 1988.

Cooper, Martin. *Ideas and music*. London: Barrie and Rockliff, 1965.

Cooper, Victoria L. *The house of Novello: the practice and policy of a Victorian music publisher, 1829–1866*. Aldershot, Hants: Ashgate, 2003.

Coover, James. *Music at auction: Puttick and Simpson (of London), 1794–1971: being an* annotated, chronological list of sales of musical materials. Warren, Michigan: Harmonie Park Press, 1988.

Copland, Aaron. *Copland on music.* London: Deutsch, 1961.

Corredor, J. Ma. *Conversations with Casals.* London: Hutchinson, 1956.

Cott, Jonathan. *Stockhausen: conversations with the composer.* London: Picador, 1974.

Cottrell, Stephen. *Professional music making in London: ethnography and experience.* Aldershot: Ashgate, 2004.

Cowell, Henry. *Charles Ives and his music.* New York: Oxford University Press, 1955.

Cowling, Elizabeth. *The cello.* London: Batsford, 1983.

Crabbe, John. *Beethoven's empire of the mind.* Newbury: Lovell Baines, 1982.

Craft, Robert. *An improbable life: memoirs.* Nashville: Vanderbilt University Press, 2002.

Craft, Robert, Editor. *Stravinsky: selected correspondence.* London: Faber and Faber, 3 Vols. 1982–1985.

Craw, Howard Allen. *A biography and thematic catalog of the works of J. L. Dussek: 1760–1812.* Ann Arbor: Michigan, 1965.

Crawford, Richard, R. Allen Lott and Carol J. Oja, Editors. *A Celebration of American music: words and music in honor of H. Wiley Hitchcock.* Ann Arbor: University of Michigan Press, 1990.

Craxton, Harold and Tovey, Donald Francis. *Beethoven: Sonatas for Pianoforte.* London: The Associated Board, [1931].

Crichton, Ronald: Editor. *The memoirs of Ethel Smyth.* New York: Viking, 1987.

Crist, Stephen A. and Roberta M. Marvin, Editors. *Historical musicology: sources, methods, interpretations.* Rochester, New York: University of Rochester Press, 2004.

Crofton, Ian and Donald Fraser, Editors. *A dictionary of musical quotations.* London: Croom Helm, 1985.

Crompton, Louis, Editor. *Shaw, Bernard: The great composers: reviews and bombardments.* Berkeley; London: University of California Press, 1978.

Csicserry-Ronay, Elizabeth, Translator and Editor. *Hector Berlioz: The art of music and other essays. (A travers chants).* Bloomington: Indiana University Press, 1994.

Curtiss, Mina Kirstein. *Bizet and his world.* London: Secker & Warburg, 1959.

Cuyler, Louise Elvira. *The symphony.* New York: Harcourt Brace Jovanovich, 1973.

Dahlhaus, Carl. *Ludwig van Beethoven: approaches to his music.* Oxford: Clarendon Press, 1991.

Dahlhaus, Carl. *Nineteenth-century music.* Translated by J. Bradford Robinson. Berkeley; London: University of California Press, 1989.

Daniels, Robin. *Conversations with Cardus.* London: Gollancz, 1976.

Daniels, Robin. Conversations with Menuhin. London: Macdonald General Books, 1979.

Day, James. *Vaughan Williams.* London: Dent, 1961.

Davies, Peter Maxwell. *Studies from*

two decades. Selected and introduced by Stephen Pruslin. London: Boosey & Hawkes, 1979.

Dean, Winton. *Georges Bizet: his life and work*. London: J.M. Dent, 1965.

Deas, Stewart. *In defence of Hanslick*. London: Williams and Norgate, 1940.

Debussy, Claude. *Debussy on music*. London: Secker & Warburg, 1977.

Delbanco, Nicholas. *The Beaux Arts Trio*. London: Gollancz, 1985.

Demény, Janos, Editor. *Béla Bartók: letters*. London: Faber and Faber, 1971.

Dent, Edward Joseph. *Selected essays*. Edited by Hugh Taylor. Cambridge; New York: Cambridge University Press, 1979.

Deutsch, Otto Erich. *Mozart: a documentary biography*. London: Adam & Charles Black, 1965.

Deutsch, Otto Erich. *Schubert: a documentary biography*. London: J.M. Dent, 1946

Deutsch, Otto Erich. *Schubert: memoirs by his friends*. London: Adam & Charles Black, 1958.

Dibble, Jeremy. *C. Hubert H. Parry: his life and music*. Oxford: Clarendon Press, 1992.

Dibble, Jeremy. *Charles Villiers Stanford: man and musician*. Oxford: Oxford University Press, 2002.

Donakowski, Conrad L. *A muse for the masses: ritual and music in an age of democratic revolution, 1770–1870*. Chicago: University of Chicago Press, 1977.

Dower, Catherine. *Alfred Einstein on music: selected music criticisms*. New York: Greenwood Press, 1991.

Downs, Philip G. *Classical music: the era of Haydn, Mozart, and Beethoven*. New York: W.W. Norton, 1992.

Drabkin, William. *Beethoven: Missa Solemnis*. Cambridge: Cambridge University Press, 1991.

Dreyfus, Kay. *The farthest north of humanness: letters of Percy Grainger, 1901–1914*. South Melbourne; Basingstoke: Macmillan, 1985.

Dubal, David, Editor. *Remembering Horowitz: 125 pianists recall a legend*. New York: Schirmer Books, 1993.

Dubal, David. *The world of the concert pianist*. London: Victor Gollancz, 1985.

Dvořák, Otakar. *Antonín Dvořák, my father*. Spillville, Iowa: Czech Historical Research Center, 1993.

Dyson, George. *The progress of music*. London: Oxford University Press, Humphrey Milford, 1932.

Eastaugh, Kenneth. *Havergal Brian: the making of a composer*. London: Harrap, 1976.

Edwards, Allen. *Flawed words and stubborn sounds: a conversation with Elliott Carter*. New York: Norton & Company, 1971.

Edwards, Frederick George. *Musical haunts in London*. London: J. Curwen & Sons, 1895.

Ehrlich, Cyril. *First philharmonic: a history of the Royal Philharmonic Society*. Oxford: Clarendon Press, 1995.

Einstein, Alfred. *A short history of music*. London: Cassell and Company Ltd., 1948.

Einstein, Alfred. *Essays on music*. London: Faber and Faber, 1958.

Einstein, Alfred. *Mozart: his charac-*

ter, his work. London: Cassell and Company Ltd., 1946.

Einstein, Alfred. *Music in the Romantic era.* London: J.M. Dent Ltd., 1947.

Ekman, Karl. *Jean Sibelius, his life and personality.* New York: Tudor Publishing. Co., 1945.

Elgar, Edward. *A future for English music: and other lectures,* Edited by Percy M. Young. London: Dobson, 1968.

Elkin, Robert. *Queen's Hall, 1893–1941.* London: Rider, 1944.

Ella, John. *Musical sketches, abroad and at home: with original music by Mozart, Czerny, Graun, etc., vocal cadenzas and other musical illustrations.* London: Ridgway, Vol. 1., 1869.

Ellis, William Ashton. *The family letters of Richard Wagner.* Edited and translated by William Ashton Ellis and enlarged with introduction and notes by John Deathridge. Basingstoke: Macmillan, 1991.

Ellis, William Ashton. *Richard Wagner's prose works: Vol. 1, The art-work of the future.* Edited and translated by William Ashton Ellis. London: Kegan Paul, Trench, Trübner, 1895.

Ellis, William Ashton. *Richard Wagner's prose works: Vol. 2, Opera and drama.* Edited and translated by William Ashton Ellis. London: Kegan Paul, Trench, Trübner, 1900.

Ellis, William Ashton. *Richard Wagner's prose works: Vol. 3, The theatre.* Edited and translated by William Ashton Ellis. London: Kegan Paul, Trench, Trübner, 1907.

Ellis, William Ashton. *Richard Wag-*
ner's prose works: Vol. 4, Art and politics. Edited and translated by William Ashton Ellis. London: Kegan Paul, Trench, Trübner, 1895.

Ellis, William Ashton. *Richard Wagner's prose works: Vol. 5, Actors and singers.* Edited and translated by William Ashton Ellis. London: Kegan Paul, Trench, Trübner, 1896.

Ellis, William Ashton. *Richard Wagner's prose works: Vol. 6, Religion and art.* Edited and translated by William Ashton Ellis. London: Kegan Paul, Trench, Trübner, 1897.

Ellis, William Ashton. *Richard Wagner's prose works: Vol. 7, In Paris and Dresden.* Edited and translated by William Ashton Ellis. London: Kegan Paul, Trench, Trübner, 1898.

Ellis, William Ashton. *Richard Wagner's prose works: Vol. 8, Posthumous.* Edited and translated by William Ashton Ellis. London: Kegan Paul, Trench, Trübner, 1899.

Elterlein, Ernst von. *Beethoven's pianoforte sonatas: explained for the lovers of the musical art.* London: W. Reeves, 1898.

Engel, Carl. *Musical myths and facts.* London: Novello, Ewer & Co.; New York: J.L. Peters, 1876.

Eosze, László. *Zoltán Kodály: his life and work.* London: Collet's, 1962.

Etter, Brian K. *From classicism to modernism: Western musical culture and the metaphysics of order.* Aldershot: Ashgate, 2001.

Ewen, David. *From Bach to Stravinsky: the history of music by its foremost critics.* New York,

Greenwood Press, 1968.

Ewen, David. *Romain Rolland's Essays on music.* New York: Dover Publications, 1959.

Fay, Amy. *Music-study in Germany: from the home correspondence of Amy Fay.* New York: Dover Publications, 1965.

Fenby, Eric. *Delius as I knew him.* London: Quality Press, 1936.

Ferguson, Donald Nivison. *Masterworks of the orchestral repertoire: a guide for listeners.* Minneapolis: University of Minnesota Press, 1954.

Fétis, François-Joseph. *Curiosités historiques de la musique: complément nécessaire de la Musique mise à la portée de tout le monde.* Paris: Janet et Cotelle, 1830.

Fifield, Christopher. *Max Bruch: his life and works.* London: Gollancz, 1988.

Fifield, Christopher. *True artist and true friend: a biography of Hans Richter.* Oxford: Clarendon Press, 1993.

Finson, Jon and R. Larry Todd, Editors. *Mendelssohn and Schumann: essays on their music and its context.* Durham, N.C.: Duke University Press, 1984.

Fischer, Edwin. *Beethoven's pianoforte sonatas: a guide for students & amateurs.* London: Faber and Faber, 1959.

Fischer, Edwin. *Reflections on music.* London: Williams and Norgate, 1951.

Fischer, Hans Conrad and Erich Kock. *Ludwig van Beethoven: a study in text and pictures.* London: Macmillan; New York, St. Martin's Press, 1972.

Fischmann, Zdenka E. Janáček-

Newmarch correspondence. 1st limited and numbered edition. Rockville, MD: Kabel Publishers, 1986.

Fitzlyon, April. *Maria Malibran: diva of the romantic age.* London: Souvenir Press, 1987.

FitzLyon, April. *The price of genius: a life of Pauline Viardot.* London: John Calder, 1964.

Forbes, Elliot, Editor. *Thayer's life of Beethoven.* Princeton, New Jersey: Princeton University Press, 1967.

Foreman, Lewis. *Bax: a composer and his times.* London: Scolar Press, 1983.

Foreman, Lewis, Editor. *Farewell, my youth, and other writings by Arnold Bax.* Aldershot: Scolar Press, 1992.

Foster, Myles Birket. *History of the Philharmonic Society of London, 1813–1912: a record of a hundred years' work in the cause of music.* London: Bodley Head, 1912.

Foulds, John. *Music today: its heritage from the past, and legacy to the future.* London: I. Nicholson and Watson, limited, 1934.

Frank, Mortimer H. *Arturo Toscanini: the NBC years.* Portland, Oregon: Amadeus Press, 2002.

Fraser, Andrew Alastair. *Essays on music.* London: Oxford University Press, H. Milford, 1930.

Frohlich, Martha. *Beethoven's Appassionata' sonata.* Oxford: Clarendon Press, 1991.

Gal, Hans. *The golden age of Vienna.* London: Max Parrish & Co. Limited, 1948.

Gal, Hans. *The musician's world: great composers in their letters.*

London: Thames and Hudson, 1965.

Galatopoulos, Stelios. *Bellini: life, times, music*. London: Sanctuary, 2002.

Garden, Edward and Nigel Gottrei, Editors. *'To my best friend': correspondence between Tchaikovsky and Nadezhda von Meck, 1876–1878*. Oxford: Clarendon Press, 1993.

Geck, Martin. Beethoven. London: Haus, 2003.

Gerig, Reginald. *Famous pianists & their technique*. Washington: R. B. Luce, 1974.

Gilliam, Bryan. *The life of Richard Strauss*. Cambridge: Cambridge University Press, 1999.

Gilliam, Bryan, Editor. *Richard Strauss and his world*. Princeton, New Jersey: Princeton University Press, 1992.

Gillies, Malcolm and Bruce Clunies Ross, Editors. *Grainger on music*. Oxford; New York: Oxford University Press, 1999.

Gillies, Malcolm and David Pear, Editors. *The all-round man: selected letters of Percy Grainger, 1914–1961*. Oxford: Clarendon Press, 1994.

Gillies, Malcolm, Editor. *The Bartók companion*. London: Faber and Faber, 1993.

Gillmor, Alan M. *Erik Satie*. Basingstoke: Macmillan Press, 1988.

Glehn, M. E. *Goethe and Mendelssohn : (1821–1831)*. London: Macmillan, 1874.

Glowacki, John, Editor. *Paul A. Pisk: Essays in his honor*. Austin, Texas: University of Texas, 1966

Gollancz, Victor. *Journey towards music: a memoir*. London: Victor Gollancz Ltd., 1964.

Good, Edwin Marshall. *Giraffes, black dragons, and other pianos: a technological history from Cristofori to the modern concert grand*. Stanford, California: Stanford University Press, 1982.

Gordon, David. *Musical visitors to Britain*. London: Routledge, 2005.

Gordon, Stewart. *A history of keyboard literature: music for the piano and its forerunners*. Schirmer Books: New York: London : Prentice Hall International, 1996.

Gorrell, Lorraine. *The nineteenth-century German lied*. Portland, Oregon: Amadeus Press, 1993.

Goss, Glenda D. *Jean Sibelius: the Hämeenlinna letters: scenes from a musical life, 1875–1895*. Esbo, Finland: Schildts, 1997.

Goss, Madeleine. *Bolero: the life of Maurice Ravel*. New York: Tudor, 1945.

Gotch, Rosamund Brunel, Editor. *Mendelssohn and his friends in Kensington: letters from Fanny and Sophy Horsley, written 1833–36*. London: Oxford University Press, 1938.

Gounod, Charles. *Charles Gounod; autobiographical reminiscences: with family letters and notes on music; from the French*. London: William Heinemann, 1896.

Grabs, Manfred, Editor. *Hanns Eisler: a rebel in music; selected writings*. Berlin: Seven Seas Publishers, 1978.

Grace, Harvey. *A musician at large*. London: Oxford University Press, H. Milford, 1928.

(La) Grange, Henry-Louis de. *Gustav*

Mahler. Oxford: Oxford University Press, 1995.

Graves, Charles L. *Hubert Parry: his life and works*. London: Macmillan, 1926.

Graves, Charles L. *Post-Victorian music: with other studies and sketches*. London: Macmillan and Co., limited, 1911.

Graves, Charles L. *The life & letters of Sir George Grove, Hon. D.C.L. (Durham), Hon. LL.D. (Glasgow), formerly director of the Royal college of music*. London: Macmillan and Co., Ltd.; New York: The Macmillan Co., 1903.

Gray, Cecil. *Musical chairs, or, between two stools: being the life and memoirs of Cecil Gray*. London: Home & Van Thal, 1948.

Gregor-Dellin and Dietrich Mack, Editors. *Cosima Wagner's diaries.: Vol. 1, 1869 - 1877*. London: Collins, 1978-1980.

Griffiths, Paul. *Modern music: the avant-garde since 1945*. London: J. M. Dent & Sons Ltd., 1981.

Griffiths, Paul. *Olivier Messiaen and the music of time*. London: Faber and Faber, 1985.

Griffiths, Paul. *Peter Maxwell Davies*. London: Robson Books, 1988.

Griffiths, Paul. *The sea on fire: Jean Barraqué*. Rochester, New York: Woodbridge: University of Rochester Press, 2003.

Griffiths, Paul. *The string quartet*. London: Thames and Hudson, 1983.

Grout, Donald Jay and Claude V. Palisca, Editors. *A history of Western music*. London: J. M. Dent, 1988.

Grove, George. *Beethoven and his nine symphonies*. London: Novello, Ewer, 1896.

Grover, Ralph Scott. *Ernest Chausson: the man and his music*. London: The Athlone Press, 1980.

Grover, Ralph Scott. *The music of Edmund Rubbra*. Aldershot: Scolar Press, 1993.

Grun, Bernard. *Alban Berg: letters to his wife*. Edited and translated by Bernard Grun. London: Faber and Faber, 1971.

Gutman, David. *Prokofiev*. London: Omnibus Press, 1990.

Hadow, William Henry. *Collected essays*. London: H. Milford at the Oxford University Press, 1928.

Hadow, William Henry. *Beethoven's Op. 18 Quartets*. London: H. Milford at the Oxford University Press, 1926.

Haggin, Bernard H. *Music observed*. New York: Oxford University Press, 1964.

Hailey, Christopher. *Franz Schreker, 1878–1934: a cultural biography*. Cambridge: Cambridge University Press, 1993.

Hall, Michael. *Leaving home: a conducted tour of twentieth-century music with Simon Rattle*. London: Faber and Faber, 1996.

Hall, Patricia and Friedemann Sallis, Editors. (Brief Description): *A handbook to twentieth-century musical sketches*. Cambridge: Cambridge University Press, 2004.

Hallé, C. E. *Life and letters of Sir Charles Hallé: being an autobiography (1819–1860) with correspondence and diaries*. London: Smith, Elder & Co., 1896.

Halstead, Jill. *The woman composer:*

creativity and the gendered politics of musical composition. Aldershot: Ashgate, 1997.

Hamburger, Michael, Editor and Translator. *Beethoven letters, journals, and conversations.* New York: Thames and Hudson, 1951.

Hammelmann, Hanns A. and Ewald Osers. *The correspondence between Richard Strauss and Hugo von Hofmannsthal.* London: Collins, 1961.

Hanson, Lawrence and Elisabeth Hanson. *Tchaikovsky: the man behind the music.* New York: Dodd, Mead & Co, 1967.

Harding, James. *Massenet.* London: J. M. Dent & Sons Ltd., 1970.

Harding, James. *Saint-Saëns and his circle.* London: Chapman & Hall, 1965.

Harding, Rosamond E. M. *Origins of musical time and expression.* London: Oxford University Press, 1938.

Harman, Alec with Anthony Milner and Wilfrid Mellers. *Man and his music: the story of musical experience in the West.* London: Barrie & Jenkins, 1988.

Harper, Nancy Lee. *Manuel de Falla: his life and music.* Lanham, Maryland; London: The Scarecrow Press, 2005.

Hartmann, Arthur. *'Claude Debussy as I knew him' and other writings of Arthur Hartmann.* Edited by Samuel Hsu, Sidney Grolnic, and Mark Peters. Rochester, New York; Woodbridge: University of Rochester Press, 2003.

Haugen, Einar and Camilla Cai. *Ole Bull: Norway's romantic musician and cosmopolitan patriot.* Madison: The University of Wisconsin Press, 1993.

Headington, Christopher. *The Bodley Head history of Western music.* London: The Bodley Head, 1974.

Heartz, Daniel. *Music in European capitals: the galant style, 1720–1780.* New York; London: W. W. Norton, 2003.

Hedley, Arthur, Editor. *Selected correspondence of Fryderyk Chopin: abridged from Fryderyk Chopin's correspondence.* London: Heinemann, 1962.

Heiles, Anne Mischakoff. *Mischa Mischakoff: journeys of a concertmaster.* Sterling Heights, Michigan: Harmonie Park Press, 2006.

Henderson, Sanya Shoilevska. *Alex North, film composer: a biography, with musical analyses of a Streetcar named desire, Spartacus, The misfits, Under the volcano, and Prizzi's honor.* Jefferson, N.C.; London: McFarland, 2003.

Henschel, George. *Personal recollections of Johannes Brahms: some of his letters to and pages from a journal kept by George Henschel.* Boston: R G. Badger, 1907.

Henze, Hans Werner. *Bohemian fifths: an autobiography.* London: Faber and Faber, 1998.

Henze, Hans Werner. *Music and politics: collected writings 1953–81.* London: Faber and Faber, 1982.

Herbert, May, Translator. *Early letters of Robert Schumann.* London: George Bell and Sons, 1888.

Heyman, Barbara B. *Samuel Barber: the composer and his music.*

New York: Oxford University Press, 1992.

Heyworth, Peter. *Otto Klemperer, his life and times.* Cambridge: Cambridge University Press, 2 Vols. 1983–1996.

Hildebrandt, Dieter. *Pianoforte: a social history of the piano.* London: Hutchinson, 1988.

Hill, Peter. *The Messiaen companion.* London: Faber and Faber, 1995.

Hill, Peter and Nigel Simeone. *Messiaen.* New Haven Connecticut; London: Yale University Press, 2005.

Hiller, Ferdinand. *Mendelssohn: Letters and recollections.* New York: Vienna House, 1972.

Hines, Robert Stephan. *The orchestral composer's point of view: essays on twentieth-century music by those who wrote it.* Norman: University of Oklahoma Press, 1970.

Ho, Allan B. *Shostakovich reconsidered.* London: Toccata Press, 1998.

Hodeir, André. *Since Debussy: a view of contemporary music.* New York: Da Capo Press, 1975.

Holmes, Edward. *The life of Mozart: including his correspondence.* London: Chapman and Hall, 1845.

Holmes, John L. *Composers on composers.* New York: Greenwood Press, 1990.

Hopkins, Anthony. *The concertgoer's companion.* London: J.M. Dent & Sons Ltd., 1984.

Hopkins, Anthony. *The seven concertos of Beethoven.* Aldershot: Scolar Press, 1996.

Holt, Richard. *Nicolas Medtner (1879–1951): a tribute to his art and personality.* London: D. Dobson, 1955.

Honegger, Arthur. *I am a composer.* London: Faber and Faber, 1966.

Hoover, Kathleen and John Cage. *Virgil Thomson: his life and music.* New York; London: T. Yoseloff, 1959.

Horgan, Paul. *Encounters with Stravinsky: a personal record.* London: The Bodley Head, 1972.

Horowitz, Joseph. *Conversations with Arrau.* London: Collins, 1982.

Horowitz, Joseph. Understanding Toscanini. London: Faber and Faber, 1987.

Horwood, Wally. *Adolphe Sax, 1814–1894: his life and legacy.* Bramley: Bramley Books, 1980.

Howie, Crawford. *Anton Bruckner: a documentary biography.* Lewiston, N.Y.; Lampeter: Edwin Mellen Press, 2002.

Hueffer, Francis. *Correspondence of Wagner and Liszt.* New York: Greenwood Press, 2 Vols.1969.

Hughes, Spike. *The Toscanini legacy: a critical study of Arturo Toscanini's performances of Beethoven, Verdi, and other composers.* London: Putnam, 1959.

Hullah, Annette. *Theodor Leschetizky.* London and New York: J. Land & Co., 1906.

Le Huray, Peter and James Day, Editors. *Music and aesthetics in the eighteenth and early-nineteenth centuries.* Cambridge: Cambridge University Press, 1988.

D' Indy, Vincent. *César Franck.* New York: Dover Publications, 1965.

Jacobs, Arthur. *Arthur Sullivan: A Victorian musician.* Aldershot:

Scolar Press, 1992.

Jahn, Otto. *Life of Mozart.* London: Novello, Ewer & Co., 1882.

Jefferson, Alan. *Sir Thomas Beecham: a centenary tribute.* London: World Records Ltd., 1979.

Jezic, Diane. *The musical migration and Ernst Toch.* Ames: Iowa State University Press, 1989.

Johnson, Douglas Porter, Editor. *The Beethoven sketchbooks: history, reconstruction, inventory.* Oxford: Clarendon, 1985.

Johnson, Stephen. *Bruckner remembered.* London: Faber and Faber, 1998.

Jones, David, Wyn. *Beethoven: Pastoral symphony.* Cambridge: Cambridge University Press, 1995.

Jones, David Wyn. *The life of Beethoven.* Cambridge: Cambridge University Press, 1998.

Jones, David Wyn. *The symphony in Beethoven's Vienna.* Cambridge: Cambridge University Press, 2006.

Jones, J. Barrie, Editor. *Gabriel Fauré: a life in letters.* London: Batsford, 1989.

Jones, Peter Ward, Editor and Translator. *The Mendelssohns on honeymoon: the 1837 diary of Felix and Cécile Mendelssohn Bartholdy, together with letters to their families.* Oxford: Clarendon Press, 1997.

Jones, Timothy. *Beethoven, the Moonlight and other sonatas, Op. 27 and Op. 31.* Cambridge; New York, N.Y.: Cambridge University Press, 1999.

Kalischer, A. C., Editor. *Beethoven's letters: a critical edition.* London: J. M. Dent, 1909.

Kárpáti, János. *Bartók's chamber music.* Stuyvesant, New York: Pendragon Press, 1994.

Keefe, Simon P. *The Cambridge companion to the concerto.* Cambridge, New York, N.Y.: Cambridge University Press, 2005.

Keller, Hans. *The great Haydn quartets: their interpretation.* London: J. M. Dent, 1986.

Keller, Hans, Editor. *The memoirs of Carl Flesch.* New York: Macmillan, 1958.

Keller, Hans, and Christopher Wintle. *Beethoven's string quartets in F minor, Op. 95 and C minor, Op. 131: two studies.* Nottingham: Department of Music, University of Nottingham, 1995.

Kelly, Thomas Forrest. *First nights at the opera: five musical premiers.* New Haven: Yale University Press, 2004.

Kennedy, Michael. *Adrian Boult.* London: Hamish Hamilton, 1987.

Kennedy, Michael. *Barbirolli, conductor laureate: the authorised biography.* London: Hart-Davis, MacGibbon, 1973.

Kennedy, Michael, Editor. *The autobiography of Charles Hallé; with correspondence and diaries.* London: Paul Elek, 1972.

Kennedy, Michael. *Hallé tradition: a century of music.* Manchester: Manchester University Press, 1960.

Kennedy, Michael. *The works of Ralph Vaughan Williams.* London: Oxford University Press, 1964.

Kemp, Ian. *Tippett: the composer and his music.* London; New York: Eulenburg Books, 1984.

Kerman, Joseph. *The Beethoven*

quartets. London: Oxford University Press, 1967, c1966.

Kerman, Joseph. *Write all these down: essays on music*. Berkeley, California; London: University of California Press, 1994.

Kildea, Paul, Editor. *Britten on music*. Oxford: Oxford University Press, 2003.

Kinderman, William. *Beethoven*. Oxford: Oxford University Press, 1997.

Kinderman, William. *Beethoven's Diabelli variations*. Oxford: Clarendon Press; New York: Oxford University Press, 1987.

Kinderman, William, Editor. *The string quartets of Beethoven*. Urbana, Ilinois: University of Illinois Press, 2005.

King, Alec Hyatt. *Musical pursuits: selected essays*. London: British Library, 1987.

Kirby, F. E. *Music for piano: a short history*. Amadeus Press: Portland, 1995.

Kirkpatrick, John, Editor. *Charles E. Ives: Memos*. New York: W.W. Norton, 1972.

Knapp, Raymond. *Brahms and the challenge of the symphony*. Stuyvesant, N.Y.: Pendragon Press, c.1997.

Knight, Frida. *Cambridge music: from the Middle Ages to modern times*. Cambridge, England.: New York: Oleander Press, 1980.

Knight, Max, Translator. *A confidential matter: the letters of Richard Strauss and Stefan Zweig, 1931–1935*. Berkeley; London: University of California Press, 1977.

Kok, Alexander. *A voice in the dark: the philharmonia years*. Ample-

forth: Emerson Edition, 2002.

Kopelson, Kevin. *Beethoven's kiss: pianism, perversion, and the mastery of desire*. Stanford, California: Stanford University Press, 1996.

Kostelanetz, Richard, Editor. *Aaron Copland: a reader; selected writings 1923–1972*. New York; London: Routledge, 2003.

Kostelanetz, Richard. *Conversing with Cage*. New York; London: Routledge, 2003.

Kostelanetz, Richard. *On innovative musicians*. New York: Limelight Editions, 1989.

Kostelanetz, Richard, Editor. *Virgil Thomson: a reader ; selected writings, 1924–1984*. New York; London: Routledge, 2002.

Kowalke, Kim H. *Kurt Weill in Europe*. Ann Arbor, Michigan: UMI Research Press, 1979.

Krehbiel, Henry Edward. *The pianoforte and its music*. New York: Cooper Square Publishers, 1971.

Kruseman, Philip, Editor. *Beethoven's own words*. London: Hinrichsen Edition, 1948.

Kurtz, Michael. *Stockhausen: a biography*. London: Faber and Faber, 1992.

Lam, Basil. *Beethoven string quartets*. Seattle: University of Washington Press, 1975.

Lambert, Constant. *Music ho!: a study of music in decline*. London: Faber and Faber, Ltd. 1934.

Landon, H. C. Robbins. *Beethoven: a documentary study*. London: Thames and Hudson, 1970.

Landon, H. C. Robbins. *Beethoven: his life, work and world*. London: Thames and Hudson,

1992.

Landon, H. C. Robbins. *Essays on the Viennese classical style: Gluck, Haydn, Mozart, Beethoven.* London: Barrie & Rockliff The Cresset Press, 1970.

Landon, H. C. Robbins. *Haydn: chronicle and works/Haydn, the late years, 1801–1809.* Bloomington: Indiana University Press, 1977.

Landon, H. C. Robbins. *Haydn: his life and music.* London: Thames and Hudson, 1988.

Landon, H. C. Robbins. *Haydn in England, 1791–1795.* London: Thames and Hudson, 1976.

Landon, H. C. Robbins. *Haydn: the years of 'The creation', 1796–800.* London: Thames and Hudson, 1977.

Landon, H. C. Robbins. *Mozart: the golden years, 1781–1791.* New York: Schirmer Books, 1989.

Landon, H. C. Robbins. *1791, Mozart's last year.* London: Thames and Hudson, 1988.

Landon, H. C. Robbins *The collected correspondence and London notebooks of Joseph Haydn.* London: Barrie and Rockliff, 1959.

Landon, H. C. Robbins: Editor. *The Mozart companion. London: Faber, 1956.*

Landowska, Wanda. *Music of the past.* London: Geoffrey Bles, 1926.

Lang, Paul Henry. *Musicology and performance.* New Haven: Yale University Press, 1997.

Lang, Paul Henry. *The creative world of Beethoven.* New York: W. W. Norton 1971.

Laurence, Dan H., Editor. *Shaw's music: the complete musical criticism in three volumes.* London: Max Reinhardt, the Bodley Head, 1981.

Lawford-Hinrichsen, Irene. *Music publishing and patronage: C. F. Peters, 1800 to the Holocaust.* Kenton: Edition Press, 2000.

Layton, Robert, Editor. *A guide to the concerto.* Oxford: Oxford University Press, 1996.

Layton, Robert, Editor. *A guide to the symphony.* Oxford: Oxford University Press, 1995.

Lebrecht, Norman. *The maestro myth: great conductors in pursuit of power.* London: Simon & Schuster, 1991.

Lee, Ernest Markham. *The story of the symphony.* London: Scott Publishing Co., 1916.

Leibowitz, Herbert A., Editor. *Musical impressions: selections from Paul Rosenfeld's criticism.* London: G. Allen & Unwin, 1970.

Lenrow, Elbert, Editor and Translator. *The letters of Richard Wagner to Anton Pusinelli.* New York: Vienna House, 1972.

Leonard, Maurice. *Kathleen: the life of Kathleen Ferrier: 1912–1953.* London: Hutchinson, 1988.

Lesure, François and Roger Nichols, Editors. *Debussy, letters.* London: Faber and Faber, 1987.

Letellier, Robert Ignatius, Editor and Translator. *The diaries of Giacomo Meyerbeer.* Madison: Fairleigh Dickinson University Press; London: Associated University Presses, 4 Vols., 1999–2004.

Levas, Santeri. *Sibelius: a personal portrait.* London: J. M. Dent, 1972.

Levy, Alan Howard. *Edward Mac-*

Dowell, an American master. Lanham, Md. & London: Scarecrow Press, 1998.

Levy, David Benjamin. *Beethoven: the Ninth Symphony.* New Haven, Connecticut; London: Yale University Press, 2003.

Leyda, Jay and Sergi Bertensson. *The Musorgsky reader: a life of Modeste Petrovich Musorgsky in letters and documents.* New York: W.W. Norton, 1947.

Lewis, Thomas P., Editor. *Raymond Leppard on music: an anthology of critical and personal writings.* White Plains, N.Y.: Pro/Am Music Resources, 1993.

Liébert, Georges. *Nietzsche and music.* Chicago: University of Chicago Press, 2004.

Liszt, Franz. *An artist's journey: lettres d'un bachelier ès musique, 1835–1841.* Chicago: University of Chicago Press, 1989.

Litzmann, Berthold, Editor. *Clara Schumann: an artist's life, based on material found in diaries and letters.* London: Macmillan; Leipzig: Breitkopf & Härtel, 2 Vols. 1913.

Litzmann, Berthold, Editor. *Letters of Clara Schumann and Johannes Brahms, 1853–1896. New York, Vienna House. 2 Vols.* 1971.

Lloyd, Stephen. *William Walton: muse of fire.* Woodbridge, Suffolk: The Boydell Press, 2001.

Locke, Ralph P. and Cyrilla Barr, Editors. *Cultivating music in America: women patrons and activists since 1860.* Berkeley: University of California Press, 1997.

Lockspeiser, Edward. *Debussy: his life and mind.* London: Cassell. 2 Vols. 1962–1965.

Lockspeiser, Edward. *The literary clef: an anthology of letters and writings by French composers.* London: J. Calder. 1958.

Lockwood, Lewis, Editor. *Beethoven essays: studies in honor of Elliot Forbes.* Cambridge, Massachusetts: Harvard University Department of Music: Distributed by Harvard University Press, 1984.

Lockwood, Lewis and Mark Kroll, Editors. *The Beethoven violin sonatas: history, criticism, performance.* Urbana: University of Illinois Press, 2004.

Loft, Abram. *Violin and keyboard: the duo repertoire.* New York: Grossman Publishers. 2 Vols. 1973.

Longyear, Rey Morgan. *Nineteenth-century romanticism in music.* Englewood Cliffs: Prentice-Hall, 1969.

Lowe, C. Egerton. *Beethoven's pianoforte sonatas: hints on their rendering, form, etc., with appendices on definition of sonata, music forms, ornaments, pianoforte pedals, and how to discover keys.* London: Novello, 1929.

Macdonald, Hugh, Editor. *Berlioz: Selected letters.* London: Faber and Faber, 1995.

Macdonald, Malcolm, Editor. *Havergal Brian on music: selections from his journalism: Volume One, British music.* London: Toccata Press, 1986.

MacDonald, Malcolm. *Varèse: astronomer in sound.* London: Kahn & Averill, 2003.

MacDowell, Edward. *Critical and*

*historical essays: lectures deliv-
ered at Columbia University.*
Edited by W. J. Baltzell.
London: Elkin; Boston: A.P.
Schmidt, 1912.

MacFarren, Walter. Memories: an
autobiography. London: Walter
Scott Publishing Co.,1905.

Mackenzie, Alexander Campbell. *A
musician's narrative.* London:
Cassell and company, Ltd, 1927.

McCarthy, Margaret William, Editor.
*More letters of Amy Fay: the
American years, 1879–1916.*
Detroit: Information Coordinators,
1986.

McClary, Susan. *Feminine endings:
music, gender, and sexuality.*
Minneapolis: University of Minnesota Press, 1991.

McClatchie, Stephen, Editor and
Translator. *The Mahler family
letters.* Oxford: Oxford University Press, 2006.

McVeigh, Simon. *Concert life in
London from Mozart to Haydn.*
Cambridge: Cambridge Univer-
sity Press, 1993.

Mahler, Alma. *Gustav Mahler: memories and letters.* Enlarged
edition revised and edited and
with and introduction by Donald
Mitchell. London: John Murray,
1968.

Mai, François Martin. *Diagnosing
genius: the life and death of
Beethoven.* Montreal; London:
McGill-Queen's University
Press, 2007.

Del Mar, Norman. *Orchestral variations: confusion and error in the
orchestral repertoire.* London:
Eulenburg, 1981.

Del Mar, Norman. *Richard Strauss:
a critical commentary on his life
and works.* London: Barrie &

Jenkins. 3 Vols. 1978.

(La) Mara [pseudonym]. *Letters of
Franz Liszt.* London: H. Grevel
& Co., 2 Vols. 1894.

Marek, George Richard. *Puccini.*
London: Cassell & Co., 1952.

Marek, George Richard. *Toscanini.*
London: Vision, 1976.

(De) Marliave, Joseph. *Beethoven's
quartets.* New York: Dover Publications (reprint), 1961.

Martin, George Whitney. *Verdi: his
music, life and times.* London:
Macmillan, 1965.

Martner, Knud, Editor. *Selected
letters of Gustav Mahler.*
London; Boston: Faber and
Faber, 1979.

Martyn, Barrie. *Nicolas Medtner: his
life and music.* Aldershot: Scolar
Press, 1995.

Martyn, Barrie. *Rachmaninoff: composer, pianist, conductor.* Aldershot: Scolar, 1990.

Massenet, Jules. *My recollections.*
Westport, Connecticut: Greenwood Press.1970.

Matheopoulos, Helena. *Maestro:
encounters with conductors of
today.* London: Hutchinson, 1982.

Matthews, Denis. *Beethoven.*
London: J. M. Dent, 1985.

Matthews, Denis. *Beethoven piano
sonatas.* London: British Broadcasting Corporation, 1967.

Matthews, Denis. *In pursuit of music.*
London: Victor Gollancz Ltd.,
1968.

Matthews, Denis. *Keyboard music.*
Newton Abbot: London David
& Charles, 1972.

Mellers, Wilfrid Howard. *Caliban
reborn: renewal in twentieth-century music.* London: Victor Gollancz, 1967.

Mellers, Wilfrid Howard. *The sonata*

principle (from c. 1750). London: Rockliff, 1957.

Mendelssohn Bartholdy. *Letters from Italy and Switzerland.* London: Longman, Green, Longman, and Roberts, 1862.

Mendelssohn Bartholdy, Paul. *Letters of Felix Mendelssohn Bartholdy, from 1833 to 1847.* London: Longman, Green, Longman, Roberts, & Green, 1864.

Menuhin, Yehudi and Curtis W. Davis. *The music of man.* London: Macdonald and Jane's, 1979.

Menuhin, Yehudi. *Theme and variations.* London: Heinemann Educational Books Ltd., 1972.

Menuhin, Yehudi. *Unfinished journey.* London: Macdonald and Jane's, 1977.

Messian, Olivier. *Music and color: conversations with Claude Samuel.* Portland, Oregon: Amadeus, 1994.

Miall, Anthony. *Musical bumps.* London: J.M. Dent & Sons Ltd, 1981.

Michotte, Edmond. *Richard Wagner's visit to Rossini (Paris 1860): and, An evening at Rossini's in Beau-Sejour (Passy), 1858.* Chicago; London: University of Chicago Press, 1982.

Mies, Paul. *Beethoven's sketches: an analysis of his style based on a study of his sketchbooks.* New York: Johnson Reprint, 1969.

Milhaud, Darius. *My happy life.* London: Boyars, 1995.

Miller, Mina. *The Nielsen companion.* London: Faber and Faber, 1994.

Milsom, David. *Theory and practice in late nineteenth-century violin performance: an examination of style in performance, 1850–1900.* Aldershot: Ashgate, 2003.

Mitchell, Donald, Editor. *Letters from a life: the selected letters and diaries of Benjamin Britten 1913–1976.* London: Faber and Faber. 3 Vols., 1991.

Mitchell, Donald and Hans Keller, Editors. *Music survey: new series 1949–1952.* London: Faber Music in association with Faber & Faber, 1981.

Mitchell, Jon C. *A comprehensive biography of composer Gustav Holst, with correspondence and diary excerpts: including his American years.* Lewiston, New York: Edwin Mellen Press, 2001.

Moldenhauer, Hans. *Anton von Webern: a chronicle of his life and work.* London: Victor Gollancz, 1978.

Monrad-Johansen. Edvard Grieg. New York: Tudor Publishing Co., 1945.

Moore, Gerald. *Am I too loud?: memoirs of an accompanist.* London: Hamish Hamilton, 1962.

Moore, Gerald. *Farewell recital: further memoirs.* Harmondsworth: Penguin Books, 1979.

Moore, Gerald. *Furthermoore: interludes in an accompanist's life.* London: Hamish Hamilton, 1983.

Moore, Jerrold Northrop. *Edward Elgar: a creative life.* Oxford: Oxford University Press, 1984.

Moore, Jerrold Northrop. *Elgar, Edward. The windflower letters: correspondence with Alice Caroline Stuart Wortley and her family.* Oxford: Clarendon Press; New York: Oxford University Press, 1989.

Moore, Jerrold Northrop. *Elgar, Edward. Edward Elgar: letters of a lifetime.* Oxford: Clarendon Press; New York: Oxford University Press, 1990.

Moore, Jerrold Northrop. *Elgar, Edward. Elgar and his publishers: letters of a creative life.* Oxford: Clarendon, 1987.

Moreux, Serge. *Béla Bartók.* London: Harvill Press, 1953.

Morgan, Kenneth. *Fritz Reiner, maestro and martinet.* Urbana: University of Illinois Press, 2005.

Cone, Edward T., Editor. *Music, a view from Delft: selected essays.* Chicago: University of Chicago Press, 1989.

Morgan, Robert P. *Twentieth-century music: a history of musical style in modern Europe and America.* New York: Norton, 1991.

Morgenstern, Sam., Editor. *Composers on music: an anthology of composers' writings.* London: Faber & Faber, 1956.

Morrow, Mary Sue. *Concert life in Haydn's Vienna: aspects of a developing musical and social institution.* Stuyvesant, New York: Pendragon Press, 1989.

Moscheles, Felix, Editor and Translator. *Letters from Felix Mendelssohn-Bartholdy to Ignaz and Charlotte Moscheles.* London: Trübner and Co., 1888.

Mudge, Richard B., Translator. *Glinka, Mikhail Ivanovich: Memoirs.* Norman: University of Oklahoma Press, 1963.

Munch, Charles. *I am a conductor.* New York: Oxford University Press, 1955.

Mundy, Simon. *Bernard Haitink: a working life.* London: Robson Books, 1987.

Musgrave, Michael. *The musical life of the Crystal Palace.* Cambridge: Cambridge University Press, 1995.

Music & Letters. *Beethoven: special number.* London: Music & Letters, 1927.

Musical Times. *Special Issue.* John A. Fuller-Maitland London: Vol. VIII, No. 2, 1927.

Myers, Rollo H., Editor. *Twentieth-century music.* London: Calder and Boyars, 1960.

National Gallery (Great Britain). *Music performed at the National Gallery concerts, 10th October 1939 to 10th April 1946.* London: Privately printed, 1948.

Nattiez, Jean-Jacques, Editor. *Orientations: collected writings — Pierre Boulez.* London: Faber and Faber, 1986.

Nauhaus, Gerd, Editor. *The marriage diaries of Robert & Clara Schumann.* London: Robson Books, 1994.

Nectoux, Jean Michel. *Gabriel Fauré: a musical life.* Translated by Roger Nichols. Cambridge: Cambridge University Press, 1991.

Nettl, Paul. *Beethoven handbook.* Westport, Connecticut: Greenwood Press, 1975.

Neumayr, Anton. *Music and medicine.* Bloomington, Illinois: Medi-Ed Press, 1994–1997

Newbould, Brian. *Schubert and the symphony: a new perspective.* Surbiton: Toccata Press, 1992.

Newlin, Dika. *Schoenberg remembered: diaries and recollections (1938–76).* New York: Pendragon Press, 1980.

Newman, Ernest. *From the world of*

music: essays from 'The Sunday Times'. London: J. Calder, 1956.

Newman, Ernest. Hugo Wolf. New York: Dover Publications, 1966.

Newman, Ernest, Annotated and Translated. Memoirs of Hector Berlioz from 1803 to 1865, comprising his travels in Germany, Italy, Russia, and England. New York: Knopf, 1932.

Newman, Ernest. More essays from the world of music: essays from the 'Sunday Times'. London: John Calder, 1958.

Newman, Ernest. Musical studies. London; New York: John Lane, 1910.

Newman, Ernest. Testament of music: essays and papers. London: Putnam, 1962.

Newman, Richard. Alma Rosé: Vienna to Auschwitz. Portland, Oregon: Amadeus Press, 2000.

Newman, William S. The sonata in the classic era. Chapel Hill: University of North Carolina Press 1963.

Newman, William S. The sonata in the Classic era. New York; London: W.W. Norton, 1983.

Newmarch, Rosa Harriet. Henry J. Wood. London & New York: John Lane, 1904.

Nicholas, Jeremy. Godowsky: the pianists' pianist; a biography of Leopold Godowsky. Hexham: Appian Publications & Recordings, 1989.

Nichols, Roger. Debussy remembered. London: Faber and Faber, 1992.

Nichols, Roger. Mendelssohn remembered. London: Faber and Faber, 1997.

Nichols, Roger. Ravel remembered.

London: Faber and Faber, 1987.

Niecks, Frederick. Robert Schumann. London: J. M. Dent, 1925.

Nielsen, Carl. Living music. Copenhagen, Wilhelm Hansen, 1968.

Nielsen, Carl. My childhood. Copenhagen, Wilhelm Hansen, 1972.

Nikolska, Irina. Conversations with Witold Lutoslawski, (1987–92). Stockholm: Melos, 1994.

Nohl, Ludwig. Beethoven depicted by his contemporaries. London: Reeves, 1880.

De Nora, Tia. Beethoven and the construction of genius: musical politics in Vienna, 1792–1803. Berkeley: University of California Press, 1997.

Norton, Spencer, Editor and Translator. Music in my time: the memoirs of Alfredo Casella. Norman: University of Oklahoma Press, 1955.

Nottebohm, Gustav. Two Beethoven sketchbooks: a description with musical extracts. London: Gollancz, 1979.

Oakeley, Edward Murray. The life of Sir Herbert Stanley Oakeley. London: George Allen, 1904.

Lucas, Brenda and Michael Kerr. Virtuoso: the story of John Ogdon. London: H. Hamilton, 1981.

Oliver, Michael, Editor. Settling the score: a journey through the music of the twentieth century. London: Faber and Faber, 1999.

Olleson, Philip. Samuel Wesley: the man and his music. Woodbridge: Boydell Press, 2003.

Olleson, Philip, Editor. The letters of Samuel Wesley: professional and social correspondence,

1797–1837. Oxford; New York: Oxford University Press, 2001.

Olmstead, Andrea. *Conversations with Roger Sessions.* Boston: Northeastern University Press, 1987.

Orenstein, Arbie, Editor. *A Ravel reader: correspondence, articles, interviews.* New York: Columbia University Press, 1990.

Orenstein, Arbie. *Ravel: man and musician.* New York: Columbia University Press, 1975.

Orledge, Robert. *Charles Koechlin (1867–1950): his life and works.* New York: Harwood Academic Publishers, 1989.

Orledge, Robert. *Gabriel Fauré.* London: Eulenburg Books, 1979.

Orledge, Robert. *Satie remembered.* London: Faber and Faber, 1995.

Orledge, Robert. *Satie the composer.* Cambridge: Cambridge University Press, 1990.

Orlova, Alexandra. *Glinka's life in music: a chronicle.* Ann Arbor: UMI Research Press, 1988.

Orlova, Alexandra. *Musorgsky's days and works: a biography in documents.* Ann Arbor: UMI Research Press, 1983.

Orlova, Alexandra. *Tchaikovsky: a self-portrait.* Oxford: Oxford University Press, 1990.

Osborne, Charles, Editor and Translator. *Letters of Giuseppe Verdi.* London: Victor Gollancz, 1971.

Osmond-Smith David, Editor and Translator. *Luciano Berio: Two interviews with Rossana Dalmonte and Bálint András Varga.* New York; London: Boyars, 1985.

Ouellette, Fernand. *Edgard Varèse.* London: Calder & Boyars, 1973.

Paderewski, Ignacy Jan and Mary Lawton. *The Paderewski memoirs.* London: Collins, 1939.

Page, Tim: Editor. *The Glenn Gould reader.* London: Faber and Faber, 1987.

Page, Tim. *Music from the road: views and reviews, 1978–1992.* New York; Oxford: Oxford University Press, 1992.

Page, Tim and Vanessa Weeks, Editors. *Selected letters of Virgil Thomson.* New York: Summit Books, 1988.

Page, Tim. *Tim Page on music: views and reviews.* Portland, Oregon: Amadeus Press, 2002.

Palmer, Christopher. *Herbert Howells, (1892–1983): a celebration.* London: Thames, 1996.

Palmer, Christopher, Editor. *Sergei Prokofiev: Soviet diary 1927 and other writings.* London: Faber and Faber, 1991.

Palmer, Fiona M. *Domenico Dragonetti in England (1794–1846): the career of a double bass virtuoso.* Oxford: Clarendon, 1997.

Palmieri, Robert, Editor. *Encyclopedia of the piano.* New York: Garland, 1996.

Panufnik, Andrzej. *Composing myself.* London: Methuen, 1987.

Parsons, James, Editor. *The Cambridge companion to the Lied.* Cambridge: Cambridge University Press, 2004.

Paynter, John, Editor. *Between old worlds and new: occasional writings on music by Wilfrid Mellers.* London: Cygnus Arts, 1997.

Pestelli, Giorgio. *The age of Mozart and Beethoven.* Cambridge: Cambridge University Press,

1984.

Peyser, Joan. *Bernstein: a biography: revised & updated.* New York: Billboard Books, 1998.

Phillips-Matz, Mary Jane. *Verdi: a biography.* Oxford: Oxford University Press, 1993.

Piggott, Patrick. *The life and music of John Field, 1782–1837: creator of the nocturne.* London: Faber and Faber, 1973.

Plantinga, Leon. *Beethoven's concertos: history, style, performance.* New York: Norton, 1999.

Plantinga, Leon. *Clementi: his life and music.* London: Oxford University Press, 1977.

Plantinga, Leon. *Romantic music: a history of musical style in nineteenth-century Europe.* New York; London: Norton, 1984.

Plaskin, Glenn. *Horowitz: a biography of Vladimir Horowitz.* London: Macdonald, 1983.

Pleasants, Henry, Editor and Translator. *Hanslick, Eduard: Music criticisms, 1846–99.* Baltimore: Penguin Books, 1963.

Pleasants, Henry, Editor and Translator. *Hanslick's music criticisms.* New York: Dover Publications, 1988.

Pleasants, Henry, Editor and Translator. *The music criticism of Hugo Wolf.* New York: Holmes & Meier Publishers, 1978.

Pleasants, Henry, Editor and Translator. *The musical journeys of Louis Spohr.* Norman: University of Oklahoma Press, 1961.

Pollack, Howard. *Aaron Copland: the life and work of an uncommon man.* New York: Henry Holt, 1999.

Poulenc, Francis. *My friends and myself.* London: Dennis Dobson, 1978.

Powell, Richard, Mrs. *Edward Elgar: memories of a variation.* Aldershot, Hants, England: Scolar Press; Brookfield, Vermont, USA: Ashgate Publishing. Co., 1994.

Poznansky, Alexander, Editor. *Tchaikovsky through others' eyes.* Bloomington: Indiana University Press, 1999.

Praeger, Ferdinand. *Wagner as I knew him.* London; New York: Longmans, Green, 1892.

Previn, Andre. *Anthony Hopkins. Music face to face.* London, Hamish Hamilton, 1971.

Prieberg, Fred K. *Trial of strength: Wilhelm Furtwängler and the Third Reich.* London: Quartet, 1991.

Procter-Gregg, Humphrey. *Beecham remembered.* London: Duckworth, 1976.

Prokofiev, Sergey. *Prokofiev by Prokofiev: a composer's memoir.* London: Macdonald and Jane's, 1979.

Rachmaninoff, Sergei. *Rachmaninoff's recollections told to Oskar von Riesemann.* London: George Allen & Unwin, 1934.

Radcliffe, Philip. *Beethoven's string quartets.* Cambridge: Cambridge University Press, 1978.

Radcliffe, Philip. *Piano Music in: The Age of Beethoven, The New Oxford History of Music, Vol. VIII.* Gerald Abraham, (Editor), 1988, p. 340.

Ratner, Leonard G. *Romantic music: sound and syntax.* New York: Schirmer Books, 1992.

Raynor, Henry. *A social history of music: from the middle ages to Beethoven.* London: Barrie &

Jenkins, 1972.

Rees, Brian. *Camille Saint-Saëns: a life.* London: Chatto & Windus, 1999.

Reich, Willi, Editor. *Anton Webern: The path to the new music.* London; Bryn Mawr: Theodore Presser in association with Universal Edition, 1963.

Reid, Charles. *John Barbirolli: a biography.* London, Hamish Hamilton, 1971.

Reid, Charles. *Malcolm Sargent: a biography.* London: Hamilton, 1968.

Rennert, Jonathan. *William Crotch (1775–1847): composer, artist, teacher.* Lavenham: Terence Dalton, 1975.

Rice, John A. *Antonio Salieri and Viennese Opera.* Chicago, Illinois: University of Chicago Press, 1998.

Rice, John A. *Empress Marie Therese and music at the Viennese court, 1792–1807.* Cambridge: Cambridge University Press, 2003.

Richards, Fiona. *The Music of John Ireland.* Aldershot: Ashgate, 2000.

Rigby, Charles. *Sir Charles Hallé: a portrait for today.* Manchester: Dolphin Press, 1952.

Ringer, Alexander, Editor. *The early Romantic era: between Revolutions; 1789 and 1848.* Basingstoke: Macmillan, 1990.

Roberts, John P.L. and Ghyslaine Guertin, Editors. *Glenn Gould: Selected letters.* Toronto; Oxford: Oxford University Press, 1992.

Robertson, Alec. *More than music.* London: Collins, 1961.

Robinson, Harlow, Editor and Translator. *Selected letters of Sergei Prokofiev.* Boston: Northeastern University Press, 1998.

Robinson, Harlow. *Sergei Prokofiev: a biography.* London: Hale, 1987.

Robinson, Paul A. *Ludwig van Beethoven, Fidelio.* Cambridge: Cambridge University Press, 1996.

Robinson, Suzanne, Editor. *Michael Tippett: music and literature.* Aldershot: Ashgate, 2002.

Rochberg, George. *The aesthetics of survival: a composer's view of twentieth-century music.* Ann Arbor, Michigan: University of Michigan Press, 2004.

Rodmell, Paul. *Charles Villiers Stanford.* Aldershot: Ashgate, 2002.

Roeder, Michael Thomas. *A history of the concerto.* Portland, Oregon: Amadeus Press, 1994.

Rohr, Deborah Adams. *The careers of British musicians, 1750–1850: a profession of artisans.* Cambridge: Cambridge University Press, 2001.

Rolland, Romain. *Goethe and Beethoven.* New York; London: Blom, 1968.

Rolland, Romain. *Beethoven and Handel.* London: Waverley Book Co., 1917.

Rolland, Romain. *Beethoven the creator.* Garden City, New York: Garden City Pub., 1937.

Roscow, Gregory, Editor. *Bliss on music: selected writings of Arthur Bliss, 1920–1975.* Oxford: Oxford University Press, 1991.

Rosen, Charles. *Beethoven's piano sonatas: a short companion.* New Haven, Connecticut: London: Yale University Press,

2002.

Rosen, Charles. *Critical entertainments: music old and new.* Cambridge, Massachusetts; London: Harvard University Press, 2000.

Rosen, Charles. *The classical style: Haydn, Mozart, Beethoven.* London: Faber and Faber, 1976.

Rosen, Charles. *The romantic generation.* Cambridge, Massachusetts: Harvard University Press, 1995.

Rosenthal, Albi. *Obiter scripta: essays, lectures, articles, interviews and reviews on music, and other subjects.* Oxford: Offox Press; Lanham: Scarecrow Press, 2000.

Rostal, Max. *Beethoven: the sonatas for piano and violin; thoughts on their interpretation.* London: Toccata Press, 1985.

Rostropovich, Mstislav and Galina Vishnevskaya. *Russia, music, and liberty.* Portland, Oregan: Amadeus Press, 1995.

Rubinstein, Arthur. *My many years.* London: Jonathan Cape, 1980.

Rubinstein, Arthur. *My young years.* London: Jonathan Cape, 1973.

Rumph, Stephen C. *Beethoven after Napoleon: political romanticism in the late works.* Berkeley; London: University of California Press, 2004.

Rye, Matthew Rye. *Notes to the BBC Radio Three Beethoven Experience, Friday 10 June 2005,* www.bbc.co.uk/radio3/Beethoven.

Sachs, Harvey. *Toscanini.* London: Weidenfeld and Nicholson, 1978.

Sachs, Joel. *Kapellmeister Hummel in England and France.* Detroit: Information Coordinators, 1977.

Saffle, Michael, Editor. *Liszt and his world: proceedings of the International Liszt Conference held at Virginia Polytechnic Institute and State University, 20–23 May 1993.* Stuyvesant, New York: Pendragon Press, 1998.

Safránek, Milos. *Bohuslav Martinu, his life and works.* London: Allan Wingate, 1962.

Saint-Saëns, Camille. *Outspoken essays on music.* Westport, Connecticut: Greenwood Press, 1970.

Saussine, Renée de. *Paganini.* Westport, Connecticut: Greenwood Press, 1976.

Sayers, W. C. Berwick. *Samuel Coleridge-Taylor, musician: his life and letters.* London; New York: Cassell and Co., 1915.

Schaarwächter, Jürgen. *HB: aspects of Havergal Brian.* Aldershot: Ashgate, 1997.

Schafer, R. Murray. *E.T.A. Hoffmann and music.* Toronto: University of Toronto Press, 1975.

Schafer, R. Murray, Editor. *Ezra Pound and music: the complete criticism.* London: Faber and Faber, 1978.

Schat, Peter. *The tone clock.* Chur, Switzerland; Langhorne, Pa.: Harwood Academic Publishers, 1993.

Schenk, Erich. *Mozart and his times.* Edited and Translated by Richard and Clara Winstin. London: Secker & Warburg, 1960.

Schindler, Anton Felix. *Beethoven as I knew him.* Edited by Donald W. MacArdle and Translated by Constance S. Jolly from the German edition of 1860

London: Faber and Faber, 1966.

Schlosser, Johann. *Beethoven: the first biography, 1827*. Edited by Barry Cooper. Portland, Oregon: Amadeus Press, 1996.

Schnabel, Artur. *My life and music*. London: Longmans, 1961.

Schnittke, Alfred. *A Schnittke reader*. Bloomington: Indiana University Press, 2002.

Scholes, Percy Alfred. *Crotchets: a few short musical notes*. London: John Lane, 1924.

Schonberg, Harold C. *The great pianists*. London: Victor Gollancz, 1964.

Schrade, Leo. *Beethoven in France: the growth of an idea*. New Haven; London: Yale University Press, H. Milford, Oxford University Press, 1942.

Schrade, Leo. *Tragedy in the art of music*. Cambridge, Massachusetts: Harvard University Press, 1964.

Schuh, Willi. *Richard Strauss: a chronicle of the early years 1864–1898*. Cambridge: Cambridge University Press, 1982.

Schuh, Willi, Editor. *Richard Strauss: Recollections and reflections*. London; New York: Boosey & Hawkes, 1953.

Schuller, Gunther. *Musings: the musical worlds of Gunther Schuller*. New York: Oxford University Press, 1986.

Schumann, Robert. *Music and musicians: essays and criticisms*. London: William Reeves, 1877.

Schuttenhelm, Editor. *Selected letters of Michael Tippett*. London: Faber and Faber, 2005.

Schwartz, Elliott. *Music since 1945: issues, materials, and literature*. New York: Schirmer Books, 1993.

Scott, Marion M. *Beethoven: (The master musicians)*. London: Dent, 1940.

Scott-Sutherland, Colin. *Arnold Bax*. London: J. M. Dent, 1973.

Searle, Muriel V. *John Ireland: the man and his music*. Tunbridge Wells: Midas Books, 1979.

Secrest, Meryle. *Leonard Bernstein: a life*. London: Bloomsbury, 1995.

Seeger, Charles. *Studies in musicology II, 1929–1979*. Edited by Anne M. Pescatello. Berkeley; London: University of California Press, 1994.

Selden-Goth, Gisela, Editor. *Felix Mendelssohn: letters*. London: Paul Elek Publishers Ltd, 1946.

Senner, Wayne M., Robin Wallace and William Meredith, Editors. *The critical reception of Beethoven's compositions by his German contemporaries*. Lincoln: University of Nebraska Press, in association with the American Beethoven Society and the Ira F. Brilliant Center for Beethoven Studies, San José State University, 1999.

Seroff, Victor I. *Rachmaninoff*. London: Cassell & Company, 1951.

Sessions, Roger. *Questions about music*. Cambridge, Massachusetts: Harvard University Press, 1970.

Sessions, Roger. *The musical experience of composer, performer, listener*. New York: Atheneum, 1966, 1950.

Seyfried, Ignaz von. *Louis van Beethoven's Studies in thorough-bass, counterpoint and the art of scientific composition*. Leipzig;

New-York: Schuberth and Company, 1853.

Sharma, Bhesham R. *Music and culture in the age of mechanical reproduction.* New York: Peter Lang, 2000.

Shaw, Bernard. *How to become a musical critic.* London: R. Hart Davis, 1960.

Shaw, Bernard. *London music in 1888–89 as heard by Corno di Bassetto (later known as Bernard Shaw): with some further autobiographical particulars.* London: Constable and Company, 1937.

Shaw, Bernard. *Music in London, 1890–1894.* London: Constable and Company Limited, 3 Vols., 1932.

Shedlock, John South. *Beethoven's pianoforte sonatas: the origin and respective values of various readings.* London: Augener Ltd., 1918.

Shedlock, John South. *The pianoforte sonata: its origin and development.* London: Methuen, 1895.

Shepherd, Arthur. *The string quartets of Ludwig van Beethoven.* Cleveland: H. Carr, The Printing Press, 1935.

Sheppard, Leslie and Herbert R. Axelrod. *Paganini: containing a portfolio of drawings by Vido Polikarpus.* Neptune City, New Jersey: Paganiniana Publications, 1979.

Short, Michael. *Gustav Holst: the man and his music.* Oxford: Oxford University Press, 1990.

Shostakovich, Dmitry. *Dmitry Shostakovich: about himself and his times.* Moscow: Progress Publishers, 1981.

Simpson, John Palgrave. *Carl Maria von Weber: the life of an artist, from the German of his son Baron, Max Maria von Weber.* London: Chapman and Hall, 1865.

Simpson, Robert. *Beethoven symphonies.* London: British Broadcasting Corporation, 1970.

Sipe, Thomas. *Beethoven: Eroica symphony.* Cambridge: Cambridge University Press, 1998.

Sitwell, Sacheverell. *Mozart.* Edinburgh: Peter Davies Limited, 1932.

Skelton, Geoffrey. *Paul Hindemith: the man behind the music; a biography.* London: Victor Gollancz, 1975.

Smallman, Basil. *The piano trio: its history, technique, and repertoire.* Oxford: Clarendon Press; Oxford; New York: Oxford University Press, 1990.

Smidak, Emil. *Isaak-Ignaz Moscheles: the life of the composer and his encounters with Beethoven, Liszt, Chopin, and Mendelssohn.* Aldershot, Hampshire, England: Scolar Press; Brookfield, Vermont, USA: Gower Publishing Co., 1989.

Smith, Barry. *Peter Warlock: the life of Philip Heseltine.* Oxford: Oxford University Press, 1994.

Smith, Joan Allen. *Schoenberg and his circle: a Viennese portrait.* New York: Schirmer Books, London: Collier Macmillan, 1986.

Smith, Richard Langham, Editor. *Debussy on music: the critical writings of the great French composer Claude Debussy.* London: Secker & Warburg, 1977.

Smith, Ronald. *Alkan.* London: Kahn and Averill, 1976.

Snowman, Daniel. *The Amadeus*

Quartet: the men and the music. London: Robson Books, 1981.

Solomon, Maynard. *Beethoven.* New York: Schirmer, 1977.

Solomon, Maynard. *Beethoven essays.* Cambridge, Massachusetts; London: Harvard University Press, 1988.

Solomon, Maynard. *Late Beethoven: music, thought, imagination.* Berkeley; London: University of California Press, 2003.

Solomon, Maynard. *Mozart: a life.* London: Hutchinson, 1995.

Sonneck, Oscar George Theodore. *Beethoven: impressions of contemporaries.* London: Oxford University Press, 1927.

Spalding, Albert. *Rise to follow: an autobiography.* London: Frederick Muller Ltd., 1946.

Spohr, Louis. *Louis Spohr's autobiography.* London: Longman, Green, Longman, Roberts, & Green, 1865.

Stafford, William. *Mozart myths: a critical reassessment.* Stanford, California: Stanford University Press, 1991.

Stanford, Charles Villiers. *Interludes: records and reflections.* London: John Murray, 1922.

Stanley, Glen, Editor. *The Cambridge companion to Beethoven.* Cambridge; New York: Cambridge University Press, 2000

Stedman, Preston. *The symphony.* Englewood Cliffs, New Jersey; London: Prentice-Hall, 1979.

Stedron, Bohumír, Editor and Translator. *Leos Janácek: letters and reminiscences.* Prague: Artia, 1955.

Stein, Erwin, Editor. *Arnold Schoenberg: letters.* London: Faber and Faber, 1964.

Stein, Erwin. *Orpheus in new guises.* London: Rockliff, 1953.

Stein, Jack Madison. *Poem and music in the German lied from Gluck to Hugo Wolf.* Cambridge, Massachusetts: Harvard University Press, 1971.

Stein, Leonard, Editor. *Style and idea: selected writings of Arnold Schoenberg.* London: Faber and Faber, 1975.

Steinberg, Michael P. *Listening to reason: culture, subjectivity, and nineteenth-century music.* Princeton, New Jersey: Princeton University Press, 2004.

Steinberg, Michael. *The concerto: a listener's guide.* New York: Oxford University Press, 1998.

Steinberg, Michael. *The symphony: a listener's guide.* Oxford; New York: Oxford University Press, 1995.

Sternfeld, Frederick William. *Goethe and music: a list of parodies and Goethe's relationship to music; a list of references.* New York: Da Capo Press, 1979.

Stivender, David. *Mascagni: an autobiography compiled, edited and translated from original sources.* New York: Pro/Am Music Resources; London: Kahn & Averill, 1988.

Stone, Else and Kurt Stone, Editors. *The writings of Elliott Carter: an American composer looks at modern music.* Bloomington: Indiana University Press, 1977.

Stowell, Robin. *Beethoven: violin concerto.* Cambridge: Cambridge University Press, 1998.

Stowell, Robin: Editor. *The Cambridge companion to the cello.* Cambridge: Cambridge University Press, 1999.

Stowell, Robin: Editor. *The Cambridge companion to the string quartet.* Cambridge: Cambridge University Press, 2003.

Stratton, Stephen Samuel. *Mendelssohn.* London: J.M. Dent & Co.; New York: E.P. Dutton & Co., 1901.

Straus, Joseph N. *Remaking the past: musical modernism and the influence of the tonal tradition.* Cambridge, Massachusetts: Harvard University Press, 1990.

Stravinsky, Igor. *An autobiography.* London: Calder and Boyars, 1975.

Stravinsky, Igor. *Themes and conclusions.* London: Faber and Faber, 1972.

Stravinsky, Igor and Robert Craft. *Conversations with Igor Stravinsky.* London: Faber and Faber, 1959.

Stravinsky, Igor and Robert Craft. *Dialogues and a diary.* London: Faber and Faber 1968.

Stravinsky, Igor and Robert Craft. *Memories and commentaries.* London: Faber and Faber, 2002.

Strunk, Oliver. *Source readings in music history, 4: The Classic era.* London: Faber and Faber 1981.

Sullivan, Blair, Editor. *The echo of music: essays in honor of Marie Louise Göllner.* Warren, Michigan: Harmonie Park Press, 2004.

Sullivan, Jack, Editor. *Words on music: from Addison to Barzun.* Athens: Ohio University Press, 1990.

Symonette, Lys and Kim H. Kowalke, Editors and Translators. *Speak low (when you speak love): the letters of Kurt Weill and Lotte Lenya.* London:

Hamish Hamilton, 1996.

Swalin, Benjamin F. *The violin concerto: a study in German romanticism.* New York, Da Capo Press, 1973.

Szigeti, Joseph. *With strings attached: reminiscences and reflections.* London: Cassell & Co. Ltd, 1949.

Tanner, Michael, Editor. *Notebooks, 1924–1954: Wilhelm Furtwängler.* London: Quartet Books, 1989.

Taylor, Robert, Editor. *Furtwängler on music: essays and addresses.* Aldershot: Scolar, 1991.

Taylor, Ronald. *Kurt Weill: composer in a divided world.* London: Simon & Schuster, 1991.

Tchaikovsky, Peter Ilich. *Letters to his family: an autobiography.* Translated by Galina von Meck. London: Dennis Dobson, 1981.

Tertis, Lionel. *My viola and I: a complete autobiography; with, 'Beauty of tone in string playing', and other essays.* London: Paul Elek, 1974.

Thayer, Alexander Wheelock. *Salieri: rival of Mozart.* Edited by Theodore Albrecht. Kansas City, Missouri: Philharmonia of Greater Kansas City, 1989.

Thomas, Michael Tilson. *Viva voce: conversations with Edward Seckerson.* London: Faber and Faber 1994.

Thomson, Andrew. *Vincent d'Indy and his world.* Oxford: Clarendon Press, 1996.

Thomson, Virgil. *The musical scene.* New York: Greenwood Press, 1968.

Thomson, Virgil. *Virgil Thomson.* London: Weidenfeld & Nicolson, 1967.

Tillard, Françoise. *Fanny Mendelssohn*. Amadeus Press: Portland, 1996.

Tilmouth, Michael, Editor. *Donald Francis Tovey: The classics of music: talks, essays, and other writings previously uncollected*. Oxford: Oxford University Press, 2001

Tippett, Michael. *Moving into Aquarius*. London: Routledge and Kegan Paul, 1959.

Tippett, Michael. *Those twentieth century blues: an autobiography*. London: Hutchinson, 1991.

Todd, R. Larry, Editor. *Nineteenth-century piano music*. New York; London: Routledge, 2004.

Todd, R. Larry, Editor. *Schumann and his world*. Princeton: Princeton University Press, 1994.

Tommasini, Anthony. *Virgil Thomson: composer on the aisle*. New York: W.W. Norton, 1997.

Tortelier, Paul. *A self-portrait: in conversation with David Blum*. London: Heinemann, 1984.

Tovey, Donald Francis. *A Companion to Beethoven's Pianoforte Sonatas*. Revised by Barry Cooper. London: The Associated Board, [1931], 1998.

Tovey, Donald Francis. *Beethoven*. London: Oxford University Press, 1944.

Tovey, Donald Francis. *Essays and lectures on music*. London: Oxford University Press, 1949.

Tovey, Donald Francis. *Essays in musical analysis*. London: Oxford University Press, H. Milford, 7 Vols., 1935–41.

Tovey, Donald Francis. *The forms of music: musical articles from The Encyclopaedia Britannica*. London: Oxford University Press, 1944.

Toye, Francis. *Giuseppe Verdi: his life and works*. London: William Heinemann Ltd., 1931.

Truscott, Harold. *Beethoven's late string quartets*. London: Dobson, 1968.

Tyler, William R. *The letters of Franz Liszt to Olga von Meyendorff, 1871–1886, in the Mildred Bliss Collection at Dumbarton Oaks*. Translated by William R. Tyler. Washington: Dumbarton Oaks, Trustees for Harvard University; Cambridge, Massachusetts: distributed by Harvard University Press, 1979.

Tyrrell, John. *Janáček: years of a life. Vol 1, (1854–1914) The lonely blackbird*. London: Faber and Faber, 2006.

Tyrrell, John, Editor and Translator. *My life with Janáček: the memoirs of Zdenka Janácková*. London: Faber and Faber, 1998.

Tyson, Alan, Editor. *Beethoven studies 2*. Cambridge: Cambridge University Press, 1977.

Tyson, Alan, Editor. *Beethoven studies 3*. Cambridge: Cambridge University Press, 1982.

Tyson, Alan. *Mozart: studies of the autograph scores*. Cambridge, Massachusetts; London: Harvard University Press, 1987.

Tyson, Alan. *The authentic English editions of Beethoven*. London: Faber and Faber, 1963.

Underwood, J. A., Editor. *Gabriel Fauré: his life through his letters*. London: Marion Boyars, 1984.

Vechten, Carl van, Editor. *Nikolay, Rimsky-Korsakov: My musical life*. London: Martin Secker &

Warburg Ltd., 1942.

Vinton, John. *Essays after a diction-ary: music and culture at the close of Western civilization.* Lewisburg: Bucknell University Press, 1977.

Volkov, Solomon, Editor. *Testi-mony: the memoirs of Dmitri Shostakovich.* London: Faber and Faber, 1981.

Volta, Ornella, Editor. *A mammal's notebook: collected writings of Erik Satie.* London: Atlas Press, 1996.

Wagner, Richard. Beethoven: *With [a] supplement from the philosophi-cal works of A. Schopenhauer.* Translated by E. Dannreuther. London: Reeves, 1893.

Wagner, Richard. *My life.* London: Constable and Company Ltd., 1911.

Walden, Valerie. *One hundred years of violoncello: a history of tech-nique and performance practice, 1740–1840.* Cambridge: Cam-bridge University Press, 1998.

Walker, Alan. *Franz Liszt. Volume 1, The virtuoso years: 1811–1847.* New York: Alfred A. Knopf, 1983.

Walker, Alan. *Franz Liszt. Volume 2, The Weimar years: 1848–1861.* London: Faber and Faber, 1989.

Walker, Alan. *Franz Liszt. Volume 3, The final years, 1861–1886.* London: Faber and Faber, 1997.

Walker, Bettina. *My musical experi-ences.* London: Richard Bentley and Son, 1890.

Walker, Ernest. *Free thought and the musician, and other essays.* London; New York: Oxford University Press, 1946.

Walker, Frank. *Hugo Wolf: a biogra-phy.* London: J. M. Dent, 1951.

Walker, Frank. *The man Verdi.* London: Dent, 1962.

Wallace, Grace, *[Lady Wallace].* *Beethoven's letters (1790–1826): from the collection of Dr. Ludwig Nohl. Also his letters to the Archduke Rudolph, Cardi-nal-Archbishop of Olmutz, K.W., from the collection of Dr. Ludwig Ritter Von Koìchel.* London: Longmans, Green, 2 Vols., 1866.

Wallace, Robin. *Beethoven's critics: aesthetic dilemmas and resolu-tions during the composer's life-time.* Cambridge; New York: Cambridge University Press, 1986.

Walter, Bruno. *Theme and varia-tions: an autobiography.* London: H. Hamilton, 1948.

Warrack, John Hamilton. *Writings on music.* Cambridge: Cam-bridge University Press, 1981.

Wasielewski, Wilhelm Joseph von. *Life of Robert Schumann: with letters, 1833–1852.* London: William Reeves, 1878.

Watkins, Glenn. *Proof through the night: music and the Great War.* Berkeley: University of Califor-nia Press, 2003.

Watkins, Glenn. *Pyramids at the Louvre: music, culture, and collage from Stravinsky to the postmodernists.* Cambridge, Massachusetts; London: Belknap Press of Harvard Uni-versity Press, 1994.

Watkins, Glenn. *Soundings: music in the twentieth century.* New York: Schirmer Books London: Collier Macmillan, 1988.

Watson, Derek. *Liszt.* London: J. M. Dent, 1989.

Weaver, William, Editor. *The Verdi-*

Boito correspondence. Chicago; London: University of Chicago Press, 1994.

Wegeler, Franz. *Remembering Beethoven: the biographical notes of Franz Wegeler and Ferdinand Ries.* London: Andre Deutsch, 1988.

Weingartner, Felix. *Buffets and rewards: a musician's reminiscences.* London: Hutchinson & Co., 1937.

Weinstock, Herbert. *Rossini: a biography.* New York: Limelight, 1987.

Weiss, Piero and Richard Taruskin. *Music in the Western World: a history in documents.* New York: Schirmer; London: Collier Macmillan, 1984.

Weissweiler, Eva *The complete correspondence of Clara and Robert Schumann.* New York: Peter Lang, 2 Vols., 1994.

Whittaker, William Gillies. *Collected essays.* London: Oxford University Press, 1940.

Whittall, Arnold. *Exploring twentieth-century music: tradition and innovation.* Cambridge; New York: Cambridge University Press, 2003.

Whittall, Arnold. *Music since the First World War.* London: J. M. Dent, 1977.

Whitton, Kenneth S. *Lieder: an introduction to German song.* London: Julia MacRae, 1984.

Wightman, Alistair, Editor. *Szymanowski on music: selected writings of Karol Szymanowski.* London: Toccata Press, 1999.

Wilhelm, Kurt. *Richard Strauss: an intimate portrait.* London: Thames and Hudson, 1999.

Will, Richard James. *The characteristic symphony in the age of Haydn and Beethoven.* Cambridge: Cambridge University Press, 2002.

Willetts, Pamela J. *Beethoven and England: an account of sources in the British Museum.* London: British Museum, 1970.

Williams, Adrian, Editor and Translator. *Liszt, Franz: Selected letters.* Oxford: Clarendon Press, 1998.

Williams, Adrian. *Portrait of Liszt: by himself and his contemporaries.* Oxford: Clarendon Press, 1990.

Williams, Ralph Vaughan. *Heirs and rebels: letters written to each other and occasional writings on music.* London; New York: Oxford University Press, 1959.

Williams, Ralph Vaughan. *Some thoughts on Beethoven's Choral symphony: with writings on other musical subjects.* London; Oxford University Press, 1953.

Williams, Ralph Vaughan. *The making of music.* Ithaca, New York: Cornell University Press, 1955.

Williams, Ursula Vaughan. *R.V.W.: a biography of Ralph Vaughan Williams.* London: Oxford University Press, 1964.

Wilson, Conrad. *Notes on Beethoven: 20 crucial works.* Edinburgh: Saint Andrew Press, 2003.

Wilson, Elizabeth. *Shostakovich: a life remembered.* Princeton, New Jersey: Princeton University Press, 1994.

Winter, Robert, Editor. *Beethoven, performers, and critics: the International Beethoven Congress, Detroit, 1977.* Detroit: Wayne State University Press, 1980.

Winter, Robert. *Compositional origins of Beethoven's opus 131.* Ann Arbor, Michigan: UMI Research Press, 1982.

Winter, Robert and Robert Martin,

Editors. *The Beethoven quartet companion*. Berkeley: University of California Press, 1994.

Wolf, Eugene K. and Edward H. Roesner, Editors. *Studies in musical sources and style: essays in honor of Jan LaRue*. Madison, Wisconsin: A-R Editions, 1990.

Wolff, Christoph and Robert Riggs. *The string quartets of Haydn, Mozart and Beethoven: studies of the autograph manuscripts: a conference at Isham Memorial Library, March 15–17, 1979*. Cambridge, Massachusetts: Department of Music, Harvard University, 1980.

Wolff, Konrad. *Masters of the keyboard: individual style elements in the piano music of Bach, Haydn, Mozart, Beethoven, Schubert, Chopin, and Brahms*. Bloomington: Indiana University Press, 1990.

Wörner, Karl Heinrich. *Stockhausen: life and work*. London: Faber, 1973.

Wright, Donald, Editor. *Cardus on music: a centenary collection*. London: Hamish Hamilton, 1988.

Wyndham, Henry Saxe. *August Manns and the Saturday concerts: a memoir and a retrospect*. London and Felling-on-Tyne, New York, The Walter Scott Publishing Co., Ltd., 1909.

Yastrebtsev, V.V. Edited and Translated by Florence Jonas. *Reminiscences of Rimsky-Korsakov*. New York: Columbia University Press, 1985.

Yates, Peter. *Twentieth century music: its evolution from the end of the harmonic era into the present era of sound*. London: Allen & Unwin Ltd., 1968.

Young, Percy M. *Beethoven: a Victorian tribute based on the papers of Sir George Smart*. London: D. Dobson, 1976.

Young, Percy M. *George Grove, 1820–1900: a biography*. London: Macmillan, 1980.

Young, Percy M. *Letters of Edward Elgar and other writings*. London: Geoffrey Bles, 1956.

Young, Percy M., Editor. *Letters to Nimrod: Edward Elgar to August Jaeger, 1897–1908*. London: Dennis Dobson, 1965.

Young, Percy M. *The concert tradition: from the middle ages to the twentieth century*. London: Routledge and Kegan Paul, 1965.

Young, Rob, Editor. *(Brief Description): Undercurrents: the hidden wiring of modern music*. London; New York, N.Y.: Continuum, 2002.

Yourke, Electra Slonimsky, Editor. *Nicolas Slonimsky: writings on music*. New York, N.Y.; London: Routledge, 4 Vols. 2003-2005.

Slonimsky, Nicolas. *The great composers and their works*. Edited by Electra Slonimsky Yourke. New York: Schirmer Books, 2 Vols. 2000.

Ysaÿe, Antoine. *Ysaÿe: his life, work and influence*. London: W. Heinemann, 1947.

Zamoyski, Adam. *Paderewski*. London: Collins, 1982.

Zegers, Mirjam, Editor. *Louis Andriessen: The art of stealing time*. Todmorden: Arc Music, 2002.

Zemanova, Mirka, Editor. *Janácek's uncollected essays on music*. London: Marion Boyars, 1989.

INDEX

I ndex to the Piano Concertos and a Beethoven time-line of significant musical and related events.

The order adopted for the listing of the individual entries in this index, for each of the piano concertos under consideration, is chronological — according to the sequential unfolding of events under discussion. Thereby, the reader is provided with both a guide to the contents discussed in the main text and a time-line of the principal events bearing on Beethoven's life and work.

ABOUT THE AUTHOR

Terence M. Russell graduated with first class honours in architecture and was a nominee for the coveted Silver Medal of the Royal Institute of British Architects. He is a Fellow of the Royal Incorporation of Architects in Scotland (retired), was formerly Reader in the School of Arts, Culture and Environment at the University of Edinburgh, a Fellow of the British Higher Education Academy, and Senior Assessor to the Scottish Higher Education Funding Council. Alongside his professional work in the field of architecture – embracing practice, teaching and research – he has maintained a lifetime's interest in the music and musicology of Beethoven. He has an equal admiration for the work of Franz Schubert and was for many years an active member of the Schubert Institute, UK. His book writings in the field of architecture include the following:

The Built Environment: A Subject Index, Gregg Publishing (1989):
- Vol. 1: Town planning and urbanism, architecture, gardens and landscape design
- Vol. 2: Environmental technology, constructional engineering, building and materials
- Vol. 3: Decorative art and industrial design, international exhibitions and collections, recreational and performing arts
- Vol. 4: Public health, municipal services, community welfare

Architecture in the Encyclopédie of Diderot and D'Alemebert: The Letterpress Articles and Selected Engravings, Scolar Press (1993)

The Encyclopaedic Dictionary in the Eighteenth Century: Architecture, Arts and Crafts, Scolar Press (1997):
- Vol. 1: John Harris, Lexicon Technicum
- Vol. 2: Ephraim Chambers, Cyclopaedia
- Vol. 3: The Builder's Dictionary
- Vol. 4: Samuel Johnson, A Dictionary of the English Language
- Vol. 5: A Society of Gentlemen, Encyclopaedia Britannica

Gardens and Landscapes in the Encyclopédie of Diderot and D'Alemebert: The Letterpress Articles and Selected Engravings, 2 Vols., Ashgate (1999)

The Napoleonic Survey of Egypt: The Monuments and Customs of Egypt, 2 Vols., Ashgate (2001)

The Discovery of Egypt: Vivant Denon's Travels with Napoleon's Army, History Press (2005)